THE WEATHER | Section

W9-BIJ-006

E CENTS Bronx and Brooklyn TEN CENTS

P ··· OURS;
···GH ··· LEET;
···R··· FIELD

Ex Libris

The Zizzis'

THUNDEROUS WELCOME

Lines of Soldiers and ··· rging to Plane Lifts from His Cockpit

··· FROM FRENZIED MOB OF 25,000

With Celebration After Day ···—American Flag Is Called For and Wildly Acclaimed.

SHOWING THE SPEED OF HIS TRIP

By EDWIN L. JAMES.

Copyright, 1927, by The New York Times Company.
Special Cable to THE NEW YORK TIMES.

PARIS, May 21.—Lindbergh did it. Twenty minutes after 10 o'clock tonight suddenly and softly there slipped out of the darkness a gray-white airplane as 25,000 pairs of eyes strained toward it. At 10:24 the Spirit of St. Louis landed and lines of soldiers, ranks of policemen and stout steel fences went down before a mad rush as irresistible as the tides of the ocean.

"Well, I made it," smiled Lindbergh, as the little white monoplane came to a half in the middle of the field and the first vanguard reached the plane. Lindbergh made a move to jump out. Twenty hands reached for him and lifted him out as if he were a baby. Several thousands in a minute were around the plane. Thousands more broke the barriers of iron rails round the field, cheering wildly.

Lifted From His Cockpit.

As he was lifted to the ground Lindbergh was pale, and, with his hair unkempt, he looked completely worn out. He had strength enough, however, to smile, and waved his hand to the crowd. Soldiers with fixed bayonets were unable to keep back the crowd.

United States Ambassador Herrick was among the first to welcome and congratulate the hero.

A NEW YORK TIMES man was one of the first to reach the machine after its graceful descent to the field. Those first to arrive at the plane had a picture that will live in their

THE LAST HERO: Charles A. Lindbergh

THE LAST HERO:

HARPER & ROW, PUBLISHERS

NEW YORK, EVANSTON, AND LONDON

CHARLES A. LINDBERGH

By Walter S. Ross

Format by Katharine Sitterly

For

JUST LUNNING

and for

WINIFRED, FRED AND LIZ

"Character," says Novalis,
in one of his questionable aphorisms—
"character is destiny."
                                    —GEORGE ELIOT

 CONTENTS

The Last Hero   ix

1 LINDBERGH TODAY   *1*
2 ORIGINS   *9*
3 BOYHOOD   *27*
4 EARLY FLIGHT   *45*
5 ARMY   *59*
6 AIR MAIL   *69*
7 THE SPIRIT OF ST. LOUIS   *78*
8 NEW YORK–PARIS   *98*
9 PARIS AND RETURN   *120*
10 "WE"   *139*
11 CELEBRATION   *146*
12 FORTY-EIGHT-STATE TOUR   *150*
13 MEXICO   *161*
14 A NEW LIFE   *170*
15 TO THE ORIENT   *181*
16 DEATHS IN THE FAMILY   *194*
17 THE HAUPTMANN CASE   *211*
18 DR. CARREL   *229*
19 DR. GODDARD   *243*
20 THE AIR MAIL CONTROVERSY   *254*
21 ENGLAND, FRANCE, GERMANY   *261*
22 AIR POWER   *273*
23 SPEAKING OUT   *285*

24   AMERICA FIRST   289

25   LINDBERGH'S PERSONAL WAR   321

26   FAMILY LIFE   333

27   CHANGE   355

28   A FREE MAN   362

Sources and Acknowledgments   370

Notes   372

Index   389

Illustrations follow page 208

THE LAST HERO

CHARLES A. LINDBERGH WAS ONCE THE MOST WOR-shiped, adored, harried, photographed, written-about, and pursued man in the world—more widely loved than any private citizen in our century.

Did he deserve all that? Did he want it?

His feat, the first nonstop flight from New York to Paris, in May, 1927—was it the epic deed of a true hero or, as one critic said, "the climactic stunt of a time of marvelous stunts"?

After the flight we made him a demigod. In "we" are included not only Americans but the French, the British, and many other peoples. We extrapolated him and his deed into a symbol of invincibility, incorruptibility, of perfect virtue—of everything, in short, that we wanted in a godhead.

Was he really a hero? Or were we creating an idol to replace our lost ideals?

We not only made Lindbergh our hero, we kept him that way. The other great achievers of his day got headlines and then vanished into vaudeville. But Lindbergh was treated differently from celebrities, stars, champions, and even Presidents. We kept him on our front pages. We followed him around. We clutched at him. We drove by his house in packed phalanxes on our day off, hoping for a glimpse of him. We did this not just for nine days, but for eight years—until he fled the country. And when he came back three years later, he was still as much of a hero as though he'd never left.

Was there—is there—something about Lindbergh that calls for this kind of adulation?

No private individual has ever had so much adoration from so many people for so long a time as Lindbergh. (In fact, even among public figures one is hard put to find a parallel. Gandhi, perhaps; Stalin; Nasser; Charlie Chaplin.) In any case, nobody ever got so much sustained attention without wanting it or working at it. Lindbergh did neither.

He was not only extraordinary as a perennial hero; history made him unique by choosing him as the last hero. This was the result of many circumstances. The most obvious was that Lindbergh's epic deed was so much a solo performance from first to last. He spent his own money and helped raise the rest. He helped design and build his own airplane. He laid out the route. He selected the time and place of takeoff. He made all the decisions about what he would carry and leave behind, where he would fly and where he would land. And, of course, he flew alone.

His modern counterparts, the astronauts, just do not have the same opportunities. If one could measure such things, they must be every bit as brave as Lindbergh. They are certainly better trained than he was. But they are government employees. They fly in machines so huge and complex and expensive that only governments can afford them. The operation has to be a team affair, involving thousands of technicians and specialists, billions of dollars of public funds, directed by computers. Very little of the work the astronauts do in space or on the ground is of their volition.

And there are other reasons for Lindbergh's unique status. The world was an innocent place in 1927, its jazzy concerns concealing a desire to reach backward into the security of the prewar era. We made Lindbergh a hero because we still believed in heroism. There are today many bold men exploring frontiers in strange lands, at the bottom of the sea, in the air, on mountains as well as outer space. But none of them—the astronauts, Sir Francis Chichester, Lindbergh's own son Jon, a record-holding deep-sea diver—has achieved a status higher than that of innovator, explorer, adventurer. They are not heroes, because the world no longer creates heroes, no longer believes in heroes.

The contrast between what we formerly made Lindbergh and what we make of him today is vast. Once a demigod, what is he now? He is not really forgotten by those who were old enough to know what was happening between 1927 and 1941, but he is not remembered by them, either. Mention of his name brings a startled reaction. Surprise, perhaps, but not the old adoration. Some remember him fondly; many recall him with bitterness. And to a whole new generation he has never been known at all. A recent informal survey of a group of high-school students at the exhibit of the *Spirit of St. Louis,* Lindbergh's old airplane, in the Smithsonian Institution, revealed that many thought he had died in World War II.

The distance between his elevation and his obscurity, between total love and nostalgia or perhaps dislike, must measure something more than the passage of time. What?

It was to answer some of these questions that this book was written. It started when Harold T. P. Hayes, the editor of *Esquire,* asked the writer "Where did Charles A. Lindbergh go?" This resulted in an article for the magazine with the question as the title Genevieve Young, an editor at Harper & Row, suggested the subject might be worth more research. She thought this might develop into a book. The writer agreed. Hence this biography.

It should be made clear that this is *not* an authorized biography. The writer has never met Lindbergh. Lindbergh has not in any way helped with this work. He has instead attempted to discourage it. In the only communication received from him by the author—it was in reply to a letter requesting an interview with Mrs. Lindbergh—Mr. Lindbergh wrote, "I prefer not to have a biography published."

Why, then, in view of his wish, has this book been written? Because, as one of his friends said, "He is an historical character partly by choice, partly by circumstance. Like it or not, he owes a debt to history." The writer feels, too, that we owe Lindbergh another look—one not clouded by crisis, or polemic, or remembered controversy. Like any human being, he has the right to be judged by the truths of our time, by current standards, by his whole life, and not just by what happened in the past. Lindbergh was formerly a magnet for news coverage. His absence from the public scene has left a vacuum. In this news void his image has sprouted myths the way old statues grow verdigris. So part of the purpose of this book is to clarify the record, not to violate his personal life.

It has for a long time been Lindbergh's policy and practice not to assist any research that might invade his privacy or indeed that of any living person. His papers are locked up in the Sterling Library at Yale University, the Library of Congress, and in his own files, and may not be seen without his permission. He refused permission to this writer. He also refused permission to Harper & Row for this writer to quote from a few letters and speeches to which he holds copyright. The interested reader is directed to the originals in the source notes at the back of this book.

Lindbergh has drawn his family and friends into a conspiracy of silence. His acquaintances and colleagues are widely separated and often do not know one another. This develops out of Lindbergh's way of living and traveling, so much alone, to so many different parts of the world, and out of his current widely separated interests in science, in aviation, in certain branches of the government, in wildlife conservation. The effect is that each group of Lindbergh's people doesn't know his relationship with other groups. Their only common denominator is Lindbergh, and they follow his lead in protecting him from what he hates most: publicity, interviews, the press.

Lindbergh has thus made it difficult for his biographers. He believes that it protects his privacy to permit them to make mistakes and produce inadequate works—"the badder the better." And this has led to the creation and perpetuation of errors about him.

How, then, can a reasonably accurate book be written about a man who has refused to make himself or his papers available?

By treating him as what he is: a historical figure, albeit a living one. In writing this book the materials of history were used—published and unpublished documents, books, magazine and newspaper articles, personal interviews with friends, colleagues, and others.

There is also the fact that even well-organized conspiracies do not achieve perfect security, and the one around Lindbergh is just a private affair. The only penalty for talking is the risk of his disapproval. Some people who know him well will take this risk in order to clarify the record. And there is much material buried in out-of-the-way places, in obscure house organs, in little-known speeches, in diaries and letters.

Lindbergh himself cannot totally hide his movements. He constantly roams the earth like some great whale, generally out of sight but having to surface here and there. Where he surfaces, he leaves some kind of record. Also, while he will not reveal himself completely, he has helped writers who were doing research on the lives of men with whom he has worked and in the process has had to disclose the roles he has played. Since he is a stickler for accuracy, these glimpses of Lindbergh may be accepted as accurate.

Thus, there are many bits of the Lindbergh mosaic scattered around. It is possible to find them and to make a picture. This does not create a definitive biography, obviously; one cannot be written without the principal papers. In all cases, however, the account of what happened or what was said has been derived from published sources, or from interviews with a witness or participant. Lindbergh's conversations reported in this book have been quoted verbatim as given by the sources; there has been no fictionalization, although sentences are sometimes abridged. In only three instances in this book is a Lindbergh dialogue reported by someone who was not a participant. A few episodes and conversations are based on the recollection of only one individual; it is unfortunate that such incidents could not have been checked with Lindbergh.

Nonetheless this book is based on known data and verifiable fact. Speculation and deduction are labeled as such. The author's judgments of Lindbergh rest on the available evidence.

W. S. R.

THE LAST HERO: Charles A. Lindbergh

1

LINDBERGH TODAY

THE FIRST THINGS TO KNOW ABOUT LINDBERGH ARE THAT he is alive and sixty-six years old. He lives in a new white three-bedroom cottage on the shore of Scott's Cove, an inlet off Long Island Sound in Darien, Connecticut. The house is the second he and his wife, the former Anne Morrow, have had on the property, which they bought in 1946. The first was a large, Tudor-type mansion with enough bedrooms for each of the five Lindbergh children, the parents, and a sleep-in cook-housekeeper. (The reason for the new house is simply that after the young Lindberghs grew up and moved out, the parents no longer needed the big house and sold it.) The youngest child, Reeve, is a student in a girl's college in the East; the second youngest, Scott, is a student in an English university. The others are married and have children. They live in widely separated places: the state of Washington, Montana, and Paris, France.

The elder Lindberghs own another small house in Vaud, Switzerland, not far from Lausanne on Lake Geneva. They use it as a base for skiing trips and as a place to write in. Neither house is guarded by savage dogs or armed men or anything else, but neither is easy to find.

In both places, Lindbergh is an early riser. Since his childhood in Little Falls, Minnesota, where he lived on a kind of farm, he has become used to waking very early—about dawn, or a little later (or earlier, in the dark, if need be).

Even on a chilly day in Darien—even in midwinter—he will often put on his swim trunks and take a swim in the Sound first thing. To get to the water, he has to walk through underbrush and trees he has allowed to grow unhindered on his land, to the break in the sea wall where he and his wife and the children have often gone swimming. Physical fitness is the necessary prerequisite for the kind of active life he likes to lead, and even at sixty-six he is still fairly lean and quite strong.

Lindbergh has often broken the ice near the shore in the winter to swim in the Sound, and come into the house "as red as a lobster," according to one eyewitness, to dry himself off in the warm kitchen.

After his swim, he will shower and shave and comb his gray thinning hair sideward over his pate. He dresses himself plainly in blue shirts, simple ties, and usually a gray suit. He does not have many clothes, although he is far from poor. His breakfast is of normal size. He swore off drinking coffee more than forty-five years ago.

If he is going on a trip, he will take a clean sock and into it drop a razor, soap, toothbrush, toothpaste, and comb. He knots the sock and puts it in his pocket. A briefcase may be his only luggage for a long trip. It usually contains the other sock, a clean shirt and underwear, and an underwater face mask. He acquired the habit of traveling light in his days as an air-mail pilot during the early nineteen-twenties. Today, he says a man can go anywhere in the world with a clean shirt and an extra pair of socks, and he acts on his own precept. The face mask is for skin diving, in case he gets a chance.

He wears a crushed gray felt fedora in cities to keep his face shielded from strangers. He may take a topcoat. (He doesn't usually wear anything heavier, no matter how cold it is; in fact, he often does not wear a coat at all.) As he goes out, he may pick up a handful of birdseed. Outside, he scatters the seed on the lawn before he goes into the garage. Feeding birds is a habit he picked up early in life from his father, the late Representative C. A. Lindbergh, a great outdoorsman. Then he puts his coat and bag in one of the family cars. This might be a Volkswagen or a Ford station wagon. When he leaves, he drives out the gate past the unmarked mailbox that keeps strangers from easily identifying his house.

When he goes to New York, as he does frequently, Lindbergh may drive himself to the Darien station of the New Haven Railroad and park his car. He will wait with the other commuters on the platform, but he will stay aloof from them unless he happens to see a friend. A few years ago, when he was meeting a friend at the station, he wouldn't get out of his car until the crowd of arriving passengers had gone, for fear he would be recognized and annoyed. On that occasion, the friend thought he had missed connections with Lindbergh until he saw with relief the tall figure get out of the car and stride toward him. (Lindbergh's walk is wide-stepping and determined.)

Now, however, Lindbergh knows that most people do not recognize him—or, if they do, seldom bother him. If he has no friends with him, he will stand alone on the platform and sit alone in the train, in a nonsmoking car, and read over whatever it is he happens to be working on. His new book, perhaps.* When the train arrives in Grand Central, he will get off and walk through the station to the Pan Am Building directly behind it. There he will take an elevator, probably to the forty-sixth floor, where Juan Terry Trippe, president of Pan American World Airways, has his office. Lindbergh has been a technical adviser to the company since 1928, then at an estimated annual salary of around $25,000. He once held a substantial amount of stock in Pan Am. When he was elected a director of the company in 1965, he owned six thousand shares. His stipend was then less than $10,000 a year.

Lindbergh might confer with Trippe about any of several new aircraft the company is interested in. This development work has been Lindbergh's main contribution to Pan Am in recent years. He had a great deal to do with adapting the first passenger jets, the Boeing 707s, for the airline, and currently he is interested in the new, huge 747, of which Pan Am has ordered several.

Finishing his work in the office, Lindbergh might head for Kennedy Airport. His habit is to take the bus. At the airport he stays in the private lounge that Pan Am reserves for important passengers until his flight is called. He usually travels first class because it is in the forward part of the ship, near the pilot's compartment, and this enables him to spend time with the crew without having to pass a lot of strangers. He frequently flies to Paris, and the jets he takes fol-

---

* This has been variously described as the rest of his autobiography; or an account of his war experiences; or a history of flight; or a book on anthropology. It may be that he is working on more than one book; but the chances are that what he is writing is autobiographical in part.

low the same great-circle route which he was the first to fly successfully, between Roosevelt Field, Long Island, and Le Bourget Airport, Paris. Lindbergh travels this way often, and sometimes much farther. Once, during the famous airlift, he dropped in at Berlin. He goes to Nairobi or to Tokyo, or wherever else he wishes. He estimated several years ago that he has flown the Atlantic well over a hundred times.*

While he is flying, Lindbergh will make notes in longhand with one of the pencil stubs he carries to write with. These notes might form part of a report to Trippe, perhaps discussing the operations of the airline. Lindbergh has always been a strong believer in a wide safety margin in passenger ships—a margin of at least 35 per cent. Put another way, he believes that no more than 65 per cent of the plane's power should be called on under normal conditions.

When he is in Paris, Lindbergh often visits his married 28-year-old daughter Anne, now Mme. Julien Feydy. Anne married Julien Feydy in December, 1963, at a family ceremony in the French village of Douzillac, in Dordogne, where Feydy's parents have a house.

Typical of a good deal of Lindbergh press coverage, the newspapers got the basic facts wrong. None of the information came from the Lindberghs directly. The *New York Times,* the Paris *Herald,* and the Associated Press recorded the wedding as taking

---

* On Tuesday, May 16, 1967, at the Lotos Club in New York, many of Lindbergh's old friends and colleagues gathered at dinner to remember him as the fortieth anniversary of his famous flight (May 20–21, 1927) approached. Lauren D. Lyman and C. B. Allen, who covered the takeoff for the *New York Times* and the New York *World,* and Harry Bruno, once Lindbergh's personal representative, were present. Later the same week there was a dinner with speeches at the Garden City Hotel, where Lindbergh lived for a week before his flight; a plaque was dedicated at the approximate spot the *Spirit of St. Louis* left the ground (from what used to be Roosevelt Field, and is now a shopping center); a pilot flew a replica of the *Spirit* around the Eiffel Tower in Paris, where Lindbergh's flight was the theme of the American exhibit at the International Air Show; and another pilot flew another replica of the plane at Lambert Field, St. Louis. Lindbergh was not present at any of these events. A friend of Lindbergh's offered to keep track of these and other anniversary celebrations. Lindbergh said, "No, thanks." On the anniversary date of his flight, he was in Indonesia tracking a rare species of rhinoceros threatened with extinction. Lindbergh told a friend he thought it futile to keep on promoting an event that took place forty years ago. "I devoted time to that in 1927 and '28," he said, "and I've written two books about it. It's not that era any more, and I'm not that boy."

place between *Jacques* Feydy and Miss Lindbergh; actually, Jacques is the name of the bridegroom's father. The papers reported that the Feydy family had a château; actually, they have a modest house. A neighbor, riding over on horseback to visit the Feydys a day or two after the wedding, came late and joked, "I got lost riding on your lands!" The bridegroom's father is professor of art history at the University of Paris.

Lindbergh favored the match between his slender blond daughter and the dark-haired Frenchman of middle height, a year or two younger than she. Lindbergh told his daughter "you'd better marry him or you'll lose him," and has displayed warmth toward his son-in-law since.

In France, Lindbergh often has business to attend to—perhaps a conference with Sud-Aviation, the French company who, with British Aircraft, Ltd., are producing the 1,450-m.p.h. Concorde airplane. After inspecting the French and British plants and analyzing their designs and tests, Lindbergh and the Pan Am engineers had recommended that their airline order six of these ships. Lindbergh is also currently interested in the status of the American supersonic jet airliner to be made by Boeing, which may be superior to the foreign product. Lindbergh and the airline's engineers will work with the manufacturers on the details of construction, to make sure the ships conform to the company's requirements. When prototypes of these craft are ready for flying, Lindbergh will probably take part in the engineering flight tests, as he has done with many other airplanes he has helped develop for his airline's use, starting back in the nineteen-twenties with the early Sikorsky flying boat.

While in France, Lindbergh might also want to see the factory people who are producing the Falcon for Pan Am. To do this, he would motor over to Brétigny, to a private airdrome where Avions Marcel-Dassault keeps its planes to take visitors from Paris to its plant in Bordeaux. Dassault builds a small executive twin-engine jet, which is almost as fast as today's big commercial jets, for Pan Am. This plane, called the Falcon, is an adaptation of Dassault's Mystère-20. Pan Am sells it to large corporations. It, too, has been adapted to the company's needs with Lindbergh's advice.

Sometimes, when he leaves Paris, Lindbergh goes on to Nairobi, in Kenya. In Nairobi he has stayed with the Chief Game Warden,

Major I. R. Grimwood, and has flown himself over the game preserve in a small plane to spot game. A few years ago he took a trip by car into the preserve. After his trip he wrote an article for the *Reader's Digest*, which was published in July, 1964.

To Lindbergh the trip had mystical significance, bringing him into contact with the past and with "the miracle of life." "For the first time [in man] life has progressed to the point where it is able to recognize itself," he wrote, "to appreciate its value, its quality, its achievement, even to question what ways of living contribute to its progress."

In the belief that "life itself is more important than any material accomplishment life makes," Lindbergh has become deeply interested and involved in preserving the species of animals that are threatened with extinction, such as the American eagle, the whooping crane, the Arabian oryx, the mountain gorilla, the blue whale, and the polar bear.

He ended his essay with the question "Is civilization progress? The challenge, I think, is clear; and as clearly the final answer will be given not by our amassment of knowledge, or by the discoveries of our science, or by the speed of our aircraft, but by the effect our civilized activities as a whole have upon the quality of our planet's life—the life of plants and animals as well as that of men."

The questions, the moralizing, the mystical quality of thought, and the strong, clear exposition of facts and ideas—occasionally interspersed with poetic and tender imagery—are all characteristic of Lindbergh's later prose. Also characteristic is his willingness to put his name to something he believes in. It had been many years since Lindbergh had published any of his writings—yet, in spite of his well-known love for anonymity and privacy, he wrote an essay to the largest magazine audience in the world.

Lindbergh has done this sort of thing several times in his life, although he knew the consequences might involve a violation of his personal privacy—an intrusion so abhorrent to him that he has been known to travel thousands of miles to avoid it.

In the United States, Lindbergh often visits the Pentagon. For most of his adult life, in and out of uniform, he has had some connection with the nation's air arm. As a youngster of twenty-two, he studied military aviation at Kelly and Brooks Fields and won his pilot's wings. When he flew the Atlantic in 1927, he was a captain in the Missouri National Guard, and was later made a colonel. He resigned from the Army in 1941 and until 1954 was a civilian.

President Dwight D. Eisenhower nominated him for a commission as Brigadier General of the Air Force Reserve in 1954, and the nomination was confirmed by the Senate. Before and since that time, Lindbergh served on several key committees for the Air Force. One of these, the von Neuman Committee, made the decision approving the Atlas missile, the motive power for our Mercury manned orbital flights into space, and recommended ways of getting it produced.

In Darien he still gets an estimated two to three hundred unsolicited letters and pieces of mail a week. He has the habit of running his fingers down the left side of the envelopes, riffling through the pile seeking familiar names and addresses. When he sees one he recognizes, he puts that envelope aside to be opened. But those bearing unfamiliar names and addresses he rejects, unopened.

Thus some of the many invitations he still receives to make speeches and other appearances are never answered. But even letters from friends do not always get a prompt reply; they sometimes wait months.

Lindbergh likes to do most chores by himself. When he collects enough unopened mail, he will load it into a trunk or carton and deliver it personally in his station wagon to the Sterling Library at Yale. He selected Yale as the repository for most of his papers because his long-time friend and employer, Juan Terry Trippe, a Yale alumnus, suggested that it would be a safe place to store them when Lindbergh left the United States with his family in 1935. The papers were on loan then, but after some years Yale requested their ownership, and since no one else had asked for them, Lindbergh made out an irrevocable deed of gift to the library with stipulations of privacy.

As this suggests, Lindbergh does have a sense of his historical importance although his sense of privacy supersedes it. He also has a deep feeling for the history of his family—so much so that he once employed a genealogist full time to dig into the origins of both branches, and recently he helped support the researches of a

Columbia University dentist who was writing a biography of Lindbergh's maternal grandfather, Dr. Charles H. Land, a dental pioneer. Lindbergh thought so much of this project, in fact, that he donated one of his most cherished awards—the thousand dollars he won, with the Pulitzer Prize, for his autobiography, *The Spirit of St. Louis*—to his grandfather's biographer.

2

ORIGINS

THE CHARACTER OF CHARLES A. LINDBERGH CLEARLY RE-
produces many traits found in his father and his grandfather. The
Lindbergh men all display the same hard, central sense of purpose,
the same fearless, even foolhardy, independence of mind and
action. In different countries, in different centuries, there is something unchanging, refractory, defiant, even downright cussed in
this family. One is not usually afforded such an uncluttered view of
repeated cause and effect in real life.

Thus, even though Charles A. Lindbergh never knew his paternal
grandfather (August Lindbergh died in 1892, ten years before his
grandson was born), the old man laid down some of the attitudes
and behavior patterns that would shape those of his grandson.

Grandfather Lindbergh was an iron man, physically and morally,
who had a stormy career as a reform politician in Sweden. Interest-
ingly, his name had not always been Lindbergh. He was born a
peasant, Ole Manson (or Mansson), in Sweden in 1810. (Swedish
peasant family names were patronyms. Ole's father was Mans. Ole's
sons became Olssons.) He farmed for his family, then for others, and
finally broke his way through the rigidly class-structured society to
become a landowner himself. Then he could run for the Riksdag
(Parliament) and he was elected to his first term at the age of
thirty-nine.

Although he was unschooled, he had strong intellectual convictions and no hesitancy in expressing them. His ideas were radical
for nineteenth-century Sweden. He began a one-man campaign
against the use of the whipping post as punishment for crime. This
enraged the country's conservatives. During his twelve years in the

Riksdag, Manson (Lindbergh) carried on this campaign, and others: he sought legal protection for servants against beatings by their masters, fought for improvements in public transportation, and tried hard to extend suffrage, which was restricted to the nobility, clergy, propertied class, and farmers. He was a good friend of the Crown Prince, who became King Charles XV of Sweden in 1859, and served as Charles' secretary.

He won his fight against the whipping post, but this victory helped cost him his career. He had been a director of the loan office of the Bank of Sweden at Malmö, in southern Sweden. His political enemies were able to construct a charge of embezzlement against him, and get him convicted. Later evidence tends to show that this conviction was more of a technical than a criminal nature, but there is no doubt that it damaged his reputation. He decided to leave Sweden.

In 1860, at the age of fifty, Ole Manson took his second wife, Louisa, aged twenty (his first wife had died), and their newborn son, Charles Augustus (named for the new king), and sailed for the United States. He started his new life with the name of Lindbergh. He explained to one of his children, some years later, that changing one's name was no disgrace. There had been too many Mansons in his locality, so he simply took another name.

A biographer of the Lindbergh family says that although August Lindbergh was hated politically by the conservatives he had fought so long and hard, he was universally respected personally. "When this Swedish peasant-gentleman announced that he was going to America the parliamentary forces he had been fighting got together and gave him a testimonial. They bought gold and fashioned it into a token. Their esteem was inscribed upon it, each word as sincere as the gold was pure," wrote Lynn Haines in *The Lindberghs*. When he got to America, Manson, now Lindbergh, traded the gold medal for a plow, thus establishing a realistic attitude toward trinkets for his descendants.

Lindbergh took his wife and baby to Minnesota, where he homesteaded a piece of forest land (known as a pre-emption) in Melrose, near Sauk Centre. He cut down trees and built a log house, twelve by sixteen feet, and began to raise a family.

He had almost no money, and cash was hard to come by. The family burned homemade candles because kerosene cost seventy-five cents a gallon. Louisa Lindbergh sold her gold watch for a cow so they had milk and butter. Game was the family's main source of meat.

Two years after their arrival in America, August Lindbergh decided to build his family a frame house. The only cash outlay would be the cost of having logs sawed into planks at the mill ten miles away, in Sauk Centre, and the nails. He had an axe to cut his own trees, and an ox to cart them to the mill. A contemporary, the Reverend C. S. Harrison, told what happened when he got to the mill. "One day he took a load of logs to the mill and, stumbling, fell on the saw. This caught him in the back and also took a stab at his right arm. [It also cut through four ribs.] Witnesses said you could see Lindbergh's heart beating through the gaping wound.

"It was hot weather and there was no surgeon within fifty miles. I followed him to his home [August Lindbergh was carried in a cart over a deeply rutted road] and we did not think that he could live. I picked out the sawdust and rags from his wound and kept the mangled arm wrapped in cold water." Through all this, Lindbergh never cried out. He had kept his arm from bleeding by applying pressure with his other hand.

There was only one horse in the area, and a neighbor mounted it and started for the nearest doctor in St. Cloud, thirty miles away. It happened that the doctor was taking care of a mother in childbirth on a nearby farm. As soon as the baby and mother were safe, the doctor left his long vigil to ride to August Lindbergh. By the time he got to the Lindbergh farm, three days had elapsed since the accident.

During those three days, Lindbergh lay patiently while his young wife, Louisa, and little Charles Augustus took turns going to the spring for cold water to bathe his wound and keep his fever down.

Writes the Reverend Harrison: "[Lindbergh's] cleanly habits and robust constitution carried him through the operation successfully. I helped the doctor and we took off the arm near the shoulder."

The doctor stitched up the wound in the back and August asked to see the amputated left arm. It was brought to him in a tiny wooden coffin. He took its hand in his remaining one and said, "You have been a good friend to me for fifty years. But you can't be with me any more. So good-bye. Good-bye, my friend."

There was a long battle against shock, infection, and loss of blood. It took the fifty-two-year-old August nearly two years to recover from this accident. He devised a belt with rings and pockets to which he could affix one end of an axe or scythe. He invented a specially balanced axe that he could swing with his one arm, and he had other tools made for his use. Then he began to chop trees and do the heavy work again.

During his long convalescence, August Lindbergh had a good chance to know his son Charles Augustus (Charlie), and vice versa. He conversed with the boy for hours—told him of his life in Sweden, his career in politics, and he talked about the world in general. Charlie Lindbergh would grow up to become the flier's father.

Young Charlie Lindbergh had more of his share of chores and responsibilities, because his father was partly incapacitated and also because August had chosen to homestead on forest rather then prairie land. The prairie could have given August Lindbergh a cash crop in the second year, but he lacked the capital to live that long without income. To clear and cultivate the forest took a long time, but the family could live off the land until they raised crops.

It early became Charlie's responsibility to keep the family supplied with meat and fish; he learned to use a gun at an age when today's children are going to nursery school. There was never a time when, if the family needed meat, he couldn't go out with his rifle and come back half an hour later with a fresh-killed deer. Once, when he was eight, he got three deer in one day. He had to be a dead shot, for ammunition cost money and he had to account for each cartridge. If he missed a bird on one shot, he lined up two on the next round. This was not so difficult in those days when flights of game birds literally darkened the sky, he later told his son.

The skins of animals had a cash value. Not deer—they were so common that a buckskin might fetch only a gallon of kerosene. But a bearskin would bring ten or twelve dollars; the pelt of a timber wolf was worth a dollar and a quarter.

The boy was often sent alone to St. Cloud on family errands, a round trip of sixty miles in the oxcart. If he met trouble—a sudden storm, a mudhole, a tree across the trail—he had to overcome it alone. He wasn't burdened with a lot of parental admonitions, nor did his parents worry him with their concern. They gave him to understand that they knew he could get along on his own.

He was an independent six-year-old spirit when his father helped start the local school. One pleasant day in 1865, August Lindbergh called his neighbors together and took them to his granary, "a fair-sized building, half log and half frame." August told them that if they would help him put in windows, a door, and a chimney, it would serve nicely for a school.

"I do not think we should wait longer to get our children started in school. All of the boys and girls must have their chance to get an education," he said, according to Lynn Haines.

The men came from the neighboring farms, bringing their saws and hammers, and in a few days had transformed the storage building into a workable schoolhouse. Not long after that, a teacher, Miss Jennie Stabler, was brought in to teach the fifteen children of the neighborhood.

As was the custom in those days, the neighbors shared in the teacher's upkeep. She boarded for a week or two with each family in turn. "When it came time for me to go to the Lindbergh home, I was always glad," Miss Stabler said. August Lindbergh "was a well-educated man and . . . interesting to converse with, although his speech was somewhat broken," she reported.

Of course, Charlie had to attend classes, but necessity did not make a scholar. He hankered for his early-won freedom and showed a rebellious spirit. His mulishness expressed itself in his frequent unexplained absences—he had the worst attendance record of any student in the school—and in the pranks he played. Once, he enraged the teacher with a trick and was told to go out and bring back a branch. "Something big and strong," said the teacher. The criminal was to provide his own means of punishment.

Charlie came back dragging a log so big he couldn't lift it, obviously useless for a whipping. The teacher sent him out for something smaller.

He came back with a twig.

Now the teacher got angry. "You know what I want," she said. "Go and get it."

He went out and did not come back at all that day.

He rejected school because he just didn't take to the discipline of

rote learning. On his own, he would read what the grownups read—
books when he could find them, and the local newspapers such as
the St. Cloud *Democrat*. It covered political news in some detail,
and it had a column of rough country humor by Josh Billings.

One thing the Lindbergh house never lacked was ideas, or talk.
Old August looked at the Civil War and the Reconstruction era with
an eye sharpened by his political experience. He saw the post-Civil
War corruption, the building of the railroads, the rise of corporations, and he talked about these things freely. His son heard
political philosophy from his father, and since he admired his
father, he accepted the old man's radical approach. Another early
influence on the boy was Ignatius Donnelly, a Minnesota orator,
who hailed the end of the Civil War as bringing unity, "with
protection for the humblest and justice to all; a land without a slave
and without an oppressor."

The Granger movement developed in the Midwest during
Charlie's adolescence, in the eighteen-seventies. This was a self-
defensive group of farmers responding to the overpowering political
and economic strength of commerce and industry. The Granger
movement sought regulation of the railroads, and set up coopera-
tives for farmers. Charlie Lindbergh read about it in Sidney M.
Owen's *Farm, Stock and Home* newspaper, and heard about it. The
Granger ideas, which were later incorporated into the Farmers'
Alliance and the Populist Party, were absorbed as part of his
growing-up process.

Except for the hit-or-miss country schooling, young Charlie Lindbergh was, in the formal sense, uneducated at the age of twenty, but
he had read widely, and talked even more. He had ideas, and he
could think. Everything he had learned contrived to point him
toward becoming a lawyer, but of course there were certain educational prerequisites.

He entered Coogan's Academy, near Sauk Centre, in his twenty-
first year. It was a private school, run by a priest. Charlie paid his
way by hunting and trapping, and he walked the ten miles to school
most days. Sometimes he would arrive with his gun on his shoulder.

When he wanted to, he could learn. He graduated from Coogan's
Academy the next year, and decided to go to the University of
Michigan and study law in the fall.

Meanwhile, to earn some money, he got a job working on the

Great Northern railroad. According to the Haineses, his neighbors, this was the beginning of his interest in transportation and distribution. "He discovered what the public was contributing in rights of way and bonds and land grants," they wrote. "He could have told you just from his own figuring pretty accurately what each mile of construction would cost. . . . Here it was, also, that he started a life-long interest in labor."

At the end of the summer he had some new ideas and a hundred dollars in cash. He went to Ann Arbor for two years and came out with a law degree. It was there that his habit of signing his first two initials, "C.A.," gave him his lifelong nickname.

"His colleagues in law school liked him without knowing why," say the Haineses. "He lived too much alone to be outstandingly popular. The professors . . . did not regard him as brilliant. . . . He too often disagreed with their conclusions and those of the learned authors."

C. A. Lindbergh told his law partner Walter Eli Quigley, years later, that he "could never see why [court] decisions made in 1725 or 1854 should apply to conditions in 1890 or 1920. The world is in constant change. Economics vary in every decade. The law must be flexible and applied with common sense." This was, of course, contrary to legal pedagogy.

He graduated from the Michigan Law School in 1884. After a year of clerking for Judge Searle, at St. Cloud, Minnesota, he moved to Little Falls and opened his own office. This town, on the Mississippi, was a center of the lumbering industry and seemed to offer a young lawyer the chance for a decent career.

Later, his sisters June and Linda came to Little Falls, followed by his younger brother, Frank, who went to law school and became his partner. The elder Lindberghs sold the family farm and moved to Little Falls, too.

For a time C.A. boarded with a family named La Fond, then married their daughter Mary. The C. A. Lindberghs had three daughters, two of whom lived.

C. A. Lindbergh wanted his children to be self-reliant. He tried to duplicate the conditions that made him that way; for one thing, he wouldn't do their thinking for them.

When one came to him with some difficulty, he would say, "Now, you have a head, haven't you?"

"Yes."

"Well, then, the best thing for you to do is think about this yourself. I'm sure you can tell what to do about it. If you are trying to do right, a mistake won't matter. I'll help you if there's any trouble."

Some years later, C. A. Lindbergh stated his theory of child-rearing: "Children manage much of the time to have their own way. That . . . is as it should be. The more child life is dominated, the easier adults are influenced. They become accustomed to having others direct them and do not think for themselves."

Lindbergh practiced law the way he had argued in law school that law should be practiced.

His first client came in soon after he opened his office in Little Falls. The man wanted to sue another man for money he claimed was due him.

Lindbergh asked him to tell the story. When the man got through, Lindbergh said, "I'm sorry you're having this trouble, but I can't take your case. Probably a suit would fail; anyway it should because the defendant is the one who ought to win."

The client was taken aback. "Ain't you a lawyer?"

C.A. said, "My fee is not the issue. The important fact is that you ought not to ask the Court to help you press a dishonest advantage over this man. Morally and, therefore, legally, you have no claim against him. He does not owe you that amount of money."

The client asked what he should do.

Lindbergh advised him to go to the other man and settle the claim; he told him how this could be accomplished.

The client listened, and agreed. "I guess you're right about it," he said. "I'll do it that way. Now, how much do I owe you?"

Lindbergh said, "Nothing. I told you that I could not handle your case."

Such obvious integrity won him a reputation as an honest lawyer, and the reputation brought many clients. He soon represented the two banks in Little Falls, and other sizable businesses. The fact that his fees were invariably lower than other lawyers' didn't hurt, either. But it was his insistence on justice that really gave him his name. When he went to court, it was almost a foregone conclusion that his client was right and would win; otherwise Lindbergh wouldn't be representing him.

He put his money into farmland, usually letting the seller set the price. Between Lindbergh's legal reputation and his sound judgment of real estate, he earned a good deal of money. After about twenty years of law practice and real-estate transactions he was worth about a quarter of a million dollars.

The record clearly shows that he was not interested in accumulating wealth for its own sake. He invested his money in many enterprises not calculated to make profits. For example, he started, financed, and lost money in two magazines which expressed his political and economic ideas.

His attitudes toward wealth (his own as well as other people's) and integrity in money matters strongly reflected his father. He looked like him, too—six feet two, blond, blue-eyed. He also had August Lindbergh's stoicism.

Once, he went duck shooting with a farmer. As already mentioned, game was so thick in those days it was not remarkable that they quickly brought down a dozen mallards over the farmer's pond.

The farmer had a well-trained spaniel who began to retrieve the birds. But the water was near the freezing point. After fetching two ducks, the dog refused to go back into the pond.

C. A. Lindbergh immediately undressed, hung everything but his shirt on some bushes, then put on his shirt and waded into the frigid water. He got the rest of the ducks and brought them ashore.

Just then, there was another flight of ducks, and he and the farmer began shooting again. Lindbergh showed no sign of cold as he stood there in his wet shirt. A strong breeze was blowing. He returned three more times to the water to get the ducks, and only then went into the house to dry himself and put on his clothes.

The bewildered farmer asked, "Haven't you any feeling, man?"

C.A. was just as stoical under the shock of his first wife's death in 1895, after only eight years of marriage. He was left with two little girls, Eva and Lillian. In 1901 he remarried, and Charles Augustus Lindbergh, Jr., was born a year later.

A farmer himself, and the son of a farmer, C. A. Lindbergh knew the problems of farmers. They were always in debt, financing their crops and their living expenses by paying interest ranging from 12 to 18 per cent. They often lost their farms on mortgages foreclosed by the lenders, who were usually out-of-state banks.

Lindbergh himself was asked to buy stock in the two Little Falls banks and go on their board of directors. He demurred, saying he had better things to do with his money. But the banks needed his name, which had become a synonym for probity with the farmers. They offered to take his note for the value of the stock, and let him pay off the debt in dividends.

Lindbergh accepted, but warned them, "You may regret it. To make money, in my opinion, is not the sole purpose of a bank."

Although he built and sold thirty-five houses and was a steady trader in farms and other real estate, Lindbergh had a reputation for never squeezing farmers. On the contrary, he frequently lent money personally to farmers who were in danger of having their mortgages foreclosed. No one knew about this except him and the borrowers.

But once, when he was strapped for cash, he brought a bundle of papers to his office and tossed them to a clerk.

"See if you can collect something on them," he said.

They were interest coupons on mortgages which he had paid to keep a number of farms from foreclosure. The total value was several thousand dollars.

The clerk drove around the countryside, seeing each of the debtors, explaining that C. A. Lindbergh needed cash, if they could spare it. He got all but twenty-five dollars of the money.

It was almost inevitable for farmers to get the idea that Lindbergh would be a good man to represent them in Congress. They began writing to him suggesting that he run. His friends also urged him to try for the House of Representatives.

Lindbergh had no stomach for public life, he said. He resisted the idea for a long time; then, in 1906, he decided to run from the Sixth District of Minnesota as the Republican candidate for the U.S. House of Representatives. His opponent, named Buckman, was a professional politician who used the usual tricks of character assassination. Lindbergh insisted on sticking to the issues. He spent very little money on his campaign, most of it on railroad fare. He used a person-to-person approach, meeting people on the farms and in mills and factories. He published only one piece of campaign literature, a pamphlet in which he stated "some of [his] views on economical questions." One of his points was "positive laws to prevent discrimination against individual persons or places." In speeches, he stated his belief that "all trade and commerce depends on transportation." His economics were classical: "Labor gives the main wealth of the world." His politics were extremely progressive: "The day is near at hand when those who furnish the energy of the world's progress will govern."

Lindbergh bucked the machine and made his points with the voters. He was elected by 16,762 votes to 13,115.

He moved to Washington in the fall of 1907, settling into a furnished apartment at 1831 V Street, N.W., with his wife, his two daughters, and his son, Charles.

On December 2, 1907, C. A. Lindbergh took Charles to the Capitol and, holding him by the hand, walked to his seat. As was customary, the new Congress had its picture taken on opening day. The photo of 1907 shows a little boy in a white sailor collar and dark suit standing behind Congressman C. A. Lindbergh.

The first votes were to select the Speaker and set the House rules. There was opposition to Joseph Cannon, the autocrat who had ruled and often frustrated the House of Representatives as Speaker, and to the rules which had helped him dominate. Lindbergh voted for Cannon and for the adoption of the old rules—a straight party-line vote.

It was the first and last time he was to be "regular." From then on he charted his career in Congress by his own principles and ideas. He opposed his party, both parties. He always worked alone— without a partner in any enterprise.

The Congressman got up at 4 A.M. and reached his office at five. He once asked a man who wanted an appointment with him to meet him at 6 A.M. He walked a good deal, and spent the first hour of the day thinking of his early life in Melrose, of his parents and their struggle to make a living. These thoughts, he said, gave him the courage to take on the day's battles and the tranquility he needed to sustain his spirit.

The panic of 1907 helped to crystallize his economic thinking. He saw farmers and small businessmen ruined in a country that was rich and productive. He concluded that the causes of such panics and depression were in the money and banking system.

His first fight in Congress was against the Aldrich-Vreeland

Emergency Currency Bill, which set out to establish the Federal Reserve System. Lindbergh opposed it as a "monstrous scheme to place under one control the finances of the country," saying, "With that power all centered in the great city banks, and these banks controlled by the trusts and money powers, the politics, as well as the business of this country, would be under its absolute dictation." He lost that fight, but never ceased attacking the "money trust."

His record in Congress added to his stature at home, and he had no trouble getting re-elected each time he stood for his seat.

In 1911, he introduced a resolution to investigate "whether there are not combinations of financial and other concerns which control money and credits." The idea was taken over by the Democrats and came into being in 1917 as the famous Pujo Committee, counseled by Samuel Untermyer. After months of hearing testimony, the committee concluded that there was indeed a money trust, and named the culprits as J. P. Morgan & Company; First National Bank of New York; National City Bank of New York; Lee, Higginson & Company of Boston and New York; Kidder, Peabody & Company of Boston and New York; and Kuhn, Loeb & Company.

As a result, Congress passed laws prohibiting interlocking directorates of banks and trust companies under federal jurisdiction. Lindbergh was pleased but not satisfied, and continued his crusade against the big money interests by writing a book called *Banking and Currency*.

He had been visited, at the time of his resolution to investigate the money trust, by an emissary of the big banks, and he told the House. At that time, he said, he was warned that if he insisted on pushing his investigation the country would be plunged into the worst financial panic it had ever known.

Lindbergh later reported an outright attempt to bribe him to suppress his book *Banking and Currency*. He told a friend some years after the event that a man had come to see him in Chicago and had engaged in what seemed a general conversation about corruption and bribery in government, and had ended by offering two million dollars if Lindbergh would suppress his book. Lindbergh refused.

The editor of a Duluth newspaper once wrote about Lindbergh: "Every effort has been made to suppress him, bottle him up, choke him off, ignore him, squash him and discipline him. . . . He has gone direct to the people and the people seem to like it."

"Indeed," the editor went on, "Mr. Lindbergh has won distinction by having it so persistently refused him. . . ."

An Old Guard politician was asked how the organization could permit such a radical maverick as Lindbergh to represent the Republican party in his district for so long. The politician said, "We spent so much money trying to lick Lindbergh that his district became too prosperous to care about a change."

As it turned out, the machine didn't have to defeat Lindbergh to get him out of Congress.

His letters show that he was relieved to give up his seat. He had made his decision not to run before his country entered the war early in 1917. But he did not leave politics. He tried to get the Republican nomination for United States Senator from Minnesota. His opponent in the primary was Frank B. Kellogg, a conservative Republican, who later was to win much fame with his postwar peace pact.

Lindbergh ran on a strongly anti-war platform. Because any criticism of all-out war in 1917 was made to seem like treason, Lindbergh lost to Kellogg. So he finished the book he had started—*Your Country at War, and What Happens to You After the War, and Related Subjects.* The book was a restatement of his previous positions.

"To a greater extent than ever before," he wrote, "the world presents the failure in some respects of the existing civilization. . . . The old order of things is what has run us 'off the track,' and . . . a new plan of things must be worked out."

He said that the campaign to help the Allies was motivated by profit, and he wanted to take the wartime profit out of all mail, telegraph, telephone, transport, banking.

"Trespass upon our rights on the high seas makes our cause just; still I do not claim it was wise to enter the war. Our purpose is humane, nevertheless I believe I have proved that a certain 'inner circle' . . . maneuvered . . . [so] that some of the belligerents would violate our international rights and bring us to war with them."

In the spring of 1918, according to Lindbergh's law partner Walter Quigley, government agents entered the plant where *Your Country at War* was being printed and ordered the owner to destroy all plates of the book and of the earlier Lindbergh book on money and banking, and all copies of both books. A few thousand copies of the former had already been printed and shipped to Minnesota, but the rest were destroyed and the book was not again in print until more than a dozen years had passed.

Also in 1918 a new political force, the Nonpartisan League, which had come into power in North Dakota, moved into Minnesota. It was made up of farmers who paid sixteen dollars a head to create a fund that enabled the League to battle the Republican right wing for party control. A full slate of candidates, headed by Lindbergh as the gubernatorial candidate, was named to fight the Republican Old Guard in Minnesota.

Three tremendous forces were against them, and more particularly against *him*. One was the fact that the war was on, and he was criticizing its conduct and aims and was therefore suspect. He even spoke against the way Liberty Loan bonds were sold by financial speculators.

Then, there was the general temper of the times. The successful 1917 revolution in Russia had made almost every businessman in the United States fear that a similar revolution could take place here. Trade unions were being influenced by Socialistic ideas. Thus exposure of the real social lags in American capitalism was resisted because the criticisms could be tabbed "Bolshevik." True, there were some very vocal left-wingers—the I.W.W., the syndicalists, the anarchists. When bombs were mailed to public officials by extremists, the whole left wing was held accountable. The fact was, however, that there were only about 100,000 persons altogether in left-wing groups, and the great majority of them were law-abiding and believed in constitutional processes.

The Nonpartisan League's program supported the war effort, but also asked for conscription of wealth, attacked profiteering, demanded a state-owned bank, as well as state ownership of terminal elevators, flour mills, and packing plants. This was very near Socialism, of course, and so the League and its candidates became the target of all the good citizens who were frightened of subversion.

There was another bloc against Lindbergh, one he had helped to antagonize during his last term in Congress. This was the Catholic Church.

In 1916 he had introduced in the House of Representatives a resolution asking for an investigation of a controversy between the

Free Press Defense League and the Church. In defending his action, and the speeches he made in its favor, Lindbergh wrote, "In my judgment, the high dignitaries of the Catholic Church made a grievous mistake in using their political influence to prevent the investigation.

"READ HISTORY. YOU WILL FIND THAT EVERYWHERE, IN ALL LANDS AND AT ALL TIMES, MANY OF THE HIGH DIGNITARIES OF THE CHURCH OF ROME HAVE BEEN THE ALLY OF OPPRESSION." He went on to say he did not blame the Church for this, but only those men in the Church who were corrupted by power.

This abortive resolution and Lindbergh's speeches were brought up strongly in 1918 by various organs of the Catholic Church. The *Catholic Bulletin*, in its last issue before the Minnesota primary election, called on Catholics to vote against the League. The Right Reverend Bishop Busch, at the graduation exercises of St. Benedict's Academy in St. Cloud, begged "the good Sisters of the Academy and all women to throw their whole soul into the prayer 'Lindbergh shall not be Governor.' "

The Minnesota Public Safety Commission was headed by John F. McGee, a Catholic, who had brought Lindbergh's resolution to the attention of the St. Paul diocese and unleashed the Catholic counterattack. The Commission had great wartime powers, and went all out to defeat Lindbergh.

With all these elements—money interests, left-wing vs. right-wing politics, and the Church issue—churning away in an already inflamed wartime situation, the 1918 Minnesota primary campaign became a vicious and unprincipled display of the democratic process. It was more like a civil war than a political campaign. There was terror and violence—and not all of it was by vigilantes. Law-enforcement officials allowed mobs to riot, sometimes aided them, and often took an illegal stand themselves.

After one meeting, Lindbergh came out of the hall to find that the friend who had driven him there had been dragged from the car by a mob and beaten nearly unconscious. There was no police protection. Alone and unarmed, C.A. faced the crowd of violent armed men and spoke to them firmly, without displaying fear. They fell back.

When the mob was at a safe distance, Lindbergh turned his back and helped his friend into the car. The two men had driven only a few yards when the spell was broken; the mob began shooting at them. Bullets hit the car. Lindbergh said to his friend, "We must not drive so fast. They will think we are afraid of them if we do."

Often Congressman Lindbergh was denied permission to rent halls in which to hold meetings. On one occasion he was actually forced out of the state for whose governorship he was contending by a sheriff who had decided to take the law into his own hands.

During the campaign, Lindbergh was vilified, calumniated, stoned, and hanged and burned in effigy. "The 1918 campaign will be remembered as long as anyone lives who took part in it," Lynn Haines wrote. "It will go down in the history of the state as one period in which Minnesota forgot the meaning of Democracy and turned loose the Cossack-minded to 'Ride' down all those who had a different point of view."

During this violent time, Lindbergh was often driven to meetings in an automobile by his son, then aged sixteen. An observer reports that Charles A. Lindbergh, Jr., did not seem to take an interest in the fierce opposition to his father, but would spend the time while C.A. spoke tinkering with the engine of the car.

C.A. survived the terror, although he was told more than once that he would not walk out of a meeting alive. At one time, it appeared that he might even win, that the Nonpartisan League would overcome being called "an American Soviet." But the Catholic backlash turned the balance during the last weeks of the campaign. The final vote was 150,000 for Lindbergh and the League to 199,000 for the Old Guard slate.

Lindbergh's contretemps with the Catholic Church and his running fight with the financial establishment had automatically made him the target of most newspapers, the great majority of which were extremely conservative. They had bank debts, and their advertisers were also beholden to bankers; it was natural that they should oppose Lindbergh with his radical economics and his unremitting attacks on the pro-war politicians as tools of big money. And, of course, the Catholic issue made Lindbergh seem a bigot. Lindbergh's partner Quigley recalled that Lindbergh was "punished by the press, receiving at times a national condemnation which would have discouraged a less courageous fighter. With the possible exception of Robert M. La Follette, Sr., no man has been more pilloried in modern American politics than Lindbergh."

Nevertheless. C. A. Lindbergh liked newspapermen most of his life. He said they were "honest, progressive, alert and desirous of playing fair with the public." "They are caught," he once said, "and like a lot of other people have to 'obey their master's voice' or stop eating."

This attitude changed, however, during his later years. From 1906 to 1916 he had never lost an election, spending five consecutive terms in Congress. But, starting with his abortive senatorial campaign against Kellogg, he never again won an election. And he attributed this to the fact that he had such a uniformly prejudiced press opposing him. He often said that the voters were not being given a fair choice, since they could not get the truth in their newspapers. During the later years of his life, he was openly bitter at newspaper bias.

The press also frustrated him in other directions. After Lindbergh's primary defeat, Bernard Baruch wired in August, 1918, offering him a position on the War Industries Board. Baruch knew Lindbergh's reputation as a banker and businessman and also that the Congressman had volunteered to help the war effort. Lindbergh wired back: "REPLYING TO YOUR TELEGRAM WILL SERVE ANYWHERE FOR THE GENERAL CAUSE. WHEN AND WHERE SHALL I REPORT FOR INFORMATION?"

He was asked to come to Washington. According to his own account, "I was sworn in, and still carry the card that was issued to me. Mr. Baruch assigned to me work of great importance, and I came back to Minnesota. I was to return to Washington within two weeks.

"When my appointment was announced in Minnesota it raised a storm of protest from the Federal Reserve Bank of the 9th District, as well as [other] Reserve Banks. . . .

"Certain of these interests, by virtue of their positions as head of Liberty Loan Committees, were willing to block the success of the Liberty Loan and even to obstruct the National Administration in its war program in order to have me removed. . . . This inspired campaign was aided by the malicious attacks of certain newspapers. . . ."

The attacks, particularly from Minnesota, became so intense that Lindbergh felt forced to resign. He wrote to his daughter Eva, "I am not blaming the Administration. They were up against it."

He never again held public office. He set up a law office in Minneapolis, but paid little attention to his practice. He was more interested in politics—he ran a disastrous race for the Senate against Harold Knutson in 1923—and in writing books about his economic and political ideas. He represented some Eastern banks and other business interests in Minnesota, and invested in Florida real estate. But his $250,000 had shrunk during his years in Congress, and his health began to interfere with his business.

In 1923 his once-volcanic energy showed signs of diminishing. He would still come to the office before dawn and work with his old-time fury, but by noon he would be tired and in the afternoon he was sometimes incoherent. He had started a new scheme, which was being well received, to create a cooperative insurance company for farmers. The purpose was to keep at home the tremendous amounts of money which Minnesotans were paying out in premiums to the Metropolitan Life and other out-of-state insurance companies. Also, Lindbergh was going to try for the governorship of his state once again.

But he never completed these projects. The reason for his declining vigors was diagnosed in February, 1924. He had a brain tumor, a malignant growth that had already invaded so much of the brain that it could not be removed. He died of the cancer a few weeks later. His body was cremated. Some months afterward, young Charles A. Lindbergh flew his airplane over Little Falls to the Lindbergh place, a mile and a half outside the town. There he banked his plane and made a slow turn over the house. With his free hand, he picked up an urn and upended it over the side of the cockpit. His father's ashes drifted down to the land he had owned.

A letter C.A. wrote a few years before his death might make his epitaph. "I will be here [in Florida] ten or twelve days now and then home again. I say home, but home to me is anywhere. I've gotten used to being at home where night finds me. It does not distress me, but guess that's because of habit, for most living things like to have a home and I would, if I really had one. Since I have none the world makes a good roomy place."

3

BOYHOOD

AFTER HIS FIRST WIFE DIED IN 1895, C. A. LINDBERGH became a romantic object: a grief-stricken widower with two young daughters who needed mothering; the fact that he was tall, handsome, well-to-do, and a successful lawyer did not detract from his appeal. Yet it was not until five years had passed that he became serious about another woman. She was younger than he by seventeen years; her name was Evangeline Lodge Land; and she was a schoolteacher in Little Falls.

The second Mrs. C. A. Lindbergh was born in Detroit in 1876. In a time when few women got any kind of higher education, she took a Bachelor of Science degree at the University of Michigan and then went on to get her Master's degree in science at Columbia University in New York. Her education was enough to set her apart from other women, and she was not merely intellectual but attractive as well. She came of a family with deep roots in North America. The first of the Lodges (her mother's family) arrived in New York sometime after the War of 1812. A Land helped found the city of Hamilton, in Ontario, Canada. Another ancestor was General Winfield Scott, who led the U.S. Army brilliantly against the Mexicans in 1847 and was the Whig candidate for the U.S. Presidency in 1852. (He lost the election partly as the result of several unfortunate extemporaneous speeches.)

Evangeline Lodge Land married C. A. Lindbergh at her parents' house in Detroit in March, 1901. She was twenty-five, he forty-two. They went on a honeymoon to California, then returned to live in Little Falls.

C. A. Lindbergh had bought a piece of land there on the banks of the Mississippi after his first wife died. It was a lovely tract of forest, more than a hundred acres, containing some tall and ancient trees whose images reflected in the river. After he remarried, he decided to build a house on it for his new wife.

When the Lindberghs came back from their honeymoon, the house was not yet begun. At first they lived in a small cabin hastily put up on the site; then construction was started on the new house. It was not going to be a modest place; it would have three stories, thirteen rooms including a billiard room, and an imposing front hall and staircase. It was the house of a man who was not only starting a new family life but was expanding his idea of what life should be; C. A. Lindbergh built in the manorial style. He even gave the place a name: Lindholm.

The couple's only child, a son, was born in Detroit at the Land house on February 4, 1902. His name was Charles Augustus Lindbergh, Jr.

The baby was brought to live at Lindholm when he was two months old. Young Charles' earliest memories are happy ones of the big house and the land. He reveled in the openness. Some of the most poetic passages in *The Spirit of St. Louis* are of his watching, from his bed on the second floor, the stars "curve upward in their courses . . . a flock of geese in westward flight—God's arrow shooting through the sky."

His nights were not all so bright. He had two childhood terrors which persisted for many years. One was a recurrent dream of falling from a high roof or precipice. Another was a phobia of the dark. "As a child, I could wander alone, tranquilly, through the most isolated places by the light of day. But at night my mind conjured up drowned bodies on the riverbank, and robbers behind every sumac clump. . . . It was what I couldn't see that frightened me . . . the imaginary horrors that took no clear-cut form."

These fears might have been reinforced by what happened when he was four. In *The Spirit of St. Louis* he describes being alone in the house with his nurse when, without warning, it began to burn. One minute he was playing with his toys, the next he was rudely yanked out of the kitchen into the back yard.

His nurse took him behind the barn to shield him from the sight. But he peeked around a corner of the building to see a huge column of black smoke consuming his home. "You mustn't watch!" the nurse cried.

He knew that something terrible was happening, and he remembers thinking, "Where is my father—my mother—what will happen to my toys?"

The place was burned to the ground. The next day his mother took him to look at it; she tried to comfort him as they poked through the ashes, saying, "Father will build us a new house." But a four-year-old mind does not easily grasp the replaceability of possessions. Before them was the still-smoldering mass of the only shelter Charles really knew—a maze of twisted pipes, melted glass, blackened fixtures, sunk into the basement and covered with soot and ashes. A few things had been saved, "but my toys, and the big stairs, and my room above the river, are gone forever. . . ."

The fire forced the family to move to Minneapolis, for the winter, into a rented apartment. Charles hated the city as a substitute for his beloved farm. It was cold; you had to be so heavily dressed that it was no fun to go out. He got measles there. It is probably the only time a doctor has had to come to see him. He spent "hours on end in dry, heated rooms, with stuffy head and whitening skin . . . pressing [his] face against a frosted window."

The Lindberghs moved back to Little Falls the next summer and stayed in a hotel while the new, smaller, but still substantial (ten-room) house* was being built. Lindbergh played with his two half sisters, Lillian and Eva, who were considerably older than he, while the carpenters and masons worked. He paddled with the girls—they blew up his water wings—and they showed him how to make teacups out of acorns.

It was a great life, all play and all outdoors. But it began to be interrupted when Charles was five years old and his father was elected to Congress. The family—including Charles—had to go to church on Sunday in Little Falls because it was fitting that a congressman's family be religious. Charles detested having to get dressed up and sit on a hard seat and listen to stupid talk about God, and he resented the reason behind it—politics.

---

* This house and the land were given some years later by Charles A. Lindbergh and his mother to the State of Minnesota as a park, a memorial to C. A. Lindbergh. The house and the park are still there; even the family's old car is in the garage.

"It's even hotter in church than behind our team of horses on the crunching road. . . . No breath of air. . . . A smell of too many people weights the sticky dampness. My legs itch under their tight stockings." When church was over, they would spend the rest of the day where there was always a cool breeze. "Through the years of my childhood, church was an ordeal to be cautiously avoided," Lindbergh writes.

Church wasn't the most disagreeable result of his father's new career in politics. Starting in 1907, Charles and his mother had to spend winters in Washington.

"For me," wrote Lindbergh, "the city formed a prison. Red brick houses replaced the woodlands on our farm. Concrete pavement jarred against my heels. . . . It was the clank of street cars, not the hoot of an owl, that woke me at night."

The resentment he felt for being deprived of his farm was not assuaged by the privileges accruing to a congressman's son, like being allowed to walk on the railing in the Capitol grounds. (A policeman gave his permission when he learned who Charles' father was.) He has never liked cities and has only rarely lived in them.

In Washington, Charles saw Theodore Roosevelt and President Taft, stood next to Woodrow Wilson when Wilson signed one of C. A. Lindbergh's bills into law. He spent hours on the floor of the House of Representatives with his father. He met Champ Clark and Robert M. La Follette, and people told him how lucky he was to be at the nerve center of the nation's policies. Yet to Charles, Washington was a penance to be endured because of his father's career; the House of Representatives reminded him of church, hot and stuffy, with speechmaking congressmen replacing the long-winded preacher.

There were some compensations. A vacant lot next door to the apartment house where the Lindberghs lived was a good place to play and he dug up a fossil leaf there. He climbed the Washington Monument, saw the Treasury presses at work printing money, and often visited the Smithsonian Institution, a place he has always liked. There were Mount Vernon and Arlington Cemetery, and Rock Creek Park to picnic in, and the zoo to visit with his mother. Washington wasn't all bad, but it certainly wasn't Little Falls.

There was one other thing which must have left a bad feeling about Washington in Charles' mind. When the Lindberghs moved there in 1907, they were a family of five. (The Congressman was forty-eight, his wife thirty-one; Lillian was nineteen, Eva fourteen, and Charles five.) It was probably the last time that they lived together as a family. After that year the two girls were sent away to school, and sometime quite early in their married life C. A. and Evangeline L. Lindbergh became estranged. Charles A. Lindbergh has never publicly commented on this estrangement or even admitted it in his autobiography. He has given ample evidence of loving both parents much more than most children love theirs. Yet the separation was there; it is felt. He writes about one parent or the other in warm and tender terms, but rarely of the two at the same time. Of the many published photographs of Charles A. Lindbergh, there are some with his father and some with his mother, but not one of the three together.

There was never a formal separation or a divorce. The Congressman told Charles that henceforth the boy would live with his mother but that he would see his father every day. However, his mother liked to travel, and from then on the pattern of his life was winters in Washington (when he did see his father every day), summers in Little Falls on the farm (when he saw his father sometimes), and in between visits to Detroit with his mother—plus numerous trips with her to different parts of the United States, once through the Panama Canal.

Evangeline Land Lindbergh was a shy and withdrawn woman who had easily won a reputation for snobbishness in Little Falls, which was only forty miles from Sinclair Lewis's Sauk Centre and spiritually right next door. She was a solitary like her husband and used to ride her horse through the countryside by herself.

From the time Mrs. Lindbergh became estranged from her husband, she devoted herself to her only child. She was a permissive mother, not generally overprotective. Lindbergh remembers her singing to him when he was little. He never mentions being physically punished by either parent, and it is likely that he never was. Evangeline Lindbergh was as stoical as her husband with Charles; she did not try to impose her ideas of what he should do or how he should behave no matter how deeply she may have disagreed with any of his decisions. And she rarely betrayed her worry over his safety—perhaps only once or twice during his daredevil flying career.

The two Detroit families she came from, the Lands and the Lodges, were both notable for their strong-minded, independent men. Both families reinforced the intransigence and Puritanism of the Lindberghs. They were not, however, so resolutely involved in the welfare of the common man as August and C. A. Lindbergh. They had more of a sense of lineage, almost aristocracy. (They were less political than the Lindberghs. Only one of Charles' granduncles, John C. Lodge, was active in local and state politics. What political beliefs the Lodges had were conservative Republican, in strong contrast with C. A. Lindbergh's extremely left-wing Republicanism.)

But, most important, both the Lodges and the Lands added another dimension to young Charles' existence: science.

Grandfather Land was a living influence in Charles' youth. During his frequent visits to Detroit, young Charles spent a great deal of time with him.

Recalling one of these visits, Charles A. Lindbergh wrote:

There he is at the gate . . . face beaming, familiar white mustache and gold-rimmed spectacles, an old black felt hat raised high in his hand to attract our attention. . . . He's not tall, and he never elbows his way to the front, but he's always there to meet us when we arrive. . . .

"Charles, we're having smelts for dinner," he says, "and you and I are going over to Canada this Sunday, to pick some flowers."

The Lands lived in a gray frame house at 64 West Elizabeth Street. The building, surrounded by apartment houses, had a sign on the door: "c. h. land, dentist."

The place was a treasure house of wonders for a small boy. "There's the stuffed head of the big Rocky Mountain sheep that I used as a target for my unloaded rifle . . . the safe which holds platinum foil and bright sheets of dental gold." There was a cabinet full of geologic samples, including a piece of a mammoth tooth. There was a human skull in a box, and Charles' toys, and a tomcat named Fluff.

Grandfather Land was much more than a dentist. He was an innovator, the first to use porcelain in dental crowns. He held patents on this and other inventions. He was also an inveterate seeker and trier. Against the industrial soot of Detroit he had invented a kind of air-cleansing system for his house, consisting of a fan which sucked outside air in through cheesecloth filters.

The house was Dr. Land's workshop, as well as his office and home. The basement and some of the rooms held much laboratory equipment, including furnaces for working porcelain and precious metals.

"My grandfather is as wise as he is old," Lindbergh wrote many years later, "and he can make *anything* with his hands." And Dr. Land was never too busy to answer young Lindbergh's questions, or to help him in his various projects—polishing the carnelians the boy had found in Minnesota, mixing clay and making molds, handling charged wires.

The talk around the Land table was different from that among the Lindberghs. The Lands were scientific determinists, interested in philosophy and the latest scientific discoveries and theories. The talk didn't "hum in my ears like a church sermon or a political speech." Science was something solid that young Lindbergh's mind could grasp; he liked the quick way he could get a definite answer in science. At the Land house he learned that "science is power." He thought he might become a scientist when he grew up, perhaps study biology and medicine, but his marks in school were poor.

He picked up some uncertainties at the Land house, too. There were debates about evolution, the missing link, and whether or not the Bible was right. (Grandfather Land said that the Bible might well be proved wrong.) Charles Lindbergh thought about this, and whether there was a God, and an existence after life. "These problems continued to throb in my mind . . . beyond childhood."

There were echoes of the same morality and principle in Grandfather Land that were so apparent in C. A. Lindbergh. Grandfather Land thought that movies were bad for children; they gave a distorted view of life. Nevertheless, following through on his ideas of free inquiry, he gave the boy nickels to go to the movies.

There were other strong male influences in Detroit. Granduncle Edwin Lodge was a physician who had his own fey way of driving an automobile. He took Charles on house calls, weaving in and out through the Detroit streets. He cared for the boy's colds and childhood cuts and abrasions. He impressed Charles with his dash and assurance.

Grand-uncle Albert Lodge was also a doctor, his house three blocks away from Grandfather Land's. He was a big, muscular man. Mrs. Lindbergh said that Albert occasionally lost his temper, Charles recalls. "Once he was riding on a Detroit streetcar and the motorman didn't pay attention when he rang the bell. The same thing had happened before, too often. Grand-uncle Albert walked to the front of the car, smashed the glass face of the fare register with his gloved fist, and said—as the astounded motorman jammed on the brakes—'Maybe you'll stop the next time I ring.' There was a note of admiration in my mother's voice whenever she told the story; but she usually added that it was wrong of my grand-uncle to do it."

The family used to speak with pride of Great-Grandfather Edwin Lodge, who had also been a doctor, owned a pharmacy, and published the *Homeopathic Observer*. He fathered eleven children by two wives. He could write the Lord's Prayer on a circle the size of a dime, and was a fundamentalist preacher who baptized his congregation members in a lake, standing up to his waist in the cold water.

Yet, in spite of their pride in the man, the younger generation were committed to following science, though it might lead to a direct refutation of old Edwin's religious beliefs.

The Lodges and the Lands, like the Lindberghs, made a point of putting principle ahead of sentiment, and reason over all. But neither family was totally consistent about it. The presence of a child could melt their rigidity.

C. A. Lindbergh's taciturnity seemed unbroken to strangers who saw him only as a stern man who gave no ground and asked no quarter. But to his daughters, and to his mother, and occasionally to an old friend, he revealed that his lone fights were sometimes depressing. His eldest daughter, Lillian, died midway in his ten years in Congress, of tuberculosis, and he never got over her death. In letters to his family, he constantly referred to his loss and apologized for inflicting his sorrow on others.

He once wrote, "The trouble with me is that I do not tell people when I am pleased."

Like other lone fighters, C. A. Lindbergh kept strangers at arm's length. Consequently he had to rely more than most men on his children for warmth and support. Being so alone in everything, he seemed to require their physical presence. He always tried to take at least one of them wherever he went—Eva, or Lillian, or Charles; particularly Charles, his first and only son.

From the time the boy was three (and he forty-six), the Congressman used to take him swimming in the Mississippi. C.A. would swim the quarter mile to the other side with Charles on his back, both of them naked, and then he would swim back. As Charles got bigger, his father urged him to swim himself.

The boy was bathing with his father when he waded into the water alone and suddenly slipped into a deep hole. The water was over his head. When he surfaced, he saw that his father was making no move to help him, but was just standing on shore, laughing. Without knowing it, Charles had started to swim. He was eight years old.

When he was only six, one of his Detroit uncles had given him a rifle and taught him to shoot it in the basement of the Land house. C.A. thought the boy a bit young to have a gun, but, recalling his own gun-toting boyhood, he allowed Charles to carry the rifle when they went into the woods. Charles pointed the gun in every direction, carried it cocked and loaded through brush, and behaved in other reckless ways. But C.A.'s principle was to offer no advice or help unless asked.

Sooner or later something would happen—and it did. A twig caught the trigger, and the gun fired. The bullet just grazed the boy's toe.

C.A. said nothing until they were near the house; then he stopped and appeared disturbed. Charles wanted to know what was troubling him.

"I'm sorry your gun went off that way," C.A. said. "It maybe will spoil our hunting. I'm afraid your mother will not let you go out with the gun any more."

Said Charles, "If you don't say anything about it, I won't either." The incident ended there.

"Father thought six was young for a rifle," Charles Lindbergh reported later, "but the next year he gave me a Savage repeater; and the year after that, a Winchester 12-gauge automatic shotgun; and he loaned me the Smith & Wesson revolver that he'd shot a burglar with. He'd let me walk behind him with a loaded gun at seven."

Charles became his father's constant companion in walking and hunting expeditions. As soon as he was strong enough to swing an axe, C.A. let him use one. When he was eleven, Charles learned to drive the family car—a Ford—on the Lindbergh land, although he was so small he had to stand up to reach the pedals. By the time he was twelve, he was permitted to drive the car elsewhere.

"Age seemed to make no difference to [Father]," Lindbergh has since written. "My freedom was complete. All he asked for was responsibility in return. . . ."

C.A. loved to have Charles with him at his office. A visiting newspaperman remarked having to step over a yellow-haired boy who was lying on the floor, reading a book. Another visitor remembered how Charles kept jumping on his father's back during a serious conversation between the two men, and how he was not reprimanded for it.

One of C.A.'s secretaries recalled an incident when the boy was helping address office mail. Charles was sitting at a long table stacked higher than his head with books and envelopes, writing as fast as he could in his sprawling script.

The secretary suggested a more efficient way of handling packages. The boy turned and said with disgust, "You can't tell me what to do. You're just a secretary working for my father."

Lindbergh, Sr., was at his desk, apparently busy, but he overheard this bit of dialogue and turned his chair. "There isn't anyone in this office working for anyone else," he said. "We are all working together. Don't forget that, son."

In 1914, when Charles was twelve, C. A. Lindbergh got a leave of absence from the House of Representatives and took him on a camping trip in north central Minnesota—a trip that was also a survey by the elder Lindbergh of the operation of the reservoir system at the headwaters of the Mississippi River. They portaged their boat to the small stream that would become the Mississippi, then floated down the river in their rowboat until they reached the family farm in Minnesota. The trip took two weeks. They cooked their own meals over an open fire—meals that were made on game they shot or fish they caught. They slept out of doors, although it rained a good deal of the time and there were swarms of black flies and mosquitoes.

"That trip with Charles was one of the happiest times in my

whole life," the father told a friend. "I found the man in him. He has good stuff, and will stick. He stood up under the discomforts of that trip as I never expected he would. A good experience that was for both of us."

On that trip, C.A. spoke to his son about his political and economic concerns for the future, as to another man. Charles did not answer, for he didn't understand many of these things; also, it disturbed him to discuss a future in which his father frankly acknowledged that he himself would not take part because he would be dead.

His father talked about the "money trust," and high interest rates on farm mortgages. The boy felt that perhaps the elder Lindbergh made these things sound more desperate than they were. C.A. said that the country belonged to the people, but they hadn't learned to run it, and he was worried about all the foreign loans we were making to a Europe at war. "The trouble with war is that it kills the best and youngest men," the father told his son.

Charles took other trips with his father, sometimes went hunting with him and other men. One of the hunters remembers how Charles would wake up in the morning, watch his father closely to see if he was asleep, then begin a pillow fight, which would end only when the father said, "That's enough, son."

However, this was only one aspect. The elder Lindbergh once told a friend that he found Charles unusually serious for his age. "I seem to be more of a kid than he does sometimes," the Congressman said.

Charles was brought up with machinery and showed a real affinity for things mechanical from an early age. The family traded up from the Ford to a Saxon car, and in the summer of 1916, when Charles was only fourteen, he was asked to drive his mother and his Uncle Charles in the Saxon from Little Falls to California. The trip had been calculated to take a couple of weeks. In thirty days they had gone only as far as Winslow, Arizona, after being held up by various mechanical difficulties and breakdowns. They had been forced to wait for repairs and, on occasion, for dry roads. It was quite a test for a fourteen-year-old, but Charles met it head on with the traditional family stoicism and resourcefulness. They arrived in Los Angeles after nearly six weeks on the road, and Charles wrote his father a letter describing the various automobiles he had seen en route and evaluating their good and bad features. He addressed the letter to "C. A. Lindbergh" and signed it "C. A. Lindbergh."

Charles' upbringing, like his father's, inculcated a strong sense of responsibility in practical things. He was capable with guns, machinery, and in matters where good reflexes and sound judgment were important. But school was something else. When he was eight, his parents decided he ought to start his studies. His mother tutored him up to his age level, then entered him in the second grade of Force School, in Washington. It was the first of eleven different schools he would attend during the next ten years, in places as widely separated as Washington and Redondo Beach, California. He records with a touch of bitterness that he never completed a full academic year in any of them before entering college—and that he never enjoyed any of them, either. He describes himself as not a good student, but puts this down partly to the errant nature of his education. Too, his physical being dominated his mind; he could study for just so long and then he had to get out and do something. He had never been able to learn abstractly; he had no use for learning for its own sake.

Charles was graduated from the Little Falls high school in 1918 at the age of sixteen, but characteristically managed to do it without much studying. In 1918 it was possible for a student in that school to gain credits toward graduation by working on a farm to raise food for the war effort. Charles left school and used the fields and woods owned by his father for this purpose. He would have preferred to join the Army Air Force or the Lafayette Flying Corps, but he was too young to enlist without parental permission, and he certainly couldn't get that from his anti-war father.

He took his schoolbooks with him, but did not expect to study much while working the farm. He would have to pass examinations but they would not be difficult. He raised heifers and sheep. He actually ran the enterprise at the age of sixteen, with a hired hand, for his father had a law office in Minneapolis (he was out of Congress by then) and had business interests that often took him East. Charles built a house for the pigs, fixed the barn for the cows, milked, acted as midwife for the animals, fought off the murderous midwinter cold of central Minnesota.

Once, he was nearly killed while plowing a field with a tractor. He had tripped the lift, preparing to turn at the end of a furrow, when the steel plow flashed by his head and smacked into the ground. The lift mechanism had jammed, upsetting the entire gangplow. If he hadn't turned his tractor at the moment he pulled the lever, he would have been crushed in his seat. The flying plowshare missed his head by less than six inches.

This experience, like several others later in life, Lindbergh absorbed and transmuted into his theory about risk and life. Farm life wasn't as safe as people thought, and there were risks in almost everything that was interesting or worth while. In fact, he figured out that "danger was a part of life not always to be shunned. . . . It was dangerous to climb a tree, to swim down rapids in the river, to go hunting with a gun. . . . You could be killed as quickly on a farm as in an airplane."

The next year, 1919, he had another brush with death on the farm. That year, at seventeen, he had taken on in addition to the running of the farm a dealership in milking machines and farm engines. Early one winter day he saddled up his pony in the five-degree cold and rode to the nearby town of Pierz. He spent the day talking to farmers about the best methods for milking cows mechanically, and finally left for home.

By evening he was still nearly thirty miles from his farm. Snow began to fall. He buttoned himself up, pulled his hat down, and nearly slept in the saddle as the pony plodded homeward. Suddenly he was jolted awake by the realization that the pony was staggering, and as he dismounted, it stopped.

He began to walk, leading the pony, for about fifteen miles. The blizzard got worse; then the snow ended and the cold became more biting. Stumbling along hour after hour, young Lindbergh finally had to lie down for a few minutes in a snowbank to ease his cramped muscles. But he and the animal made it back to the farm.

In 1920 he had had two years of raising sheep and cows and could see that he wasn't getting anywhere. He actually liked farming, loved the farmer's life, and did it well—but it wasn't fully satisfying. What he really wanted to do was to go to Alaska and to fly an airplane. These were not sudden whims. The Alaska idea came from Vilhjalmur Stefansson, the Minnesotan who had become a famous arctic explorer. Stefansson told Charles that Alaska was the last frontier, the last chance he'd have to prove himself a man the way his father had done on the American frontier.

And as for flying—that idea started when, as a small boy, Charles would lie on his back, completely hidden in the tall grass in Little Falls. Then he could look directly overhead and see the clouds sailing by, and nobody could see him. "How wonderful it would be," he thought, "if I had an airplane—wings with which I could fly up to the clouds and explore their caves and canyons—wings like that hawk circling above me." With an airplane, he could ride the wind.

One summer day—he's not sure of the year—he recalls hearing an engine. Nothing unusual in that, since a number of automobiles had passed by on the road that summer. He went on playing in his upstairs room with the river stones he and his mother had collected.

Then he realized that the sound was coming not from the road but from the other side of the house. He climbed out the window onto the roof.

"Flying upriver below higher branches of trees, a biplane was less than two hundred yards away—a frail, complicated structure, with the pilot sitting out in front between struts and wires." It was one of his first looks at an airplane, one of the "pusher" types with the propeller behind, pushing the plane.

Charles watched it fly out of sight and then ran down to tell his mother the breathtaking news. His mother knew about it; she'd read in the *Transcript* that a pilot was coming to the town, but she'd forgotten to tell Charles about it. The pilot was taking people up for rides at a dollar a minute, she said. Not only was this terribly expensive; it was terribly dangerous. A wing could fall off—the engine could stop—you could be killed.

Impressed by his mother's anti-airplane arguments, Charles did not ask to fly. But the sight of a plane had buttressed his dreams of flight with the substance of the real thing. And as for the dangers of flying—he'd heard grownups talking about such living pilots as Orville and Wilbur Wright, Glenn H. Curtiss, and Lincoln Beachey. Dangerous and expensive flying might be, but if it was done with skill, one could survive.

One time when he was quite young, in Washington, Charles' mother took him to nearby Fort Myer, Virginia, to see an air show. There were six planes and a small grandstand to watch from while the planes took off and raced a motorcar around a track. In another event the pilots flew over a chalked outline of a battleship and "bombed" it with oranges thrown by hand. The pilots sat out in front of the planes, with their caps turned backward. Like the plane Charles had seen in Little Falls, these were biplanes with the propeller mounted behind.

At this meet a plane was seen to falter and to descend behind some trees to make a forced landing. Charles never learned whether or not the pilot had been hurt.

It is not possible to determine whether these planes or the one at Little Falls were the first Charles had seen, but there is no doubt that Fort Myer was his first look at an organized exhibition of flying.

All these experiences coalesced with his identification of freedom with flying, his interest in things mechanical, and his theory of the relativity of risks and his belief that the only real achievements were physical; i.e., conquering fear and fatigue. He had to be a flier.

But the urge to vanquish the Alaskan frontier and the desire to fly were countered by the more prosaic notions of his parents. Both were graduates of the University of Michigan; both thought he ought to have a college degree. Since he was a dutiful son, he determined to try to do what they wanted.

He decided to study mechanical engineering at the University of Wisconsin in the fall of 1920. He would have preferred aeronautical engineering, but most of the courses he wanted to take were given at the Massachusetts Institute of Technology. His grades were not good enough for him to get into the Institute.

Before leaving the farm he decided he should find tenants to take over the livestock and the land. He interviewed several people and selected a married couple; then he was ready to leave.

From the time he learned to drive, Charles always had some means of transportation—each one faster than the last. His first personal vehicle was an Excelsior motorcycle, which he got in his late teens. He rode it much too quickly for the comfort of the Little Falls citizenry, but he had been given "independence with responsibility" by his father and he continued to exercise them both.

When fall came, he rode to Madison, Wisconsin, on his motorcycle and entered the University. One schoolmate says he kept the machine in his room, constantly tinkering with the engine when he wasn't riding it, interfering with sleep in the dormitory. But this may be apocryphal, because Lindbergh was living with his mother, who had taken a job teaching in Madison to be with her son.

There was a hill in Madison which he liked to speed down on the machine. He told a friend that it should be possible to descend the hill at full throttle and make the turn at the bottom without braking, if one calculated the centripetal and centrifugal forces properly and leaned at the proper angle. He tried it once and fell off. Since he was going so fast, he might have been seriously hurt, but he broke no bones, merely scraped himself badly. He got up and went back a second time, and made it.

He also had the idea of testing how far he could leap the machine into the lake bordering the campus, but was dissuaded by his two friends (both male) from trying this experiment. With one of his friends he designed and built a motor-driven iceboat. It was equipped with a small gasoline engine and an airplane propeller, and attained some very high speeds before it cracked up.

He still hated school and studying and spent most of his time out of doors on the motorcycle, or in rifle and pistol shooting. He had joined the University R.O.T.C. and had become a member of both the rifle and the pistol teams. He practiced in the shooting gallery or on the range, and was an excellent shot. He and the captain of the rifle team had a little game between them. They used to shoot twenty-five-cent pieces out of each other's fingers from a distance of fifty feet. This further implemented Lindbergh's theory about risks being relative—particularly when the same boy tried to talk him out of flying because it was too dangerous.

Lindbergh knew that progress depended on education, that he wouldn't have his motorcycle if someone hadn't studied and invented it, but he couldn't understand why study couldn't be better balanced with the more interesting pursuits of life.

He knew one thing for sure: studies or no, diploma or no, he had no intention of following his father into the law or into politics. He'd seen enough of politics to know he hated the life in Washington, and of the law his father had told him, "A lawyer's tied to his office and his desk. It isn't the kind of work you'd like."

At the end of his freshman year, Lindbergh went to R.O.T.C. artillery school at Camp Knox, Kentucky, for six weeks. He had the motorcycle with him, and when the artillery course was finished he rode alone to Florida, at the age of nineteen, with forty-eight dollars in his pocket. This was a time when any kind of motor travel was risky and unreliable. At one point he had to walk his machine through ten miles of wet sand—there was just no road. But he made it to Jacksonville, and back to Little Falls, fighting his battles with weather and machinery, stopping only when he was too worn out to move. He returned with nine dollars.

He went back to the University of Wisconsin in the fall with the renewed resolve to do well in engineering. But he was still the poor student whose body was master of his mind. His mathematics was only passable. His English composition was marked down for punctuation and spelling.

Lindbergh was repelled by the idea of spending his youth on "formulae, semicolons, and our crazy English spelling. I don't believe God made man to fiddle with pencil marks on paper. He gave him earth and air to feel. And now even wings to fly. . . ."

He thought that if he were studying something related to his concerns, like aeronautics, he might do much better. "I would work hard to understand the magic contours of a wing." But there weren't many aeronautics courses at Wisconsin, and with his marks M.I.T. was ever more remote and impossible.

Lindbergh could see no future for himself at Wisconsin. He talked things over with his two friends in Madison—one was Richard Plummer, who shared Lindbergh's cycling enthusiasms, the other Delos Dudley, the son of the University's assistant librarian. Dudley wrote to several flying schools for literature (he himself was much interested in aviation) and gave it to Lindbergh. One of these places was the Nebraska Aircraft Corporation, which was producing the Lincoln Standard Turnabout Airplane—and giving flying lessons as a promotional device to help sell their product and to carry part of the firm's overhead.

During the second half of his sophomore year at Wisconsin, Charles told his parents he wanted to quit school and learn to fly. C. A. Lindbergh was dead set against the idea. He said, "Flying is too dangerous and you're my only son." He offered him a choice of careers in business or farming. He even got his friends to try to reason with Charles. But in the end C. A. Lindbergh capitulated and later even helped the boy borrow some money at the bank to buy his first airplane.

Mrs. Lindbergh, when she heard the news, showed concern in her face, but not in her words. "All right," she said. "If you really want to fly, that's what you should do."

"You must go," she told him later. "You must lead your own life. I mustn't hold you back. Only I can't see the time when we'll be together much again." She was right; they did not spend very much time together after that, although they were always in close touch.

At the end of March, 1922, Lindbergh left the University of Wisconsin. He had not completed his sophomore year. On his Excelsior, he headed for Lincoln, Nebraska. There he enrolled as a student flier with the Nebraska Aircraft Corporation.

After Lindbergh became committed to a flying career, Mrs. Lindbergh moved back to Detroit. She got a job teaching science there in the Cass Technical High School.

![decorative laurel ornament] EARLY FLIGHT

IN APRIL, 1922, WHEN LINDBERGH STARTED LEARNING TO fly, commercial aviation in the United States was far behind that of Europe. Airplanes designed and built in Europe had dominated most of the air war of 1914–1918. It was in Europe that regular airlines had begun to carry passengers. (KLM started in 1919 between Amsterdam and London.) There were one or two local scheduled airlines in the United States.

At that time there were 1,200 civilian airplanes in the U.S. (as compared with more than 106,707 today). Almost all were former warplanes, sold off as government surplus. Most of these wood-and-fabric crates could hold only one or two passengers or a pilot and a small bit of cargo. Passengers were weighed; a man over two hundred pounds might be refused a ride or forced to pay extra. Half the planes were operated by established companies, which means they were based on fields where they could be serviced and would carry passengers over a short radius to nearby points. There was no up-to-date weather information. There was a single government-operated airway system to permit the mail to be flown from California to New York, with frequent stops for refueling and change of pilots.

The aircraft industry, built so swiftly during the war, was floundering. There was no government regulation of planes or pilots. If you had $300 or so, you could pick up a surplus warplane and fly it.

When Lindbergh reached Lincoln, Nebraska, in April, 1922, he had never been near enough to an airplane to touch one. He approached the plant at Nebraska Aircraft Corporation as an acolyte approaches an altar. "I can still smell the odor of dope [cellulose acetate or nitrate] that permeated each breath," he reported thirty years later, "like ether in a hospital's corridors. I can still see the brightly painted fuselages on the floor, still marvel at the compactness of the Hispano-Suiza engine."

The Hispano-Suiza was a water-cooled V-8 engine which turned out 150 horsepower. By comparison, the V-8s in today's automobiles are often more than twice as powerful.

The Nebraska Aircraft Corporation's plant was not a large one. The company's main business was buying up old Army training planes and converting them to civilian use. These Lincoln Standard Turnabouts were, like other Army ships, biplanes—two wings gave more strength and lift in combat—and were powered with the Hispano-Suiza engine.

The Lincoln Standard Turnabout had an open cockpit aft for its pilot and a second open cockpit forward in which two passengers could be carried. Unlike the earlier planes of Lindbergh's childhood, this one had its propeller mounted forward, which made it a "tractor," pulling rather than pushing. Its top speed was ninety miles an hour.

The Nebraska Aircraft Corporation president, Ray Page, looked over the gangling six-foot-three-inch Lindbergh and took him on as a student in his "school." Lindbergh paid $500 tuition in advance. Actually, there were no other paying students. Nevertheless there were pilots and mechanics who could teach flying and maintenance.

About a week later, on April 8, one of the company's planes was hauled out to the nearby airfield by truck. The wings were lashed parallel to the fuselage. Lindbergh stood by and watched every detail of how the plane was assembled and made ready for flight.

The wings were taken carefully out of the tow truck and attached to the fuselage, and the wires operating ailerons, flippers, and rudder were hooked up. The fuel was strained into the tank (an impurity could cause a crash), and the engine was tuned up. Lindbergh noted how the engineer tested the tautness of cables with his fingers. He had been warned that a pilot had to know about all these things and more; he had to be able to repair his plane in the field where he might be alone, far from any expert assistance. The fragile wings, wooden spars and ribs covered with fabric stretched tight with dope (that first smell of the factory) often needed mending, spark plugs had to be cleaned regularly, valves ground or changed. "You had to know how to lockstitch, how to bind the ends of rubber rope, how to lap a propeller hub to its shaft," Lindbergh recalls.

The next day, April 9, 1922, Lindbergh made his first airplane flight in the front cockpit of the Standard, sitting alongside a farm boy named Bud Gurney, who worked in the factory to earn his lessons. The pilot's name was Otto Timm. First the engine was started by hand; a mechanic pulled strongly on the propeller and then dodged out of the way when the eight cylinders began firing. The pilot was watching his instruments as Lindbergh twisted in his seat to look at him; Timm taxied the plane to the end of the sod field and turned the tail to the wind. Again he studied his instruments as he revved up the engine. This flying was serious business, Lindbergh thought. Then Timm let the motor throttle down and nodded to the mechanics. They pulled the wheel chocks out.

The plane bumped down the field and turned into the wind whose direction was shown by the wind sock. Again Timm stopped to study his instruments and check the field. Then he began his run and takeoff. Suddenly the bumpy ride became smooth as the plane left the ground.

A novice has a poet's eye, Lindbergh noted. "I lose all conscious connection with the past . . . in this strange, unmortal space, crowded with beauty, pierced with danger," he wrote many years later about his first flight. Now he sees things with a professional eye—he has learned to look downward for a mile the same way a man on the ground learns to judge things a mile away horizontally. Now he can read the contour of a hillside that to his novice's eye would have looked flat, but never has he "seen the earth below so clearly, as in those early days of flight."

Lindbergh's regular instructor was Ira Biffle, a hard-bitten, tough-talking man who'd taught many pilots to fly during the war. But Biffle had lost his taste for flying after one of his close friends had died in a crash. Lindbergh would be at the field every day on his motorcycle, but Biffle might not come. Then, later, at the factory, he would tell Lindbergh—who had by now acquired the nickname of "Slim"—that the air was too turbulent that day, to meet him in the late afternoon at the field when the wind had died down. Sometimes—not often—he would keep the appointment, and there would be time for a few takeoffs and landings in the dual-control plane before it got too dark. But most of the time Biffle never showed up at all.

Lindbergh doesn't comment on this, but the fact that he reveals Biffle's dereliction is a comment in itself. However, he obviously had sympathy for Biffle's problems; more than a dozen years later, when Biffle was dying in a Chicago hospital, Lindbergh sent a $50 check with a personal note expressing hope for his recovery.

Biffle's negligent attitude restricted Lindbergh's flying to only about eight hours in the first five or six weeks he spent at Lincoln. Then, in May, Lindbergh learned from Bud Gurney that Ray Page was going to sell the training plane to a barnstorming pilot named Erold Bahl. If Lindbergh wanted to solo, he would have to do so immediately. Lindbergh spoke to Biffle about it, but Biffle said he had to leave Lincoln for another job. Lindbergh went to Ray Page and asked permission to solo. Page said there was no question that Lindbergh had shown ability as a flier, but planes were expensive, and if he wanted to solo he would have to put up a bond of $500 to cover damage in a possible crack-up.

Lindbergh didn't have the money. He had already invested $650, including his expenses, to get eight precious hours of flying instruction. Anyhow, he knew that one solo wouldn't make him a pilot. What he needed was more experience. He asked Erold Bahl if he could go along with him as helper on the barnstorming trip. He even offered to pay his own expenses. Bahl hesitated, then said he could come. They left in May on a month's tour.

Lindbergh kept the plane clean, pulled through the propeller, and got passengers, from the crowds that gathered, at $5 a ride. After a few days, Bahl said he would pay Lindbergh's expenses because he was doing such a good job.

Later, Lindbergh suggested that Bahl might draw bigger crowds if he (Lindbergh) stood on a wing as they flew over the town preparatory to landing. Bahl was an extremely conservative flier who flew in a business suit and thought that flying ought to be safe—although he sometimes took off in weather that other, more colorful pilots would not brave. It was all a matter of judgment, he said. He told Lindbergh to climb out on the wing, if he wished, "but watch how you step on the spars." (The space between the wooden spars—the long horizontal beams that supported the wing —was covered only with thin fabric.) "Don't go farther than the inner-bay strut." The strut was the brace between the upper and lower wings. These were all the instructions Lindbergh got the first time he stepped out of the cockpit while the plane was in the air. He wore no parachute. Most pilots didn't own them then.

After the trip with Bahl, Lindbergh came back to work in the factory at Lincoln for fifteen dollars a week. He had a small amount of money in the bank but was determined to live on what he could earn.

That was June, 1922. That same month a parachute maker named Charles Hardin came to Lincoln to demonstrate his product. He did it in the most convincing way. Lindbergh watched Hardin strap on his harness, climb into a plane, and a few minutes later dive into space, a dot in the sky at an altitude of 2,000 feet. As Lindbergh watched tensely, the white chute blossomed in the air and Hardin drifted down, his life hanging from fragile threads beneath the delicate white canopy. Hardin landed safely, collapsed the fabric, and strolled off. Lindbergh was much impressed.

A day or two later he knew he had to jump. Suddenly he was exhilarated. "I had a feeling of anticipation mixed with dread, of confidence restrained by caution, of courage salted through with fear. . . . What gain was there for such a risk? I would have no pay in money for hurling my body into space. There would be no crowd to watch and applaud my landing. Nor was there any scientific objective to be gained. No, there was a deeper reason for wanting to jump, a desire I could not explain. It was the quality that led me into aviation in the first place, when safer and more profitable occupations were at hand. . . . It was a love of the air and sky and flying, the lure of adventure, the appreciation of beauty. It lay beyond the descriptive words of men where immortality is touched through danger, where life meets death on equal plane; where man is more than man, and existence both supreme and valueless at the same instant."

He asked Ray Page's permission to make a jump, and then approached Hardin and his wife. "I'd like to make a double jump," he said.

A double jump is a parachute jump in which the jumper uses two chutes, one after the other. He cuts himself away from the first after it has opened, and then opens the second and comes to earth.

When Lindbergh broached the idea of doing this kind of jump to the Hardins, they were taken aback. Lindbergh had to give a good reason for wanting to try this stunt. "I might want to buy a parachute," he said. He even asked the price, to lend verisimilitude to his request.

He told Hardin he had read that Hardin had used as many as ten chutes on one drop, and he asked with a feigned innocence, "It isn't more dangerous with two chutes than with one, is it?"

Hardin was on the spot. His sales story had been that all his parachutes were equally safe. If that was true, it followed that a double drop was no more risky than a single one. He had to agree to lend Lindbergh two of his chutes for the double drop. He also made Lindbergh a price of a hundred dollars for one parachute.

Lindbergh and Hardin took great care to see that everything went well. Together they packed the parachutes, laying the cloth out on the grass, methodically folding it accordion style, and laying the lines out straight, to run free between sheets of paper. The vent (a small opening at the top) of the second chute was tied to the shroud ring of the first chute, so that the second chute would string out full length as the first chute was cut away from the jumper.

Then the chutes were packed in a canvas bag tied to the plane near the end of the wing, to make sure the jumper cleared the tail surfaces of the ship.

Lindbergh strapped on his jumping harness and climbed into the front cockpit. Suddenly the cockpit which had seemed such a flimsy spot became as safe as a bank vault by comparison with the wing tip and that faraway canvas bag of parachutes.

When the plane reached an altitude of 1,800 feet, the pilot banked toward the field. This was the signal for Lindbergh to begin his long walk along the wing to the bag at the end. He put a leg over the side of the cockpit as he had often done before, but now he would have to walk far out, carefully stepping on the fragile spar. There was nothing but thin wires to hold onto. At last he reached the end and sat down on the wing to snap the ends of the parachutes to his harness. Then, as the plane throttled down, he let himself fall under the wing. At this point he was being held aloft by a bowknot on the mouth of the parachute bag, a knot he had tied himself. Once he untied that knot, he would be falling, with only a parachute to brake his descent.

He had no choice now, second thoughts or no. He pulled the knot and fell free. There was a jerk. The first parachute blossomed open quickly. After a few seconds he cut the rope holding the first chute to the second. It drifted off. Not being an experienced jumper, he did not realize that he should feel a second tug indicating the opening of the chute. There was no tug. He was falling free, dangerously near the ground. Instead of stringing out as it was meant to do, the second chute was a useless wad of folded fabric. He knew nothing of this at the time. Fortunately, there was enough altitude so that the speed of his descent forced air into the second parachute and it opened by itself. Lindbergh swung in the shrouds, content with his achievement, ignorant of his close call. He took a small camera from his pocket and began photographing the chute over his head.

Hardin came over to apologize for using the wrong string to tie the two chutes together; he normally used twine but had forgotten to bring it with him. The string had broken before freeing the second chute; that was why it hadn't opened.

"Slim, that was just grocery string," Bud Gurney told Lindbergh later. "It was so rotten you could pull it apart with your finger. I cut off a piece to try." But Lindbergh was unworried. He had done what he had set out to do.

"How soundly I slept that night—as I always have after a jump! I simply passed out of mortal existence a few seconds after my head hit its pillow; and when I became conscious again the sun had risen. There wasn't a dream in memory."

With that jump, Lindbergh had apparently exorcised his childhood dream phobia of falling. "Strangely enough, I've never fallen in my dreams since I actually fell through air."

A very skillful pilot named H. J. ("Shorty") Lynch came to Lincoln that June to pick up a Lincoln Standard plane—the last one in the plant—which he was taking to Kansas. Ray Page paid Lynch to give Lindbergh a few more flying lessons. Lynch told Lindbergh that he was ready to solo but that he couldn't get Page to risk a plane.

With Lynch taking the last plane from the factory and with no instructor available, there was nothing to hold Lindbergh in Lincoln. Lynch mentioned that he just might be doing some barnstorming in Kansas, and might be able to use an assistant—especially one who could wing-walk and make parachute drops.

"Don't count on it," he said. When he got to Kansas, he might send Lindbergh a wire.

Meanwhile, Lindbergh settled his finances with Ray Page and Hardin; he traded his claim to the right to solo, the wages due for several weeks' work in the factory, and twenty-five dollars in cash for a new Hardin muslin parachute.

At that time the lifespan of an aviator was about 900 flying hours. Lindbergh knew the vocation was risky, but he felt it was possible to surmount the risk, and that in any case it put him on a higher level of existence. "In flying, I tasted a wine of the gods. . . . I decided that if I could fly for ten years before I was killed in a crash, it would be a worthwhile trade for an ordinary lifetime."

Also there was Wilbur Wright, who had flown actively for more than fifteen years and was still very much alive. And there were others—some of them men who flew at Lincoln.

The same thing was true of parachutes. Lindbergh was the only jumper at the Lincoln field, and was regarded by nonjumpers as being something like a man in a condemned cell in prison. But he knew that most parachute deaths were caused by avoidable errors; that if one packed one's chute carefully, and it was well made to start with (Hardin's chutes were well made, as Hardin himself had proved countless times), then the risk was negligible. There were dangers in landing but these, too, could be canceled by careful management of the terrain.

At Lincoln, Lindbergh studied the tricks of exhibition flying. A young mechanic named Pete, in exchange for free rides on Lindbergh's motorcycle out to the flying field, gave him the trick of "hanging by the teeth." In reality, the man who hung was securely held by a harness and a wire cable invisible to the crowd below. Lindbergh knew that men had been killed wing-walking, but that was the result of disregarding foreseeable failure. "The day I stood on the top wing of an airplane while it looped, I was tied on as safely as though I'd been strapped in my cockpit." He wore a harness he had made himself. There were heel cups to snug his feet and four wire cables from a heavy leather belt around his waist that held him to strong points on the wing.

The biggest safety (or danger) factor for the stunt man was the pilot. Lindbergh studied and analyzed the style of every flier who passed through Lincoln. Lynch was one with whom he felt he'd be safe. So when he got the hoped-for telegram from Lynch in July, 1922, asking him to come on the barnstorming tour, he took his parachute and left by train for Bird City, Kansas.

He was met there by Lynch, who was flying the plane he'd picked up in Nebraska. The next day Lindbergh made his first jump for Lynch. After that, they barnstormed through Kansas, Nebraska, Wyoming, and Montana. They took with them a dog who loved to fly and would stand strapped to the outside on the plane's after cowling.

Lindbergh was still "Slim" to his pals but to the public he was "DAREDEVIL LINDBERGH" on the promotion posters. Wherever he went, he was an object of awe—on a small scale, already a local hero. Of course there was danger, but in all that year of flying, jumping, and wing-walking Lindbergh says he was never as close to being killed as he had been the day on the farm when the plow zipped by his ear.

After the barnstorming tour ended, in October, 1922, Lindbergh decided to run the Yellowstone River alone in a boat he bought for two dollars. He made twenty miles the first day, but the rapids knocked the calking from between the planks and soon he was bailing more than he was sailing. At the end of the second day he gave up, traded the boat for a ride to the railroad, and took the train back to Lincoln, where he'd left his motorcycle.

He had jammed a piston on the cycle racing a car, so had to repair the machine before he rode to Detroit (a three-day trip) to see his mother. After a visit with her he spent the rest of the winter with his father, on the farm and in Minneapolis.

Lindbergh still had not soloed when he decided to buy an airplane. He'd heard they were selling war-surplus "Jennies" cheap in Georgia. The Jenny got its name from its initials; its full name was the Curtiss JN-4D. It was a biplane which had been used for training pilots in World War I. It was very slow—top speed seventy-five miles an hour.

Lindbergh had a little money saved from his stunting career the summer and fall of 1922, and his father signed a note at the bank so that he could borrow more. He went to Souther Field, Georgia, in April, 1923, with cash and checks in his pocket. There, from the large stock of surplus Army trainers on the deserted airfield, he selected a Jenny. He paid five hundred dollars, more than he'd expected but only half the price asked for the plane. For this sum he got a complete airplane, a new Curtiss OX-5 engine (90 horse-power, V-8, water-cooled), a fresh coat of olive-drab dope on all the plane's fabric surfaces, and an extra twenty-gallon gasoline tank installed in the fuselage.

To save money, he lived alone on the field while the plane was being assembled and painted. Everyone there just assumed that Lindbergh was a pilot—why else would he buy a plane? So when the plane was ready to fly, no one asked any questions. You didn't need a license to fly a plane in 1923. Souther Field was big and smooth. Lindbergh thought he could get the plane into the air and down again without cracking up. So he just said to the chief mechanic, "Let's push her out on the line."

He wrote later, "How I wished I'd had my training in Jennies instead of Standards! I'd flown in a Jenny for only thirty-five minutes at the flying school." Enough to realize that it landed differently from a Standard. It was a problem in the air; it didn't have enough power.

Lindbergh thought he'd try out the plane on the ground by taxiing back and forth across the huge field. He taxied downwind to the opposite corner of the field. So far, so good. Then he headed back, into the wind. This time the Jenny began acting strangely. He tried to straighten it out, and before he knew it, he was airborne. He cut the throttle, came down too fast, gunned the engine, went up with one wing low, closed the throttle, yanked back on the stick, and luckily hit the ground on one wheel and a wing skid.

It was a hard bounce, but somehow he didn't break anything in that frail wooden craft. He didn't know what had happened; perhaps a puff of wind had pushed him higher than he'd intended. He decided to wait for a calmer time of day before risking his plane a second time.

Meanwhile a young man dressed in the usual pilot's boots and breeches had been watching. He came over and introduced himself as Henderson. Unasked, he offered to get into the front cockpit to help Lindbergh iron out the kinks, and asked if the Jenny's dual training controls were still hooked up. They were.

Lindbergh, embarrassed by his obvious ineptitude, made excuses for the poor performance. Henderson waved them off, saying lots of pilots got rusty over the winter. He climbed into the forward cockpit, and Lindbergh flew the plane. He made a half-dozen takeoffs and landings, and at last Henderson told him he could solo. But he suggested that Lindbergh wait for the late afternoon when the breeze had died.

That afternoon, just before dark, Lindbergh got into the plane alone and took off. He climbed to 4,500 feet, seeing the field get smaller and smaller, exulting in the freedom of flight. He finally landed because the sun was going down. It wasn't a good landing but a safe one. He had, at last, soloed.

He spent another week at Souther practicing takeoffs and landings, gaining confidence. But his cash was running low and he felt he had to start earning some money by taking up passengers. He decided to work his way through the South to Texas, then wind up in Minnesota.

A pilot warned him that he was taking a dangerous route across the country, that he'd be safer following the Gulf Coast. "But my engine was new; and my inexperience great. I'd not be bluffed by a few swamps and hills." With four hours of fuel in his tanks, he was sure he could find an emergency landing field if necessary.

He sent his suitcase home by railway express. "Then I rolled up an extra shirt, a pair of breeches, a toothbrush, some socks, spark plugs, tools, and other spare equipment in a blanket, and strapped the bundle down in the front cockpit with the seat belt." Also in the roll was an aged compass he'd bought the day before but hadn't bothered to install in the plane. He would fly by following railroads, rivers, and the sun—and install the compass when he was grounded by bad weather. He also bought and left behind two extra wooden propellers (price $20) as replacements for those he might damage in landing.

On the morning of May 17, 1923, he took off and headed for Montgomery, Alabama.

The first day he made Meridian, Mississippi, easily. The next day he headed west. Running into storms, he lost his bearings and the ground below looked forbidding; at last he selected a pasture that seemed ideal. He landed safely. Wanting to get his plane to the trees at the edge of the field, to tie it down against the storm, he taxied into a hidden ditch, almost turned over, and splintered his propeller.

He thought he was in Louisiana, but was still in Mississippi, near

Maben, having flown north instead of west. He settled into a nearby hotel, wired Souther Field for one of his new propellers, and meanwhile installed the compass he had bought in Georgia. When the propeller arrived, he lapped it to the shaft, then made a test flight.

He needed passengers to earn his way. At first the citizens of Maben were reluctant, but when he persuaded one passenger to ride, others followed. He made expenses, including the price of the propeller, the first day.

He stayed in Maben for two weeks, during which time he carried nearly sixty passengers. He was learning more about flying all the time, including the fact that he couldn't loop the Jenny—it was so low-powered it tended to stall before he could get it over. When he left, he had $250 more than when he had arrived.

His father was running in Minnesota for the United States Senate in a special election to fill the seat of Knute Nelson, who had died in office. After flying across country, Charles picked up his father in Marshall, Minnesota, in June, 1923, and gave him his first airplane ride. C. A. Lindbergh may have been scared; Charles hints that his mouth was set a little tighter than usual, but he would not admit fear to his son. Charles took the ship over the town, and C.A. dropped a few hundred handbills from the air. Quigley says C.A. told him, "I don't like this flying business. See if you can't get Charles to study law."

However, this was to be the beginning of a political campaign by air. But two days later the scheme ended in a crash. Lindbergh had taken off with his father from Glencoe for a flight to Litchfield, and the plane was barely fifty feet in the air when it nosed down, breaking a wing and a propeller. Some attributed the crash to sabotage (a cut wire), but Lindbergh makes no mention of it in his autobiography. C.A., according to an old friend with whom he stayed, had his glasses broken and "blood washed from his face."

By the time the plane was repaired, the campaign was over. C.A. had lost another election, in this one deserted by even his own Farmer-Labor supporters. It was the last time he was to run for office.

"That was the summer [1923] I landed at our Minnesota farm," Lindbergh writes. "I'd looked forward to bringing my own airplane home ever since I began flying."

He'd never before seen the farm from the air—seen it entirely. Now he could recognize the landmarks in an over-all pattern, could see how he'd misjudged the size of fields and woods from the ground. He studied the wind by the blowing poplar leaves, stalled in over a fence, and landed in a soft meadow. The neighbors were as impressed as he'd hoped they would be. Already, at twenty-one, he had made something of a mark in the world.

Later that month Charles A. Lindbergh met his mother in Janesville, Minnesota, and gave her her first flight. Although she had been unenthusiastic about his going into aviation, she proved an eager passenger. She liked flying so much that Lindbergh took her with him on a ten-day barnstorming tour. Later in his career, when he became an air-mail pilot, she would often ride with him, sitting on the mail sacks in the front cockpit.

The Jenny was so underpowered that every pound of weight made a difference in its performance. On short local flights with passengers, Lindbergh would keep his fuel tank only partially filled to save a few pounds. Once, with a very heavy passenger, he barely cleared the tops of trees on takeoff.

The plane's range was short even when carrying its full load of gas. And there was no system of airfields and no beacon lights at all for flying at night (except between Chicago and Cheyenne, for the new experimental air mail). Lindbergh was his own pilot, navigator, ground crew, field personnel. He would sometimes run into bad weather. Then he would have a limited time to decide where to land, and he had to pick a field from the air that was safe enough to land on—not an airfield, just a field.

He learned the strengths and weaknesses of every strut and spar; he knew the insides of the engine so well he could almost work on it in the dark. He might damage his ship, but never beyond repair; he fixed it and flew it again, usually without any help.

Once, trapped by a storm, he was forced to choose between a rocky hillside and a swamp. He stalled into the swamp; the plane's wheels sank into the ooze before its forward momentum had halted, and it nosed down and flipped over. Lindbergh was left hanging upside down in the cockpit, held in only by his safety belt. The position seemed ludicrous, but it was also dangerous. Pilots had broken their necks by unleashing themselves too quickly from this position and falling on their heads. To complicate his problem, his safety-belt release had jammed; he had to work his way out of the topsy-turvy cockpit by loosing the ends of the belt where they were attached to the plane and turning himself over carefully by main strength. Meanwhile a couple of local children claimed that they had seen him dead in the cockpit.

This was when he made his first headline: "AIRPLANE CRASHES NEAR SAVAGE" (Minnesota). The story said, inaccurately, that he had nose-dived the plane from three hundred and fifty feet in the air into the swamp and landed it on its propeller. Only the propeller had been damaged. He sent for a new propeller, and got some farmers to push the plane to hard ground, where he could make his repairs and take off.

The lack of power in the Jenny meant that it rarely flew high and never fast, so a crash was not apt to be fatal. Still, pilots—older, more experienced pilots—were being killed frequently in such slow ships. The fact that Lindbergh survived his crashes unhurt must be more a tribute to his fast thinking, quick reflexes, and skill than to his good luck.

5

BARNSTORMING WAS A PRECARIOUS LIVING, NOT ONLY BE-
cause of the flying risks but because so many pilots were doing it.
The market was becoming glutted; Lindbergh would sometimes fly
into a town only to learn that it had already been barnstormed out
by other pilots. Also, the unwritten price of $5 a ride per passenger
was being cut by some money-hungry pilots to $2.50. Lindbergh
refused to lower his price but says he gave a good ride for the
money. If one wanted to get ahead in flying, commercial aviation
seemed to be the answer. But to bridge that gap Lindbergh would
need more training and more prestige as a pilot.

A stranger who saw Lindbergh working on his plane one summer
day in 1923, in southern Minnesota, suggested that he join the Army
Air Corps. "They train pilots on DHs with Liberty engines," the man
said. The DH was the De Havilland (DH-4B), the Army's observation plane of World War I, and the Liberty was its 400-horsepower
engine. The plane had a top speed of a hundred and twenty-five
miles an hour. Besides this, the man said, the Army gave you
mechanics to take care of your plane. The Army flying course took a
full year, but when you graduated you were a second lieutenant—
and you didn't have to stay in the Army for the full three-year
enlistment. You could resign on two weeks' notice and join the
Reserve.

Lindbergh had to balance his current freedom against the regimentation of Army life, his future as a barnstormer against his
future as pilot after he was entitled to wear an officer's wings. He
really was as free as a bird—literally able to fly any place his fancy
took him. But he could see that time was running out for barn-

stormers. The Army course was by far the best flying school in the country; when you graduated from it, there was no doubt that you were a thoroughly qualified pilot. So he opted for the Army, got recommendations from two of his father's friends, and wrote his letter of application. He was interviewed at Fort Snelling that fall.

That same fall, 1923, Lindbergh was in the air one day when he got the idea that it might be interesting to attend the air races in St. Louis; they were being held that week at Lambert Field.

After he got there, he was sorry he'd given in to the impulse. He found Lambert crowded with high-powered planes. Small civilian craft like his Jenny had to be parked on a hillside a mile away. This was a shock to a lone barnstormer who had become used to being greeted in small towns as a kind of demigod from the skies. In most places where he flew, the people had never seen a pilot before, but in St. Louis he was surrounded by pilots—men with national reputations, like Captain Frank Hawks with his red racing plane. Lindbergh was extremely conscious of his second-class status at Lambert Field. His plane was the slowest; he himself looked disreputable, for, as he says, a barnstorming pilot didn't have much baggage allowance in his low-powered plane.

He wandered around looking over the fast aircraft, judging their designs with his eye. For no good reason, he decided to fly his Jenny during the open hours. (Civilians could fly into Lambert in the late afternoons when the races were over.) He went through the usual maneuvers of unlashing wings, pulling through the propeller, and giving the engine three minutes of idling to check temperature and pressure. Then he opened the throttle. "I heard shouts of rage behind me. I looked back to discover a great cloud of dust thrown up by my slipstream. In it I could see, vaguely, gesticulating pilots. . . . I'd been used to flying from sod-covered pastures, not from a crowded and newly graded airport, baked dry by Missouri's sun."

One of the race officials ran over and chewed Lindbergh out. "Where did you learn to fly? Don't you know enough . . . Where do you come from? What's your name?" And so on. Lindbergh says he felt like a forty-acre farmer stumbling through a state fair, and decided to leave St. Louis the next day. Certainly there was no joy in flying around Lambert Field.

Then, by chance, he bumped into his former fellow-student, Bud
Gurney. Gurney had won a parachute-jumping contest, and come in
second in another. He needed someone to take him up for the
double-drop contest. Would Lindbergh? Lindbergh would.

Gurney told him that Jennies had been marked up in price as the
interest in aviation was rising. Lindbergh might sell his plane at a
profit, particularly if he would instruct the buyer how to fly it.

Lindbergh set a price on his plane and sold it for more than he
had paid for it. Lessons to the buyer were included. At the same
time, he got another pupil, a man who'd bought a Hisso-Standard
and didn't know how to fly.

At this time Lindbergh had had two hundred and fifty hours of
seat-of-the-pants flying. He'd learned something from a half-dozen
pilots—things to emulate, things to avoid. He had developed ideas
about flying that he could put into practice. He learned more by
having to codify his experience for novices. In order to instruct, you
had to know the exact limits of your plane—if you stopped a
student making a mistake too soon, he would lose his confidence; if
you let him go too long, there would be a crash.

Late that fall he soloed his student in the Jenny and flew with
him to his home in Iowa, as a final check. Lindbergh took the boy's
promissory note for the balance due on the airplane, and gave as his
last instruction "Don't fly below a thousand feet when you don't
have to; and when you go over [a] town, always stay high enough
to glide to a field if your engine fails." He wondered, after that, how
much experience you could really transmit. The last time he saw his
Jenny, it was flying two hundred feet over the railroad station
where he was waiting for his train to St. Louis.

Lindbergh supported himself during the late fall and early winter
by various piloting jobs at Lambert Field while waiting to take his
Army entrance examination. He took the exams at Chanute Field, in
Illinois, on January 1, 1924. He would get the results—whether or
not he was to be admitted to the Army flying school—sometime
later. The school would not open until late in March, so he had
nearly three months to wait *if* he was admitted.

He had made friends in St. Louis with a man named Leon Klink,
who had bought a plane known as a "Canuck." The Canuck was
similar to the Jenny, but with slightly better performance. Klink

wanted to learn to fly, and Lindbergh felt that he could teach him and make expenses at the same time by barnstorming in a warmer part of the country.

It was bitter cold when they left St. Louis late in January, 1924. They flew south in the Canuck, stopping in Kentucky, Tennessee, Mississippi, Alabama. Pickings were thin; they were just barely covering expenses. They decided to head for the Atlantic Coast and then cross the country to the Pacific. In February at the post office in Pensacola, Florida, Lindbergh got the long-hoped-for acceptance into the Army flying school. He was told to report to Brooks Field, San Antonio, Texas, on March 15, 1924.

That was still a month away, enough time for him and Klink to get to California. Lindbergh could enlist on the Coast and take a train back to Texas.

Lindbergh had promised to give a ride to the sister of a friend before leaving. So the next morning he took the Canuck up for a quick check, his usual procedure before carrying any passengers. Over the water, at only two hundred feet of altitude, the motor cut out for no ascertainable reason. Lindbergh banked for shore. If he had been a few feet higher, he could have reached the field safely. Instead, he crashed into some sand hillocks, crushing the landing gear, splintering the propeller, and driving the left wheel up through a spar of the lower wing.

On his previous mishaps he'd had few witnesses. This time he got the full Navy treatment—sirens, fire trucks, etc.—and felt humiliated. But the base commander gave him and Klink help in moving the plane into a hangar and even spare parts to repair it.

Lindbergh and Klink fixed the plane and were ready to take off by February 20. This would make the trip to California and back to Texas by March 15 a rather near thing. But by carrying extra fuel to increase the plane's range, they thought they would make it. Two five-gallon cans of gasoline were lashed to the wing next to the fuselage. "It was quite a job leaning out of my cockpit, into the slipstream, and unlashing one of those cans; and then, empty, lashing it back again. But with the aid of a steamhose slipped over the nozzle, I hardly spilled a drop," Lindbergh writes. They made San Antonio in five flights. At their next stop, in Camp Wood, Texas, they found no decent landing field, so they blithely put down in the town square.

Of course, the town went wild with curiosity and excitement. There was nothing extraordinary to Lindbergh about landing in a large square. But the wind shifted, and the planned takeoff the next morning had to be redirected, down one of the town streets. It was a possible runway, but had one dangerous point between two telegraph poles. They were only two or three feet farther apart than the wingspan of the Canuck. Lindbergh thought about it. "After all, one drove a car regularly between objects with only a few inches clearance. Why shouldn't one do it with an airplane?"

He would mark the exact center of the street and keep the plane headed perfectly straight; this would give him at least a foot clearance on each side. But something went wrong. Three inches of the right wing failed to clear the pole; the plane spun around and crashed into a hardware store.

There was a splintered propeller and a damaged wing tip. To repair these, they would need a new propeller and a can of dope. The store owner refused payment for the damage done to his shop by the Canuck; it had been an interesting experience and good advertising, he said.

Waiting for the materials from Houston and making the repairs took another three days. Then the wind was right and they could take off from the town square with a full load of gas.

The next day there was more trouble—a dagger-plant cactus ripped a wing. This time they were far out in the country and it took eight days to get materials and fix the wing. By then it was too late to fly to California, so Klink took the train to California and Lindbergh flew what was left of the Canuck to Brooks Field, San Antonio.

It was a rather mutilated airplane. Part of the fabric had ripped away from one wing, the splices showed as ungainly bulges, the homemade stitching was coming loose, and one wheel was minus a tire. The crewmen couldn't believe a plane could fly in that condition, but Lindbergh assured them that it would—and he had a chance to demonstrate it when he was told by a corporal (under orders from the major) to get the damned thing off the field. He flew it to Stinson, a nearby commercial airfield, and returned to enlist in the Army on March 19, 1924, at the age of twenty-two, one of a hundred and four cadets.

The training was as rigid and detailed as any in the world. The plane used was the same kind Lindbergh had owned (and had sold), the Jenny, but the Army Jenny had the powerful 150-horsepower Hispano-Suiza engine instead of the 90-horsepower OX-5 in Lindbergh's former plane. The Army, since the war, had installed left-hand throttles in all their planes. Lindbergh had flown only ships with right-hand throttles.

Flight training started in April. The new controls seemed strange to Lindbergh, and his first landing was not a three-point one as he'd expected. But after three rounds of the field, his master sergeant turned him loose for solo and, what's more, in the sergeant's own plane. There was no doubt Lindbergh could fly.

But Lindbergh had never learned to discipline himself to classrooms and textbooks. His first grades at the Army school came in at 72 per cent—just two points above passing.

This scared Lindbergh. For the first time he was in a school from which he wanted to graduate, and he forced himself to become the good student his college instructors had said he could be. "Photography, motors, map-making, field service regulations, ratio theory, military law—twenty-five courses we took in our first half-year of training. I spent as much as seven hours writing an examination."

During this time he lived a bit of a dual life. On base it was all regulation and regimentation. A couple of miles away was Stinson, the field where he'd parked the Canuck. Leon Klink had returned from California and wanted to take the Canuck back to St. Louis—but first he had to learn to fly it.

So Lindbergh would spend his morning flying Army acrobatics, go to ground school in the afternoon, and then in the evening instruct Klink in solo flying, sideslips, landings, and all the things necessary to a cross-country pilot. At night he would study.

And study effectively. By the end of June nearly half the class of hand-picked cadets who had started with Lindbergh had been washed out of school—but he had moved up to second place in the class. His grades were averaging better than 90 per cent.

It was difficult for him to force himself into Army button polishing, bedmaking, and all the other rigidities and formalism. Lindbergh was only a surface conformist; the more he was pushed into a mold, the more his inner drive toward personal freedom asserted itself. One manifestation of his galled spirit was in practical jokes. Physical humor had always been a part of Army life, and Lindbergh added to it his own wild originality. For example, a sergeant who had made his life unpleasant had the habit of getting drunk, rolling into the barracks, and snoring all night loud enough to keep everybody awake. Lindbergh took this as long as he could. Then, one night when the sergeant barreled in stoked with whiskey, ready to sleep it off, his bed wasn't there. Lindbergh had put it up on the roof.

This same cadet sergeant had been the victim of a previous practical joke. When the man was off in San Antonio, a dead skunk was put in his pillow. By the time he returned, the odor was so pervasive that everyone was sleeping out of doors. For the next two weeks the sergeant had to keep his bed outside while the others slept peacefully in the barracks.

By September, only thirty-three of the hundred and four élite young men remained in Lindbergh's class. This hard core of superior students moved to Kelly Field, ten miles from Brooks, for the second six months of training in the De Havillands Lindbergh had heard so much about.

He was warned about the DHs. They had more power than the Jennies, but once they stalled they needed a lot of altitude to recover flying speed. And they couldn't be stunted like the stouter Jennies. "Their wings aren't tied on that strong," the instructor warned. "If you pull the stick back too hard, they're liable to leave you." The standards of flying were more precise at Kelly than at the other bases. Procedures were rigidly standardized. There was training in formation flying, bombing, strafing, gunnery, photography— just about everything a pilot would need to know. Six weeks before graduation, the cadets were divided into four groups representing pursuit, bombardment, observation, and attack. Lindbergh had been trying hard for pursuit, the most difficult and rewarding of the four. He got it.

In February, 1924, at the Mayo Clinic in Rochester, Minnesota, the doctors diagnosed the brain tumor in C. A. Lindbergh.

"He will sink into a coma within a few days and never come out of it," a neurosurgeon told C.A.'s law partner Quigley. He suggested that the family be sent for.

Charles got leave to come up from San Antonio, but the furlough was necessarily brief considering the concentrated nature of Army training. When Charles had to go back, he rode to Minneapolis with Quigley, who reported, "I could see that he was deeply moved over his father's condition, but outwardly he was stoical."

He had never lost the desire to fly off on his own. One day when the ceiling was low and the visibility poor—the kind of day a cadet could safely disobey air regulations because no instructor could see him—from his plane he spotted another DH in the air. He chased the other plane, and the two did a series of complicated maneuvers in a mock dogfight. Then Lindbergh got close enough to see that there were two men in the other ship, which meant that one of them must be an instructor. He would be washed out of the school for stunting if the instructor reported him. He waited in agonized uncertainty for days, but nothing happened.

At Galveston, where the cadets took gunnery practice, Lindbergh had his first real Army emergency. He was part of a nine-plane formation, flying in three groups of three planes each. Lindbergh was left wingman in the top unit, with Cadet Phil Love leading and a Lieutenant McAllister on the right. Love mock-attacked a DH flying below them at an altitude of 5,000 feet, with Lindbergh and McAllister flying in to confirm the "kill." Lindbergh dived a bit more and then turned left at the same time that he pulled his plane into a climb toward the empty space above the DH.

In his official report at the time he wrote, "I saw no other ship nearby. I passed above the DH and a moment later felt a slight jolt followed by a crash. My head was thrown forward against the cowling and my plane seemed to turn around and hang nearly motionless for an instant. I closed the throttle and saw an SE-5 [a scouting plane of the type Lindbergh was flying that day] with Lieutenant McAllister in the cockpit, a few feet on my left. He was apparently unhurt and getting ready to jump.

"Our ships were locked together with the fuselages approximately parallel. My right wing was damaged and had folded back slightly, covering the forward right-hand corner of the cockpit. Then the ships started to mill around and the wires began whistling. The right wing commenced vibrating and striking my head at the bottom of each oscillation. I removed the rubber band safetying the belt, unbuckled it, climbed out past the trailing edge of the damaged wing, and with my feet on the cowling on the right side of the cockpit, which was then in a nearly vertical position, I jumped backwards as far from the ship as possible."

The locked ships spun almost straight down and threatened to strike Lindbergh, but they didn't. He recorded seeing McAllister floating down. Lindbergh landed safely in a plowed field, and noted that he lost his goggles, a vest-pocket camera, and the rip cord of his parachute.

His report, the earliest example of Lindbergh's published prose (it was published both in the Army newsletter and in the New York *World*), is written so clearly and simply that one wonders why he had so much difficulty with English composition in college. It is interesting to contrast this account with his telling of the same incident in *The Spirit of St. Louis* thirty years later.

The crash: "Then it happened. I heard the snap of parting metal and the jerking crunch of wood, as my forehead bumped the cockpit's cowling and my plane cartwheeled through the air. I yanked the throttle shut. . . . For an instant, after that first crashing bump, both planes seemed to hang motionless in space. . . .

"A trailing edge of the broken top wing folded back over my cockpit and vibrated against my helmet, shaking sight from my eyes and thought from my brain. . . . Our planes were revolving like a windmill."

He jumped. "How safe the rushing air had seemed when I cleared those planes—like a feather bolster supporting me. My hand was on the rip cord but I didn't dare pull it, for the planes were right above me, spinning, and spewing out a trail of fragments to the sky. . . . My parachute had no more than flowered out when I was below the cloud layer."

He also recorded in his book something he had not included in the Army account. When the other pilots saw the two ships collide, they broke formation; all of them, including instructors, headed out of the mist toward the two parachutists. "Every few seconds, a pair of wings saluted by—too close for comfort," Lindbergh wrote.

Also, he told how he got razzed for losing his rip cord, usually the accident of a novice jumper.

For this emergency jump he and McAllister became members No. 12 and No. 13 in the Caterpillar Club, the organization of men who had had to jump from airplanes to save their lives. (Caterpillar after the insect which manufactured the silk from which parachutes were then made.)

It was all treated as a joke. An hour after the jump, two fresh SE-5s had been made ready for Lindbergh and McAllister and they were flying again.

But it was sheer chance that had saved them. The parachute was such a new idea in 1925 that Lindbergh's class was the first to be issued chutes.

The incident took place only nine days before graduation. Lindbergh was top man in his class, which had narrowed down to eighteen at the end. He was commissioned Second Lieutenant Charles A. Lindbergh in the Army Air Service Reserve in March, 1925.

6

AIR MAIL

THE END OF THAT MONTH FOUND LINDBERGH ON THE
way back to St. Louis. He had applied to the Army for a commission in the Regular Air Service after his graduation, but hadn't received an answer. He was free to take a civilian job, and had already been offered one dusting crops in Georgia for two hundred dollars a month. He'd turned that down because it was not enough money.

He went to St. Louis because it was the most hospitable place he had found in all his travels. From the time he flew in to the air races in the fall of 1923 until the day he left with Leon Klink in the Canuck in January, 1924, he had been made welcome and had become, as he says, "an accepted member of the city's little group of pilots."

At twenty-three, Lindbergh was a veteran flier. He didn't look it. He was six feet three inches tall and almost skinny (although in those days he was known for having an enormous appetite), and had a baby face. He did not drink or smoke; he had tasted liquor and didn't like it, and considered smoking a form of stimulation that might interfere with the steadiness of his nerves and the speed of his reflexes. For a similar reason he had given up coffee in college; at that time he felt that caffein might induce a tremor in his hands that would make him a less efficient marksman in rifle and pistol shooting. Yet among the chain-smoking, hard-drinking, hard-nosed pilots, Lindbergh was given respect and admiration.

Jobs were open to him that he could not have had a year before. Air mail, for instance. The federal government had started an air-mail route in 1918 and had been flying mail between New York and

California since 1920. Now feeder lines from other areas were going
to be added to that single cross-country line, and the pressure from
Congress and business was to get the government out of the
business. The new lines were to be let by contract to private
bidders. Two brothers named Robertson, both ex-war pilots, had set
up the Robertson Aircraft Corporation in St. Louis and had entered
a bid to fly the mail between St. Louis and Chicago. (Chicago was
one of the coast-to-coast stops.) Major Bill Robertson offered Lindbergh, whom he had been watching carefully, the job of chief pilot
if and when the Robertson company got the contract.

Lindbergh accepted the proposition; this was what he wanted—a
permanent, responsible job in aviation. But meanwhile there would
be a long wait. He could find plenty of students to teach at
Lambert; he transported passengers (on shares in other men's
planes) and did stunt flying with an aerial circus which included his
old friend Bud Gurney.

He also tested planes. In St. Louis at the end of May, 1925, after
the aerial circus had run its course, he found a new plane, designed
and built by an engineer at Lambert Field, that needed testing.
Powered with an OXX-6 (100-horsepower) engine, the plane had a
wide fuselage to make passengers comfortable. It was a stubby ship
covered with plywood. Lindbergh flew it and found that it answered well to certain maneuvers, but in stalls it was "mushy" and it
had other undesirable characteristics.

The last trial was the tail spin. He couldn't get it to spin right at
all, so he tried the left. That went well; the plane came out of the
spin promptly. Then he tried it again, and suddenly his controls
didn't respond. They were blanketed by the wings and fuselage.

The plane was spinning and falling as Lindbergh tried every last
desperate maneuver to bring it out. He rode it down for nearly two
thousand feet, trying to save the ship, and then he looked below
and knew he had to jump or crash. He was barely three hundred
and fifty feet from the ground.

He made a fast roll out of the cockpit and pulled his rip cord as
soon as he cleared the plane. "The ground was right there, leaping
at me. Trees and houses looked tremendous. There seemed scarcely
enough room for a parachute to string out."

The chute did open, but no sooner was Lindbergh swinging

under it than he saw the plane head straight for him. It was less
than a hundred feet away.

He was "braced for death. . . . Every muscle, every nerve, was
tensed for the tearing blow on flesh." The shrouds of the parachute
were twisted, and as Lindbergh swung around, somehow the plane
skinned by without touching him or the chute.

"If the hand of death ever cracks the door that lets life's senses
peek beyond life's walls, it should have cracked it then," he wrote.
"Danger had swept all unessential detail from my mind—it was
clear as a pane of glass. . . . You couldn't come much closer to
death than that." He got no glimpse of the hereafter then. But on
later occasions he had the notion there was something just beyond:
"I've felt the presence of another realm . . . a realm my mind has
tried to penetrate since childhood."

To fulfill his Reserve training requirement, Lindbergh spent two
weeks instructing on military aircraft at Richards Field, near Kansas
City. He made his third parachute emergency jump at this time,
dislocating his shoulder in landing. In August, 1925, while carrying
passengers at the National Guard camp near Nevada, Missouri, he
got a letter from Captain Wray Vaughn, president of the Mil-Hi
Airways & Flying Circus at Denver, Colorado, offering him a pilot's
job at four hundred dollars a month. This would enable him to
make some money while waiting for the Robertsons' contract to
come through, and also, said Lindbergh, it would give him a chance
to fly around among the deep canyons and high mountains and
study, by the behavior of his own plane, the action of downdrafts
and other air currents and turbulences on aircraft. The fact that he
might be killed in the pursuit of this knowledge fitted in with his
ideas about personal risk and the value of life, and added some salt
to the idea.

"I've never chosen the safer branches of aviation. I've followed
adventure, not safety. I've flown for the love of flying, done the
things I wanted most to do. . . . Why should man want to fly at
all? . . . What justifies the risk of life? . . . I believe the risks I
take are justified by the sheer love of the life I lead."

He took a train to Denver and was met by Vaughn, who could
hardly believe that this gangling boy was the veteran flier they had
hired. Lindbergh in turn was not overjoyed to find at Humphrey's

Field, where his new employers were located, that the company's assets consisted of exactly one airplane, and that this was the very same Lincoln Standard he had barnstormed in with Lynch three years before. Its age was not really concealed by a coat of fresh paint.

When Lindbergh took the ancient crate into the air and put it through its paces, any doubts that Vaughn might have had about his new pilot vanished. "There was never another like him," he said later.

The Mil-Hi company made contracts for Lindbergh to fly this ship to small country fairs in Colorado and provide entertainment in the way of acrobatics during the day—he had a wing-walker who did stunts as well—and fireworks by night. With their barkers, carrousels, and Ferris wheels, these itinerant fairs were one of the few touches of glamour in the lives of country people, and Lindbergh's stunts and fireworks were the high point of the proceedings.

The towns where fairs were held seldom had decent landing fields, and none had lights for night landing. At best there would be a large area of level sod. Since the fireworks were to be shot off from the plane at night, there had to be some means of lighting the fields for takeoff and landing. It would have been impossible for Lindbergh to fly at night if he hadn't been able to persuade people with automobiles to park them at the airfield and turn on their headlights when he took off and relight them when they heard the engine of his plane returning to land.

There were countless close calls in this hit-or-miss kind of flying, but the worst was over a Colorado town that Lindbergh had never seen before. He was flying with Vaughn as his passenger. They had a contract to shoot off fireworks to close the local fair; the contract called for the performance to take place in the air sometime between darkness and midnight.

They were delayed in arriving because some passengers had come late for a ride. Vaughn and Lindbergh had waited for these people because it meant another twenty dollars for the Mil-Hi company. Then a further complication, lack of oil in the plane, delayed them still longer. By the time they got their oil, the sun had set and Lindbergh wanted to stay where he was for the night. Vaughn said they would lose two hundred and fifty dollars if they didn't shoot off the fireworks. He said he knew where the field was;

it was only fifteen minutes away, and there would still be a little light left. Lindbergh could always be counted on to rise to a challenge. He took off with Vaughn in the front cockpit.

Reaching the town, whose lights were already on, Vaughn couldn't locate the landing field. "By that time, ditches and fences had merged with darkness," Lindbergh wrote. "I'd done just what I'd been warned against as a student. I'd let night catch me in the air. . . . I had to land. And I couldn't see what was below."

He headed away from town. The last touch of reflected light in the sky gave him a hint of what was on the ground, but only a hint. He headed toward a large, dark spot which he thought might be a stubble field, warning Vaughn to brace himself for a crash. He set the plane down. Amazingly, there was no sound of rending fabric, just a bumpy landing. It was after nine-thirty.

Vaughn got a car to take him to town to get the fireworks. He told Lindbergh to buy boards and hardware and make a platform for the plane from which the fireworks could be touched off. Two automobiles furnished illumination for this work. When everything was organized and constructed, it was half past eleven.

Vaughn insisted on going through with the show, even though Lindbergh said that everyone would be in bed. "Our contract doesn't expire till midnight," Vaughn said.

There was only one car left at the field and its lights failed. Without some light, a takeoff was impossible. In desperation, Lindbergh asked Vaughn to use his flashlight to illuminate a strawstack on the field. With only this feeble dot of light, he took off into the night sky.

He climbed to 1,800 feet—he wanted to go higher but it was already ten minutes to midnight. First he began throwing over the fire bombs. He would pick one up, pull off the cap, rub the igniter, and toss it over the side. There were seven seconds between ignition and explosion, but it was safer to allow only five. If a bomb went off in the cockpit, he could be badly burned, blinded, and would almost certainly crash.

After the bombs it was time to ignite the Roman candles. Four were attached to each upper wing. Lindbergh nosed down and closed the switch. The flames streamed behind the plane. So bright was the light that Lindbergh lost his bearings. Only the city lights could tell him which way was down. At last he set off his flares, almost as bright as the sun. Then, when his eyes got readjusted to the darkness, he took out his watch. It was eleven-fifty-seven; the contract had been fulfilled with three minutes to spare. He headed back for the field and found it nearly impossible to see the feeble light of the flashlight on the ground. He circled and circled, and finally committed himself to a risky landing. Again he made it. Thank God, he thought, for the huge size of Colorado fields.

That winter he was back in St. Louis, instructing, test-flying and laying out the air-mail route from St. Louis to Chicago. The Robertsons had won their contract and, as promised, appointed Lindbergh chief pilot. He hired two other men, ex-Army buddies, Phil Love and Thomas Nelson, as pilots. Like Lindbergh, they had had their share of close calls. Love had just survived the crash of a crop-dusting plane that hit the earth so hard his teeth bit into an iron bar in the cockpit. He carried the bar with the impress of his teeth with him to prove it.

Along the 285-mile route between St. Louis and Chicago, Lindbergh selected nine landing fields, one about every thirty miles. These were not really airfields—just fields one could land in, with a small cache of gasoline and a telephone and someone nearby to help the pilot. They were not lighted; nor did the planes—rebuilt Army salvage DHs with Liberty engines—carry landing lights for the first few months. If a pilot had to land at night, he dropped a parachute flare from the plane. Each plane carried only one flare. Like just about everything else connected with civilian flying in 1926, the Robertson operation was a shoestring affair.

Organizing the airline was a major part of Lindbergh's life, but just as important to him was the fact that he could involve himself in a steady commitment to the Army. He enlisted in the Missouri National Guard, where he instructed wartime pilots in the newest techniques of flying and attended armory drill one night a week. He also lectured on navigation, aerodynamics, and other things he had learned in the Army and from personal experience. He was promoted to First Lieutenant in the Guard.

In April, 1926, Lindbergh flew the first air mail from St. Louis to Chicago, the sacks piled into the front cockpit of the plane. The contract called for five round trips a week, and during the spring and summer the Robertson line fulfilled it with 99-plus per cent efficiency. A letter which arrived at the St. Louis post office before three-thirty in the afternoon could, by a series of close connections, reach the New York City post office in time for the next morning's delivery, a saving of one day over train mail.

Nevertheless, the Robertson company's mail sacks were often almost empty, since businessmen seemed to figure that the less than 1 per cent chance of delay, plus the extra expense of air-mail postage, overbalanced the saving of a day in mail delivery. But Lindbergh and his pilots kept flying doggedly through night and storm; they were convinced that if they proved their efficiency long enough they could break down the prejudice against air mail.

The lack of weather information and ground lights was a serious handicap, sometimes bordering on tragedy. One night Lindbergh was flying north toward Chicago when he ran into fog. He tripped his single flare, but it did not ignite. Not being able to see the ground, he flew on toward Chicago, where the airfield had lights. But the Chicago field was so blanketed by fog that even though the ground lights were turned on (as he was told later) he could not see to land. He left the metropolitan area, hoping to pick up one of the transcontinental beacons along the government's airway, but the fog was too thick to find a beacon. By this time he had located the reason his flare hadn't lit—a slack release cable. He headed for open country with the hope of seeing a pasture at the edge of the fog where he could land. He saw a light on the ground which might indicate a break in the fog and he dropped his flare by pulling on the cable. It ignited and drifted earthward, but its light showed only the enveloping mist.

Now the engine began missing; he was running low on fuel. He turned on the emergency tank, which gave him another twenty minutes of flying time. He still couldn't find a landing place. Then, when the engine died, he jumped and pulled the rip cord of his parachute. It opened.

Thinking the plane completely out of fuel, he hadn't bothered to cut the ignition switches. But the forward tilt of the descending craft evidently drained a last reserve of gasoline into the carburetor. The turning propeller started the engine again while Lindbergh was dangling in his parachute, and the pilotless ship began flying in circles. Again, for a breathless minute, he thought he was going to be hit. The wheeling plane dived toward him—and missed him by a hundred yards. Then it came back and made five spirals, each one a little farther away than the last, before he lost track of it. When he reached for his flashlight to see what he was dropping toward, he found it had fallen from his pocket.

Lindbergh was lucky again. He hit a cornfield and was unhurt. Soon he was picked up by a farmer who had heard the plane crash. Lindbergh introduced himself as the pilot to the goggle-eyed farmer. They tried to find the wreck, but it was impossible to locate in the dark.*

On the farmer's party line, Lindbergh called St. Louis and Chicago to report the interruption in mail service, and he asked anyone listening to give news of the plane if it was found. A few minutes later a call came in; the plane had crashed two miles away. The farmer drove Lindbergh there and he found the mail sacks intact in the smashed cockpit. He took them to the nearest post office to have them put aboard a train.

In September of 1926, five months after he began flying the mail, Lindbergh was in the air on his way to Chicago, having just left Peoria. It had been a perfect day—too perfect for him. "There's . . . nothing to match yourself against," Lindbergh mused. "On such an evening you might better be training students . . . no tricks of wind, no false horizons."

He welcomed night with its moon. It made him feel even more detached from earth. "Why return to that moss; why submerge myself in brick-walled human problems when all the crystal universe is mine?"

He let his mind rove, wondering why he couldn't float like the moon, wondering how much fuel a plane could carry if it was loaded with gasoline. Then he became annoyed at the immediacy of his problem—he would have to land in Chicago in less than two hours. Why didn't he have a plane that could fly directly to New York?

Such a plane had been built, he knew—the Wright-Bellanca. It was of a new type, single-winged—a monoplane. With only one wing, it had less drag and more speed than the biplanes Lindbergh had been flying. It could carry a great load. Of course, it was terribly expensive; it cost at least $10,000 as against only about

---

* This and another emergency jump Lindbergh made while flying the mail cost the Robertsons half their fleet. They did not blame him, as neither was his fault.

$1,000 for the Army biplanes the Robertsons used. Still, with a Bellanca one might really run a commercial airline between, say, St. Louis and New York.

Again his mind began to wander between the fantasies of flight and the realities of aviation. If he had a Bellanca and filled it with tanks instead of passengers and freight, how far would it fly? With the engine at low speed, it might stay aloft for days, like the moon. And then the practicality. "Judging from the accounts I've read," Lindbergh wrote in his autobiography, "[the Bellanca] is the most efficient plane ever built. It could break the world's endurance record, and the transcontinental, and set a dozen marks for range and speed and weight. Possibly—my mind is startled at its thought —I could fly nonstop between New York and Paris."

THE SPIRIT OF ST. LOUIS

THERE WAS A REMARKABLY SHORT DISTANCE IN LIND-bergh's mind between the desirable and the possible. No sooner did the New York-to-Paris idea strike him than he began testing the limits of reality against the boundaries of his purpose.

First there was Lindbergh himself. "Why shouldn't I fly from New York to Paris? I have more than four years of aviation behind me, and close to two thousand hours in the air. I've barnstormed over half of the forty-eight states. I've flown my mail through the worst of nights."

And the things he'd done. Four years before, he had been a college dropout, dreaming about flying a plane. That dream had become reality. And so with his other dreams—the parachute jumping, the Army flying school, and now, at twenty-four, chief pilot of an air-mail line and a captain in the Reserve, training and lecturing men older than himself.

A man who could do all those things in four brief years could do just about anything he had to in the air. He decided then, that night in his mailplane, to start organizing a flight to Paris.

There was a good reason for selecting New York to Paris as the challenge—rather than, say, Los Angles to Hawaii. When the war ended in 1918, the Atlantic Ocean was regarded by pilots as aviation's major obstacle—probably because European alliances and trade focused so much of America's attention in that direction and vice versa.

First to organize a flight across the Atlantic was the United States Navy, in May, 1919. They had four huge flying boats known as "NC" ships. These large biplanes were powered by four Liberty engines apiece, and carried crews of five men. They were designed to take off from and land on water.

The Navy used three of these boat-hulled craft, each weighing more than fourteen tons loaded, to try to fly from Newfoundland to the Azores. Twenty-one destroyers were stationed at intervals of sixty miles across the Atlantic, shooting up star shells and sending out radio signals to guide the airplanes.

The chief mechanic at the Lincoln plant where Lindbergh learned to fly had been a member of the expedition. He had told Lindbergh about the countless emergencies, forced landings, and engine trouble the lumbering craft had encountered. The weather reports proved inaccurate; they ran into fog and many other problems. Although no lives were lost, only one of the three boats reached the Azores, 1,380 miles away, and then made another hop on to Lisbon. That was the first halting transatlantic flight, and it had taken millions of dollars and the efforts of thousands of men to make it possible.

The London *Daily Mail* offered a prize of $50,000 for the first *nonstop* heavier-than-air flight across the Atlantic. Two British fliers, Captain John Alcock and Lieutenant Arthur Brown, decided to try for it in a Vickers-Vimy biplane powered with two 350-horsepower Rolls-Royce engines. In June, 1919, five weeks after the Navy's NC ships crossed the ocean, Alcock and Brown took off in their plane from St. John's, Newfoundland, the closest point on the North American continent to Europe. Flying most of the way by dead reckoning through fog, the two men reached Clifden, Ireland, in sixteen hours and twelve minutes—a distance of 1,936 miles. Their plane landed in a bog and nosed over. It was somewhat damaged, but neither man was hurt.

Alcock and Brown thus made the first successful nonstop transatlantic crossing in an airplane, and won the *Daily Mail* prize. However, their triumph was dimmed by the fact that Alcock, a veteran pilot with more than 4,500 flying hours, was fatally injured a week later on another flight.

Perhaps inspired by the *Daily Mail* prize, Raymond Orteig, a New York hotel owner who was born in France, offered a prize of $25,000 for a nonstop flight between New York and France in either direction. His offer was first made before the Alcock and Brown flight in 1919, and was renewed five years later, in 1924.

The reason the Orteig prize lay unclaimed for so long was simply that there was no plane capable of making a nonstop flight between New York and France, a distance of 3,315 miles, until the mid-nineteen-twenties. The nonstop distance record in those days was just over 2,500 miles, from New York to San Diego. This was set in 1923.

But, as Lindbergh had noted, in 1926 there was the Bellanca plane, and there were now others which could be calculated to fly nonstop from New York all the way to Paris. Several aircraft designers and builders were working on other long-range planes.

The same month that Lindbergh got his idea about the flight, September, 1926, the papers were full of an actual attempt of a famous French war ace, René Fonck, to make the flight. The glamorous Fonck, a dashing figure, had a big airplane designed by the famous Igor Sikorsky and built in Long Island, New York. It was a biplane carrying three powerful air-cooled radial engines. (Air cooling and radial design produced higher power at lower weight than the earlier water-cooled aircraft engines.) On September 21, 1926, Fonck's big plane started its run for takeoff from Roosevelt Field. It never got off the ground. At the end of the runway it crashed and burst into flame. Fonck and his co-pilot Lawrence Curtin escaped without serious injury, but the mechanic and the radio operator in the same plane were burned to death.

Lindbergh thought a lot about that accident. Why hadn't Fonck cut his switches before the crash? But he also thought, "Who am I to judge his crisis-action? . . . Fonck had to decide in seconds what his critics had had days to talk about. And what pilot is immune to errors? We all commit them, as every honest man will say."

Still, there were things he didn't understand. Instead of being stripped of useless weight, Fonck's plane had been upholstered in leather, and even carried a bed. It had two radios, four men in the crew (you didn't need four men to fly to Paris, certainly), and even a hot dinner for the celebration in Paris. At the last minute a bag of croissants had been put aboard. It was all faintly ridiculous; more than that, it had contributed to tragedy. If Lindbergh could get the right plane to fly to Paris, he would fly alone, strip the plane of useless accoutrements, take only the barest necessities to cover the trip and emergencies.

But where would he get the plane? He had a few thousand

dollars in a Detroit bank, carefully saved against a bad season or a crash—not nearly enough to buy a plane like the Bellanca. How would he get the rest of the money? He would need some kind of business organization to back him. What would attract businessmen to help him? Well, if he could bring off the flight, it would help put St. Louis on the map in a big way. And as a financial proposition—if he won the Orteig prize of $25,000, that would cover the investment necessary to buy the plane. The backers would own the plane, free and clear, *and* have all their money repaid. So the venture could even be profitable.

He thought of the St. Louis businessmen who flew, like Harold Bixby, a banker who owned a brand-new plane; Harry Knight, a broker who was taking flying lessons; and Earl Thompson, to whom Lindbergh had given flying instructions in Thompson's gold-painted Laird. He determined to see Thompson first, since he knew him best. Meanwhile he drew up a plan of attack.

He divided it into seven categories: "Action, Advantages, Results, Cooperation, Equipment, Maps, and Landmarks." Under the first step he had eight subcategories: 1) Plan, 2) Propaganda, 3) Backers, 4) Equipment, 5) Cooperation of manufacturers, 6) Accessory information, 7) Point of departure, and 8) Advertising. Under "results" he had only two: "1) Successful completion, winning $25,000 prize to cover expense," and "2) Complete failure."

The thirty-seven points he covered all had pertinence; there was no pipe dream in the lot. Everything showed a firm grasp of the realities of the world around him as well as of the practicalities of the flight. For example, under "Equipment" four of the five items he listed he was eventually to take with him—raft, rockets, clothing (waterproof), condensed food, and still (water). Only waterproof clothing was omitted by reason of its weight, and because he later figured that if he was forced down he could cut strips of the doped fabric from his plane and use them for protection.

He drew up a prospectus to make his project attractive to St. Louisans. "St. Louis is ideally situated to become an aviation city. We have one of the finest commercial airports in the United States, and we will undoubtedly become a hub of the national airways of the future."

It was only two or three days after he began to dream of Paris that Lindbergh got an appointment to see Earl Thompson. He opened the interview by saying he had come to ask Thompson's advice about an idea. He explained about the Orteig prize. He said that he thought a modern plane could make the flight and he would like to try it—to advance aviation, and advertise St. Louis. But he said he was too young and inexperienced to undertake the venture alone. Besides, he didn't have the money. "I can furnish two thousand dollars myself," Lindbergh said, "but the right kind of plane will probably cost at least ten thousand. I think the Wright-Bellanca could probably make it," Lindbergh added.

Thompson's voice sounded disturbed as he began asking questions. The Bellanca was a single-engined plane, wasn't it? And designed to fly over land?

It was true the Bellanca was a land plane but a land plane of a new type, Lindbergh said. And that single engine was a new kind of engine—the Wright "Whirlwind"—a radial engine of nine cylinders, air cooled, which weighed only 500 pounds, developed 220 horsepower, and ran for an average of 9,000 hours between failures. This made it about 9,000 per cent more dependable than the engines Lindbergh had been flying. The Wright-Bellanca had been designed by the famous airplane designer Giuseppe Bellanca precisely to show off the best characteristics of the Whirlwind engine.

Lindbergh told Thompson that a one-engine plane would be much cheaper than one with three engines. A three-engine plane might cost around thirty thousand dollars. Besides, three engines only increased the chance of engine failure. If one failed over the ocean, you couldn't expect to return on the other two. And, went Lindbergh's clinching argument, René Fonck's plane had had three engines, hadn't it? And it never got into the air.

Thompson was interested in Lindbergh's plan, but with reservations. He still thought Lindbergh ought to have the security of three engines, perhaps a plane like the Fokker.

A salesman for the Fokker company, plane builders whose chief designer was the brilliant Dutchman Anthony Fokker, happened to be at Lambert Field, and Lindbergh questioned him about a transatlantic plane. The man said the Fokker people had made a study of the New York-to-Paris flight, and could build a three-engine plane for spring, 1927, delivery to make the flight. The cost? Ninety thousand dollars. Before Lindbergh could gulp, the man went on smoothly to say that of course they would have to be satisfied with the operating personnel. They wouldn't sell a tri-motored Fokker to just anyone, he said, eying the baby-faced Lindbergh. And he made it plain that under no conditions would they sell a single-engine plane for a flight across the Atlantic.

Nevertheless, Lindbergh kept on with his plan. He got a pledge of a thousand dollars from Major Lambert, after whom the St. Louis airfield was named, to help buy the Wright-Bellanca. Lindbergh's boss, Major Bill Robertson, also helped; he gave Lindbergh encouragement and allowed him occasional time off from the mail route to arrange his personal business.

The St. Louis *Post-Dispatch* had carried front-page stories of both of Lindbergh's emergency jumps from his mailplanes, so Lindbergh was well known to Roy Alexander, a young aviation reporter on the paper.* One day in the fall of 1926, Lindbergh telephoned Alexander and asked if he planned to be at Lambert Field that afternoon.

Alexander, a flier himself, said yes, and Lindbergh asked him to stop by the Robertson office. Alexander met Lindbergh with Bill Robertson, and Lindbergh immediately said he proposed to fly across the Atlantic ("as though he were talking about going to the grocery store," Alexander recalled recently) and win the Orteig prize. Alexander asked why Lindbergh thought he could do it, and Lindbergh explained that the new Wright J-5 engine had changed everything. At that point, Alexander says, Lindbergh was talking in terms of a three-engine ship.

He said he would need thirty-five thousand dollars to make the flight, a lot of money in those days. Alexander offered to set up an interview with his managing editor and the chief of the editorial page, with the idea that the *Post-Dispatch* might back the flight. He made an appointment for Lindbergh to come to the paper at noon the following Tuesday.

"I said, 'For God's sake, wear your uniform,'" Alexander recalled. "Slim looked about thirty in his captain's uniform and he looked nineteen in that shiny blue serge suit."

But Lindbergh showed up at the interview in the blue suit with a cloth cap. "I said, 'For Christ's sake, Slim, why didn't you wear your uniform?'

* Later editor of *Time* magazine.

"He said, 'I didn't think it would be the right thing. I didn't want to go under false pretenses.' And that was the guy—a man of rock-like, sometimes senseless, integrity."

The managing editor turned Lindbergh down cold. "We have our reputation to consider," he said. "We couldn't possibly be associated with such a venture!" He thought Lindbergh was too young and couldn't know enough navigation. He seemed to take it as a personal affront that Lindbergh was willing to risk his life on so hazardous an enterprise.

Similar reactions by other mature people were bound to force Lindbergh to question his own premises, but he still thought he could make the flight if he could get the right plane and the necessary backing. He began to consider how an unknown pilot could approach the Wright people about buying the Bellanca, and finally decided on the dramatic impact of a long-distance telephone call. Such a call was a rarity in 1926; a man who made one certainly meant business. It would surely gain him the ear of the man he wanted to reach. Lindbergh made his call to a Wright executive in Paterson, New Jersey, and he was more than cordially received. His judgment had paid off. He made an appointment to visit the plant.

Before starting on the trip to Paterson, Lindbergh decided he had to look like a businessman. The only decent suit he owned was the captain's uniform. With the advice of a well-dressed National Guard officer, Lindbergh ordered a custom-tailored civilian suit. He also bought an overcoat and a felt hat, to look like the successful businessmen he'd seen, and a scarf, gloves, and so on. It all came to more than a hundred dollars. Wasting money on such window dressing galled him, but he figured it might be just as important to his purpose as it would be to buy the plane later. He took the train east in November, 1926.

The Wright company was interested in selling the Bellanca, but they were thinking of selling it to a manufacturer—Huff Daland—and thought that Lindbergh had better talk to them. He saw Giuseppe Bellanca, who said he thought the plane would fly to Paris but suggested an endurance flight test beforehand to make sure. If the Wright company would not sell his plane to Lindbergh, he said, he could design and build another, but it would take time.

The Wright people tried to talk Lindbergh into a three-engine ship. "We didn't want to put our reliance on a single engine over the ocean," Ken Boedecker, one of the old-time Wright mechanics recalled.

But Lindbergh said, "I fly single-engine mailplanes. If my engine quits on takeoff, I'm just as much out of luck as I would be if it quit over the ocean."

As it turned out, the Wright-Bellanca was not for sale to Lindbergh for a transatlantic flight. It wound up in the hands of a man named Charles A. Levine, who owned the Columbia Aircraft Corporation.

There were weeks of such setbacks. Lindbergh had garnered some backing, but not nearly enough. Meanwhile he kept on flying the mail through the bitterly cold winter of 1926–27. He spent more than one night alone on one of the small fields between St. Louis and Chicago, grounded by snow or fog. Every so often during such nights, he would put all his strength into turning over the cold-stiffened engine to keep it from freezing altogether. (There were no self-starters on airplanes in those days.) When he was at Lambert Field, he would take long walks and make plans to raise money.

Meanwhile, in Europe and America, airplanes to fly from New York to Paris were actually being made and tested. Lindbergh was falling so far behind that his project seemed hopeless.

He decided to make one last-ditch effort to raise the money. He asked his two air-mail pilots to take over the mail schedule for a few days while he braced the businessmen of St. Louis.

He went to see Harry Knight, the young broker, who was president of the St. Louis Flying Club. Instead of being turned down summarily, as he had expected, Lindbergh was surprised to find Knight taking a real interest. What's more, Knight called up his friend Harold Bixby at the State National Bank and asked him to come over and listen. The two men asked Lindbergh the usual questions about single-engine *versus* multiple-engine planes. He went through his arguments, which by now were well rehearsed. Finally, Bixby said he wanted to think over the proposition for a few days. He made an appointment with Lindbergh for the following Wednesday at his office.

Elated, Lindbergh went back to Lambert and his mail route, an hour-by-hour battle against blizzards and engine trouble. The next day he was grounded for a while in Springfield by clouds, then after taking off had to turn back to that field to repair his engine. Later, the Chicago airport was supposed to be socked in by clouds, but Lindbergh found a five-hundred-foot ceiling there and landed safely. No one expected him; Phil Love, a very good pilot, hadn't even been able to take off that day from Chicago.

It was Tuesday night and Lindbergh had his appointment with Bixby the following morning. He had to get back to St. Louis. He decided to take off into a night that the other pilots considered too hazardous to fly in. Once more, he made it back to St. Louis.

The next morning Bixby kept him waiting for a few minutes at the bank. Then he came out to usher him into his office. He said, "Slim, you've sold us on this proposition of yours. It's a tough job you're taking on, but we've talked it over and we're with you. From now on you'd better leave the financial end to us." He said that if Lindbergh could stick to a reasonable budget and would put in his two thousand dollars, they and Lindbergh's other backers would take care of the rest.

Now Lindbergh could prospect for a plane. There were two good possibilities. The Travel Air Company, in Kansas, was turning out a monoplane very much like the Wright-Bellanca that might suit his purpose. There was another company farther away, on the Pacific Coast—Ryan Airlines—that was manufacturing a high-wing monoplane reported to give good performance. Travel Air being nearer, Lindbergh wired them first.

They wired back refusing to accept his order.

Lindbergh decided to try Ryan. Signing the telegram with the name of the Robertson Aircraft Corporation—Lindbergh's boss had given him permission to use the company name—Lindbergh wired Ryan on February 3, 1927, asking if they could produce a plane capable of flying nonstop between New York and Paris and, if so, to "please state cost and delivery date."

Lindbergh was used to waiting weeks for replies. He got an answer the next day. Ryan telegraphed that a plane similar to their Ryan M-1 monoplane could be built in three months for about six thousand dollars, plus engine.

Lindbergh wired again asking if they could cut the time to two months, because of the mounting competition, and also asking for specifications. If he could get a reliable plane by April, when the weather would start to become good enough for a transatlantic flight, he might still be the first.

The flight to Paris was becoming a race with various entrants announcing themselves. In the United States, Commander Richard E. Byrd, backed by Rodman Wanamaker, was getting together a four-man crew to fly a three-engine ship designed and built by Anthony Fokker. The Wright-Bellanca became another contender in the hands of its new owner, Levine, who had hired several top American pilots, headed by Clarence Chamberlin. The Army Air Corps had several bombers on order from the Huff-Daland company. They authorized the company to sell one of these, stripped down, to Lieutenant Commander Noel Davis of the U.S. Navy, who, with Lieutenant Stanton H. Wooster, was planning to make the flight to France.

On February 6, 1927, Lindbergh got an unexpected wire from Giuseppe Bellanca: "WILLING TO MAKE ATTRACTIVE PROPOSITION ON THE BELLANCA AIRPLANE FOR PARIS FLIGHT." He suggested that Lindbergh come to New York. Lindbergh had the utmost confidence in Bellanca as an aircraft designer and as a man. Although he was preparing to visit the Ryan people in California, he quickly changed his plans and went to see Bellanca.

Bellanca presented him to Charles Levine and Clarence Chamberlin. Levine offered to sell the Wright-Bellanca for fifteen thousand dollars. This was more than Lindbergh had expected to pay. He said he would have to go back to St. Louis and ask his backers.

The backers approved the purchase. Harold Bixby handed Lindbergh a check for fifteen thousand dollars. And at that time he asked, "What would you think of naming it the *Spirit of St. Louis?*"

With the check in his hand (made out to him personally), Lindbergh was slightly agog at the trust his partners put in him. "All right, let's call it the *Spirit of St. Louis,*" he said.

He took another train back to New York to see Levine. "We will sell our plane," Levine told him, "but of course we reserve the right to select the crew that flies it."

Lindbergh was "dumfounded . . . more chagrined than angry." There was no use talking about that, he said. What Levine was offering was no longer an outright sale but just the chance to paint "Spirit of St. Louis" on the plane's nose.

Lindbergh picked up his check and started to go. But Levine wasn't that sure; he might change his mind. He asked Lindbergh to call him the next morning.

When he got Levine on the telephone the next day, Lindbergh heard him say, "Good morning. Well, have you changed your mind?" Lindbergh hung up, too angry to reply. He is still angry in retrospect at having his hopes lifted, being asked to make two round trips to New York, and losing precious time, only to wind up empty-handed. He wasn't the only one who reacted that way to Levine. Levine had a talent for rubbing people the wrong way.

Lindbergh returned to St. Louis discouraged, thinking that time was so against him in winning the transatlantic race he might better forget it and think about flying the Pacific instead. But Knight and Bixby told him to stick to his original plan, to go and see the Ryan people.

On February 23, 1927, he arrived by train in San Diego, California, where the Ryan Airlines had their factory near the waterfront. The odors of the airplane plant mingled with those of dead fish from a nearby cannery. It was obviously not a rich or successful company. Lindbergh met the executives and factory personnel, most of them very young men. He discussed the price of a plane with B. F. Mahoney, the president. The airframe would be six thousand dollars. The engine and instruments would be extra; Mahoney said he would resell them to Lindbergh at cost.

Then came the key question. "Will you guarantee to give us a plane with range enough to fly from New York to Paris?" Lindbergh asked.

Mahoney hesitated. "The risks are too high," he said. "It isn't as though we were a big company with a lot of money in the bank." At six thousand dollars, Ryan would be making no profit; there was no margin for a guarantee.

Lindbergh had to decide whether or not to risk his partners' money without a guarantee. He decided to rest his decision on his assessment of the chief engineer, Donald Hall. He liked Hall instantly. They spoke the same language; their minds worked in the same direction.

Hall asked about where he was going to put the cockpits for the pilot and the navigator. Lindbergh told him he would need only a single cockpit. "You don't plan on making that flight alone, do you?" Hall asked.

Lindbergh explained that he would be better off with extra gasoline than with an extra man.

Hall instantly grasped the advantages of solo flight. The fuselage could be shorter and lighter; the plane could carry another three hundred and fifty pounds of gasoline.

Suddenly both Lindbergh and Hall realized they were talking about a New York–Paris flight without knowing the exact distance. They piled into Hall's old Buick roadster and headed for the public library. There, with a bit of string, they measured the mileage on a globe—about 3,600 statute miles. Then the plane should be able to fly at least four thousand miles, Hall figured, perhaps more. But Lindbergh said those four hundred extra miles would be plenty of margin. He expected to fly with a tail wind.

Back at the plant, Lindbergh got from Mahoney a firm price of $10,580 for the plane with a Wright J-5 engine. Special equipment, such as an earth inductor compass which Lindbergh wanted, would be extra, at cost.

Lindbergh wired Knight on February 24 saying he thought they should go ahead with Ryan. The next day Knight wired approval, Lindbergh placed the order, and Hall and Lindbergh began working out the design together.

The idea of flying alone which so unnerved other people was almost a congenital necessity with Lindbergh. It had been drummed into him by his father that "one boy's a boy. Two boys are half a boy. Three boys are no boy at all," a saying that grew out of the old Indian war days in Minnesota. But it turned out to be true in the air, too. Lindbergh had to consult his associates on certain earthbound details; otherwise he was on his own. He had no flying partner to convince; he had no responsibility for another man's life. His movements were not tailored to somebody else's limitations. When his experience and his senses told him something ought to be done, he was in a position to make the decision and carry it out.

The airplane was going to be designed and built around Lindbergh and nobody else. This would take a bit more time than adapting a tested design, but had the advantage of creating a ship just for Lindbergh's purpose. The allowance for the pilot was his own weight, one hundred and seventy pounds, and there would be a specially hollowed place over his head in the cabin to allow for his folded six feet three inches. The pilot's seat was a cut-down wicker chair.

The first thing to be decided was where to *put* the cockpit.

Lindbergh wanted it enclosed—and he wanted it behind the gas tank. Experience had shown that men who sat in front of gas tanks usually died in crashes while those behind the tanks had lived. The tanks would block his forward view in flight (the engine blocked it on the ground), but it gave him a safety and efficiency factor. He could see ahead by banking the plane. He would dispense with night-flying equipment—he couldn't afford the weight—and also with a parachute, which weighed twenty pounds. He would manage without gauges on the gas tanks, too, since they were heavy and rarely worked. He would figure fuel consumption by the revolutions per minute (r.p.m.) and his grandfather's nickel-plated watch.

He decided to fly the great-circle route—the shortest route between two points on a curved surface—rather than follow the longer ship lanes where he might be picked up if he were forced to land. He needed ships' charts, and would have to figure out how to lay out the course. He could have got help from the naval officers at San Diego, but decided not to ask; it would betray his ignorance and make people question his flight even more than they were already doing. He tried to buy the charts he needed in a local ship chandler's store, and found that the nearest supply was in San Pedro. He borrowed one of the Ryan monoplanes and flew up to get his charts; he was flying monoplanes at every chance, since his flying experience had been almost exclusively in biplanes. In San Pedro he found Mercator's projections of the Atlantic, extending far enough inland to show both New York and Paris. He also found charts of time zones, magnetic variations (invaluable for compass readings), and prevailing winds. To fly from San Diego to New York, he would rely, as he always had, on Rand McNally railroad maps of the states. You could buy them in a drugstore for fifty cents each.

Working from instructions printed on the charts, Lindbergh laid out his great circle from New York, curving northward through New England, Nova Scotia, Newfoundland, arcing eastward across the Atlantic, and then southward past Ireland, England, and on to Paris.

"What freedom lies in flying!" he exulted as he looked at his handiwork. "What godlike power it gives to man! I'm independent of the seaman's coast lines or the landsman's roads; I could as well have drawn that line north to the Arctic, or westward over the Pacific, or southeast to the jungles of the Amazon. I'm like a magician concocting magic formulae. The symbols I pluck from paper, applied to the card of a compass, held straight by rudder and stick, will take me to any acre on the earth where I choose to go."

Since the plane was calculated to cruise at about a hundred miles an hour, he marked off intervals of a hundred miles on the great circle, deciding to adjust his course each hour to allow for winds, drift, and other variables. Every day required some basic decisions, but these nearly always boiled down to the same choices in Lindbergh's mind: "Safety at the start of my flight means holding down weight for the take-off. Safety during my flight requires plenty of emergency equipment. Safety at the end of my flight demands an ample reserve of fuel. It's impossible to increase safety at one point without detracting from it at another."

A stamp collector offered him a thousand dollars to carry a pound of mail to Paris—a truly tempting chance, since his finances were tight and the weight small. Still, with the kind of ruthless logic that guided his decisions, Lindbergh—after consulting his partners— refused. If he was going to take an extra pound, it had to contribute more toward the flight than money.

It may not seem to the casual air traveler of today that taking a pound of letters might affect the flight, but Lindbergh calculated every controllable ounce that went into the plane. He took no radio, because naval radios were too heavy and inaccurate when they were needed most—near the coast. He traded the radio for an extra ninety pounds of gasoline. He took no sextant to help him plot his deviation from course, because he wouldn't be able to work it while flying. He ripped spare pages out of his notebook to save weight. He cut holes in the charts he carried of areas over which he did not expect to fly. He even designed special lightweight flight boots with soft soles to save a few ounces. For food on the flight, he would take only five sandwiches and a quart of water. (There was another gallon of water and emergency rations for a forced landing.) He said, logically, "If I get to Paris, I won't need any more, and if I don't get to Paris I won't need any more either."

He left nothing to chance that could be estimated. When the Wright engine arrived and was being installed in the plane, a mechanic dropped a wrench on one of the fins that provided air cooling and cracked it. It was only one fin; it had nothing to do with the moving parts of the engine; still Lindbergh demanded that the jacket be replaced. The mechanic wanted to know why, and Lindbergh said, "I don't swim so well."

It was a race against time and weight; the entire Ryan factory staff worked day and night on Lindbergh's plane. Donald Hall stayed at his desk for as long as thirty-six hours at a stretch. At last the wing—of wood and canvas—was finished and ready to join to the fuselage, which was made of metal tubing. And then, for one ridiculous hour, it seemed that they would not be able to get the wing out of the upper floor of the plant; it was too long. But they managed by edging it out of a pair of upper doors onto the top of a railroad box car.

In March, 1927, news stories chronicled the progress of the Byrd flight; Sikorsky announced that a new plane was being built for René Fonck; the American Legion was backing Commander Noel Davis to the tune of a hundred thousand dollars in his bid for the Orteig prize (his ship would be called *American Legion*). From the other side of the Atlantic, Captain Charles Nungesser and Lieutenant Coli announced that they would definitely compete for the prize in a biplane with a single 450-horsepower engine. They would take off from France.

Clarence Chamberlin and Bert Acosta stayed up in the Wright-Bellanca for more than fifty-one hours—a new world's-endurance record flight, which Bellanca had predicted for his plane. And Lindbergh's name began appearing in the news. His application for the Orteig prize was accepted on March 28 by the National Aeronautic Association, which was charged with administering the prize. Actually, Lindbergh had mailed his application in more than a month earlier, as soon as he could furnish the necessary information about his plane. But the committee had waited until now to ask for further data about the plane and his flight plan. According to the rules, Lindbergh would not become eligible for the prize for sixty days from the date of his filing—which meant May 27, 1927.

Major Clarence M. Young, commander of Captain Lindbergh's Reserve squadron, came to visit him at San Diego. Young was the new chief of the recently formed Air Regulation Division of the United States Department of Commerce. He offered encouragement and some advice about the new government air licenses. The *Spirit*

of St. Louis would need more than a name; it would now need a
number, Young said. He would issue an "N-X" number (211) for
the plane—"N" was the international identification code letter for
the United States, and "X" meant "experimental," which gave
Lindbergh latitude in changing the design of his craft without
seeking government approval.* He would also see that Lindbergh
got one of the new pilot's licenses that were now being issued.

As the time approached for the flight tests of the new airplane,
Lindbergh began for the first time to be annoyed by reporters.
Publicity was an essential part of his plan; it was on the basis of
publicity that he had sold his backers on the flight. But at the end of
April, 1927, he noted, "What started as a pleasant relationship with
local journalists now involves elements of tension." He didn't want
the press around when he was making his flight tests in the *Spirit of
St. Louis* for several reasons. He had to concentrate on the tests.
The accuracy of data recorded might make the difference between
life and death for him. A slight error could mean a crash, and "One
makes errors more easily when onlookers get in the way, and ask
questions, and smoke cigarettes near fumes of gasoline. Also, plans
often go wrong; and the less said about them in advance, the
better."

On April 28, 1927, the *Spirit of St. Louis* was finished. It stood in
front of the hangar, sleek, silver, the most beautiful airplane Lindbergh had ever seen. He would test it himself. He climbed in. He
looked over the instruments, tried the controls. He told the
mechanic to go ahead and spin the propeller. The motor caught,
and Lindbergh tested the dual ignition, cutting out first the left and
then the right magneto. The motor fired smoothly, powerfully, with
either one. Then he signaled for the wheel chocks to be pulled
(Douglas Corrigan was the young mechanic who pulled them—
later to become famous as "Wrong-Way" Corrigan). Unrestrained,
Spirit accelerated faster than any plane Lindbergh had ever flown.
The plane, lightly loaded, took off in a hundred and sixty-five feet,
in just over six seconds. It flew very well, although it was not too
stable. While Lindbergh was in the air, a Navy Hawk fighter flew
over to take a close look at this new bird. Instinctively, Lindbergh
banked his plane for combat position, and the two went into a mock

---

* It was also called "Ryan NYP." The initials stood for "New York–Paris."

dogfight for several minutes. Then he controlled his playful ten-
dencies and turned back to the Ryan field. The story that appeared
in the papers next day added to his growing mistrust of the press.
He had, it seems, been involved in a "near crash" and had "narrowly
escaped disaster" when his plane nearly collided with a Navy
fighter.

He ran more tests in the next days. He got the plane's speed up to
a hundred and thirty miles an hour over the Army's speed course.
He found that it would take off with three hundred gallons of
gasoline (a hundred and twenty-five less than planned for the Paris
flight) in about a thousand feet. He didn't dare try out the plane
with a full load of gas. The surface of the airfield at Camp Kearney,
where the tests were made, was rough and stony; he might blow a
tire. Too, although the plane was designed to take off and lift the
load, it was not meant to be landed with so much weight. And he
had to figure that he was working at an altitude of nearly six
hundred feet in his Pacific Coast tests; in New York he expected to
take off almost at sea level, where the air would be much heavier
and more buoyant. So, balancing one thing against another, he
decided to let the tests stop at three hundred gallons. He was now
ready, except for weather, to fly the *Spirit of St. Louis* eastward.

April was a month of accident and tragedy for Lindbergh's rivals
for the Orteig prize. The Bellanca, after setting the endurance
record, cracked up when one of its wheels came off during a later
flight. Commander Byrd's huge three-engine Fokker, with designer
Anthony Fokker piloting the ship, crashed after a test flight. Everyone in the crew was injured, except Fokker. Commander Davis and
his co-pilot, Lieutenant Stanton H. Wooster, were killed when their
multi-engine ship, the *American Legion*, crashed in Virginia.

This spate of disasters dismayed Lindbergh. "My God! Every one
of the big multi-engine planes built for the New York-to-Paris flight
has crashed." And he felt confirmed in his decision to have the
cockpit aft, for if the fuselage wasn't crushed and the gasoline
didn't catch fire, the pilot would probably not be injured in a crash.

In France there were now at least three planes being readied for
the flight to New York. It was predicted that Nungesser and Coli
would soon be ready to take off.

On May 4, Lindbergh completed the flight tests of the *Spirit of St.
Louis*. As far as he could tell, the ship was satisfactory for the New

York-to-Paris flight. He wired his partners he would fly into St. Louis in forty-eight hours.

But he was held back for four days by bad weather. Meanwhile, on May 8, 1927, Nungesser and Coli took off in their heavily loaded biplane from Le Bourget Field north of Paris. Reading about it in San Diego, Lindbergh was certain they would make New York. He began to study the charts he had assembled for the transpacific flight.

For the next two days the Nungesser-Coli flight could be charted from the newspaper stories. Their plane, *White Bird,* was sighted at various points along the route. There were even those who swore they had seen *White Bird* over Boston, but nobody claimed to see it after that. The sightings may have been illusory. *White Bird* just disappeared. After it left France, its fate was never learned.

Hearing that Lindbergh was ready to fly east, Guy Vaughan, of the Wright Aeronautical Corporation, telephoned him offering the services of the company's press representatives, Bruno & Blythe, in New York. The Wright people had a legitimate interest in the flight, since Lindbergh was using their engine. He accepted their offer of help.

On May 9 Lindbergh was still grounded in San Diego, wondering why a flier had to be so dependent on his eyes that he couldn't fly through storms and fogs and night; why better instruments couldn't be invented to help him see his way through bad weather. Another obstacle was being raised; with Nungesser and Coli presumably down at sea, the American Ambassador to France, Myron Herrick, wasn't sure if it would be good for Franco-American relations if an American flier took off for Paris at this moment. Might not the French feel insulted? Particularly if the American made a successful flight? Also, some humanitarians were afraid that Lindbergh might be needlessly sacrificing himself; there were attempts by outsiders to get his partners to persuade him to give up the scheme. He had run into this kind of fearful opposition from the time he tried to sell the *Post-Dispatch* on his flight. He felt there was only one way to dissipate this fear: to prove his plane and himself worthy by making a successful nonstop, overnight flight from San Diego to St. Louis.

At last the weather broke, and Lindbergh was ready to take off. He allowed himself to carry a small suitcase of personal belongings because he was taking only enough gas for the fifteen-hundred-mile flight to St. Louis—little more than half the plane's capacity.

As usual, he had planned everything long in advance of takeoff, as far ahead as he could see. In his notebook he had written such messages to himself as "Stop mail: leave address. Wire day of arrival to Knight." And he did not forget to add, when he had arrived at St. Louis, to wire Ryan Airlines performance data on their ship. They had put everything into it; they would want to know. At each stop, there was always the notation "Notify papers." And under "Paris Arrival," his list started with "Arrange for care of ship." Third on the Paris list were cables to St. Louis, Ryan, Wright, Mother, Standard Oil, Union Oil—everyone who had helped with the plane, engine, fuel, or had a legitimate personal interest in the pilot.

He left San Diego at 3:55 P.M. on May 10, 1927. The time was selected to give him three hours of daylight to locate any trouble with the ship and to bring him over the flat plains of Kansas at dawn. It would be the first time he would fly through an entire night. He was stopping at St. Louis because the flight to Paris was a St. Louis project.

The *Spirit of St. Louis* took off well; then the planes that flew with him as an escort—witnessed by the press ("It looks as though I won't have to bother much about adequate publicity from now on," Lindbergh noted)—dropped off as night approached. He began climbing for the flight over the Rockies. At 8,000 feet over Arizona it was cold, and he was still climbing to avoid the peaks. At this altitude, for the first time, the motor began missing. He was over mountains in the dark, without any idea just where he was. Suddenly all the months of work were threatened. He was faced with a forced landing in a situation that would almost certainly destroy the ship and probably himself. He began scanning the night-shrouded valley for a smooth place where he might land upwind and mitigate the damage.

He circled desperately, trying to penetrate the darkness with his eyes. The motor was still rough, but the ship was staying aloft. He couldn't figure out the trouble; there was no sign from the instruments of what it might be. And then miraculously, as he flew at a lower altitude, the motor smoothed out and began firing rhythmically. He cautiously adjusted the fuel mixture, and it continued to function well. Now he had to choose between going forward and trying again to climb over the mountains or turning around and heading for San Diego, nearly five hours behind, and chancing a crash landing on the desert or in the sea.

He chose St. Louis, began climbing, and headed east. He thought the trouble was probably in the engine temperature; he would use more power—he had plenty of reserve fuel—and watch his mixture more carefully. And when he got to New York, he would have an intake heater installed.

As he gained altitude, the motor began missing intermittently again, but he found he could handle it. The main thing was to be able to fly over the highest peaks. He would take advantage of several minutes of smooth running to climb, then nurse the ship through a coughing spell while he clung to his altitude. Almost foot by foot he crawled up to 13,000 feet, high enough to cross the mountains.

Once on the other side, he was able to fly at a lower altitude better suited to the engine, and he had no more trouble. He reached St. Louis a little after six in the morning—about three hours ahead of schedule. He had flown only fifty miles off course and without the benefit of his new earth inductor compass, which had stopped working and could not be fixed until he reached New York. Below was Lambert Field. Like a kid showing off his new bike, he buzzed the field, then climbed over the town and gave himself a joy ride before touching down at 6:20 A.M. The trip had set a new speed record from the Coast of fourteen hours and twenty-five minutes— an average of better than a hundred miles an hour!

Lindbergh's pilot's license was waiting for him; his partners were brimming with plans for dinners and other festivities. But he explained that although he would stay if they insisted, he thought he ought to get along to New York while there was still a chance to be first to Paris. They agreed; he stopped in St. Louis overnight, had his plane serviced, and took off the next morning for New York. He didn't tell them about the engine trouble over the Rockies.

8

NEW YORK – PARIS

LINDBERGH LEFT ST. LOUIS A LITTLE AFTER 8:00 A.M. ON May 12, and arrived at Curtiss Field, Long Island, near New York City, in just over seven hours. Added to the first leg from San Diego to St. Louis, he had an elapsed flying time across the United States of less than twenty-two hours, a new record.

Men with cameras were scattered all over the field, some of them just where Lindbergh wanted to touch down. They crowded around before his engine stopped, putting themselves in real danger from the whirling propeller. This was a hazard that had always worried Lindbergh. He noticed from his earliest flying days that people on the ground seemed irresistibly drawn to the turning propeller without knowing how much damage it could inflict. He had always been afraid that one day he might injure someone who ventured too close. Now he was being crowded by newsmen who seemed to feel it their professional privilege to go anywhere.

Why couldn't they wait? he thought. He'd be glad to pose himself and the ship where they wanted, and no one would get hurt.

One of the first people to introduce himself to Lindbergh was Dick Blythe, of the firm of Bruno & Blythe, who handled press relations for the Wright company. But even as Blythe was shaking Lindbergh's hand, the photographers were crowding around from all sides, cursing, shoving, taking pictures from every conceivable angle with movie and still cameras. Each moment Lindbergh felt less comfortable with these newsmen; they were much different from the easygoing Pacific Coast types.

"I've got a hangar for you," Blythe said above the noise.

"How much is it going to cost?" Lindbergh asked. He had fifty

dollars in cash in his pocket; there was only about $2,000 or so left
of the $15,000 put up by the *Spirit of St. Louis* organization.

After his plane was safely stowed, Lindbergh gave performance
data on the Wright engine to Joe Hartson, of the Wright company.
Then Hartson, Blythe, and Lindbergh drove to the Garden City
Hotel, in nearby Garden City, where Lindbergh would stay while
his plane was being serviced. He wanted to live at the field, but
there was no place to sleep.

On the way, Lindbergh asked who Blythe and Bruno were.
"They're your buffers," Hartson told him. "Both fliers. They're
O.K." Lindbergh nodded and agreed to retain Bruno and Blythe as
his press and business representatives.

At the hotel, Hartson suggested that Lindbergh take a double
room with Blythe as his roommate. Lindbergh nodded again. He
said nothing.

That night, according to Dick Blythe, "We bedded down like two
strange wildcats, each in his own hole."

The next day Lindbergh was back at Curtiss Field. Wright was
giving him all the mechanical aid he needed. (His mechanic was Ed
Mulligan.) They couldn't afford to play favorites, since their
engines were in the three planes gathered at Curtiss and nearby
Roosevelt Field, all preparing to take off for Paris. The planes were
the Bellanca, Byrd's tri-motored Fokker *America*, and the *Spirit of
St. Louis*. Also at the field were representatives of all the companies
whose products Lindbergh was using. Brice Goldsborough, of the
Pioneer Instrument Company, was ready to install a new earth
inductor compass and any other instrument he needed. A man from
the Vacuum Oil Company was there to sell him oil and gasoline
when he wanted it.

Flying into New York, Lindbergh could see that Curtiss Field
was too small for his takeoff with a loaded plane. The best place
would be Roosevelt Field, with a runway almost a mile long.
Admiral Byrd had this field under lease, and had put a lot of money
into building the long runway. Still, Byrd offered to let Lindbergh
use the field when the *America* wasn't using it. Byrd even offered
Lindbergh his weather information. There was a lot of camaraderie
of that sort among the pilots, even though they were engaged in a
highly competitive race.

Bernt Balchen, the famous pilot and navigator who was flying

with Byrd, and Brice Goldsborough checked Lindbergh's charts.
They laid out the route, "a flattened great circle," Balchen says,
allowing for the winds at that time of year. "You just follow the
coast to Newfoundland," he told Lindbergh, "then follow 107
straight across and you'll find Europe."

But why hadn't the Bellanca left? What was holding Byrd back?
The Bellanca was repaired, but there was dissension about who
would pilot it. There was even the threat of a lawsuit by one pilot,
who said he had been hired to make the trip and then dropped.
As for Byrd, one member of his crew was still hospitalized, and he
was still testing the *America*.

The delays only focused more attention on the race. Blythe told
Lindbergh that newspaper interest was becoming more intense with
every day. Who knew what might happen next? There had already
been four men killed trying to fly nonstop to Paris—Davis, Wooster,
and the two in Fonck's crew the year before. Two men were
missing—Nungesser and Coli were still the objects of a Navy search
at sea—and three men in the *America*'s crew had been injured.
Death and danger were the reasons for all those crowding, cursing
photographers, and the prying reporters who asked Lindbergh such
silly questions as "Do you carry a rabbit's foot?" "What's your
favorite pie?" "How do you feel about girls?"

The reporters were hungry for color. They nicknamed Lindbergh
"the Flyin' Fool" and "the Flyin' Kid" and reported his conversation
as if it had been written by Zane Grey. "These fellows must think
I'm a cowpuncher," Lindbergh muttered to a friend.

The papers emphasized the dangers of the flight, and retold with
embellishments the stories of the men who had died, and the men
who had been injured, and the men who had been lost at sea trying
to make it. To be sure, the flight was extremely risky. Some of the
businessmen who had refused to back Lindbergh were motivated
by the idea of protecting him. A group of air transport executives
summoned Harry Bruno to a conference, as Lindbergh's representative. "Bruno, why are you mixed up in this suicidal stunt flying?"
one of them asked. "Four men lost in four weeks—you are sending
men to their deaths. You'll ruin aviation in America." Bruno defended the flight as not a stunt but a feasible, well-planned enterprise. Still, many in aviation were convinced that no good could
come of it.

The newspapers continued to emphasize this side of the story. In one day, May 13, they printed so much inaccurate and sensational news about Lindbergh—the accent always on danger and impending disaster—that they got his mother worried. She had been staying in Detroit, out of the limelight, out of her son's way. On the night of May 13, while he was at dinner, Lindbergh got an unexpected telegram from Mrs. Lindbergh saying that she was arriving in New York the next day.

Lindbergh certainly did not want her in New York while he was so busy with flight preparations, and also he didn't want her exposed to the prying press. But it was too late to head her off. She was already aboard the train when he got the wire.

When she arrived, Lindbergh refused to pose kissing his mother in front of the camera. He took her with him into the hangar and they spent some little while alone together. She stayed for only a few hours. When it came time for Dick Blythe to drive her to the Garden City station, he stepped back so that she could say goodbye to her son in private.

She patted Charles on the back. She did not kiss him. "Goodbye, Charles. And luck," she said.

"Goodbye, Mother," Lindbergh replied.

And that was the end of the incident. Mrs. Lindbergh returned to Detroit. She did not stay to see her son take off because, she said, she would only be in the way and distract him from his work.

On Saturday, May 14, the day his mother went back to Detroit, Lindbergh took two Wright experts up for separate flights to check his engine. He asked each, first Ken Boedecker and then Ed Mulligan, to set his fuel mixture at the most efficient reading. At each setting, he made a pencil mark. The two men had chosen points a sixteenth of an inch apart. Later, Ken Boedecker asked Lindbergh which he had used on the flight. "Neither," Lindbergh replied. "I set the mixture directly between the two."

During his second landing, some photographers got in the way of the plane, and to avoid hitting them Lindbergh damaged his tail skid. The thing that annoyed him most was that instead of being penalized for violating the field regulations, the photographers got a better picture and the reporters turned the accident they had caused into "news." They said Lindbergh had landed too fast and had thereby damaged his plane.

"Accuracy, I've learned, is secondary to circulation," Lindbergh reported bitterly. "A thing to be sacrificed, when occasion arises, to a degree depending on the standards of each paper. But accuracy . . . is vital to my sense of values. . . . Every aviator knows that if mechanics are inaccurate, aircraft crash. If pilots are inaccurate, they get lost—sometimes killed. In my profession life itself depends on accuracy."

Blythe told Lindbergh that all this attention meant he had "taken the show." The reporters didn't know what to make of Lindbergh; they had heard little of him, and suddenly he turned up in New York with a new transcontinental speed record in his pocket and his plane almost ready to push on to Paris. They were intrigued, and so was the public.

This meant good publicity for the *Spirit of St. Louis*, just what Lindbergh had wanted for his partners. But it was getting out of hand. The minute Lindbergh showed his face outside the hangar, he was surrounded by people and police. At the hotel, reporters watched every entrance, so that he couldn't take a walk without being followed. The only time he was free was when he was alone in his room, so he took to eating there. "The attention of the entire country is centered on the flight to Paris," Lindbergh reported, "and most of all on me—because I'm going alone, because I'm young, because I'm a 'dark horse.' Papers in every city and village are headlining my name. . . . Newspaper, radio and motion picture publicity has brought people crowding [around]." On Sunday, thirty thousand people came out to the flying fields. And he was being inundated with mail, requests for autographs, money offers from newspapers to write his story. This last was a new idea. Certainly E. Ray Lansing, a member of the *Spirit* organization, ought to have the story for his St. Louis *Globe Democrat*. But in other cities it might be sold separately. So Lindbergh gave the St. Louis rights to the story to Lansing; then Harry Knight called the *New York Times* to sell syndication rights to that paper. Arthur Hays Sulzberger, of the *Times*, got on the telephone and dictated an agreement which Knight accepted for Lindbergh. Then Sulzberger dictated a memorandum in New York for the files. The *Times* paid $1,000 to bind the contract and promised to pay an additional $4,000 for world rights to Lindbergh's story if the flight was successful (a successful flight was defined as one arriving within fifty miles of France). If the flight was unsuccessful, the *Times* promised to pay an additional $1,000. And if Lindbergh did not make the flight, the initial payment of $1,000 was to be returned by Knight.

Frederick Birchall, the *Times* managing editor, cabled his Paris bureau chief, Edwin James, that world rights had been bought, and "Lindbergh instructed silence" to all except accredited *Times* correspondents. In the event of failure and rescue, Lindbergh was to communicate with the *Times* in any way he could.

"Up to date, our project has been successful beyond my wildest dreams," Lindbergh wrote. One thing gave him special satisfaction: "My reputation as a pilot has been established." This, according to Harry Bruno, was Lindbergh's main motivation—not fame with the public, not money, not even when it was hurled at him, but prestige as a flier. He had never been bawled out by his boss for losing those two mail ships, but the other pilots had ribbed him unmercifully. "He *knew* that he was as good as any pilot in the business," Bruno says. Now, in New York, here he was, "an unknown kid, swooping out of the sky to challenge the greatest fliers in the world—and making them admit that perhaps he had the stuff it took to make his challenge stick."

But Lindbergh's elation over his breakthrough had a dark side. "The way the tabloid people acted when my mother came, left me with no respect for them whatever. They didn't care how much they hurt her feelings or frightened her about my flight, as long as they got their pictures and their stories. Did she know what a dangerous trip her son was undertaking? they asked. Did she realize how many older and more experienced aviators had been killed in its attempt?" When Lindbergh and his mother refused to embrace before the cameras, the tabloids made pictures using photographed heads of the Lindberghs pasted on other bodies. This was a favorite journalistic trick of the tabloids—the "composite photograph."

Lindbergh was not only disgusted with this kind of press coverage; he could see that his time was being taken up more and more by the demands of publicity and promotion, and less and less was given to his plane and the flight. He had to fly as soon as he could. His plane was ready. The engine had been serviced, the compasses installed. But he was grounded, as were all the others, by a bad weather system that hung over the Atlantic.

There were few outlets for his energy. After a couple of nearly totally silent evenings with Lindbergh, Dick Blythe woke with a yell one morning at 5 A.M. as he was being doused with the contents of a pitcher of ice water. Lindbergh stood there holding the pitcher and grinning. "That'll teach you to wear pajamas," he said. A day or two later, Blythe, who wore a mustache, awoke with his nose full of shaving soap. Lindbergh loomed over him with a razor in his hand. "I've always had an ambition to shave off half a mustache while its owner was asleep," he told Blythe.

The two men became very close friends. Blythe slipped away one day with Lindbergh and took him, incognito, to Coney Island. Lindbergh had a good time on the rides, eating hot dogs, and so on, until a woman spotted him and yelled, "There's Lindbergh!"

"Get me out of here," said Lindbergh, and Blythe immediately took him back to the hotel.

The weather was still too bad to take off. Lindbergh was introduced to the chief of the New York City weather bureau, Dr. Kimball. Kimball gave him all the help he could, but told Lindbergh he didn't get much useful information about the weather up north along the great-circle route.

As Kimball's forecasts showed continuing bad weather, Lindbergh began accepting invitations to visit people, like Colonel Theodore Roosevelt, Jr. Roosevelt insisted on giving him letters of introduction to people in Europe, including Ambassador Herrick. Although he had turned down the pound of mail from the stamp collector, Lindbergh felt he had to carry Roosevelt's letters after accepting the Colonel's hospitality. He also took with him, out of friendship, a letter for the postmaster of Springfield, Illinois, and another for Gregory Brandewiede, who had helped him lay out the air-mail route between St. Louis and Chicago. None of Lindbergh's partners asked him to carry anything for them.

During these days of waiting for fair weather, Lindbergh met many famous men of aviation; Al Williams, René Fonck, Tony Fokker, Chance Vought, Grover Loening. They had been his idols, names in the newspapers, and now he was one of them, accepted as their equal. He also met some reporters who knew their business and stuck to questions about aviation and his flight, which he was always glad to answer. He still remembers with respect Lauren D. (Deac) Lyman, of the *New York Times* (now a consultant to United Aircraft); Bruce Gould, of the New York *Post* (later for many years editor of the *Ladies' Home Journal*); and C. B. Allen, of the New York *World* (now a consultant to Martin Marietta).

Harry Guggenheim, the aviation enthusiast, was at Roosevelt Field making test flights with Commander Byrd one day when he heard that the *Spirit of St. Louis* was at Curtiss being prepared for the Paris flight. Guggenheim was a rich man, a former wartime Navy flier, the catalyst for bringing several millions of dollars of his father's fortune into aviation education and civil aviation. The Daniel Guggenheim Fund for the Promotion of Aeronautics, of which Harry was a trustee, was then the only important source of finance for aviation experimentation.

Harry Guggenheim hurried over to Curtiss Field to see Lindbergh and his plane. He recalls looking inside *Spirit* and noting that "very little room had been left in the cockpit for the pilot. I remember saying to myself, 'This fellow will never make it. He's doomed.'" Lindbergh's comment on this was that "the cockpit probably looked cramped since it was designed to fit me closely. Actually there was plenty of room for the pilot, more than in most planes of the time—an essential for long-distance flying."

While Guggenheim was examining the plane in the company of Charles Lawrance, the designer of the Wright Whirlwind engine, Lindbergh showed up. He was introduced to Guggenheim and they posed for some pictures together. Then Guggenheim left, saying, "When you get back to the United States, come up to the Fund and see me." He says there was more optimism in his words than in his heart.

Lindbergh still had more than a week to go before qualifying for the Orteig prize. So he phoned Harry Knight in Detroit and asked him if the organization would permit him to fly anyhow as soon as the weather was good. As usual, he got prompt and positive assurance of support from his partners. "When you're ready to take off, go ahead," Knight told him.

On May 19, after spending a week in New York, Lindbergh continued to get bad weather reports. So he picked up B. F. Mahoney, president of Ryan Airlines, who had just come to New York, and visited the Wright engine plant with him, Dick Blythe, and another man, in Paterson. That night Bruno set up a dinner for Lindbergh at the Newspaper Club in New York, and Blythe arranged for him to see a hit musical, *Rio Rita*, and visit backstage.

As Lindbergh was driving the group across Forty-second Street in Blythe's car around six o'clock, it was rainy and dismal. Someone suggested it might be a good idea to check with the weather bureau. He stopped the car and Blythe telephoned Kimball. Surprisingly, the forecast was for clearing skies over the Atlantic.

Blythe telephoned Bruno at the Newspaper Club, suggesting that Bruno tell the dinner committee some story that would cover Lindbergh's nonappearance without revealing his plans. But a cartoonist from the *Daily Mirror* was in the booth next to Bruno's. Overhearing the conversation, he promptly telephoned his office, and by nine o'clock that evening the *Mirror* was out with headlines announcing Lindbergh's departure.

Lindbergh turned the car around and headed for Long Island. There was a lot to do in a hurry. A recording barograph had to be installed in the plane by the National Aeronautic Association to make a paper tracing of time and altitude. Without this machine, the record of the flight would not be officially accepted.

They stopped for a quick dinner in a small restaurant at Queensboro Plaza. Around the corner at a drugstore, Blythe bought five sandwiches "to go" (two ham, two beef, one hard-boiled egg), wrapped in wax paper for the Paris flight.

At the field, Lindbergh was astonished to find no activity in the rival groups. Possibly Byrd and Chamberlin didn't believe in the changed weather forecast, which, to be sure, was somewhat conditional.* Lindbergh applied the same test to his flight that he had to his air-mail flights; if the reports seemed good enough, "I'll take [the] responsibility on my shoulders, where it belongs." If he got things moving now, he would be ready to fly at daybreak and could make a last-minute weather decision then.

The tanks of *Spirit* had come out a bit larger than Hall had figured, and would hold an additional twenty-five gallons. This was an extra hundred and fifty pounds of weight, but it could mean a hundred and sixty miles of added range for the airplane. On the other hand, the engine had shown that it needed less oil than had

---

* Actually, the Chamberlin plane, *Columbia*, was grounded by a court injunction. Byrd's *America* was not ready. Byrd came over to bid Lindbergh farewell; he was, in fact, the last person to say goodbye to him. Both planes later made the transatlantic crossing. Chamberlin, with Levine as passenger, flew nearly to Berlin on June 4–6, 1927. Byrd's plane took off on June 29. Flying by instruments almost all the way, the *America* was ditched in the sea off Brest.

been calculated, so Lindbergh was saving thirty-five pounds on oil. The original gross weight of the ship had been calculated at 5,135 pounds. With the extra gasoline, minus the oil, it would now weigh 5,250 pounds. The plane had not been designed to lift the extra hundred and fifteen pounds, but Lindbergh decided to take them and risk a difficult takeoff in order to add to his flying radius. Mulligan and Boedecker began checking the engine and kept at it all night.

While he was making his plans, he was besieged by promoters who offered him huge sums of money for personal appearances, for movies. He had several times stayed up forty hours at a stretch, working hard most of the time; now he was facing a thirty-five-hour flight and he wanted to be fresh for it. So, close to midnight on May 19, he set a friend as a guard outside his hotel-room door and tried to get a few hours of sleep. Harry Bruno, driving out to the field about this time, found the road jammed with about ten thousand cars. The *Daily Mirror* headlines had done their work.

Usually, when Lindbergh put his head on the pillow, he went to sleep. But not this night. A poker game was going on among the correspondents at the hotel. Excitement mounted when the pot reached $400. Just at that point, Lindbergh came into the room and said, "Can't you let me get some sleep? I've got to get up early in the morning." Sam Schulman, a former International News Service cameraman recalls that this had little effect on the group.

Lindbergh went back to bed and twisted and turned, thinking of all the calculations he had made, all the decisions he had weighed. Had he done right to omit the radio? The parachute? To take on those extra pounds of gasoline? He had just begun to drift off when— slam!—his personal guard broke into the room with a completely irrelevant question. "Slim, what am I going to do when you're gone?" *That* murdered sleep.

He finally gave up and got up. He dressed and went downstairs into the hotel lobby and out on to the stone porch. It was about 2:45 A.M. The *New York Times* man covering the hotel, Johnny Frogge, saw him looking into the darkness at the dripping trees.

"Are you going this morning, Captain?" Frogge asked.

Lindbergh waited a minute. "I don't know," he said.

"When will you know?" Frogge asked, anxious to catch the last edition.

"I don't know." Lindbergh repeated.

He was, as Deac Lyman said later, not being evasive, only honest. He really hadn't decided if he was taking off that day or not.

He drove out to Curtiss Field at three o'clock in the morning of May 20 without having slept. The weather was bad, but getting better. Nobody would take the plane from the hangar in the drizzle without Lindbergh's approval. He looked at the skies, smelled the wind, thought of what the weatherman had said about a high-pressure system moving in from the west, figured that if he started at dawn he could always turn back if he ran into too much bad weather.

He ordered the plane hauled out of the hangar. Its tail was tied to a truck that would tow it the short distance to Roosevelt Field. It was not a happy occasion. The plane—shrouded against the weather, lurching tail first through the mud—seemed heavy and lifeless. Reporters, policemen, mechanics sloshed along on foot through the squelching ooze. To Lindbergh, it seemed more like a funeral procession than the beginning of a joyous adventure in the air.

A light east wind was blowing, so the *Spirit of St. Louis* was towed to the west end of the Roosevelt runway. At the other end of the runway was a steamroller that had been used to pack it down. Beyond that were telephone wires to clear, and beyond that Merrick Avenue.

Deac Lyman and C. B. Allen walked down to the steamroller and crouched near it. "We knew the story would either be there or in Paris," Allen said recently, "and we wanted to be ready to help if necessary. The steamroller was plenty of protection for us."

The tanks were filled. Chief Abram Skidmore and Inspector Frank McCahill, of the Nassau County police, were worried about the danger. Everybody knew that the plane was loaded to the last ounce with gasoline. Harry Bruno agreed to follow the takeoff in his open car. Skidmore and McCahill were with him, holding fire extinguishers.

Lindbergh climbed into the cabin and closed the door. Ed Mulligan pulled the propeller, and Ken Boedecker held a booster coil to give the cold engine a hot spark. Once the engine started, he cut the wires to the coil, as Lindbergh would not need it again and did not want to carry the extra weight. The engine kicked over, and Lindbergh kept opening and closing the throttle. It wasn't revving up as high as expected. "They never rev up on a day like this," Boedecker said, but his face looked worried. Lindbergh shut the engine off. Boedecker and Mulligan made a hasty check of fittings and connections. Everything was in order—the wires, the valve springs, the fuel lines.

Again Mulligan pulled the propeller, and once again Lindbergh tried to get the engine up to full power. It was still low. (Boedecker says it was fifty revolutions below optimum performance. But Lindbergh disputes this. He says it was thirty revolutions low. "If it was fifty low, I wouldn't have taken off," he told Boedecker many years later.) Adopting Lindbergh's figure, the Whirlwind was still about 1.5 per cent below full power. The plane was already overweight, its greased tires sinking into the rain-soaked clay of the runway.

Now, to complicate things further, the wind shifted from east to west, from head to tail. True, it was only the slightest breath of wind, barely enough to move the wind sock, but it was blowing the wrong way. It added another tiny element of danger to an already perilous situation. If Lindbergh decided to take off into the wind, the ship would have to be towed to the other side of the field. The engine was too light and would overheat if he taxied the heavy ship through the soft ground. Taking off westward also meant a hazardous course over hangars and houses, almost certain death if things went badly. And there would be the loss of vital time—just enough time, perhaps, to bring him to the Irish coast after dark instead of before sunset as he hoped.

Everybody was watching him. The decision was his—his alone. Boedecker said that the engine was functioning as well as possible in that kind of weather. The test flights had shown that the plane had plenty of lift, but now he was asking it to lift a thousand pounds more than it ever had before—in mist, off a mud runway, with a tail wind. And with an engine at less than full power, and with moisture condensing on its lifting surfaces. Of course, Lindbergh could start his takeoff and then cut power at the halfway mark and hope not to crash by coasting to a stop. There were no brakes on the wheels, no reversible-pitch propeller such as today's aircraft have, to slow the plane on the ground.

Wind, weather, power, load—those were the thoughts churning in his mind. And then the churning stopped. "It's less a decision of logic than of feeling," he said later. "The kind of feeling that comes when you gauge the distance to be jumped between two stones across a brook." He knew that no one would blame him if he didn't take off; no one would doubt his courage. Still, "sitting in the cockpit . . . the conviction surges through me that the wheels *will* leave the ground, that the wings *will* rise above the wires, that it is time to start the flight."

He pulled down his goggles. Boedecker asked, "Do you want us to kick the blocks?" Lindbergh nodded. Boedecker and Mulligan knocked out the blocks. Lindbergh checked his instruments again and gave the engine full throttle. Eight or ten men pushed against the wing struts to help lift the plane loose from the gluey earth. *Spirit* began to move under its own power, at first agonizingly slow. It seemed that the overloaded plane could never rise above the ground; its wheels were cutting furrows in the clay instead of riding high and quick. At the halfway mark, the controls were mushy but tightening; he tried to lift the plane and the wheels did leave the ground for a split second. It was 7:52 A.M.

Bruno was following close behind in his roadster, with the policemen and the fire extinguishers.

Now Lindbergh was certain; he was committed. He continued to roar down the runway, picking up speed as he lurched along. He bounced into the air, still without enough flying speed. (A couple of "kangaroo leaps" was Bruno's description.) But at last the plane broke contact with the ground and Lindbergh nursed it slowly aloft. There was still a thousand feet to the telephone wires. He climbed very slowly, attaining speed as he went, and cleared the wires by twenty feet. Bruno and Skidmore turned toward each other in the front seat as the car skidded to a halt. "By God, he made it!" they shouted in unison.

Lindbergh flew along Long Island, and then, following the first leg of his great-circle course, he pointed across Long Island Sound toward Connecticut. He had never flown over so much water in his life, but he knew that between land and water there was always an area of turbulence. With his wings and fuselage overstrained, Lindbergh could not afford to add anything to the burden. He trembled with each shock of turbulence, watched his wing tips bend too much, waiting for the rending sound that would signal he had pushed things too far. Those were an uneasy few seconds, but a thousand feet out over the water the air became smooth as glass. The wings stopped vibrating. Now with each passing moment his ship became lighter as it consumed fuel, and a less likely prey to turbulence. He crossed the Sound and flew over Connecticut. At the end of his first hour he began to fill the hourly log that would tell him what he needed as he went along, particularly about fuel consumption. He recorded wind velocity (zero), true course, compass variation. His altitude was 600 feet, his air speed 102 m.p.h., the tachometer showed only 1,750 r.p.m., 50 below the normal cruising speed. He had plenty of reserve power as he cruised across Rhode Island and Massachusetts.

Between Massachusetts and Nova Scotia there were two hours of flight over open water. This would really test his navigating skill. If he could stay on course without familiar landmarks to guide him, he could be confident of doing the same thing over the North Atlantic. The drone of the engine seemed to emphasize the fact that he hadn't slept for more than twenty-four hours. Also, he had been flying for nearly four hours, a good day's flight. He began to get sleepy, very sleepy. And there were still thirty hours ahead of him, part of it at night and most of it over ocean. Overwater flight, he was learning, had a certain monotony that made sleep ever more desirable. His eyelids wanted to close. In fact, his eye did blink closed several times; perhaps he slept for a second or two without knowing it. During the third hour of flight, the cockpit was suddenly lit by warm sunlight. He looked out and saw a bit of mud on the wing, thrown up from Roosevelt Field by the wheels. It irritated him to think he had cut every unneeded ounce from his plane and was now forced to carry a tiny load of mud all the way to Paris.

Suddenly a green coast leaped at him; it was the shore of Nova Scotia. Checking his charts against the shape of the shore line, he found that he had made landfall at the mouth of St. Mary's Bay, only six miles off his course, only two degrees away from his calculated objective, well within the five-degree margin for error he had allowed himself. This was very good navigating indeed. A six-mile error here was the equivalent of a miss of about fifty miles at Ireland. And his plane had averaged a hundred and two miles an hour. Already it was about four hundred pounds lighter in fuel than when he started.

In his mind, Lindbergh had set three checkpoints which would determine his flight plan. The first one was halfway down the runway at Roosevelt. The second was this one, Nova Scotia. If he found it socked in by fog, or if he was totally lost—showing that flying by compass would not work—he planned to turn back to Long Island. His next and last would be halfway across the Atlantic, the point of no return. Before that, if he ran into trouble he could turn back; after that, he would have no choice but to press on.

Over Nova Scotia and Cape Breton Island he met heavy rain, fog, turbulent air. He began to worry about his wings again, and his lack of parachute. Why had he traded those twenty pounds of safety for extra gasoline? Why hadn't he put dump valves on his fuel tanks so he might lighten his load, if necessary, and save his plane? He knew the answers, but doubts began to gnaw at him. Had he made the right decisions? If he lived, he would know.

He flew for three hours over Nova Scotia, then headed out over another two hundred miles of open water toward Newfoundland. Once more, sleep began to overtake him; his eyes grew heavy, and he forgot to keep his plane on course. He began to dream of lying in a snowbank in Minnesota, that winter when he was seventeen and became snowbound with his pony. Those clouds looked so soft out there . . . just like the Minnesota snowbanks. But he wrenched himself awake to take an interest in the ice fields that appeared below. He began to make plans for a forced landing on ice. He adjusted his engine revolutions to allow for the lightened weight of fuel he was now carrying after nine hours of flight. At last the mountains of Newfoundland showed themselves, and Lindbergh had to make a decision. Should he fly off course a bit—only a few minutes off—to dip his wings to St. John's, the last settlement he would see before Ireland? Or should he stick to his rigid schedule?

No plane had ever flown from St. John's eastward without first landing there. It was there that Commander Read and his three flying boats refueled and took off for the Azores on the Navy flight eight years before, in 1919. It was from St. John's, too, that Alcock and Brown had flown to Ireland the same year.

It would be fun to dive on St. John's and then continue across the Atlantic—another joke he could play. But this one had possibly serious consequences. After having cut everything to the bone to save fuel, he would be wasting a quarter of an hour's flight for a bit of fun. No, he couldn't do that. But then he continued to think—

flying over the city would give the inhabitants one last fix on his plane and his course. They would know he had made it this far, which would reassure his partners, and they would know where he was heading and at approximately what speed. If he didn't get to Europe, they could figure he must be down somewhere along the route between St. John's and Ireland. This knowledge would narrow the search for him as he waited, floating on his rubber raft.

He altered course toward St. John's. It took only a moment to dive down over the edge of the city. Men looked up and saw him. Then he flew out to sea, nearly two thousand miles of it before him. As he broke his last tenuous connection with the land, he checked his fuel and his ignition. He was heading toward night.

"To the pilot of an airplane without flares or landing lights, night has a meaning that no earthbound mortal can fully understand," Lindbergh has written. "Once he has left the lighted airways there are no wayside shelters open to a flyer of the night. He can't park his plane on a cloud bank to weather out a storm, or heave over a sea anchor like the sailor and drag along slowly downwind. He's unable to control his speed like the driver of a motorcar in fog. He has to keep his craft hurtling through air no matter how black the sky or blinding the storm. To land without sight is to crash."

Now he was committed to the night and to the sea. After an hour he had to climb to get above fog. Then a storm began developing and he had to climb higher to get over it. He was at 10,500 feet. Suddenly he noticed how cold it was inside the plane, and this warned him through the haze of sleep that there was danger outside. Ice—ice that could deform the airy shape of a wing, that could overload the plane and force it into the sea—ice was forming. He could see some of it by the light of his flashlight. He was inside an ice cloud, one of those terrible, soft things that would not cause a plane to crash immediately but were an all-embracing threat. "They enmesh intruders," he wrote. "They're barbaric in their methods. They toss you in their inner turbulence, lash you with their hail-stones, poison you with freezing mist. It would be a slow death, a death one would have long minutes to struggle against . . . climbing, stalling, diving, whipping, always downward toward the sea."

He wanted to panic, to turn and dive, but he kept himself from moving too precipitately. The *Spirit of St. Louis* was an extraordinarily sensitive airplane that required careful flying every minute; it wasn't an old Standard that could be kicked around in the sky. He maneuvered his way out of the ice clouds and back into clear air. The ice was not so thick on the plane's wires now.

Lindbergh had had removable glass windows built for the plane, windows he could insert from inside the cockpit. At one point during the flight he considered using them to keep out the cold, and also to add streamlining and extra range to the ship. But they would cut him off from sensory contact with the passing air; they would dull the sound of the engine; they would keep the cabin warm—and that might only make sleep irresistible. He had sacrificed several miles' worth of gasoline for the windows, which weighed about three or four pounds, but he never put them in.

Sleep continued to threaten him. He had never known such a terrible urgency to close his eyes, to drift off. He began to doubt that he could stay awake to complete the flight; sleep and ice seemed determined to kill him. He shook himself. He stuck his mittened hand out the window to deflect cold air into his face. He slapped himself, hard, and didn't feel a thing. He noticed his head was hurting; his altitude, still over 10,000 feet, had allowed the air cushion on which he was sitting to expand just enough to force his helmet against the top of the cockpit.

By fighting every second—and probably by occasionally falling asleep for a few seconds, or nearly—Lindbergh thrashed his way in the twilight zone of sleep. The air became clearer, then warmer. He could see the moon. Below, he knew, must be the Gulf Stream; if he was forced down into that body of water, he could live for a long time.

And then, during the seventeenth hour of flight, he passed the third of his three checkpoints, the point of no return. Before he had been flying away from safety; now he was moving toward it with every passing second.

He had now gone about forty-eight hours without sleep, and the need to close his eyes became the most demanding thing in his life. He actually pried his eyes open with his fingers, but they closed anyhow. His body was in revolt. "Every cell of my being is on strike, sulking in protest, claiming that nothing, nothing in the world, could be worth such effort; that man's tissue was never made for such abuse." He had to stay awake to live; he knew that, and he

kept telling himself that basic truth over and over. He was still
filling out his log, hour by hour. At the end of eighteen hours he
knew he was approximately halfway to Paris. He had planned on a
private celebration—a sandwich and some water—but he wasn't
hungry enough to eat, and he didn't want any more water. (He had
taken a couple of sips since the start of the flight.) He just kept
flying like an automaton, dull, spiritless, yet always sensitive to
danger. If his turn indicator or his air-speed indicator showed a
change, he reacted instantly.

For the next five hours he battled sleep and fog; he was so tired
and so often socked in that he couldn't take proper readings, and so
neglected his log. Now he kept a record only of the hours of fuel
consumed from the various tanks. The sun rose, but the usual
morning arousal failed to take place within him. He was flying in a
stupor, wasting fuel by not properly setting his mixture and by
allowing the engine to turn over faster than necessary. After some
hours he saw the sea and could tell from the direction of the spume
that a strong wind was blowing, a wind that was helping him—a
tail wind. But sleep still threatened. How could he keep on flying
for another ten hours? How could he navigate to find his landfalls?
"But the alternative is death and failure," he thought. "Death!
For the first time in my life, I doubt my ability to endure."

His body was suffering from lack of oxygen. He thrust his head
out of the window and took great gulps of air. That helped, but he
still wanted sleep. He fought the fog in his brain, he fought the
plane; he was fighting to stay alive. And then, as though he were
getting over an acute illness, for no discernible reason he began to
feel alert again. His strength returned. His eyes stayed open
without an effort. He could see and feel and smell. He looked at his
watch. It was just about twenty-four hours since he had started out
and he was well into his third sleepless day. Somehow he had flown
past the need for sleep, just as he had slipped through clouds. The
world was suddenly new and bright.

With his head clear, he began planning ahead. He was totally
unsure of his position. He might have drifted hundreds of miles off
course during his hours of drowsiness; if he had, and his error was
to the south, he might have to fly an additional thousand miles over
ocean to reach land. Should he, then, throttle down to save fuel? On
the other hand, if he was headed toward Ireland, as he thought, and

he slowed down, he might not get there before dark. Once again it was his philosophy of risk that made the choice. "If security were my prime motive," he thought, "I'd never have begun this flight at all." Security demanded that he slow down and conserve fuel; instead, he speeded up the engine, gave it a richer mixture, and saw the air-speed indicator rise, by seven miles an hour, to an even hundred.

During his battle with sleep, he had been the prey of hallucinatory visions. He recalled his childhood, his youth; he thought he saw dragons; he thought he saw islands in the middle of the sea. Now he did see something, and it was real—porpoises. He wasn't knowledgeable enough about sea life to know whether this meant he was close to land or not.

But when during the twenty-sixth hour of flight he sighted a sea bird, he was reasonably sure he was approaching land. Birds could rest on waves, but they nested on shore. Then supposition merged into certainty when he saw some fishing boats down below. This was the most exciting moment of the flight, he said later.

In the past, Lindbergh had been able to talk to people on the ground by flying low and throttling back on his engine. He tried this with a fishing boat. But when he circled, shouting, "Which way is Ireland?" nobody even came out on deck. He had no idea of how far off course he might be; he had only his compasses to guide him, and they had not been reliable during the night. He circled another boat, shouting. This time a man stuck his head out of a porthole, but he only gawked; he never answered. He didn't even point.

At last Lindbergh gave up in disgust. He had wasted precious minutes of fuel and daylight trying to get the uncommunicative fishermen on deck. He headed eastward.

Within the hour (the twenty-seventh of the flight) he thought he saw land. It had to be Ireland, even though it was much too early to be this close. As he drew nearer, he could see the high mountains, too high for Brittany or Cornwall, and the fields; they were much greener than one would find in Scotland. It *had* to be Ireland. It was. He was more than two hours ahead of schedule; that tail wind had pushed him a couple of hundred miles nearer. He flew over a village. It was beautiful. Everything was beautiful. People streamed into the streets, waving, waving. He felt he had returned to life, to earth.

He arrived over the Irish coast at a point only three miles off his course—Valentia and Dingle Bay. He had figured he might make it within fifty miles. That would have been extremely good dead reckoning. But three miles! "Before I made this flight I would have said carelessly that it was luck. Now, luck seems far too trivial a word, a term to be used only by those who've never seen the curtain drawn or looked on life from far away."

He had kept his watch—his grandfather's nickel-cased watch—set at New York time. It was now 11:52 A.M. in New York—of May 21, the day after he took off. In a few hours he would be in Paris, if all went well. And all was going well. He tried out his switches; both sets of spark plugs were firing. He decided to use up all the fuel in the nose tank to give the plane a heavier tail; this would lessen chances of nosing over on landing.

Four hours from Paris, he again revved his engine and got up to an air speed of 110 m.p.h. At this speed he would reach the shore of France while it was still daylight and give himself an edge in the event of a forced landing.

For a while he wondered if he shouldn't fly farther than Paris. He had plenty of gasoline left. Without gauges, but by calculating time, speed, and distance, he assumed that there was at least enough gasoline in the plane to fly on to Rome. That would be a feat! Another seven hundred miles beyond the impossible goal of Paris!

But then he remembered how it had been over Cleveland one night, when his plane wasn't expected. He had circled and circled, not finding the lights of the airport, and had just about given up hope and decided to search for a field on the outskirts of town when the airport lights went on. The man on the ground said that of course they turned the lights off at night when they didn't expect a plane. Why should they waste all that electricity? Lindbergh was afraid the same thing might happen to him if he pushed on beyond Paris to cities where no one expected him.

It was still daylight when he saw the coast of France. Now Paris was only a little more than an hour away. He was three hours ahead of schedule. That would surprise the people, all right! He thought of what he would do after he arrived. He had no visa; that might be a problem. He had to buy a suit; he had only the flying clothes he was wearing. Maybe he could take his plane on a tour of Europe—even fly on around the world. At the very least, he expected to fly it home. It would demean the *Spirit of St. Louis* to return to the United States on board a ship.

As he passed the 3,500-mile mark, he knew he had broken the world's record for nonstop airplane flight. In a kind of celebration he ate a sandwich—his first food in more than thirty-five hours. It didn't taste very good, but he chewed it down, following each mouthful with a swig of water. He certainly didn't have to conserve his supply of water any longer. He crumpled the paper wrapping and started to throw it out the window. Instead, he stuffed it into the bag. He didn't want his first contact with France to be litter.

As he angled in toward Paris at 4,000 feet, he thought how wonderful a plane the *Spirit of St. Louis* was—"Like a living creature, gliding along smoothly, happily, as though a successful flight means as much to it as to me. . . . *We* have made this flight across the ocean, not *I* or *it*."

Soon he picked up the patterned lights of the Paris streets, the Eiffel Tower—he circled it, naturally—then headed northeast toward Le Bourget. He thought he saw the airport, but it seemed terribly close to the city, so he flew past to make sure there wasn't another field farther along. He returned to Le Bourget—it was Le Bourget, all right—and wondered why they had all those floodlights lit, but no beacons, no approach lights, no warning lights. He banked over the field to get an idea what he was landing in, then circled lower. The wind sock showed a gentle wind.

He came in lower. He could see what seemed like a lot of automobiles on a road nearby. What were they doing there? The plane felt funny; he was coming in as slowly as he dared, almost stalling, yet he might very well overshoot the field. He was flying out of the lighted area into unknown, unseen hazards. He sideslipped, held the nose up, finally felt his wheels touch. Should he stay on the ground and possibly run into a building? Or should he gun the engine and take off again for another landing? He chose the earth; the plane rolled more slowly, but it was rolling into darkness. He couldn't see a thing. At last he could turn, and began to taxi over toward the hangars. It was 10:22 P.M. Paris time, thirty-three and a half hours after he had left Roosevelt Field.

Le Bourget had been empty a moment before. Now, suddenly, out of the darkness burst an avalanche, a flood, a torrent of running figures. People. They were spreading all over the field; they would engulf the plane; they might get hurt by the propeller. He cut the engine, hoping the propeller would not be turning over when they reached him. The *Spirit of St. Louis* was resting in the center of Le Bourget Airport.

9

PARIS AND RETURN

LINDBERGH HAD BEEN AWARE IN NEW YORK THAT HE
had become a celebrity. But he had no idea that his new status
would continue to enlarge.

He did not know how much was being written about him in
Europe, and saw very little of it in the United States. He could not
know that already the hero-making process was irreversibly under way.

When he was sighted over New England or Nova Scotia or over
St. John's, each incident made a headline and a fresh edition of the
newspapers. The same bits were pouring over the radio, too. Many
recall how Lindbergh was in everybody's mind, and how they
talked about little else that day.

Then, for eighteen hours, between St. John's and Ireland, because
he took no radio and did not fly over shipping lanes, there was a
total blackout of news. The world's interest became the world's
concern; almost literally did the inhabitants of America and Europe
hold their breath.

In Yankee Stadium, New York City, the night of May 20, the first
night Lindbergh was in the air, two heavyweights, Jim Maloney
and Jack Sharkey, fought before a crowd of 40,000. "Joe Humphreys, a little announcer with a bow tie and voice of brass," wrote
John Lardner, "arose in the pool of light in the center of the
darkness and called for silence and prayer." Humphreys said
Lindbergh was now 300 miles at sea, past Newfoundland. The
entire place went silent and everybody stood with bared heads.

All along his route and in countries far beyond, men prayed for
Lindbergh.

He was completely unaware of this. In his mind he was still a kind of tourist, an American without a visa. He had the letters of introduction from Colonel Roosevelt—taken out of courtesy, to be sure, but he had the intention of using them. In his pocket was a $500 bank check to pay his expenses.

When his plane burst out of the sky over Ireland, its sighting was reported immediately around the world. And each subsequent sighting, over Plymouth, England, and over Cherbourg, France, added to what was now a fire of world frenzy.

Lindbergh flew on, occupied with his piloting problems. But on the ground, in France, people were streaming toward Le Bourget Airport. A young French boy who lived in Maisons-Lafitte, a village about twenty miles from the airport, took his push-bike and with his friends started toward Le Bourget. As they moved along the roads, they ran into increasingly heavy traffic. "Cars, trucks, carts, horses, bicycles, people walking. It was like during the war," he said. For the last few miles, there was no use trying to ride the bike. He just got off and pushed. Outside the airport he put it on the ground with all the other bikes and went to join the mob, which had by now become so large nobody could count it—or control it.

"When I circled the aerodrome it did not occur to me that any connection existed between my arrival and the cars stalled in traffic on the roads," Lindbergh reported. "When my wheels touched earth, I had no way of knowing that tens of thousands of men and women were breaking down fences and flooding past guards."

The French had made elaborate preparations to receive and protect him. There were many civil police at the airport and then, as the mob began to gather, a regiment of soldiers was detailed to Le Bourget. They affixed bayonets to their rifles. But it would have needed much more of the French Army, better armed than these soldiers, to restrain the pent-up emotion of the people. Nobody knows how many there were—perhaps a hundred thousand, perhaps many more. There is no photograph of the event, for the good reason that the crowd swept over everything—steel fences, police, soldiers, and newsmen—in an irresistible surge toward the *Spirit of St. Louis.*

When the *Times* bought Lindbergh's story, Birchall had cabled Edwin James to "prepare to isolate [Lindbergh]," and had wired all ships at sea for any sightings of Lindbergh. On May 21, James deployed his staff around Le Bourget and got off a story telling how "25,000 pairs of eyes" had watched the plane landing. (Later, James elevated the number to 150,000 "gone insane with joy.")

James had thought he had everything organized. There were a car and a chauffeur, a telephone line to New York, stenographers, photographers. J. Carlisle MacDonald was one of the *Times* men assigned to isolate Lindbergh.

As soon as *Spirit* landed, MacDonald and James lunged across the field. MacDonald was six feet from the ship when the propeller stopped. He waved at Lindbergh, but could not attract his attention. Immediately, he was hit in the back by a bicycle and knocked down; he crawled under the plane with James to escape being crushed to death. They came out under the tail. MacDonald remarked, "I wish the editor who sent that message had been here to isolate him."

Before Lindbergh could open the plane door, he was surrounded. He could feel parts of the plane crack; he could hear the fabric ripping. The machine that had become for him a living creature, bearing him toward life, was being rent by the mob. "Are there any mechanics here?" he shouted. Nobody answered. "Does anyone here speak English?"

He opened the door to climb out, but he did not set foot on the ground. Hands reached and pulled him out; he was spread-eagled on top of the crowd like a helpless tortoise on its back. His stiff muscles did not help him. There was real danger that he would be dropped and crushed to death in his hour of triumph.

He wrote that after finding he was powerless to put his feet on the ground, "It seemed wisest to relax . . . [it became evident that] the men under me were determined that no matter what happened to them, I would not fall."

He felt his soft leather helmet being snatched from his head. That was the work of a couple of French pilots, Detroyat and Delage. They took the helmet and put it on the head of another American, a tall man. Someone shouted to the crowd that the other man was Lindbergh. Then, for the first time in the half hour since he had landed, Lindbergh was put on the ground. In the darkness, his flying suit blended inconspicuously with the crowd, and the two French fliers were able to hustle him into a small Renault automobile. They drove to a hangar and put him in a side room, dimming the lights so that he could not be readily seen.

Now that the noise of the crowd was shut out and Lindbergh's ears had stopped ringing from the incessant exhaust of the engine, he could hear Detroyat and Delage ask him if he needed a doctor, or a bed, or anything else. No, he said, but he was worried about the *Spirit of St. Louis.* They refused to permit him to go out and look after the ship, but assured him it would be protected. Then Lindbergh asked about customs and immigration—he was still a little uneasy about his lack of a visa. The men only laughed and joked about that.

Major Pierre Weiss, of the French Air Forces, whose nonstop distance record (to Persia) Lindbergh had just broken, appeared and ordered that Lindbergh be taken to the military part of the airport, about a mile away. The official reception committee, including Ambassador Herrick, was cut off by the mob on the other side of the field.

It was two hours before Lindbergh met Herrick. He was immediately impressed with the old Ambassador's perceptiveness and kindness. Herrick welcomed Lindbergh, made sure he was all right, and then said he was taking him back to the Embassy.

Lindbergh accepted gladly, but insisted on making sure first that his plane was in a hangar, under guard. The sight of it was almost enough to make him cry. There were gaping holes in the fabric of the fuselage, torn out by souvenir hunters; someone had actually ripped a grease reservoir off the engine. What was worse, the log that Lindbergh had kept so faithfully had disappeared. It was never found.

The Ambassador could not be located again in the surging throng, so Lindbergh was taken to Paris by Delage, Detroyat, and Weiss in the little Renault. Entering the city by some side roads, they passed the Opéra and then drove (possibly up the Champs Elysées; Lindbergh remembers a "long avenue") to the Etoile. They stopped near the inner ring of the spacious circle and got out of the car. Then they walked under the Arc de Triomphe, and Lindbergh found himself standing with the French pilots, the flame of the tomb of the Unknown Soldier burning at his feet. The Frenchmen said they wanted this to be his first stop in Paris.

They reached the American Embassy at 2, Avenue d'Iéna before Ambassador Herrick arrived. The official limousine had got stuck in the huge traffic jam between Le Bourget and the center of the city.

Someone thoughtfully provided Lindbergh with food. When Herrick arrived at 2:00 A.M. he went to see Lindbergh immediately, and asked if he was too tired to see the reporters. Lindbergh said that he was not too tired, but that he had a contract to tell his story exclusively to the *New York Times*.

MacDonald of the *Times* was still trying to reach Lindbergh; he never got close to him again at Le Bourget. He drove in to Paris, the twelve-mile trip taking three hours. He had no idea where Lindbergh might be, and was worried that another paper might reach him first. He tried the American Embassy.

The building seemed quiet; only a few lights were on. But the Ambassador's son Parmely Herrick said, "Come on in, Mac. He's upstairs talking to Father." There were no other reporters in the Embassy.

In the Ambassador's bedroom, MacDonald saw "a boy of a man" swathed in the Ambassador's pajamas, much too large for him, seated on the edge of the bed with a huge sandwich in one hand and a glass of milk in the other. It was hard to believe that this youth was the conqueror of the Atlantic.

Edwin James wrote later that when MacDonald told Lindbergh "we intended to isolate him, [Lindbergh] answered: 'There seem to have been a million other people with the same idea.'"

Lindbergh gave MacDonald a half-hour exclusive interview. It was two-thirty in the morning, yet MacDonald found Lindbergh "wide-awake, coherent and most cooperative." When the other reporters arrived, Lindbergh was not going to see them. He said to MacDonald, "You [the *Times*] had the faith to back me when not many others would, so I have faith in you."

"I could barely believe he was true," MacDonald wrote. "In deference to the world importance of the story, I took it upon myself to release him from the contract and let the other correspondents talk to him. I never regretted it. Through all the giddy weeks afterward, when syndicates and movie moguls bid millions for his story, he remained true to the *Times*."

When Lindbergh was asked how much farther he could have flown, he said, "A thousand, or at least five hundred miles." Some enterprising reporters got a mechanic at the airfield to drain the tanks of the *Spirit of St. Louis* to see how much longer the plane might have gone on. The mechanic did not know the system for draining the plane's five tanks, and found only twenty gallons of gas. This made a dramatic but inaccurate story. "Actually," Lindbergh says, "eighty-five gallons of gasoline and fourteen and a half gallons of lubricating oil remained on board after the flight from New York—enough to have carried the *Spirit of St. Louis* more than a thousand miles farther eastward, under existing wind conditions."

"What about you?" the reporters asked. "Could you have flown on? Weren't you too tired?"

"I could have flown half as far again," Lindbergh said. And he added, "You know, flying a good airplane doesn't require nearly as much attention as a motorcar."

Lindbergh's first Paris interview was a remarkable display of poise, politeness, and good taste, particularly for one in his state of fatigue. It was 4:15 A.M. before the reporters left him alone and he could go to sleep. It had been sixty-three hours since he had last slept. Thoughtful Ambassador Herrick wired Lindbergh's mother that her son was safe and well, and sleeping "under Uncle Sam's roof."

(The young boy who came to see Lindbergh at Le Bourget left with the crowd. When he went to get his bicycle, he found it was stolen. "So I did what anyone else would do—I took somebody else's," he said. Many years later, he told Lindbergh this story and Lindbergh grinned and said, "I hope you got a better one.")

There were headlines on the front pages of special editions of the important newspapers of Europe, such as *Aftonbladet, Le Figaro,* and *La Prensa.* Newspapers all over America bannered Lindbergh's flight and sold more copies than they ever had before. The staid *New York Times* used its three-bank, eight-column, front-page headline, usually reserved for only the largest international events like wars and revolutions, to announce Lindbergh's arrival. Most of the paper's front page and a good part of its first five inside pages were devoted to him and his flight.

The *Times'* reporting was reasonably accurate. But the farther away from Paris one went, the more fictional were the newspaper accounts of Lindbergh's arrival. The Chicago *Tribune* quoted him as asking, on arrival, "Am I here?" The Denver *Post* gave it as "Well, here we are." And the *Post* said Lindbergh referred to his cockpit as a "death chamber." "If I had believed that, I would never have started on the flight," Lindbergh comments. Since the reporters were all swept away by the mob before they could see him, they could only have surmised what his first words had been.

Lindbergh woke in Paris about noon on May 22. The courtyard and the ground floor of the Embassy were filled with nearly three hundred reporters, photographers, and newsreel cameramen. A crowd in the street that had started gathering the night before was chanting "Vive Lindbergh!" It filled the Avenue d'Iéna. It was so large, in fact, that Herrick demanded police protection for the Embassy and got it. Lindbergh breakfasted on grapefruit, oatmeal, bacon and eggs, toast—and this menu became important news. He borrowed a blue serge suit from the Ambassador's son, and was interviewed by Carlisle MacDonald and Edwin L. James, of the *Times*, for his by-line story. Then, to satisfy the crowd, he went out onto the front balcony of the Embassy with Herrick and waved and smiled. It was his first formal appearance before a large audience.

An unnamed diplomat who witnessed this was later interviewed by writer Fitzhugh Green. (Captain Green was asked by Lindbergh to write up the receptions given to him for Lindbergh's first book, *We.*) The diplomat told Green that the people kept on cheering long after one would have expected their interest to subside. "I suddenly had a feeling they were applauding mechanically, as if their attention were rooted on something that fascinated them," the man said.

"I glanced up at Lindbergh to see if he was doing anything he shouldn't do. No, he was just smiling and his ruddy face was alight with appreciation.

"I looked from Lindbergh to the crowd. Then I realized that something was going on right before my eyes that I couldn't see. Lindbergh's personality was reaching out and winning the French just as surely as his flight had reached out and found their city."

Lindbergh hadn't quite completed all the reminders on his list, like wiring Ryan, the Vacuum Oil Company, the Wright people, and the Champion spark-plug manufacturers how well their products had performed. So he sent the wires. He had the idea of flying to England to use the new transatlantic telephone to call his mother; however, a special wire had been run to Paris just so that he could make the call. He spoke to Mrs. Lindbergh from the Embassy before meeting the press. The call was another infallibly right gesture to reassure the world that the boy they were idolizing was all that he should be.

Probably he was guided by Ambassador Herrick to do some of the things he did in Paris, like visiting the mother of Nungesser, one of the French pilots who had been lost. But the way he handled these situations was his own. Lindbergh told Mme. Nungesser he thought her son would be found. And he told French aviators at a lunch that what Nungesser and Coli had tried to do was much more difficult than what he had done; flying from east to west meant bucking head winds all the way. Wherever he went, he won the crowd with his quick, ready smile, his boyish appearance. Although he was called Captain Lindbergh, he never wore anything but civilian clothes.

He was often called on to speak. He had only English, but he used it well. There were a few simple themes; often a speech would be only a hundred words long. He would talk about Franco-American friendship. He would talk about the future of aviation. If he mentioned himself, it was usually as "we," which Jimmy Walker, Mayor of New York, characterized later as an "aeronautical we," including the plane. He didn't get much chance to fly, except very early one morning when he took up a French Army Nieuport and stunted it over Paris, to the delight of his French colleagues.

There was one medal after another, starting with the Chevalier Cross of the Legion of Honor, personally given by the President of France. He lunched with Blériot, the first man to fly the English Channel. He visited French heroes of the war, Marshal Foch, Marshal Joffre.

Ambassador Herrick was a shrewd man, and a man of good will. It was his intention to try to rebuild the good Franco-American relations that had been dissipated since the Versailles Treaty and the Kellogg-Briand Pact. In Lindbergh he found the perfect instrument. At lunch with the French Aero Club Herrick said, "This young man from out of the west . . . shows you that the heart of the United States beats for France."

Lindbergh, the symbol of American good will, was also used by his government as an unofficial ambassador to Belgium and England.

On Saturday, May 28, Lindbergh went to Le Bourget at 8 A.M. and spent several hours checking over the *Spirit of St. Louis*. The fabric covering of the fuselage, which had been so badly damaged by the crowd, had been replaced, and the fuselage itself repaired. He took off about one o'clock, circled the Eiffel Tower, and dropped a note of thanks to the French people in the Place de la Concorde. Then he headed for Brussels. He circled Senlis and Valenciennes en route. The flight to Evère Aérodrome, Brussels, took two hours and fifteen minutes. There was a tremendous crowd at the airport.

But Albert, King of Belgium, had given firm orders that Lindbergh must not be mobbed. The reception was warm, but the crowd was kept under control. Lindbergh was greeted by the Prime Minister of Belgium and taken to the American Embassy, where his host was the Chargé d'Affaires (the Ambassador was in the United States). He visited with the King and Queen, inspected airplanes, and the next day (Sunday) was welcomed by the Burgomaster of Brussels, M. Max, in the town square.

Later that day, May 29, Lindbergh flew to Croydon Aerodrome in London in two hours and thirty-five minutes. A crowd nearly as large as the one that had greeted him at Le Bourget eight days earlier was gathered. And the crowd was, if anything, less controllable than the Le Bourget mob. No sooner had the *Spirit of St. Louis* touched down than they broke through the police barricades and rushed the plane. Lindbergh was certain that people would be hurt by the moving ship, or the propeller, so he quickly took off again. He circled the airport for five minutes while police pushed and hauled at the mass to try to clear a place where he could land safely. On the second touchdown, he was able to halt the propeller just before the mob pelted up to him. Officials of the Royal Air Club in an automobile managed to reach the *Spirit of St. Louis* a second or two ahead of the pack and got Lindbergh safely away before the first clutching hands could touch him. But the plane could not be totally protected; a stabilizer was damaged by the crush and had to be repaired before Lindbergh could fly the ship again.

As in Paris, the official welcome was canceled by the crowd. Sir Samuel Hoare, British Secretary for Air, and the American Ambassador, Alanson B. Houghton, were prevented from carrying through the prepared ceremony. Instead, Lindbergh mounted a control tower for safety, and shouted a few words to the crowd. Then the Ambassador's limousine pushed through the crowd and Lindbergh jumped into it, and they got him away with only one window broken.

There was another huge mob outside the American Embassy, where Lindbergh stayed. That night he dined there with the Ambassador and some of Herrick's friends. Lindbergh revealed to the Ambassador his plans after London. He wanted to return to the United States by air, flying the *Spirit of St. Louis* eastward across Europe and Asia to the Bering Strait, thence via Alaska and Canada back to his starting place at Roosevelt Field. He had been studying maps and was convinced that the flight was feasible.

However, the Ambassador explained that the United States government had other ideas. President Calvin Coolidge had decided to send the cruiser *Memphis*, flagship of the U.S. European Fleet, to take Lindbergh and his plane back to the United States. Lindbergh at first objected. It would insult his plane, he said, to carry it back in a box across the ocean it had so gallantly spanned. The Ambassador reminded Lindbergh that he was a captain in the Reserve, and that Coolidge was his Commander in Chief—but, of course, returning by ship was not an order, merely advice. Lindbergh got the point, and gave up his plans to fly around the rest of the world. On May 31, *Spirit* was flown to Gosport, England, there to be disassembled, crated, and put aboard the *Memphis*.

Lindbergh stayed in England until Friday, June 3. During that time he was constantly fêted, met Prime Minister Stanley Baldwin, the Prince of Wales (later to be King, and now Duke of Windsor), King George, and Queen Mary. King George V decorated Lindbergh with the Royal Air Force Cross, given only once before to Americans (the crew of the NC ship that first flew the Atlantic). Sir Samuel Hoare hailed Lindbergh at a luncheon of the Air Council. The Prince of Wales asked Lindbergh what he was going to do after he returned to America. "I'm going to keep on flying," Lindbergh told him. He was still under contract to the Robertson company to fly the air mail. He also met Lord and Lady Astor, attended a Derby, placed a wreath on the tomb of Britain's Unknown Soldier.

The British Royal Air Force lent him a plane to fly to Paris. He was grounded by fog for a while at Lympne, England, then followed a British mailplane to Paris. He stayed there one day, flew back to Cherbourg on June 4, and boarded the *Memphis*.

Aboard ship, just as at Pensacola at the time of his crash in the Canuck, and at San Diego where the *Spirit of St. Louis* was built,

Captain Lindbergh got along very well with Navy personnel. Perhaps too well for the Army's comfort. They may have felt that the Navy was stealing their hero by transporting him home. The Secretary of War, Dwight F. Davis, jumped Captain Lindbergh two ranks and made him a full colonel in the United States Officers' Reserve Corps.

Awaiting Lindbergh, President Coolidge invited Mrs. Evangeline Lindbergh to come to Washington, D.C., for the reception scheduled on the *Memphis's* arrival, June 11. Mrs. Lindbergh was asked to wire the time of her arrival so that she could be met at the train. But she left Detroit without replying. Instead of going to Washington on Thursday, June 9, she got off the train in Baltimore and spent the night in a hotel. It was only on the next day that she got to Washington. The President finally located her and had her brought to the executive mansion. (It was not the White House, which was being repaired at the time, but a temporary official residence at Dupont Circle.) Mrs. Lindbergh dined there Friday evening, June 10, with President and Mrs. Coolidge. Also present was Dwight W. Morrow, at that time a partner in J. P. Morgan & Company. Two years before, Morrow, a former college classmate of Coolidge's, had been head of a special Air Board, appointed by Coolidge to investigate the charges and countercharges about air power made by Colonel Billy Mitchell. Now Morrow was being considered by Coolidge for another job, Ambassador to Mexico.

The cruiser *Memphis* was met at 5 P.M. that same day by four destroyers, two Army blimps, and forty airplanes from the Army, Navy, and Marine Corps as it steamed up Chesapeake Bay.

Aboard one of the destroyers, the *Goff,* was Dick Blythe. At the request of Major General Mason M. Patrick, chief of the Army Air Corps, Blythe had with him a colonel's uniform especially tailored by the Army for Lindbergh's lanky frame, from measurements in his War Department file.

Blythe gave Lindbergh the uniform, as requested by General Patrick. He put it on, Sam Browne belt, riding boots, silver eagles, and all. It fitted perfectly.

"Not so bad . . . for a mail pilot," Lindbergh said, regarding himself in the mirror.

"You can't wear it," Blythe said.

"What do you mean I can't wear it?"

"Look, dumbbell," Blythe said. "Up to now you weren't an Army man, or a Navy man, but a plain civilian with a job, and your way to make in the world. Nobody could claim you and nobody could be against you."

"I was always a Captain in the Air Reserve," Lindbergh said.

"But you went to Paris as a civilian," Blythe replied. "The public remembers you in that old blue serge suit. You can get a new one, but you don't wear the uniform. Look, you're aboard a Navy vessel, yet there isn't a man in the crew who isn't on your side. But suppose you put on an Army uniform . . ."

"Why couldn't I wear a Navy overcoat over this?" said Lindbergh.

"It's June. People would think that you had gone crazy," Blythe said.

"I've got to wear the uniform," Lindbergh insisted. "It was made for me and I've been ordered by my superior officers to have it on when I land. I have no choice."

Blythe said quickly, "Besides, it's a lousy fit."

"Where doesn't it fit?" Lindbergh asked.

"It's terrible. No superior officer can expect you to wear a uniform that looks so bad."

Lindbergh began to argue; then he stopped suddenly and grinned. "I got you," he said. "You're right. Give me a hand with these boots, will you?"

When the sun rose in Washington, on Saturday, June 11, there was no doubt it would be a hot day. The heat that began to build over the city had a special quality, a kind of breathlessness. There was a nervous going to and fro; policemen were busy roping off streets. People looked skyward as airplanes kept droning back and forth in unaccustomed numbers. Crowds began to gather early along Pennsylvania Avenue behind barricades. People looked out of open windows, craning for the surge of movement that would mean Lindbergh's arrival. Tension was building, minute by minute.

About ten o'clock the *Memphis* was sighted off Alexandria, and the city of Washington suddenly exhaled in a whoop of factory whistles, automobile horns, church bells, and fire sirens. The din was overpowering. Airplanes were now thick in the sky; fifty pursuit planes darted back and forth over flights of slower bombers. The huge dirigible *Los Angeles* zigzagged above the cruiser as it moved upriver.

"What do you think of it?" Blythe shouted into Lindbergh's ear as they stood on the *Memphis's* bridge.

"I wish I could see it from the air!" Lindbergh yelled back.

There was no lull in the noise, which was amplified by the shouts of people as the *Memphis* came closer. At eleven o'clock there was a fifteen-gun salute for Admiral Burrage, of the *Memphis,* and a twenty-one-gun salute for President Coolidge. The *Memphis* came alongside the Navy Yard dock and a gangplank was run up. The Admiral, in summer full dress, descended and a moment later came back with Mrs. Lindbergh on his arm. The cheering rose by several decibels. She went into her son's cabin and the two were left alone for several minutes.

Finally they appeared. Lindbergh was wearing the blue serge suit. (Bearing out Blythe's judgment, one of the Washington papers wrote, "He returned as a plain citizen dressed in the garments of an everyday man." And the other papers copied.)

Crowds in windows and along the shore cheered some more as they walked down the gangplank. The official reception began. There were three Cabinet officers (Navy, War, and the Postmaster General), the former Secretary of State, an Admiral, a Rear Admiral, and Major General Patrick. All perspired in uniforms and silk hats and cutaways, forming a fine contrast to the simply dressed Lindberghs.

The crowd was getting restless. They rushed the Marines, who stood with fixed bayonets. Lindbergh was hustled into an automobile and the parade began.

Slowly it wound its way through Washington, bracketed by cheering multitudes, many of whom wept openly. Finally the parade halted at the Washington Monument. There President and Mrs. Coolidge waited on a huge reviewing stand to greet Lindbergh, surrounded by ambassadors and their families. A photograph taken from the top of the monument shows people scattered as far as the lens can see.

Lindbergh and his mother mounted the stand, and Coolidge came forward and took his hand. "Those closest to Mr. Coolidge say that rarely has he shown the unrestrained cordiality he put into that simple greeting," wrote Fitzhugh Green.

Then the President went to the rostrum, which was lined with microphones for every radio network in the country and many local stations, and began an address that was second in length only to his State of the Union Message to Congress. For the laconic Coolidge, the number of words he used was as much a measure of his enthusiasm as the emotional content of his speech, which was warm. He set Lindbergh's feat in the context of the great achievements of aviation by other Americans, starting with the Wright brothers. He attributed to Lindbergh "the same story of valor and victory by a son of the people that shines through every page of American history." He disposed of Lindbergh's radical father in a short sentence, gave more attention to Mrs. Lindbergh, "who dowered her son with her own modesty and charm. . . . She has permitted neither money nor fame to interfere with her fidelity to her duties." He ran through Lindbergh's own career, quoting liberally from the War Department file in which Lindbergh's superiors had called him "intelligent, industrious, energetic, dependable, purposeful, alert, quick of reaction, serious, deliberate, stable, efficient, frank, modest, congenial, a man of good moral habits and regular in all his business transactions."

"One of the officers," said Coolidge, "expressed his belief that the young man 'would successfully complete everything he undertakes.' This reads like a prophecy."

He ended the address by pinning the Distinguished Flying Cross on Lindbergh's lapel, the first such award ever given.

Lindbergh responded with one of his terse, adroit speeches. In only about a hundred words, he delivered the simple message that the people of France and of Europe had nothing but good will for America.

Fitzhugh Green reports that "Just as when Lincoln finished his Gettysburg Address his listeners sat stunned at the very brevity of it, so was there a curious silence immediately following Lindbergh's utterance. Then came long applause . . . men and women clapped until their palms were numb. Again many wept, a radio announcer whose stock-in-trade was routine emotional appeal broke down and sobbed."

That night the Lindberghs dined with the Cabinet. Later that week he was praised by the National Press Club for reinstating the realization that "clean living, clean thinking, fair play and sportsmanship, modesty of speech and manner, faith in a mother's prayers, have a front-page news value." The Postmaster General, Harry S. New, presented Lindbergh with the first special air-mail stamp—the first time a stamp was issued by the United States Post Office to honor a man still living.

He laid another wreath on still another Unknown Soldier's tomb. He visited wounded veterans at Walter Reed Hospital. He got the Cross of Honor of the United States Flag Association from Charles Evans Hughes, soon to be Chief Justice of the United States Supreme Court.

In his acknowledgments, Lindbergh was always modest, pointing out that his feat was the culmination of twenty years of achievement by American aviation and industry, that what was needed was more support for commercial aviation in this country.

On Monday morning, June 13, Lindbergh received a life membership in the National Aeronautic Association at a breakfast meeting at the Hotel Mayflower. Then he went to Bolling Field, where the *Spirit of St. Louis* had been reassembled by Army mechanics. He got into the plane about 7:30 A.M. only to find that the engine was firing unevenly. It was too risky to fly. So, very reluctantly, he left his plane and flew an Army pursuit ship to New York. He was accompanied by more than twenty other craft. There were celebrations in Baltimore, Wilmington, and Philadelphia as the party flew over those cities.

Lindbergh arrived at Mitchel Field, New York, near noon. There he got into an amphibian plane and took off again, landing the ship in the channel just above the Narrows, between Brooklyn and Staten Island.

The water sparkled in the June sunshine as he planed to a stop. Ahead of him stretched a tremendous fleet—probably more than five hundred boats in all—that covered the water of lower New York Bay like a moving carpet. There were excursion boats, yachts, tugs, motorboats, launches, fireboats, dredges. A police launch came alongside Lindbergh's plane and took him to the *Macom*, the official yacht of the Mayor of the City of New York.

Every one of the boats was tooting its whistle or blowing its horn, and so were the factories of New York. The din was so loud that conversation was impossible aboard the *Macom*, where Lindbergh stood on top of the pilothouse for the trip to the Battery. Overhead the air vibrated with the sound of airplane engines. Fireboats lent their power streams to the spectacle, offering moving arches of water to the procession.

Lindbergh was interviewed in the *Macom's* cabin by reporters, but it was not a successful interview because of the noise and his refusal to discuss his emotions.

When the *Macom* tied up at the Battery, there were about three hundred thousand people massed at the waterfront. Lindbergh and Mayor James J. Walker got into Official Car No. 1, a large touring car with the top down, and began the slow ride to City Hall, inching between the crowds.

The police estimated that between three million and four and a half million people were out in the streets—so many, in fact, that they issued a special warning to householders not to leave their homes unguarded. Ticker tape and confetti rained down on the open car, with the bareheaded Lindbergh and the silk-hatted Mayor perched on top of the rear seat. New York had never seen anything like the storm of paper. It far exceeded the Armistice Day celebration that had ended World War I. It cost the city more than sixteen thousand dollars to clean it up the next day.

At City Hall the parade stopped for the welcoming ceremony. Walker made a graceful and witty speech kidding Lindbergh about the letters of introduction he had taken to Paris. "If you have prepared yourself with any letters of introduction to New York City, they are not necessary," he said. And he pointed out that he himself was, like Lindbergh, the son of an immigrant. He ended by pinning the Medal of Valor on Lindbergh's lapel.

Lindbergh replied with a deft, short speech. The receptions at Le Bourget and again in Brussels and London had been tremendous, he said, and Washington had been "marvelous." But after an hour in New York Lindbergh knew that nothing could outstrip the greeting of that metropolis.

The parade continued uptown, stopping at Madison Square, Twenty-third Street and Fifth Avenue, where Lindbergh laid a wreath at the World War memorial. And all along the route there were people, people who had been standing since eight in the morning (it was now well after noon) to glimpse Lindbergh. At St. Patrick's Cathedral, Lindbergh descended from his car to meet Cardinal Hayes.

The parade wound into Central Park, where Governor Alfred E. Smith pinned another medal on Lindbergh: the New York State Medal of Honor. New York gave an entire day to Lindbergh in an outpouring of emotion never equaled, before or since. It was not until five in the afternoon that the official reception was over and Lindbergh could meet his mother alone in the apartment of Harry H. Frazee at 270 Park Avenue, where they were able to rest in some kind of seclusion for an hour or so.*

That night there was a sumptuous banquet for "eighty of New York's most prominent people," with Lindbergh as guest of honor, at the Long Island estate of Clarence Mackay, head of the Postal Telegraph Company.

There was a dinner for four thousand people at the Hotel Commodore the next night, a banquet that strained every resource of that large hostelry. Charles Evans Hughes made the welcoming speech.

"We measure heroes as we do ships, by their displacement," he said. "Colonel Lindbergh has displaced everything. . . .

"He has displaced everything that is petty; that is sordid; that is vulgar. . . .

"America is fortunate in her heroes; her soul feeds upon their deeds; her imagination revels in their achievements. There are those who would rob them of something of their lustre, but no one can debunk Lindbergh, for there is no bunk about him."

On Wednesday, June 15, Lindbergh had dinner with Rodman Wanamaker aboard Wanamaker's yacht. (Wanamaker had tried to underwrite a transatlantic flight as early as 1914, and was the patron of Commander Richard E. Byrd and his *America.*) Afterward they attended a light opera, and after that a charity benefit at another theatre. At 1:30 A.M. Lindbergh left by a back door and was driven to Mitchel Field. Still wearing his evening clothes, he borrowed a helmet and flew his Army plane back to Washington. He left at 3:05 A.M., picked up the *Spirit of St. Louis* at Bolling Field, Washington, and flew it back to Mitchel Field, arriving at 7:30 A.M. He had promised to fly *Spirit* to St. Louis the following day, June 17.

Raymond Orteig had decided to waive the sixty-day waiting pe-

---

* Frazee was a friend of Grover Whalen, New York City's official greeter, and offered his apartment at Whalen's suggestion. The New York City police had said they could not guarantee Lindbergh's privacy in a hotel. Frazee had not known Lindbergh and was unconnected with aviation.

riod for the Orteig prize. On June 16, he handed Lindbergh a specially hand-lettered check, carrying the design of the *Spirit of St. Louis,* drawn on the Bryant Park Bank for $25,000. For some unexplained reason, the check was dated June 17, 1927.

The next morning, Friday, June 17, Lindbergh got up very early and was driven out to Mitchel Field. At 8:17 A.M. he took off in the *Spirit of St. Louis.* He flew over the Wright plant in Paterson, New Jersey, where his engine had been built. At 11:16 A.M. he was over Columbus, Ohio. A little later, over Dayton, a flight of thirty Army pursuit planes rose to escort his plane onward. He passed over Indianapolis and Terre Haute, Indiana, and later over St. Elmo and Scott Field, Illinois. At about five o'clock in the afternoon he was near St. Louis. A damp fog hung over the city, so Lindbergh dropped to a lower altitude and circled St. Louis to give the people a chance to see "their" plane in the air.

St. Louis had been awaiting him impatiently for nearly four weeks, ever since he arrived in Paris. They put planes in the air to welcome him, and the earthbound population was out in full force, in the streets and on roof tops. When he set down at Lambert Field, after a flight from New York of nine hours and twenty minutes, he was protected by soldiers from the mob that had gathered to welcome him.

He was put up at the house of Harry Knight, a large estate where he could be sheltered from strangers.

The next day, Saturday, June 18, came the triumphal parade in the city that had named his plane. St. Louis did itself proud. All who could get to a window overlooking Washington Avenue, or stand on the street, were out to welcome the hero they could claim as their own. There weren't as many people as in New York, of course, but there were enough, and the enthusiasm and excitement were just as great as New York's.

On Sunday, June 19, Lindbergh flew his airplane over the old fair grounds in Forest Park, St. Louis, in an exhibition for his "home town."

Afterward there was another of the endless receptions. This one was held at the Knight estate. A small gathering of St. Louis's upper crust was there. Lindbergh stood around making polite conversation. Then he spied Dick Blythe standing near a newly planted tree. He walked over casually and said, "Hello, flier," and at the same time pushed Blythe on the chest. A guy wire holding the tree was directly behind Blythe's legs, and he went over backward on the lawn.

Blythe picked himself up, laughed with the others, and then suddenly tackled Lindbergh. As Lindbergh went down, Blythe sat on his back and shoved his face into the grass, rubbing it back and forth.

"You dirty bum," he said half angrily. "You will make a dunce out of me, will you? Well, I'll show you who's the bigger dunce!"

Blythe told Bruno later that every time he pushed Lindbergh's face into the dirt, a shiver ran down his spine. He had no idea of how the nation's hero would take being publicly chastised.

As Bruno tells it, "Slim got up, brushed the grass from his knees, and wiped the moist dirt from his face. Then, without a word or a glance, he walked into the house, while the company stared at Blythe in horror.

" 'I've done it now,' thought Dick. 'This ends us with Lindbergh.'

"Up in their room, he found Slim seated on the bed, evidently expecting him. His face was still smeared with dirt, and he was smiling like a tickled kid.

" 'Say, wasn't that slick the way we got out of that?' Lindbergh said. 'I was so filled up with listening to this hero guff that I was ready to shout murder.' "

Blythe and Lindbergh used the incident as an excuse to spend an afternoon quietly—one of the very few Lindbergh could get. On June 22, Lindbergh went to Dayton, Ohio, to see Orville Wright. He was an overnight guest in the Wright house. "The visit was a sincere gesture," wrote Marvin W. McFarland, in *The Papers of Wilbur and Orville Wright*, "and Orville Wright never forgot it." Lindbergh wanted the visit to be private, and refused to attend any public functions in Dayton. However, as soon as word got out that he was in the Wright house, crowds appeared and began to trample the shrubbery and lawns around the mansion. In order to save his place from harm, Orville Wright asked Lindbergh to show himself in public. Lindbergh obliged with a brief appearance on the balcony, and only then did the mob disperse. After that, Lindbergh made no more public appearances for several weeks.

10

AFTER MEETING LINDBERGH AT THE TEMPORARY WHITE House the first day the flier arrived in Washington, Dwight Morrow telephoned his friend Harry Guggenheim that afternoon in New York. He said, "Harry, almost everyone in the country is after this young fellow, trying to exploit him. Isn't there something you and the Fund [the Daniel Guggenheim Fund for the Promotion of Aeronautics] can give him to do, to save him from the wolves? Something that will give him a chance to catch his breath before he commits himself to some proposition he might regret?"

Harry Guggenheim had already formed a good impression of Lindbergh at Curtiss Field before the Paris flight, and had seen something of what he had been up against. He told Morrow he would be glad to help.

Offers had begun flooding in on Lindbergh before he took off for Paris. One man wanted him to sign a motion-picture contract for two hundred and fifty thousand dollars. Another offered Lindbergh a fifty-thousand-dollar guarantee to go into vaudeville. The only offer Lindbergh accepted was the one from the *New York Times* for the exclusive rights to his story. He was a little sorry about the way it worked in the beginning. He would talk to Carlisle MacDonald or Edwin James for a while and they would write stories over Lindbergh's by-line, which he did not have time to correct or often even to read before they were cabled to New York.

George Palmer Putnam, the book publisher, asked his friend Frederick Birchall, of the *Times*, for help in reaching Lindbergh with a proposition to write a book about his flight and life. Birchall aided Putnam in composing the message and in getting it to Lindbergh in Paris via the *Times* Paris office. Lindbergh says he was under the impression that the book would be written about him in the third person, based on interviews, and signed by the real author. He thought he was only supposed to check the facts and write a foreword to the book. He undertook the venture, he says, because he needed the money. He was down to less than $1,500 of the original $15,000 put up by his backers. He had learned, he told a friend, that "after the flight a hundred dollars didn't go as far as ten dollars did before I took off." He needed cash for personal expenses, and he wanted to repay his backers. So he signed a contract with Putnam's.

World syndication rights to the *New York Times* stories brought a great deal of money to the paper. Lindbergh signed a new contract to keep writing for the *Times*. The New York office decided that they did not wish to profit from his feat; they wired publisher Adolph S. Ochs, then in London, to this effect, and Ochs concurred. "I heartily approve all net revenue to Lindbergh," he cabled, "plus generous Times payment."

The Paris office was informed of this decision. Birchall wired James that the *Times* was not going to hold Lindbergh to the $5,000 contract but was turning over to him all receipts from his stories, minus expenses. The *Times* also paid Lindbergh's backers, as per the contract. James was told to advance Lindbergh what money he needed, and that an accounting would be made later. The total amount that Lindbergh got from the *Times* for his stories was $60,000.

Putnam said that Lindbergh made a contract with Carlisle MacDonald to write his book. MacDonald returned with Lindbergh aboard the *Memphis* and interviewed him during the voyage. When he got back to the United States, he moved into Putnam's house in Rye and was "reinforced with secretaries" by the publisher.

He did "a good job and a quick one," Putnam wrote. "Hot from MacDonald's typewriter the copy was rushed to our printing plant in nearby New Rochelle." By Putnam's recollection, the galley proofs of the ghost-written book titled *We*—Lindbergh's often quoted expression—were sent to Lindbergh ten days after he arrived. The publisher's hurry was understandable. He had orders on hand for 100,000 copies.

But when Lindbergh saw that the book was written in the first person singular, he said "no." Putnam said that Lindbergh "found no fault with what MacDonald had written." Simply, he'd "changed his mind."

Lindbergh's recollection is that "For one thing it was inaccurate. For another . . . I didn't want a ghost-written book to come out over my name."

His impulse was to throw up the job. But Putnam's had all those orders on hand "[I]rate customers were stalking us with knives," Putnam said. So Lindbergh declared he would write it himself. Putnam wanted to know when he would get to it. Lindbergh thought he might have some time in the autumn—and here it was only June. "At that juncture high blood pressure pretty nearly overcame us," Putnam said.

Lindbergh was picking his way through hundreds of demands on his time, trying to maintain some kind of schedule of public appearances he felt were obligatory, or helpful to aviation, or both. Yet he had signed that contract. He promised to turn out a manuscript "at least 40,000 words in length."

Harry Guggenheim and his wife, Carol, hearing of his problem, invited Lindbergh to stay in their house, Falaise, a Norman-style mansion of thirty rooms on Sands Point, Long Island, while he wrote the book. Lindbergh stopped all public appearances and holed up at the Guggenheim house.

"I didn't know what I was letting myself in for," Lindbergh said later. "I don't think I ever would have gotten it done if they hadn't offered me that retreat. For the next three weeks it was sometimes as much as fourteen hours of work a day."

In twenty-one days he turned out 45,000 words about himself and the flight. He wrote in longhand, on legal-size sheets of yellow paper. In the upper right-hand corner of each page was a number— the exact number of words on that page. George Palmer Putnam said, "One could almost see him counting and saying to himself with a sigh as he cast up the total, 'Well, *that* many are out of the way, praise be!' "

Fitzhugh Green was hired by Putnam's to write up for *We* the receptions given Lindbergh in Europe and the United States. He signed his portion of the book, which was written in the third person and introduced by Lindbergh. Green got $4,000 for his work.

For a "nonprofessional" book, *We* is a bravura performance. It is terse, clear, readable. But it is also inhibited. One reason was that

Lindbergh was pressed for time. He had agreed to start a good-will flight to all forty-eight states for the Guggenheim Fund in July, and that deadline was almost at hand. Often he did not have time to reread what he had written. There was no time for corrections, or for inserting nuances of thought. Also, "Being young, and easily embarrassed, I was hesitant to dwell on my personal errors and sensations," he said. And he knew the eyes of the world were on him. He knew he was a symbol of aviation. If he put in the whole, unvarnished truth about the dangers and problems in flying, he might weaken the public image of aviation, which was none too sturdy to start out with.

Lindbergh's first royalty check from We was for $100,000. The book continued to sell. (MacDonald got $10,000 for his aborted version.) Later, a collector offered Putnam $30,000 for Lindbergh's manuscript. Putnam wanted to accept the offer; he thought that he and Lindbergh ought to split the $30,000. Lindbergh said, "If it's yours, you do as you wish. It it isn't, I want it." The manuscript was his, and he got it.

One day, while he was writing We, Lindbergh accepted an invitation to visit William Randolph Hearst, the most powerful newspaper publisher in America and a prestigious producer of movies, in Hearst's apartment in Manhattan. Hearst was also probably the most omnivorous collector of art objects in modern times. Among the treasures in his apartment was a unique pair of silver globes, one terrestrial and one celestial, made in 1700. Lindbergh admired them greatly.

Hearst offered him a contract calling for a payment of $500,000 plus 10 per cent of the profits if Lindbergh would star in a film about aviation. He made a strong pitch about how much good a really well-made and accurate motion picture could do for flying and commercial aviation in the United States.

Harry Guggenheim recollects that Lindbergh was strongly tempted by this idea. Hearst urged, "Sign it [the contract], and I'll put it in my safe here. It'll stay there till you have a chance to talk things over with your friends. Then, if you change your mind, come back and we'll destroy the contract."

Lindbergh signed and went back to Falaise. He told Guggenheim about the deal. Also present was Colonel Henry C. Breckinridge, a lawyer, who was to represent Lindbergh for many years. The two men said that Hearst was undoubtedly planning to use Lindbergh *not* to promote aviation but to assist the career of an actress named Marion Davies, who would certainly be co-starred. Hearst was famous for the sums he poured into pictures starring the pleasant but untalented Miss Davies, who was his mistress. Lindbergh was not at all sure that Hearst was insincere about promoting aviation.

The argument raged until three in the morning at the Guggenheim mansion, and finally Lindbergh gave in. The next day he asked Hearst to make good on his promise to tear up the contract, and Hearst kept his word.

He did better than that. Shortly thereafter a package arrived for Lindbergh containing the two silver globes he had admired at Hearst's apartment. It was a truly priceless present.

The Hearst offer was the only time Lindbergh came close to commercializing his fame. Almost certainly it was not the money that tempted him. "In one week if he'd accepted all the jobs, chances to sign testimonials and endorsements, and other commercial 'opportunities' presented to him, he could have picked up five million dollars," Harry Bruno says. Bruno and Blythe were in a position to know, since they were acting as Lindbergh's personal representatives. "We spent twenty hours a day saying no," Bruno adds.

"In my presence," Bruno writes, "Lindbergh declined a vaudeville contract to which was attached a $1,000,000 guaranty. A motion picture offer of $1,000,000 met a like reception. Two lecture bureaus guaranteed him $100,000 each, in vain. Radio offers passing over my desk, and all declined, in themselves would have netted him a sizeable fortune." Lindbergh also turned down many presents, such as "a home in Flushing Meadows, a live monkey, a fifty-thousand-dollar offer for a cigarette endorsement, and several motion-picture contracts—one of which carried a figure of five million dollars," according to Esther B. Mueller, of the Missouri Historical Society.

Putnam said that Lindbergh made nearly $200,000 from *We*. He received awards of $25,000 each from the Raymond Orteig Trustees and the Vacuum Oil Company. Lindbergh had endorsed the Vacuum oil used in his plane, and the company ran his endorsement in advertisements; he also gave endorsements to other products he had bought and used—Champion spark plugs, and the Waterman fountain pen with which he kept his log.

While Lindbergh was still in Europe, one unnamed tycoon and

three of his associates sent for Dick Blythe, as Lindbergh's agent, and asked what Lindbergh was going to do when he got back.

"Well, under his contract with Robertson, he still has to fly the mail for a while," Blythe told them. "But after that, he'll be free to accept better offers."

"That won't do," said the tycoon. "He'll be exploited, cheapened, ruined. We want to save him from that."

"How?" asked Blythe.

"We want to endow him," said the rich man. His friends nodded in agreement. "We four want to settle a million dollars on Lindbergh so he'll be in a position to refuse all offers that mean exploitation."

"And what do you gentlemen expect in return?" Blythe asked.

"Not a damn thing," said the leader of the group. "We only want to protect him. The thing can be done completely without publicity."

Blythe thought a minute. "That's fine of you, gentlemen," he said, "but the answer is no. Captain Lindbergh won't take money he hasn't earned. . . . Even if we advised him to take it." And he remained obdurate, even when the men "hinted at using pressure to make him take it."

Later, when Lindbergh returned to this country, Blythe told him of the offer. "Total strangers!" Lindbergh said, somewhat angry at the thought. "What do they think I am, a philanthropy?"

On another occasion, a group of businessmen ponied up another million dollars and offered it to Lindbergh on the condition that he stop flying. "You're the symbol of aviation," they argued, "and if you keep on flying, sooner or later you'll crash. You'll undo all the good your flight has done. You might even be killed."

Lindbergh turned down that million dollars, too.

Sometimes money was sent to him without any notice. The Aero Club of France forwarded 150,000 francs which Lindbergh returned with the request that the money be distributed among the families of men who had died in aviation; the sum of 5,350 crowns from the Stockholm newspaper *Svenska Dagbladet* was returned to that paper with the request that the money be used in aviation.

Some of the honors bestowed on Lindbergh have been noted. There was also the Wright Brothers Memorial Trophy as well as citations and awards from thirty governments. Hardly a city of any size in the United States, and in many other countries, did not strike off some kind of gold medal, or plaque, or special gold key for Lindbergh.

Including those silver globes from Hearst, Lindbergh received more than fifteen thousand presents from sixty-nine countries. Their value was estimated (conservatively) at more than $2 million.

He accepted the honors, and the money awards listed, but did not keep the medals, keys, presents, and other objects of value given him. All this hoard of treasure he loaned, on request, to the Missouri Historical Society in St. Louis. During a ten-day show in 1927, eighty thousand people visited the exhibition. After that, the awards, scrolls, and presents were left on permanent loan at the Society. In the first year, 1927–28, nearly a million and a half people visited the Jefferson Memorial Building, which housed the trophies.

Among the presents were a stickpin with a picture of the *Spirit of St. Louis* carved on a single large diamond. A huge pearl was sent to Mrs. Lindbergh. The presents also included such things as a set of the works of O. Henry (from the citizens of Greensboro, North Carolina); a mesh bag (for his mother) from Plainfield, Massachusetts; and a chest of silver (Providence, Rhode Island), a dress sword (Hamburg, Germany), a cane carved from a tree in the Mark Twain garden (Hartford, Connecticut). There were also portraits in gold, tapestry, oil, water color, and pen and ink, and carved busts in bronze, silver, ivory, plaster, and soap; *Spirit of St. Louis* models in solid gold and embroidered in silk; books, pillows, jewelry, toilet articles, religious objects, good-luck tokens, a Gutenberg Bible. There was even a police dog (donor unknown), lifetime gold passes to all National League baseball games, to Shubert theatres, automobiles from Franklin, Ford, and Cadillac—La Salle, a five-seater monoplane (from Ryan).

In 1935 Lindbergh and his mother drew up and signed an irrevocable deed of gift for the medals, awards, and presents they had received. Part of the Lindbergh collection is on permanent exhibition [the rest is in storage] at the Jefferson Memorial Building, in Forest Park, St. Louis, Missouri. In the collection is the handwritten manuscript of *We.*

11

CELEBRATION

THE CELEBRATION OF LINDBERGH STARTED LIKE THE fêting of other folk heroes of the day—gangsters, marathon dancers, golf champions, and so on. But it acquired a quality of its own and far outstripped the others. A number of factors combined to make him and his flight more significant, better loved, and longer-lasting in the public consciousness than other doers and other deeds.

Some, like Lindbergh's appearance, youth, and "lone eagle" status, have been noted. There were many others—even such accidents as the weather that broke in his favor. The skies cleared over the Atlantic just in time to permit him to arrive in Paris on a Saturday evening in May—the perfect hour in the week, in the best season of the year, to attract a crowd. His airplane had been named by a home-town booster after a Midwestern United States city, but the name of that city and the plane also happened to be the name of one of France's beloved saints. It is probable that most Frenchmen took this coincidence as a gesture of amity, and reacted accordingly. Certainly, considering the climate of Franco-American relations at the time, they would probably not have reacted so warmly to Byrd's *America* or to Levine's *Columbia* as they did to the *Spirit of St. Louis*.

Then, there was the era, a time after a war that nobody had wanted and nobody won—a time of disillusionment, the Lost Generation, mad speculation in stocks, inflation, a loss of values, a kind of moral vacuum.

In this atmosphere Lindbergh himself was a refreshing change. It was not only what he had done, but the way he did it, and even more the way he behaved afterward. Frederick Lewis Allen, the historian, in *Only Yesterday* sums up this aspect, which was mentioned by many of Lindbergh's welcoming orators: "For years the American people had been spiritually starved. . . . Romance, chivalry and self-dedication had been debunked; the heroes of history had been shown to have feet of clay, and the saints of history had been revealed as people with queer complexes. . . . Something that people needed, if they were to live at peace with themselves and with the world, was missing from their lives. And all at once Lindbergh provided it. Romance, chivalry, self-dedication—here they were, embodied in a modern Galahad for a generation which had forsworn Galahads."

It was as if Lindbergh had been bred for this purpose, like a prince carefully tutored to meet royal occasions. The tough example of his father, the stoic attitudes of his mother, the strong fruits of a lonely unsettled childhood and of Lindbergh's years of solitary fights to prove himself against death and danger—all merged into the epitome of the hero the world had waited for.

It was not just a pasteboard ideal, either, that the twenty-five-year-old Lindbergh provided. He stood up to everything that was demanded of him, and more. If he had been normally venal, if his head had been easily turned or even turnable, if he had betrayed any of the weaknesses the world was deploring in itself or had been missing any of the virtues which the world was looking for in him, Lindbergh might have been another nine-days' wonder. But he lasted. He had staying power.

Lindbergh fulfilled more than an emotional need in the American people. He was also a godsend to newspapers, magazines, and radio. American newspapers sold 50 per cent more copies than usual of the issues that carried news of his flight and his receptions. Fitzhugh Green estimates that, as a result of Lindbergh's flight, more than 25,000 extra tons of newsprint was used by newspapers in May and June of 1927. And, of course, radio and magazines profited, too, from an increased and attentive audience.

In a very real sense, everything Lindbergh was given redounded to the benefit of the giver. When the heads of governments in England, France, and Belgium fêted him, they shared his glory. When the Navy brought him home in a warship, the Navy got very good publicity. The suppliers who gave him presents were only trying to cash in on his fame.

Dwight Morrow had foreseen the dangers in exploitation. So had others. Harry Bruno writes, "Ordinarily our job was to get publicity for our clients; with Lindbergh it was to shield him from all but the inescapable phases of it. It proved the biggest and one of the most difficult tasks we'd ever had. The mail came in literally by truckloads. Several extra telephone lines had to be installed in our offices and our hotel apartment, and I kept a night secretary on duty in the room next to my bedroom."

There were also the social climbers to watch out for. If Lindbergh had accepted even 10 per cent of the weekend invitations he received, "he'd have looked like a social climber himself," says Bruno. There were other dangers. When Lindbergh was invited to a public banquet, it was often because the sponsors wanted to use his name as bait to sell expensive tickets and raise money.

A leading theatre in New York once offered Lindbergh a private midnight show, exclusively for him. Bruno and Blythe went over the guest list and the names all looked very good. There would also be plenty of police protection. But Bruno got a tip from a reporter that the star of the show was going to use the occasion to have herself photographed with Lindbergh.

The manager of the theatre and the actress were waiting for Lindbergh in front of the theatre when he arrived with Dick Blythe. The photographers were also waiting, flash guns poised. Lindbergh got out of the car, the actress came forward, but just before the shutters clicked, Dick Blythe stepped casually between Lindbergh and the lady. Result: she was left with a lot of pictures of herself reaching for Blythe instead of Lindbergh.

The purpose of thwarting this ruse was, of course, to protect Lindbergh from having his name linked romantically with the lady—or with any lady not of his own choosing. He was, at the time, as Bruno says, "the most popular and eligible male in the world."

Women literally flung themselves at him, sometimes singly, sometimes en masse. He accepted an invitation to a private club on Long Island, thinking he would be among well-mannered people, but he found the young matrons and unmarried women panting after him even harder than the girls in the streets. Once, when he was lunching in a restaurant, a middle-aged woman came over and peered into his mouth to see what he was eating.

It was no accident that he was forced to hide in a millionaire's house to write his book, or to stay in another rich man's house in St. Louis. It was only in the mansions of the wealthy that he could get some privacy.

He could no longer walk anywhere freely; he was mobbed wherever he went. If he ate in a restaurant, people came up to his table and asked for his autograph; the knife and fork he used, the plate, the napkin, all became souvenirs for hunters. He never had any used personal linen. If he sent anything to a laundry, it didn't come back; he was always buying new shirts and underwear. If he checked a hat, it was somehow "lost." If he wrote a bank check, it would not be cashed but kept as a souvenir for his autograph. Everything around him had acquired magic.

It was a rare day when he could get a few peaceful hours alone with a friend. People stiffened when he entered a room. Someone said it was as if he carried Medusa's head; they all turned to stone. The spotlight was always on him. Undeniably exciting at first, it became an increasing irritant. "It blinds you," Lindbergh said. "After a while, you can't see other people, but they can see you."

Lindbergh has described his predicament as being something like Midas's. Everything he touched turned to publicity. Midas nearly starved to death when even his food was transmuted into gold. Lindbergh lived in an emotional desert withered by his blinding fame.

Midas survived by renouncing his gift; Lindbergh had no choice in the matter. His fame had become an entity with a life of its own. He had beaten the sea and the wind and the night, but he couldn't overcome his own image. No matter what he did, he only added to its luster. He wanted to go back into some kind of private life; his fame wouldn't let him. It dictated his movements, his associates, his schedules—he was only the pilot of the *Spirit of St. Louis* now; something else was telling him where to fly.

He didn't like it; in fact, he hated it. It was something he hadn't calculated, and couldn't control. In the beginning, he rolled with it. He smiled, made speeches, posed, made himself available. But after a while the smile appeared with decreasing frequency, finally degenerated into a frown. No matter. The photographers pictured him looking tense and unhappy, and the editors promptly captioned it Lindbergh's "flying face." He could do no wrong.

FORTY-EIGHT-STATE TOUR

HARRY GUGGENHEIM HELPED LINDBERGH FIND A WAY TO put it all to good use. As he had promised Dwight Morrow, he got the trustees of the Daniel Guggenheim Fund to give Lindbergh something to do by underwriting a Lindbergh air tour of all forty-eight states in the *Spirit of St. Louis*. The purpose was to use Lindbergh to promote commercial aviation, but this was one way he wanted to be used.

The tour was set up by the Fund with the cooperation of William P. MacCracken, Jr., Assistant Secretary for Aeronautics of the U.S. Department of Commerce. MacCracken delegated Donald E. Keyhoe, of the Department, to go along as Lindbergh's aide.

Keyhoe was introduced to Lindbergh by Harry Guggenheim at Mitchel Field in late June or early July, 1927. He was a little overawed by the prospect of spending several months with the most famous man in the world.

Guggenheim suggested that they find a map so "the colonel can indicate in general how he wants us to plan the tour."

The three men gathered in front of a large map of the United States, and in ten minutes Lindbergh had pointed out the cities where he wanted to land. Keyhoe said something about using the transcontinental air-mail route through the Rockies. Lindbergh quickly decided against it. "We'll save time by flying straight over the mountains," he said.

The Department of Commerce planned to send Keyhoe in one of their planes ahead of Lindbergh, so that he could check the landing fields and the arrangements to restrain the crowds. Lindbergh said he would like to have his ex-Army buddy and air-mail pilot, Phil Love, pilot the advance plane, and this was approved.

Once Lindbergh's good-will flight was announced, almost every city in the United States wanted to be included on the schedule. Keyhoe and the Guggenheim Fund hammered out the itinerary under a bombardment of phone calls, telegrams, and personal visits from civic officials.

Keyhoe's second meeting with Lindbergh took place at Falaise about July 12. Present were Guggenheim, Lindbergh (they had just returned from fishing), Keyhoe, and Milburn Kusterer, the tour advance man who was to travel by train. Ivy Lee, the Guggenheim press agent, was in charge of public relations.

After listening to an outline of the tour, Lindbergh took over the meeting. "We must remember two things," he said. "First, we must always be on time—if we have to get up in the middle of the night to do it. We want to show people that aviation can come through on time. . . . Now, the second is about landing at airports. Sometimes the crowds forget and rush out onto the field. . . . I've seen a propeller kill a man, and I don't intend to have anyone hit by my ship if I can help it. I'd rather skip a city entirely than take a chance by landing into a crowd."

Guggenheim backed him on both points and at the same time made it clear that Lindbergh was in charge of the tour.

Guggenheim sent letters to the mayors of all the cities on the schedule. He asked them to make no plans that would keep Lindbergh from going to bed at nine o'clock in the evening. "I hope you will pardon me for being so explicit," Guggenheim wrote, "but . . . Colonel Lindbergh is making a very difficult trip . . . with a view to promoting interest in aviation rather than with a view to receiving personal plaudits [which he can best accomplish] by limiting his activities." Guggenheim also warned that there was to be no commercial exploitation, that no admission was to be charged to see Lindbergh, and that Lindbergh could not accept personal invitations.

The *Spirit of St. Louis* had been resting at Teterboro Airport, in New Jersey, since July 4. On July 19 Lindbergh flew it to Mitchel Field. And the next day it was ready for takeoff on the first hop of the tour, to Hartford, Connecticut. The Department of Commerce plane piloted by Phil Love left a half hour early, to give Keyhoe time to check the Hartford field. But it ran into a rainstorm which forced a detour, and Love lost more time because of an incorrect map. Keyhoe and Love made it into Hartford just ahead of Lindbergh. "Don't tell Slim about it," Love begged Keyhoe. "He'll kid me for the next six months, getting lost on a simple little run like this."

Hartford was primed for the event. Citizens were straining at the police barricades. Photographers were poised, the mayor's committee was there ready with a welcome. As in previous Lindbergh visits, the noise was incessant and very loud. Shouts, whistles, sirens, bells, automobile horns—any way noise could be made, Hartford made it. Lindbergh rode through it all bareheaded, sitting atop the rear seat of an open limousine. His face had assumed what several of his friends described as his "public mask," an impassive, impersonal regard. Only his eyes moved. They seemed to see all the tiny details of what was happening.

As they passed an orphanage, a small crippled girl stood watching the parade. For a second Lindbergh's expression changed into a tiny smile, and he saluted with his hand. This caused people to turn toward the child, and immediately Lindbergh assumed his public face. But a reporter had seen the incident, and was already writing it up.

Almost everyone reacted sharply to Lindbergh's appearance, and in different ways. Those who had been cheering suddenly became silent when they saw him. Silent people suddenly began shouting and cheering, to subside in embarrassed silence as soon as he had passed. People with cameras ready forgot to snap the shutters, and each time the motorcar slowed down, those nearby rushed in to try to shake his hand.

After the parade he was interviewed at the local hotel. A female reporter asked, "Is it true, Colonel, that girls don't interest you at all?"

Lindbergh smiled. "If you can show me what that has to do with aviation, I'll be glad to answer you," he said.

"Then aviation is your only interest?" she kept on.

"That is the purpose of this tour, to promote aviation," Lindbergh said.

"Are you always so evasive?" she asked.

"I shall be glad to tell you anything I know—on aviation," he replied. But the girl wasn't interested in aviation.

After the interview, Lindbergh relaxed with Love and Keyhoe and joked about not having any lunch. Somehow this simple item had been omitted from their flight schedule. At their future stops, he said, he wanted lunch ordered the minute they arrived at the hotel. "Phil, that'll be your job," he told Love, "you don't have anything to do but fly, anyway."

Before Love could answer, there was a knock at the door. Keyhoe suddenly saw a "lightning-like transformation" in Lindbergh. The easygoing Slim was gone to be replaced with the serious Colonel of public events.

The man at the door was a local committeeman who had stopped in to ask what to do with all the presents that had been sent to the party. Lindbergh looked over the flowers, fruit, and candy and suggested sending them to hospitals and orphanages.

That evening there was a banquet at which Lindbergh said his few words for aviation. When he returned to the hotel with Keyhoe, Love was taking a warm shower and singing.

Lindbergh listened, then said, with a gleam in his eye that Keyhoe soon learned to recognize, "We ought to do something about that. You stand here and be ready to close the door."

He picked up a large pitcher of ice water and went to Love's room. A few moments later the singing stopped abruptly and Lindbergh appeared, running, with Love not far behind. Keyhoe slammed the door just behind Lindbergh and ahead of the sprinting Love. Lindbergh turned the key and ignored the noises Love was making outside the door.

The next morning breakfast was brought by no fewer than four waiters, each wishing to take turns serving Lindbergh. They all wanted autographs, too. Lindbergh took Keyhoe into the next room and said he'd be glad to give the men autographs, but felt that it would save a great deal of time if the waiters left and they waited on themselves.

The habit of the Lindbergh party of eating breakfast and lunch in their rooms gave one reporter in another town an important news story. He reported that, only two hours before leaving for a banquet, Colonel Lindbergh had the following luncheon brought to his room:

4 club house sandwiches
3 pimento cheese sandwiches
1 potato salad
1 double order potatoes au gratin

1 order sliced tomatoes
1 pot of coffee
2 bottles of milk
1 fruit salad
1 apple pie à la mode

The headline was "COLONEL LINDBERGH EATS HEARTY MEAL BEFORE BANQUET." Of course, there was a great deal of interest in the fact that Lindbergh ate all that was served to him at the banquet that night.

At another town a photographer broke away from police surveillance and got directly in front of the *Spirit of St. Louis* as Lindbergh was taxiing the ship across the field. On the ground the ship was blind toward objects dead ahead by reason of its big gas tank forward. Lindbergh did not see the man. He opened his throttle to take the plane over a rise. The whirling metal propeller headed directly toward the photographer. Someone shouted a warning at Lindbergh and he cut his switch. The propeller missed the man by only a couple of inches.

Apparently unaware of how close he had come to death, the photographer began to laugh. Lindbergh beckoned him over. "Do you know you just missed being killed?" he asked. He did not raise his voice. "We're trying hard to complete this tour without hurting anyone, but if everyone acted as you did we wouldn't get very far. . . . Don't ever cross in front of an airplane again."

After that Lindbergh asked Keyhoe to wire Kusterer to tighten security at all fields. And he told Keyhoe and Love to make extra sure that no one got in front of his ship again.

When the party was ready to leave Boston on July 23—on the fourth leg of the trip, to Portland, Maine—they found the field closed in by fog. The weather report also showed fog beyond Portland.

An airport official commiserated about losing a day on the schedule so early in the trip. Lindbergh paced up and down, looked up at the mist, and then ordered his ship rolled out.

"You're going ahead, through all that?" the man asked.

Lindbergh said, "It isn't as bad as it looks. . . . I've seen worse days on the mail. The only trouble will be at Portland, if the airport is covered with fog."

He carried no parachute during the tour. He said, "Parachutes should not be used except in military work, air mail service, testing, and experimental flying. I'm better off in the *Spirit of St. Louis* without a chute. It would give me less room and less freedom in handling the ship. And this plane lands so slowly that I could stall it almost anywhere. Dropping with a chute in the mountains might be a lot worse than sticking to the ship."

The *Spirit of St. Louis* had the best contemporary instruments for blind flying—compass, bank and turn indicator, altimeter, air-speed meter. But such flying depended much more on the pilot's ability to grasp quickly what the instruments told him and to make instantaneous adjustments than on the instruments themselves.

Love and Keyhoe urged Lindbergh not to fly, but he insisted that he had to stick to the schedule or the trip would be worthless. He took off against their objections, and *Spirit* instantly disappeared into the mist. Love waited awhile; then, when the fog seemed to be lightening, he took the other plane up on a test flight. But while he was in the air, the fog rolled in thickly and he couldn't land at Boston. After a while his plane was heard heading away from the airport. With both planes gone, Keyhoe and Ted Sorenson, the mechanic on the tour, decided to drive to Portland. They skidded for hours over the wet roads. When they finally reached Portland, they found that Love had landed safely in an unbelievably tiny field, but there was no sign of Lindbergh. "Where's Slim?" Love asked.

After a few nervous minutes, word came through that Lindbergh had landed safely at Concord, New Hampshire. Lindbergh got on the telephone and told Keyhoe that he had reached Portland on time, but had been unable to land. He had circled over the town for an hour and a half in fog before heading away. "Tell the people at Portland I reached the city on time," he said. "I could have landed about twenty miles from [Portland], but I didn't want to leave the *Spirit of St. Louis* unguarded."

The next day was also foggy but he managed to land at Old Orchard Beach, near Portland. Then, a day late, he went through with the official ceremonies.

Lindbergh's method of navigation was to lay out all his hops along straight lines, regardless of such useful trails as rivers and railroads. Then he would mark off his route in units of ten miles and arrange his maps in sequence.

"It's the best lesson in geography you can have," he told Keyhoe. "You start out from plain country, with nothing but the map to indicate a mountain range a hundred and fifty miles away. After a while you start looking for the bluish haze that means the mountains, and pretty soon it shows up. It's something like sighting land coming in from the sea. It's always interesting."

He loved to read the map, holding it in one hand and flying the ship with the other, even when he knew the terrain below.

Lindbergh also had a kind of sixth sense, perhaps developed during combat training, of what other pilots in nearby ships might do. Certainly he felt at home enough with Love to play games in the sky. Once, he saw Love flying the advance plane from the cabin instead of the pilot's seat by means of cords he had attached to the controls. Lindbergh maneuvered *Spirit* in front of the other plane and banked to give it the full backward blast of his propeller. Love's plane bucked and jumped in the air, sending baggage flying and the passengers sprawling. Love clawed his way to the cockpit just as Lindbergh banked to the other side and caught the ship in a second backwash of his propeller. Love could only shake his fist. His ship wasn't fast enough to enable him to give the same sort of treatment to Lindbergh.

On another occasion, Lindbergh learned that a couple of enterprising newspaper photographers had, contrary to agreement, hired airplanes to follow him and get pictures of him flying the *Spirit of St. Louis* in the air. The other ships had started their engines as he climbed into his plane. "Let them go ahead," he told Love. (By this time on the tour, the "advance" plane was taking off *behind* Lindbergh so as not to leave him unprotected on the ground. There were always last-minute requests that would delay his takeoff if Keyhoe wasn't around to act as buffer. Once airborne, Lindbergh would delay over their destination until Love had time to land and see that he had a clear field.)

As Lindbergh's plane rose into the air, the photographers' planes plowed behind him into his dust cloud. He had barely become airborne when the photographer in the leading plane stood up in his cockpit and pointed his camera at Lindbergh. The *Spirit of St. Louis* immediately went into a steep climbing turn and was out of range before the photographer could adjust his focus. By now airborne themselves, Love and Keyhoe could follow the dogfight as the two photographers' planes "attacked" and Lindbergh constantly took evasive action; he sideslipped, dived, turned, climbed, always outmaneuvering the two ships. At last, after a good fifteen minutes, the frustrated photographers gave up the chase and their planes turned back to the airport. The next day Lindbergh asked Keyhoe to get him the newspapers from the city they had visited the day before. There were big stories in both papers about the visit but no new aerial photographs of Lindbergh's plane. Lindbergh grinned as he gave the papers back to Keyhoe.

Although Lindbergh kept strangers at arm's length, he insisted on seeing anyone whom he had known before Paris. At one stop, a sailor attracted his eye by shouting, "Slim!" from the crowd. Many people used his familiar nickname to claim friendship, but they were usually trapped by Love or Keyhoe. This time, Lindbergh instantly recognized the sailor and told Love, "That chap helped me out at Pensacola several years ago. Be sure that no one turns him away when he comes up to the rooms."

In Butte, Lindbergh arranged to meet and fly with Shorty Lynch, who had taken him barnstorming only a few years before. And all along the route he was open to visits from any of the barnstormers and test pilots—the heart of aviation of the day—of whom he had been one; he was not only available but really happy to see them. Professor William A. Williams of the University of Wisconsin history department, whose father was one of this group of pilots, recalls that "all these men knew Lindbergh, and had profound respect for his flying and his character. There was a strong, if intangible, feeling [among them] that Lindbergh would do great things for flying, and a great satisfaction when he did."

Williams was a small boy the summer of 1927. He recalls that Lindbergh wired his father, William Carleton Williams, to meet him in Omaha, Nebraska, on August 30. The elder Williams accepted and in return asked Lindbergh to fly a bit out of his way between Des Moines, Iowa, his previous stop, and Omaha, so that young Bill Williams could see the *Spirit of St. Louis*. He told Lindbergh how to recognize the house, which was in Atlantic, Iowa, two blocks south of the main highway linking Des Moines and Omaha. "So,"

Professor Williams wrote recently, "my mother put me out in the big front yard with a sandwich and some milk, and I waited. It was a magnificently sunny day. Sure enough, at the almost exact time he'd told my dad, Lindbergh and the *Spirit of St. Louis* came winging in over the top of the house; you can imagine my joy, etc., etc. It was a great moment and I treasure it even now in the retelling."

Lindbergh managed to see his mother in Grand Rapids, Michigan, and take her for a short flight. A photo by Keyhoe shows the two of them with wide grins. (Keyhoe had a camera and asked permission of Lindbergh to take pictures through the trip. Lindbergh readily consented, but usually when Keyhoe went to snap something, he found part of his camera missing. Once, a fish fell out of the lens.)

In Detroit, at Ford Airport, Lindbergh persuaded Henry Ford, Sr., to take his first (and only) airplane ride in the *Spirit of St. Louis*. Ford's company had been flying the air mail (it was the first private company to do so in the United States) and, like many other early airlines, was also manufacturing the planes it flew. But Ford himself did not trust airplanes. The Ford plane, originally designed by William B. Stout, was an all-metal monoplane with three Liberty engines (later redesigned to take the Wright Whirlwinds), known as "the flying washboard," because of its corrugated metal exterior, or "the tin goose." It was the early work horse of commercial aviation, but Ford gave up manufacturing it after a few years because he couldn't make aviation pay.

In one city the police escort on motorcycles revved their engines often to keep from stalling at slow speed, sending dense clouds of smoke back over the limousine in which Lindbergh rode. At the end of that parade his face looked haggard, with dark shadows of soot under his eyes, and he was photographed this way. He had also often been photographed after landing with the imprint of the goggles around his eyes, giving somewhat the same haggard appearance. By the time the tour reached Chicago, on August 13, MacCracken, of the Department of Commerce, was waiting for them. It seemed that as a result of the photos there was much public clamor that the tour should be ended because it was undermining Lindbergh's health.

MacCracken said that it would be a good idea for Lindbergh to get a physical checkup and have the results made public. The checkup showed that he had lost some weight but was otherwise healthy. The Guggenheim Fund also released a telegram sent by Mrs. Lindbergh, who had flown with her son only a couple of days earlier. She said she had found him "in excellent health."

The last official day of the tour was in Philadelphia, October 22, 1927, more than three months after the start. There Lindbergh laid a wreath on the Liberty Bell. Some photographers did not catch the gesture, so Lindbergh re-enacted it for them, although he said that he was no actor.

The party slept in Philadelphia. The next day they flew to Mitchel Field, New York, in an hour and fifty minutes, by way of Trenton and New York City. (Flying over many cities in which they did not have time to land was part of the tour. Over each such place Lindbergh would do several slow 180-degree turns to give the citizenry a chance to see the ship in the air. Then he would drop a canvas bag with an orange streamer attached. The bag contained a message, "Aboard 'Spirit of St. Louis' on Tour; Greetings," and explaining why there was no time for a separate stop, and appealing for aid to civil aviation. It was signed by Lindbergh, Guggenheim, and MacCracken.)

The plane touched down in Mitchel Field on October 23, 1927, at exactly two o'clock in the afternoon, ninety-five days after the tour had started. In that time, they had flown 22,350 miles and spent about 260 hours in the air. They had stopped in eighty-two cities and had spent at least one night in each of the forty-eight states. They had flown through all kinds of weather, including fog, rain, and snow, and only once (between Boston and Portland) had they been delayed.

When the *Spirit of St. Louis* touched down at Mitchel Field, Lindbergh posed for the photographers once more. Then he said goodbye to his buddies and handed a package to Keyhoe, saying, "Will you take care of these?"

The packages contained gold wrist watches for each of the men, engraved as souvenirs.

One small by-product of the tour: as requests were constantly being received by the party to fly over cities that had not been part of the original schedule, Lindbergh got the idea of exacting a price for such visits. He would require that the city paint its name prominently on some roof top so that it would provide a future trail mark for cross-country fliers. One city, on only half an hour's notice, managed to get three such signs painted on tops of buildings, and Lindbergh, in gratitude, spent extra time showing off the *Spirit of St. Louis* in the air over that town.

The trip cost the Guggenheim Fund $68,721.27, of which $50,000 went to Lindbergh. Although it had the side effect of further popularizing Lindbergh, the tour probably accomplished what it set out to do: to make the country more air-conscious, to get more support for civil aviation. In 1927, the year of the tour, there were 1,036 landing fields and airports in the United States, of which only a handful were lighted. By the end of 1930 there were 1,782 air-fields, and 640 had lights. This rapid 72-per-cent growth in the number of fields could be laid to many factors, but not the least was the tremendous publicity engendered by the Lindbergh tour.

Lindbergh's activities also gave a strong boost to air mail. In September, 1926, the month that he got the idea of flying to Paris, the U.S. air-mail services carried a total of 79,841 pounds of mail. A year later, during the September of the Guggenheim tour, American airlines (by this time the government had dropped out of the air-mail business) carried 146,088 pounds of air mail—an 84-per-cent increase.

13

MEXICO

LINDBERGH FLEW THE *Spirit of St. Louis* TO TETERBORO, New Jersey, on October 25, 1927, and left it there. He spent the next month resting and relaxing.

A man several years Lindbergh's senior recalls meeting him at a house party on Long Island about this time. The group of young men and women walked on the beach, which, like all Long Island North Shore beaches, was full of pebbles. A game started of skipping rocks along the water.

The older man was much chagrined at this turn of events. "I've always admired baseball players and wished I could be one, but all my life I've thrown like a girl," he confided to Lindbergh, who told him he had had the same trouble himself ever since he'd dislocated his shoulder in a parachute jump. Lindbergh suggested that they take a walk instead.

The man remembers this incident vividly forty years later as one of the most thoughtful things that had ever been done for him.

Lindbergh did not have too much time for this sort of byplay, however. Dwight Morrow had become Ambassador to Mexico and was greatly interested in furthering good relations with that country. He had an idea that Lindbergh could help.

Morrow invited Lindbergh to visit him at his estate, Next Day Hill, in Englewood, New Jersey. He introduced Lindbergh to his family, among them his dark-haired, brown-eyed daughter Anne Spencer Morrow, a sensitive, shy, introspective girl of twenty-one. The Ambassador talked over an idea he had with Lindbergh: another good-will flight, this one to Mexico City. It would fit in very well with Morrow's plans, which, in contrast to earlier attitudes of the United States toward her southern neighbor, can be summed up by what Morrow said: "I know what I can do for the Mexicans. I can *like* them."

This was Lindbergh's reaction to Morrow's proposal:

After returning from Europe and completing a flying tour of the United States with the *Spirit of St. Louis* I wanted to make another long-distance nonstop flight before retiring the plane from use and placing it in the museum. The plane and engine were practically new and in a number of ways the *Spirit of St. Louis* was better equipped than any other plane for long flights. I was particularly interested in the future possibilities of long distance flying and wanted to make a flight under different conditions than I encountered on the New York–Paris trip. The flight to Mexico was made during the long December nights, under conditions of storm and fog during nearly the entire night, and over country varying from high mountains to low coast line. I wanted to experiment with these conditions and if possible to demonstrate that flying could be made practical under them.

In addition to the technical side I loved any opportunity to fly, particularly in the *Spirit of St. Louis*, and I was fascinated with the idea of going to Mexico City when Mr. Morrow made the suggestion.

Morrow even had an idea of how the trip should be made—like the Guggenheim tour, in short stages. He did not want any kind of flight that would put Lindbergh in danger; certainly Lindbergh's idea of flying nonstop appalled him.

However, Lindbergh was quite set on a nonstop flight between Washington, D.C., and Mexico, D.F., as a dramatic demonstration of the close linkage of the two capitals. "You get me the invitation," he told Morrow, "and I'll take care of the flying."

Morrow, a blunt man himself, appreciated this kind of talk and there was no further argument. In due course an official invitation was extended through diplomatic channels by President Plutarco Elías Calles, of Mexico, to Lindbergh to visit his country.

Lindbergh was getting ready to fly the *Spirit of St. Louis* from Teterboro to Washington for the official start of the new tour when he heard that Dick Blythe was in critical condition in a Brooklyn hospital. Blythe had had an operation, and instead of rallying had begun to hemorrhage.

Lindbergh immediately phoned Harry Bruno and asked, "How's Dick?"

"Not so good," Bruno said. "He may need a transfusion. I'm just going to the hospital now."

"Pick me up at Harry Guggenheim's office," Lindbergh said. "I've got to see Dick before I leave."

Bruno drove Lindbergh to the hospital, and Lindbergh sat by the bedside kidding Blythe as long as he was permitted.

Outside the room he said to Bruno, "About that transfusion. . . . I want you to let me furnish the blood."

"Forget it," Bruno said, pointing out that Lindbergh had an important appointment in Washington the next day.

"Promise me," Lindbergh said. "Or I don't leave this hospital."

Bruno had to agree. The next day, Lindbergh called to find out Blythe's condition. Bruno said that the doctors had told him Blythe was doing well and would not need a transfusion. Lindbergh did not believe him at first, and made Bruno swear that he was telling the truth. Only then would he leave.

On December 7, 1927, Lindbergh flew *Spirit* to Washington. On the eighth he attended a meeting of the board of regents of the Smithsonian Institution and was given the Langley Medal by the chancellor of the Institution, Chief Justice William Howard Taft. (The medal is one of aviation's highest awards, although it is named after Samuel Pierpont Langley, a man whose aviation experiments failed often enough so that his name was for a while ridiculed.)

A couple of days later, Lindbergh was invited to be a guest of the House of Representatives. The House went into recess for the occasion, and each member filed by the dais to shake Lindbergh's hand. After he left, the representatives passed a bill unanimously to award Lindbergh the Congressional Medal of Honor, previously reserved only for military heroes, and sent it on to the Senate. On Monday, December 12, the Senate passed the same bill unanimously and sent it to President Coolidge to be signed. The medal would be given to Lindbergh later on.

On December 13, 1927, the *Spirit of St. Louis* was ready to fly to Mexico. The nonstop trip would cover 2,100 miles, just a bit more than half the distance between New York and Paris, so Lindbergh did not need a full load of gasoline. He carried seventy-five fewer gallons than on the Paris flight; instead of being overloaded, the plane was about four hundred pounds under its maximum gross weight.

Bolling Field was wet and muddy, as Roosevelt Field had been when he took off for Paris nearly seven months before. The *New York Times* described it as a "hummocky, soggy, puddle-bespattered morass." Even with its lightened load, *Spirit* did not run easily or take off quickly into the lowering clouds. But Bolling Field was large enough for Lindbergh to gain good flying speed. He lifted the plane and headed toward the southwest.

He flew through clouds until nightfall. By that time he was over the western mountains of North Carolina. He had added to the plane's complement of instruments a new and highly sensitive altimeter. He needed all his skill in navigating by instruments that night, for he was flying in winter and away from the sun, and so had many hours of darkness before he would see daylight again. When dawn did break, he was on course, over Houston, Texas. Then he followed the Gulf Coast down to Tampico, Mexico. There he had to climb to get above the fog, and he lost his bearings; he headed north of his projected course. When the fog cleared below, he found himself flying over desolate country he couldn't identify from his map.

"There were numerous railroads below," Lindbergh reported, "but I could not find corresponding ones marked on my maps. I tried unsuccessfully to read the names of railroad stations. I climbed then to high altitude and obtained my approximate position from the direction of watersheds. Later I flew over a city and after coming down to low altitude could read the words 'Hotel Toluca' on the side of a building. I found Toluca on my map to be only a short distance [west] from Mexico City."

He looked at his watch: it was past three o'clock in the afternoon of December 14, 1927 (one hour earlier by Mexican time).

Lindbergh's estimated time of arrival in Mexico City had been noon. Ambassador Morrow had taken his family out to Valbuena Airport at eight-thirty in the morning. By twelve o'clock a crowd of a hundred and fifty thousand people were gathered to greet Lindbergh, among them President Calles.

There was no sight of Lindbergh, and no word. The plane had been reported passing over Tampico at nine-fifty that morning, and after that there was only silence. Morrow, not a very calm man, began to get extremely anxious. So did almost everybody in Mexico and the United States. On the Guggenheim tour, Lindbergh had established a reputation for near superhuman promptness. The feeling was, therefore, that if he was late there could be only one reason: he had crashed. As the sky remained empty and silent for two hours past Lindbergh's ETA, the apprehension grew into certainty. Morrow began to think he had sacrificed Lindbergh for political expediency.

A bright sun overhead did nothing to lighten the massed gloom below. But suddenly out of the void came word that Lindbergh had been sighted over Toluca, and the mood changed immediately.

In a few minutes his plane appeared from the west, and the crowd went wild. Lindbergh followed his usual tactic of flying over the field before he landed. He managed to set down without being mobbed, a tribute to the Mexican officials. He had been in the air for twenty-seven hours and fifteen minutes.

Morrow was overjoyed to see him. Mrs. Morrow wrote in her diary, "Dwight and Capt. Winslow went over to the plane and brought him back to the grandstand in our open car. Dwight brought him to the President, who welcomed him and gave him the keys of the city. Lindbergh only said 'Thank you' very simply. The throng on the field shouting and screaming with joy was indescribable. As we went to the car our clothes were almost torn off. Dwight, Constance [a Morrow daughter], Lindbergh, General Alvarez, and I were in the car, Burke driving. Ceto and two officers on the running board. Oh! The crowds in the streets on the way to the Embassy! On trees, on telegraph poles, tops of cars, roofs, even the towers of the Cathedral. Flowers and confetti were flung every moment. We took him to the Chancery and to the balcony to wave to the crowd. He had soup and a bath while the Staff had a buffet lunch. We all drank to him in champagne. Then he came out and met all the Staff, telegraphed to his mother, and saw the reporters. We left him sleeping tonight as we went to the University Club dinner for Will Rogers."

The Mexican welcome was probably as large and impressive as any that had gone before, and if emotion could be measured, it probably topped them all in a sheer outpouring of unrestrained joy—and relief. And it was not just the charismatic hero the Mexicans were welcoming; they were opening their hearts to another gesture of amity from their fearsome neighbor to the north. Lindbergh had risked his life—the late arrival had added some gilding—to bring them reassurance that Uncle Sam was not going to eat them up.

An editorial in the New York *World* echoed the American reaction: "It is just eleven months since Secretary Kellogg . . . charged that a Bolshevist government in Mexico threatened the peace of the United States. The Mexican government . . . is the same [one] with which a new Ambassador has succeeded in establishing unusually cordial relations. . . . The flight of Lindbergh follows a series of events which indicate a real shift in sentiment and a thoroughgoing change in policy." Coolidge issued a formal statement and Calles hailed Lindbergh's feat as a harbinger of "closer spiritual and material relations."

Not since the days of the conquistadors had Mexico seen anything like the following week. There were bulls dedicated to Lindbergh in the arena, and the presentation of the gold-threaded capote from the leading torero, José Ortiz (the cape is now in the Lindbergh collection). There were exhibitions of Mexican folk dancing in his honor, rides through the floating gardens, rodeos staged for him. He was formally received by the Mexican Chamber of Deputies. Memories of this triumphal week are preserved in some of the huge murals in Mexico City buildings, painted by Juan O'Gorman and other Mexican painters.

In Mexico, Lindbergh was the guest of the Ambassador. He renewed acquaintance with the Morrow family, including the dark-eyed Anne. The Morrows invited Mrs. Lindbergh to come to Mexico to spend Christmas with them and her son. Mrs. Lindbergh sent her regrets; she didn't want to interfere with her son's activities. But the Morrows persisted, and she relented when Henry Ford offered to have her ferried down in a Ford tri-motor airplane.

(This would not be her first flight in one of these metal monoplanes. After the ride with her son in August, in Grand Rapids, Michigan, she had been flown back to Detroit in a Ford tri-motor. Her trip then had been at night, and a reporter had asked Lindbergh if he was worried about his mother's safety. "I don't see why I should be worried," he said. "She is in a good ship, flying with an experienced pilot. She is as safe as she would be in a train or a motorcar.")

As the plane carrying his mother to Mexico neared Mexico City on December 22, Lindbergh went out to Valbuena Airport and took off in the *Spirit of St. Louis*. He met the Ford in the air out of town and escorted it back to Valbuena.

This time, landing the *Spirit of St. Louis* was a problem. Lindbergh records in his log: "Three short flights, made to avoid injuring anyone in crowd which overran field 0 hrs. 15 min." And he goes on to add, "Took off before end of first and second landing rolls. Then landed in adjoining field to attract crowd. Took off before first people reached my plane. Returned to Valbuena Airport and taxied *Spirit of St. Louis* into hangar."

The reception given Mrs. Lindbergh was nearly as overwhelming as that given her son a week before.

After Christmas she was flown back to Detroit, and Lindbergh took off on his good-will flight to seventeen Latin-American countries. His first hop lasted seven hours and five minutes and brought him to Guatemala City, Guatemala. His longest flight was the last one on the tour, fifteen hours and thirty-five minutes from Havana, Cuba, to Lambert Field, St. Louis, on February 13, 1928. On this flight both of his compasses malfunctioned while he was crossing the Florida Strait at night. Not being able to see any stars through the heavy haze, he flew nearly three hundred miles off course.

In each of the countries in which he landed, he demonstrated his friendliness toward the inhabitants and helped to re-establish the image of Uncle Sam as a benevolent fellow.

Throughout the 9,000-mile Latin-American tour, except for the time he got lost over Mexico, Lindbergh always landed safely and on time, once more demonstrating the reliability of air transportation. There were dramatic moments. There were times when he was almost forced down. There was a fifteen-minute period between San Salvador and Honduras when he flew through the roughest air he had ever encountered, but somehow he always managed to avoid trouble by skillful flying. In fact, his record of success in country after country was so consistent that one managing editor wired a reporter, "NO MORE UNLESS HE CRASHES." This might have been prompted by editorial envy. Lindbergh was himself writing up the trip under an exclusive contract with the *New York Times*, for a reported $50,000.

On the ground, he threaded his way through a series of complicated political situations. He followed protocol, and was cordial toward the press, although he made it clear to his friends he wanted to retire to private life as soon as possible.

"The New York–Paris flight is past," Lindbergh told Keyhoe. "I suppose that it helped aviation by interesting the people, and probably it had a certain amount of pioneering value. But we need to go ahead in commercial flying, and we should not live in the past. I wish that people would just remember my flight to Paris as something that happened in 1927, and then forget about me."

Keyhoe replied that it would be impossible. "You are a public figure," he said, "and everyone insists on keeping you in the foreground."

"I can either be in public life, or go back to private life. It might help aviation if I were to keep on visiting cities and talking about flying, but I think that there are more important things to be done. I'd like to be free to work on some of the scientific problems we ought to solve . . . there is still a lot of research to be done."

Coolidge presented him with the Congressional Medal of Honor at the White House on March 21, 1928. The ceremony had to be gone through three times, once in the President's study and twice more on the lawn for the newsreel cameras. "The first time," Lindbergh told Harold Nicolson, the English journalist-historian-diplomat, a few years later, "I was kind of moved by the thing. After all, I was more or less a kid at the time and it seemed sort of solemn to be given that thing by the President of the United States. But when we had to go through the whole damned show again on the lawn—me standing sideways to the President and looking an ass—I felt I couldn't stand for it. Coolidge didn't seem to care or notice. He repeated his speech twice over in just the same words. It seemed a charade to me."

The Smithsonian Institution had asked for the *Spirit of St. Louis*. After the Latin-American tour, Lindbergh made only two more flights in the plane. The first was around St. Louis on February 14. The second was from Lambert Field to Bolling Field on April 30, 1928. The 725-mile trip took only four hours and fifty-eight minutes. There was a strong tail wind.

"At Bolling Field," writes Lindbergh, "the *Spirit of St. Louis* was presented to the Smithsonian Institution. It was dismantled, and reassembled in the museum in Washington, where it now rests, in permanent exhibition, with the Kitty Hawk biplane of Orville and Wilbur Wright."

His logs show that the *Spirit of St. Louis* made 174 flights, the shortest about 5 minutes, the longest 33 hours, 30 minutes, and 29.8 seconds (to Paris). Its total flying time: 489 hours and 25 minutes.

On April 1, Lindbergh had accepted delivery of a new monoplane, built for him by the Mahoney Aircraft Company. (Mahoney had changed the Ryan company's name to his own. The company no longer exists. The Ryan Aeronautical Company, of Harbor Drive, San Diego, is a successor company, started by T. Claude Ryan, the man who had originally founded Ryan Airlines.) It was a luxury "brougham" version of the *Spirit of St. Louis,* with leather seats for three passengers in the cabin and without the huge gas tank forward. The engine was a present from the Wright Company—a nickel-plated J-5 Whirlwind. And the plane had an electric self-starter.

14

🌿 A NEW LIFE

IN FEBRUARY, 1925, THE U.S. CONGRESS PASSED THE
Kelly bill, which was intended to take the government out of air-
mail transportation and encourage private operators to fly the mail
under government subsidy. Postmaster General Harry S. New realized that this shift would set the pattern for future commercial
aviation in the United States; the air-mail lines would eventually
become the air-passenger lines. So he carefully excluded the air-mail
contract bids of blue-sky promoters and inadequately financed
businessmen from those acceptable to his department. In effect,
New started to move the center of gravity of American aviation
from the gypsy fliers and barnstormers to more business-like types.
It was under New and the Kelly Act that the Robertson Aircraft
Corporation got its contract which gave Lindbergh his job as an air-
mail pilot.

Now that the government was giving subsidy support to flying,
and with the added inspiration of an easy money market, many
banks and underwriters became interested in the aviation industry.
Soon thereafter, under the stimulus of Lindbergh's Paris flight and
Guggenheim tour, the public became aware that aviation was a
coming thing. Harry Guggenheim released an open letter to in-
vestors warning them of "ill-advised, economically unsound aviation
enterprises" and telling them to "be extremely wary of investing
. . . money with unknown promoters . . . until the science, art
and operation . . . [of the industry] . . . have been more thoroughly perfected." Nevertheless, in the stock-market boom of 1927–
29, aviation stocks outpaced the general market average. In 1929
alone, the public poured $400,000,000 into aviation securities. Any

company with the word "air" or "aviation" in its title could sell its stocks. Even the price of the stock of the Seaboard Air Line—an East Coast railroad—spurted suddenly when some members of the investing public decided that with such a name the road must be truly an airline.

The Daniel Guggenheim Fund played an important part in pushing aviation forward. In 1927 the Fund made a grant to Western Air Express, one of the private-contract fliers of air mail, to explore the possibilities of carrying passengers over its route between Los Angeles and Salt Lake City. Using this grant to buy the latest-model passenger planes, the company quickly turned a profit on the passenger business. Within two years it had earned enough to repay the grant.

As by far the best-known personality in aviation, Lindbergh was constantly being asked to join various aviation deals and schemes. Most of those offering deals wanted him as a front man to push securities or raise money. But Lindbergh had already outlined his own ground rules. He wished to be private, and he wanted to make a genuine contribution.

With the help of people like Harry Guggenheim and Colonel Breckinridge he carefully analyzed the offers and decided to accept two. Both were with airlines which were well-financed, serious enterprises. And they did not just want his name; they wanted his competence. One was Pan American Airways, Inc.; the other Transcontinental Air Transport (TAT).

Pan American had been formed by Juan Terry Trippe, a young ex-Navy bomber pilot and graduate of Yale's Sheffield Scientific School. Trippe had started one of the earliest air-passenger services in the United States in 1923, an air-taxi line from Long Island using surplus Navy planes. In 1925, with the backing of a Vanderbilt and a Whitney, he organized Colonial Air Transport and won a contract to fly air mail between New York and Boston. But Trippe had always had his eye on an overseas line.

Partly to offset Scadta, a German owned and operated airline flying in Colombia ("too close to the Panama Canal to be ignored," according to Major Henry H. Arnold, of the Army Air Service), and another German airline, Lufthansa, both of which were seeking to set up a more extensive network between points in Latin America, the Caribbean, and the United States, two American companies—

Pan American, Inc., and one called Florida Airways—were compet-
ing for an air-mail contract between Havana, Cuba, and Key West,
Florida. At this point Trippe stepped in and bought out the two
American lines. He formed them into Pan American Airways, Inc.,
late in 1927. With the air-mail contract between the United States
and Cuba as his base, he set up passenger service between Miami
and Havana. A lot of the passenger business in those prohibition
days was made up of Americans seeking a place where they could
get a decent drink and do some legal gambling.

Trippe had the idea of expanding this airways overseas, and he
was encouraged by men like Arnold to set up a regular air and
passenger service between the West Indies, Central America, and
Mexico. The Kelly Foreign Air Mail Act of 1928 gave him important
help in the form of higher subsidies for overseas air mail. (The
justification was that overseas carriers had to install their own
airfields, emergency landing fields, beacons, etc., all of which were
being provided by the U.S. government to mainland carriers.)

Trippe needed Lindbergh's technical help. So did TAT, which
was owned by a holding company, North American Aviation, run by
Clement M. Keys and backed by Blair and Company, Hayden, Stone
& Company, and General Motors.* Keys, a former *Wall Street
Journal* reporter, was a demon organizer who started National Air
Transport, which is now part of United Airlines. He started TAT
in 1928 to give coast-to-coast transportation to mail and passengers.

For both companies, TAT and Pan American, Lindbergh undertook to be technical consultant. He could work for both because
the lines were noncompeting. TAT was strictly within the borders of
the United States; Pan American was an overseas carrier. Both
needed someone who knew how to survey air routes, assess weather
conditions, find landing fields, arrange practicable schedules, and
select or help adapt the necessary aircraft. Lindbergh's training,
experience, and interests fitted him to do exactly this type of work.

He went to work for TAT in May, 1928. His job was to lay out the
route for the company between New York and California. At first
this service combined both airplanes and trains. Passengers left
New York at night by train. In the morning they transferred at

* Two Lindbergh backers, Harold Bixby and Harry Knight, were directors.
And the Wright Aeronautical Corporation was part of the complex.

Columbus, Ohio, to a plane which flew through the day to Wichita, Kansas. At night they were put back on another train to New Mexico. The following day they arrived in Los Angeles by plane.

The coast-to-coast trip took forty-eight hours. This was twenty-four hours faster than a straight train ride, but it also cost more and was not popular.

Harry Bruno was press agent for TAT (but no longer for Lindbergh) and says he continued to try to keep Lindbergh's name from being "unduly exploited." However, it was Bruno who, in a TAT publicity story, followed the company's name with brackets in which he wrote ["The Lindbergh Line"].

"The moment Keys saw it his face lit up," reports Bruno. " 'Great!' he said. 'We're not using Slim's name in advertising, but we can through constant repetition of the slogan "The Lindbergh Line" in news stories get the public to realize what Lindbergh has done for air transportation.' And 'The Lindbergh Line' became the name of the service."

Lindbergh was not wholly averse to such identification. TAT made a promotional film showing the ease and comfort of its relatively quick method of transportation. It is called *Coast to Coast in Forty-eight Hours.* It shows well-dressed people climbing aboard a train and follows them through their various embarkations and debarkations in passenger planes through the trip to the West Coast. At one point in the film the airborne camera shows Lindbergh flying a small plane alongside the passenger ship, and the narrator makes the point that this intrepid pilot is the same man who laid out the airline.

Laying out the TAT line took most of the spring and summer of 1928.* In October, Lindbergh accepted an invitation to hunt at the Chihuahua ranch of the Mexican Secretary of Agriculture. From there, he flew to Mexico City on invitation to visit the Morrow family.

Lindbergh had become friendly with Anne Spencer Morrow since the time he had met her in Englewood in 1927, before the Mexican flight. He saw her several times after that in New York, at the

---

* In June, Lindbergh was invited to a reunion of the class of 1924 of the University of Wisconsin, at Madison. He spent a pleasant afternoon with his former classmates, the most honored member of the group although he had no diploma. That lack was made up by the University when they awarded him an honorary LL.D. at the commencement exercises.

family's town residence, during the fall of 1927. Her family was then already in Mexico. Lindbergh began to use an incognito with the servants when he rang her up on the telephone. They met again in Mexico in December, on his good-will flight, and saw a good deal of each other during the two weeks Lindbergh spent as the Morrows' guest in the Embassy.

In many ways they were opposite. Her interests were literary; she yearned to be a writer; she had graduated with special honors from Smith College. Lindbergh, the college dropout, was interested in mechanical things that went fast, and in science. Where she was very contemplative he was adventurous. But they shared many traits of character. They were both shy; both were solitaries; both had lively, questing minds. They both loved nature. They had very similar ideas about integrity and service and what one owed to one's country.

Lindbergh had learned to camouflage his personal interests from the press. But he couldn't keep them from speculating. Many papers reported the rumor that Lindbergh was interested in Anne's pretty sister, Constance.

By this time, he was beginning to fly around Central America for Pan American, so his flights to Mexico to see Anne could be made to seem like business trips. However, after his November visit to the Morrows, his second in 1928, certain Mexican newspapers began to hint at a romance. This was promptly denied by the Morrows, but when Lindbergh continued to fly in and out of Mexico, each time managing to spend some time with the Morrows, the rumors got stronger. The Morrows had bought a house in Cuernavaca, and Lindbergh spent several weeks there walking with Anne and giving her flying lessons in his Curtiss biplane.

One day in February, 1929, he was flying the mail for Pan American on his way into Havana—he was behind schedule by reason of heavy seas and a detour to survey possible landing fields on a couple of British islands—when the Morrows issued the following statement: "Ambassador and Mrs. Morrow have announced the engagement of their daughter, Anne Spencer Morrow, to Col. Charles A. Lindbergh."

When Lindbergh landed in Havana, reporters clustered around to ask him about this one-sentence announcement. "Well," he said blandly, "I see you know all about it. . . . I will confine my remarks to aviation."

In February, 1929, the plane that Lindbergh was flying with his fiancée in Mexico lost a wheel on takeoff. Such a thing was to be expected and coped with by the pilot, but Lindbergh was not alone. Inside the cabin he packed Anne with cushions before attempting to land. Then he brought the plane down on one wheel and a wing tip. After a short run, the wing dipped and the plane nosed over. Anne was unhurt, but Lindbergh wrenched his shoulder—the same shoulder he had dislocated in one of his emergency parachute jumps. Lindbergh said later, "Landing on one wheel and a wing tip with a lightly loaded plane isn't very dangerous when a pilot is well acquainted with his craft. It's not likely to cause much of a crack-up, and it has been done a great many times. The newspapers always make it seem a good deal worse than it really is." In Mexico, there had been a full contingent of press and motion-picture photographers at the field to shoot Lindbergh's flight, and they recorded his mishap. But no pictures got out. Mexican Army personnel at the field confiscated all the film that had been taken of the incident.

Hidden but steady warfare had started between Lindbergh and the reporters. He insisted on continuing to confine his cooperation with the press to matters he considered to be of legitimate public interest; namely, his flying and business activities. They, of course, had a public to satisfy and wanted personal news about his emotions, his private life, his relations with Anne and his mother.

These cross-purposes inevitably produced tensions. Yet the personal attitude of reporters was kept well hidden in their accounts of Lindbergh's activities. Once, when he flew some members of the Morrow family to Maine in an amphibian plane, Lindbergh had to put down in Portland for refueling. It so happened that a group of photographers had gathered at the field to cover another story; when they saw Lindbergh, they rushed over and wanted interviews and posed pictures. He refused. He was there to get some gasoline and continue his flight.

After he took his fuel aboard, the heavily laden plane became stuck in a mudhole on the runway. The reporters and photographers would not help him pry the wheels loose. Lindbergh struggled alone for a half hour with the ship until he could get it rolling and take off, according to the late Morris Markey, an eyewitness reporter. But the papers next day omitted all mention of the delay. They wrote only that Lindbergh had stopped off for fuel.

It was now nearly two years since the Paris flight, and Lindbergh was still as sought-after as in the beginning. Only in sequestered surroundings, where his movements could be shielded, could he relax with people he knew.

In May, 1929, Mrs. Lindbergh visited the Morrow home in Englewood, New Jersey. There was a big reception on Saturday, May 26. On Sunday the twenty-seventh the Morrows invited a number of friends informally by telephone to drop in for a visit, perhaps for lunch. Dr. Brown, the minister of the church the Morrows attended, was among those invited. In the middle of the afternoon, Mrs. Morrow began circulating among the guests, asking them into the living room. When she had got them all there, she suggested that they stand up when Dr. Brown did.

Everybody obeyed, not certain exactly what was happening. When Dr. Brown stood, they stood, and then a side door opened and Anne Spencer Morrow entered dressed in a white wedding dress. It had been made secretly. She was carrying a bouquet of flowers. She came and stood beside Lindbergh, and the wedding service was read. Then, without fuss, the young Lindberghs changed into the clothes they had been wearing before the ceremony and drove off in a car.

They reached a secret hideaway before the reporters found out that they had been married. It took ten days to track them down in York Harbor, Maine, where Charles and Anne Lindbergh were spotted aboard a sailboat. Then reporters and photographers in a speedboat began circling the Lindbergh craft, while Anne ducked into the cabin. Lindbergh had to stay on deck. For eight hours they kept up this harassment, yelling and hurling bottles at the Lindbergh boat. After that, the couple began cruising down the Maine coast.

Some days later, at Mitchel Field near New York City, Lindbergh and his wife made their first public appearance as a married couple in connection with a demonstration of aviation safety for the Guggenheim Fund. Lindbergh was interviewed afterward, and a reporter asked if it was true that Mrs. Lindbergh was pregnant. He turned pale and did not reply.

Lindbergh's two employers both grew rapidly during these years. TAT combined with Western Air Express, the company that had shown such success in passenger air travel, to form Transcontinental & Western Air Express (TWA) and dropped the rail service from its schedule. This merger was helped along by Herbert Hoover's Postmaster General, Walter F. Brown, who used his ample powers from Congress to promote similar large consolidations of air-mail and air-transport companies. Brown carried forward the policies of Harry New, his predecessor, to select only financially powerful groups as beneficiaries of air-mail contracts. These subsidies went to a small group of companies, and resulted in the establishment and expansion of some of today's major American carriers: TWA, American Airlines, United Airlines, Northwest-Orient-Airlines. By the time Brown left office in 1932, all these lines plus feeder lines formed a network of passenger air service from coast to coast in the United States. And the government, which had paid out $34,500,000 in mail subsidies to help achieve this system, was spending only half as much in subsidies as it had in the beginning.

Brown favored Pan American as the "chosen instrument" of the U.S. Post Office overseas. He even got the State Department, under Secretary Henry L. Stimson, to intervene on Pan American's behalf when another U.S. company tried to block one of Trippe's expansion plans in South America. When the government called for bids on overseas mail contracts, Pan American had already surveyed the routes and established franchises with the governments involved. They were able to beat out competition and get air-mail contracts, even though they sometimes had to bid very low to do so.

In 1929 Pan American had four air-mail contracts. Wall Street looked on it as a prime investment, calculating that the company would receive, in government mail subsidies alone, fifty million dollars during the next ten years. Thus, Trippe and his associates were able to float a large stock issue to pay for their expansion.

In February, 1929, Lindbergh made the first air-mail flight, two thousand miles, between Pan American's Dinner Key seaplane base, in Miami, and Panama. He made the trip in three days, flying a Sikorsky S-38, by way of western Cuba, Honduras, and Nicaragua.

After this, Pan American moved to increase its bases farther south.
By the end of its first three years of operation, Pan American had
completely encircled South America with air service. (The line had
formed a joint company with the Grace shipping and banking
interests to do this.) The company reported at the end of 1929 it
had "forty-four multi-engined transport planes, 1,200 employees,
seventy-one airports on two continents, and twenty-six ground
control radio stations."

With Lindbergh as technical consultant, the company ordered
and launched in October, 1931, the amphibian Sikorsky S-40—
"American Clipper"—then the largest transport ever built in the
United States. Lindbergh made the first regular flight in this plane
that month.

The early scientific atmosphere and attitude of the Land household had planted in Lindbergh a lifetime interest in new ideas and
explorations. Accordingly, he combined his survey of Central
America for Pan American with aerial prospecting for archaeological
sites. It was one of the earliest uses of the airplane as an aid to
archaeology; he could see ancient patterns in the ground from the
air that were not visible to men below.

Lindbergh told the Carnegie Institute that he had discovered a
ruined Mayan city while flying over Yucatan. At his suggestion,
Carnegie and Pan American jointly financed an expedition to explore the site. Anne went along with the expedition, doing her full
share of the work; Lindbergh never coddled her. Nobody outside
the family knew it, but she really *was* pregnant.

Their first child, Charles Augustus Lindbergh, Jr., was born on
Anne's twenty-fourth birthday, June 22, 1930, at the Morrow house
in Englewood. Full security was maintained; not even the child's
name was given out for more than two weeks. Then Lindbergh
handed to reporters, whom he had agreed to meet, some snapshots
he had taken of the baby.

As Deac Lyman wrote several years later, the Lindberghs lived in
a state of siege. They could not go out of the house without being
assaulted by curious strangers, reporters, and photographers. They
were not much safer at home. Bribes were offered by newspapers to
household servants to betray family confidences; one reporter tried
to get a job as a servant in the house. Their telephone was tapped.

The Lindberghs could not even go to a movie without disguising themselves.

"It's all right for your Prince of Wales and people like that, because they have an organization to protect them," Lindbergh told Harold Nicolson. "I don't. But then they have to be polite whereas I don't, so it works out either way."

They rented a farmhouse near Princeton, New Jersey, and moved there. Meanwhile, Lindbergh bought a large tract of land of about four hundred acres, farther north and west, in Hopewell, New Jersey, and began putting up a house on the land. He and Anne had few friends; an occasional visitor would drop in on them. Donald Keyhoe remarked how Lindbergh straightened up as he entered his house; how the tenseness that marked his demeanor in public fell away; how he could laugh easily and play with the baby and the dog.

Charles A. Lindbergh's marriage into the Morrow family has been adduced by some critics as one piece of evidence that he had sold out to the same interests his father had fought. It is true that his father-in-law, Dwight W. Morrow, had been a partner in J. P. Morgan & Company for thirteen years. But it is also true that Morrow's work in the bank, and before that in a large firm of corporation lawyers, had had the effect of making private utilities and other powerful groups more responsive to the public interest. Morrow was not an acquisitive man. He had almost a horror of wealth; he once woke up and told his wife, "I have had the most horrible nightmare. . . . I dreamt . . . that we had become rich. But *enormously* rich." He was visibly shaken by the experience. Yet he was so talented that, like C. A. Lindbergh, he made money almost in spite of himself and he did become very rich. One could not call him a tycoon, however; his money was not used as power. Nor was it used to procure more than a modest share of the world's goods. He was generous with his family. He spent money on travel and he liked to buy books. He lived very well, but not extravagantly, in Englewood, New Jersey. He was always more interested in what he could do for his country than what he could gain for himself. When President Coolidge, who had been his classmate and friend at Amherst College, asked him to become Ambassador to Mexico, a backwater of a job without a future (because Coolidge was not going to run again for the Presidency), Morrow talked it over with Coolidge and then wrote to his partner, J. P. Morgan, who did not want him to leave the bank. "What in substance he said to me," Morrow wrote to Morgan, "was that you were probably right that I could do more good where I was [in J. P. Morgan & Company] than in Mexico. He said, however, that that was not the whole story; that it was not the business of the Government to do good but to prevent harm, that when Governments tried to do good they generally got themselves and other people into trouble, that he felt that I should probably prevent a good deal of harm if I went to Mexico now. The upshot of it was that I told him he was the President and that if he thought I ought to go, I was willing to go." And he went. Later, he was asked to run for the U.S. Senate from New Jersey. He did so, and won, and in winning he did not compromise his ideas. He was the first candidate to come out for the repeal of the prohibition amendment, when his advisers thought such a stand political suicide. But it was typical of Morrow that he would not pussyfoot; he did not go for cheap compromises or evasions In short, he was very much like C. A. Lindbergh. If Charles A. Lindbergh gained from marrying into the Morrow family, it was not in the financial sense; his wife had been brought up to the same ideals as he had. His parents-in-law had the same kind of integrity as the Lindberghs and the Lands.

15

TO THE ORIENT

routes across the Atlantic and Pacific. There could be no doubt, watching him, that he meant Pan American to encircle the globe.

In 1931, to help forward this purpose, Lindbergh planned a very long exploratory flight by way of Canada, Alaska, and Kamchatka (Soviet Union) to China to survey a possible great-circle air route from the United States to the Orient. This route had been first attempted as part of the first round-the-world flight by four Army biplanes seven years previously. Only three of the four planes got as far as China in that effort, although the full resources of the Army and Navy had been behind it, and there had been many skilled pilots and mechanics aboard those craft.

Now Lindbergh was setting out to fly the same course in a lone monoplane carrying himself as pilot and his wife as radio operator.

In her chronicle of the trip, *North to the Orient*, Mrs. Lindbergh acknowledged the commercial purpose of the flight. But she and her husband had other, more personal motives for making it—a love of travel and the thrill of flying to the far and glamorous East which evoked pictures of Ming porcelains and Marco Polo.

The plane they used had been ordered by Lindbergh the year before. In 1929, at the Cleveland Air Races, Lindbergh was in the market for a fast plane. The Lockheed company had been experimenting, not too successfully, with a low-wing monoplane. Lindbergh spoke to the company's designer, Gerard F. Vultee, who sketched a ship of this type for Lindbergh on a piece of Cleveland hotel stationery and drew up preliminary specifications.

Lindbergh told them to go ahead and build it. Now, of course, he had the money, $17,825, to pay for a ship built to his own needs.

He went out to Burbank, California, and, as he had done with the *Spirit of St. Louis,* lived at the plant while the ship was being built. He put on overalls, ran errands, got materials for the plane from stock, even brought the mechanics sandwiches. His presence attracted visitors and reporters. One day a company executive took him to lunch at a nearby hot-dog stand. When the man put in an expense voucher for eighty cents for the meal, the incident made national headlines.

Also at the plant was Colonel Roscoe Turner, a colorful pilot with a reputation for fast flying and high living. Turner wore a Sam Browne belt, riding breeches, highly polished boots, or sometimes spats and a derby—in contrast to Lindbergh's dirty overalls. But, like Lindbergh, he was a practical joker.

It started when Lindbergh wound a copper wire around the rubber cord stretched across the entrance to the hangar where his plane was being built. The wire was attached to a booster coil. One day Turner came for a visit. He picked up the rope to enter the hangar. Lindbergh flipped a switch sending an electric current through the wire. Turner's reaction showed that he had a command of speech as colorful as his costumes.

He got even a few days later by using the same coil. He wired it to a metal box of nuts and bolts. Then, when Lindbergh came to pick out some small part for his plane, Turner closed the switch and it was Lindbergh's turn to jump and howl.

The plane was finished in October, 1929. Its fuselage was of the modern, monocoque construction; i.e., the shell of plywood was its own support. It had a 600-horsepower Wright engine, nearly three times as powerful as the engine in the *Spirit of St. Louis.* It was also a ton heavier than *Spirit*—over 7,000 pounds gross weight—and so it had to have great lifting power. It had a range of 2,000 miles.

The Lindberghs christened the fast ship—top speed 185 m.p.h.—*Sirius* after the brightest star in the sky. It was painted black, with red trim. On April 20, 1930, they took off in the *Sirius* and flew it to New York. Including one stop for gas en route, they made it from Glendale, California, to Roosevelt Field, New York, in fourteen hours and forty-five minutes. This was a new, but unofficial, transcontinental speed record—more than seven hours faster than Lindbergh's record in *Spirit* three years earlier.

The ship was later modified to use retractable landing gear, and even later than that, for the northern flight to the Orient, Lindbergh decided to have the *Sirius* equipped with pontoons.

"Of course, we'll have to use pontoons instead of wheels up there," Lindbergh told his wife as he studied the map of Canada. He was explaining how safe the trip would really be.

She wanted to know why pontoons were necessary over land.

He said there were a lot of lakes in northern Canada. "The Canadian pilots always use seaplanes." Along the coast of Siberia they would find plenty of sheltered landing spots on water, and if the worst came to worst and they had to, they could land in the open sea. For that, they had the rubber boat.

Mrs. Lindbergh pointed out that if they came down in the middle of the Bering Sea, "it would be quite a long row to Kamchatka."

"We might sail to shore," Lindbergh said, "but otherwise we wouldn't have much chance of being found without radio."

His wife asked if he could operate a radio.

He had studied radio in the Army, he said, but she would have to be the radio operator.

The next day he brought home a practice set of buzzers so she could begin to learn how to send Morse code. When she pressed the key, "there was a little squeak which brought four dogs and the baby [Charles, Jr.] scrambling into my room," Mrs. Lindbergh recalls.

They would need a third-class license to operate the radio for anything but emergency calls. This meant passing an examination in sending Morse code at fifteen words a minute, and other tests on the care and operation of vacuum-tube apparatus and on radio communications laws and regulations.

"Now, Charles, you know perfectly well that I can't do that," said Anne Lindbergh. "I never passed an arithmetic examination in my life. . . . I never understood a thing about electricity."

"It's too bad you didn't take more," he said, "but it's not too late; we'll start tonight. I don't know much about radio; we'll work on it together."

They sat with clean pads and sharp pencils while their instructor lectured them.

They would start with the vacuum tube the instructor said.

And after a lengthy explanation of the vacuum tube the instructor was ready to move on to the next subject.

Anne Lindbergh asked where the vacuum tube was.

The instructor's face mirrored several emotions before he said, "*This* is it," as though talking to a child.

It was just like studying French at Smith; when she missed a few words, the rest became gibberish. At college her mind used to go blank and she would hope to get it all explained after class.

This time she used her college textbooks on physics and the diagrams given by the radio expert, and pieced it all out with her husband's explanations. At last came the written examination, one hot day. Anne and Charles Lindbergh went together to take the test. She finished first. They both passed, but he got the higher grade.

Then they went out to the plane in its hangar for the practical test of sending messages. A radio operator on Long Island listened for her signal.

He asked, in code, who was sending. She spelled her name, and asked if her sending was all right.

He replied, "Pretty---good---just---like---my---wife's---sending."

Although this was a dot-dash conversation, "I could hear the tone of his voice, the inflection, the accent on the *my*, the somewhat querulous, somewhat kindly and amused, somewhat supercilious, husbandly tone," Anne Lindbergh remembered.

Meanwhile the route was being planned, caches of gasoline were set out across Canada, a radio of the type Pan American used in its South American flights was installed in the *Sirius*.

Lindbergh balanced the possible emergencies they would encounter on the flight—polar landings, ocean landings, forced landings in insect-ridden country—against the weight of the equipment they could carry to meet these contingencies. For weeks before the departure, the floor of their room was covered with heaps of electrically heated flying suits, gloves, helmets, parachutes (they would take them on this trip), revolvers (a .38 and a .22). The .22 was part of the parachute-jump equipment, which included matches, Army rations, fishhooks, line, compass, a rubber boat, and other things needed for a forced landing at sea. Each item was weighed on the baby's scale. Mrs. Lindbergh read books on nutrients to help select the most essential foods (tomatoes were good against beri-beri). Lindbergh endlessly added to and subtracted from lists. He weighed a shotgun: six pounds. And each shell weighed nearly two ounces. "Think what that would mean in food!" he said.

"Or *shoes*," said his wife. She was trying to get along on two pairs, since they had allowed themselves only eighteen pounds each of personal luggage—including the suitcase.

She went into a shop and said, "I want a pair of shoes that I can wear at balls and dinners, and also at teas and receptions, and also for semisport dresses, and also for bedroom slippers." And, she added, she would like them to have low heels.

"Try our 'Growing Girl' department" was the clerk's exasperated reply.

On July 27, 1931, they were ready to begin the long flight. They were starting from College Point, on Long Island, where they would take off from Flushing Bay for Washington, D.C., on the first leg.

The weather was dark and steamy when they gathered at the ramp. Of course, the takeoff was a matter of international importance; every kind of newspaper, most magazines, and all newsreels and radio stations were represented.

On one side, Lindbergh was answering technical questions. Other reporters asked Anne Lindbergh about the danger—wasn't she afraid? And about her clothes, and where she stowed the lunch boxes. These conventionally feminine questions depressed her, and she gave noncommittal replies.

As the mechanics rolled the plane into the water, Mrs. Lindbergh overheard a radio announcer covering the departure. He described her, on that sweltering day, as being dressed in a leather flying helmet and leather coat and high leather flying boots.

She looked down at herself in wonderment. She was wearing a cotton blouse and light sneakers and no helmet. Then she realized that the man thought he had to describe her in conventional flying gear because that was what people expected to hear.

On the flight to Washington, Anne Lindbergh tried out the radio. It didn't work. She wondered what the reporters would write; perhaps that she didn't do any radio sending because she couldn't get the coils into place. But her husband passed her a note telling her to check the fuses—and then passed her a fuse so that she would know what to look for. Then he wrote:

"Don't look so gloomy. Probably due to a short circuit when they installed the compass light—get it fixed at North Beach on our way to Maine."

They arrived in Washington in an hour and twenty-five minutes, stayed overnight, and flew back to New York the next day. On July 29 they took off for the Morrow summer home on the island of North Haven, in Maine, where Charles, Jr., was being cared for by his grandparents.

In the past, Anne Lindbergh had been accustomed to take a sleeper train from New York, then a ferry and a small boat to North Haven. It had been a long, leisurely overnight trip, during which one could savor the slow change from New Jersey to Maine, from school to vacation. But the *Sirius* cut through all that and brought her there in a swift, slashing two and a half hours. She really wasn't ready to greet her parents and her friends; she needed a night in the familiar Morrow house before she could adjust to being there. They stayed less than twenty-four hours, and the next day were off in brilliant sunshine for Ottawa.

That night they dined with experts and discussed the trip. There were aviators, explorers, meteorologists, surveyors, scientists—the people who knew just about all there was to know about northern Canada. And they all argued with Lindbergh.

The big question was: why had he chosen that route?

"Well," said Lindbergh, "it's the shortest."

But it wasn't much shorter than the route along the Mackenzie River, which would be much safer. And there were only Hudson's Bay posts and Mounted Police stations to stay in, they told him.

Lindbergh smiled and said, "Well?"

So they began to tell him about the tremendous tide in Hudson Bay, which might drag the plane from its mooring or leave it high and dry . . . the terrible fogs . . . and "glass water," which you couldn't see and which could cause a dangerous crash . . . and the magnetic pole that would throw the compass out, and the terrible mosquitoes. . . .

One man remarked that he wouldn't take his wife over that country. Lindbergh replied that *his* wife was crew.

They tried to cajole him into taking another route nearly as wild and just a bit longer.

Lindbergh looked them in the eye and said distinctly, "I like to feel that in flying I can mark one point on the map for my position and another point for my destination, and that I can draw a straight line between the two, and follow it. I don't like to deviate for possible difficulties en route. I'd rather prepare for the difficulties."

They played their last card. If something happened to Lindbergh, they couldn't take the responsibility.

"All right," he snapped. "If we can't take that route we'll go back and go over Greenland!"

That would be even worse, they said, and at last they began to come around. They gave him advice about landing places, special photographic maps of anchorages, wing ropes, special life preservers that couldn't be got anywhere else. And, at last, a word of encouragement: they knew he would make it.

Lindbergh wasn't that sure of himself. He had from the beginning literally flown in the face of accepted ideas of the possible. Privately he sometimes wondered, "Is aviation too arrogant? . . . Sometimes, flying feels too godlike to be attained by man. Sometimes, the world from above seems too beautiful, too wonderful, too distant for human eyes to see, like a vision at the end of life forming a bridge to death. Can that be why so many pilots lose their lives?"

However, he kept such self-doubts carefully concealed from other people. To the world he offered a set face, masked with firm, unshakable purpose. He would defend his plans, and he would justify later the snap decisions he made en route.

They took off from Ottawa the next day, August 1, and made Moose Factory, Canada, without incident. They continued along Lindbergh's chosen route to Alaska, managing to avoid all the threats which the experts had warned of.

Point Barrow, Alaska, the northernmost stop on the trip, was a disappointment in one respect: the gasoline that was supposed to be there for the *Sirius* had not arrived. The ship did carry enough gasoline to reach the next stop, Nome, but with not much margin for error. They took off on August 11, and headed south toward Nome. Although it was the time of year when one might expect to find almost perpetual daylight in the arctic, astonishingly at eight-thirty in the evening the light was beginning to disappear. It was the first twilight they had seen in a week. It was so dark in Anne Lindbergh's cockpit, in fact, that she could barely read the message her husband handed her to radio to Nome asking what time it got dark.

They were short of fuel and would have to land somewhere before night.

There was no answer from Nome, but a relay station picked up the message and made contact for them. The station radioed that Nome was putting out flares on the river for the Lindberghs, and would light them when the plane was expected. That would be in an hour and a half, Lindbergh wrote in a message for his wife to radio back.

They were flying over a mountain range whose deep valleys were ominously filled with shadow.

Suddenly Lindbergh pulled the plane up into a stall and throttled back on the engine. It was quiet enough for his wife to hear him shout, "Tell him there's fog on the mountains ahead. We'll land for the night and come into Nome in the morning."

She had barely enough time to get the message off, then had to reel in the antenna as Lindbergh was diving toward the water. He had to get down before the light was completely gone. The plane whistled seaward and smacked the water lightly. It seemed to run on for miles before it slowed. It must have been a down-wind landing; in that dim light any landing was an achievement. When the plane came to rest on the dark water, the shore was an indistinct shadow perhaps a half mile away. Lindbergh climbed on a pontoon and threw out the anchor. It made a great splash, but sank so little that the rope floated. The water was barely three feet deep. A little shallower, and he might have wrecked his pontoons. They were at an inlet called Shishmaref.*

---

* Many years later a fellow flier and arctic expert, John Grierson, asked Lindbergh why he hadn't checked sunset time at Nome before he left Barrow. "That sort of error we made early in our flying careers—but once running out of daylight we carried the lesson permanently in our pocket," Grierson commented.

Lindbergh attempted to defend himself by categorizing the Shishmaref No. 4 on a list of hazards in which No. 1 represented most danger—danger of death— and No. 4 the least—risk of unimportant damage to the aircraft. He also emphasized his belief that danger cannot be totally avoided and may be increased by too much forethought and preparation. He admitted in the letter that he had made many mistakes in his life.

Grierson did not let him off so easily, and continued to criticize the landing as a hangover from Lindbergh's barnstorming habits.

Lindbergh defended himself in a second letter, and capped the debate by writing the introduction to Grierson's book *Challenge to the Poles* in which the correspondence is reproduced.

Later, on August 19, flying south from Petropavlovsk, Kamchatka (Soviet Union), to Japan the Lindberghs saw fog in the distance. Suddenly there was fog all around and a storm system up front. Lindbergh turned north and found fog there, too.

He pushed back the cockpit cover, put on his helmet and goggles, and raised his seat so he could see better. "Here we are again," thought Anne Lindbergh, recognizing by this familiar buckling on of armor that the fight had begun.

Her mind turned back along a long corridor of fears. There was a time over the Alleghenies, another over the San Bernardino Mountains, when they had been trapped in fog, and both times there had been a river that Lindbergh had followed, flying down the valleys between the towering mountains, until they had found safety. There was no river out here; they couldn't even see the ocean.

And they couldn't stay up forever. They had already been flying for six hours. Alongside a peak, the plane nosed downward, "Like a knife going down the side of a pie tin, between fog and mountain. Will he say afterward, 'It was nothing at all'?" Mrs. Lindbergh wondered.

Lindbergh tried to fly his way down the side of the mountain, alternating between patches of visible flight and areas of blind flying, with jagged peaks springing at the plane. There were tantalizing glimpses of the sea, but not enough visibility to land. "Oh, God!—we'll hit the mountain!" Anne Lindbergh thought. Then the engine roared, and they were climbing again. She caught her breath and thanked God for the blue sky overhead.

She was watching her husband's face as he sat up high, staring out of the cockpit. "The wind flattened his face, made the flesh flabby, the brows prominent—like a skeleton." It forced his mouth into an expression of fear.

Suddenly she felt the plane nose downward once more and realized he was going to repeat the maneuver. She made a mental resolve never to fly again. "Really, it was too much." Lindbergh flew straight down the side of another mountain, skimming over bushes and rocks, almost feeling his way toward the water. They plunged downward, and over a cliff, and the water was there fifty feet below. There was no choice but to keep on going at the same angle. The surface of the water appeared only in brief glimpses; it might disappear altogether. Suddenly the pontoons were spanking the tops of waves, very hard. The ship bounced once . . . twice . . . three times. It seemed as though it might break up. At last they stopped.

Lindbergh turned around and looked at his wife's face. "What's the matter?" he asked.

"Nothing," she said. "I'm so happy to be down."

He laughed.

There was the sound of waves on a shore, although the shore line was invisible. They taxied slowly until they found the edge of an island in the lee of the wind. Lindbergh cut the engine and dropped anchor.

They had hit the surface much too fast. The impact had buckled the spreader bar bracing the two pontoons. Mrs. Lindbergh radioed their position, which they reckoned near a Japanese island called Ketoi. The Japanese radioed an offer to send a ship, but Lindbergh declined help. However, the ship came anyway, and it was just as well that it did. For the weather grew stormy, and without help Lindbergh could not have repaired the spreader bar for takeoff. Also, the sailors saved the plane from being dashed to pieces when its anchor rope was accidentally cut against a rock.

There were no fewer than three such forced landings, any one of which would have made a less skillful pilot crash. But Lindbergh, except for that hard landing at Ketoi Island, did not damage his plane during ten thousand miles of flying.

However, he nearly lost his life in another kind of situation. When he and his wife had landed in Nanking, China, they found the Yangtze River in flood. Tremendous areas were inundated and cut off by the rising water. The Lindberghs offered to help. They made a number of flights for the National Flood Relief Commission, to map the flooded land. Hundreds of villages were underwater. People driven out of their houses were living in sampans. There was no way of reaching them; the water was too shallow for motorboats, and of course the roads were impassable. The month was September and there was no hope that the waters would subside until spring at least. It was a heartbreakingly frustrating experience to fly over these people who were slowly starving or dying in epidemics and who couldn't be helped.

On one of the survey flights, Lindbergh had seen the walled city of Hingwa standing above the flood, isolated by at least twenty-five miles of water from the nearest dry land. The Commission thought that this city would be a useful place for distributing food and supplies. So Lindbergh loaded his plane with two doctors—one Chinese, one American—and medicines. Leaving his wife in Nanking, he flew to Hingwa.

He landed on some flooded fields near the city. The natives in sampans were fearful of the plane. The Chinese doctor managed to wave one or two close. He stepped from the plane's pontoons into a sampan and handed an old woman in the boat a package of medicines. She sat on it.

Now there were other sampans approaching. They saw the old woman with the package of medicines. They thought it was food. They wanted their share. More and more sampans began crowding against the *Sirius*. The Chinese doctor's sampan was sunk by people climbing aboard. They were all making chopstick motions with their fingers. They were desperate for food. The Chinese doctor moved into another sampan, and it, too, sank under the weight of the people who followed him.

The plane was being threatened by the heavy prows of the sampans, which could have knocked holes in the pontoons. The American doctor in the plane asked Lindbergh if he had a gun. "Yes —a thirty-eight revolver," Lindbergh said, "but someone in that crowd may have a rifle, probably several—fatal to show a gun in a crowd like that." By now there were literally hundreds of boats and thousands of people, sullen, menacing, packed around the plane.

Suddenly a man put his foot on one of the plane's pontoons. Lindbergh took out the gun which he had been hiding and pointed it at the man. Men on the other side of the plane moved to board the craft. Lindbergh whipped the gun back and forth, shooting from one side to the other, over the heads of the boarders. The maneuver made each group think that someone on the other side had been hit; they began to fall back.

The Chinese doctor saw that he could do nothing. He managed to reach the plane, only to be confronted with the revolver. He stood up and shouted before Lindbergh recognized him and let him aboard. Meanwhile the American doctor hauled in the anchor. Lindbergh in the front cockpit was ready to take off. A single sampan remained stubbornly in front of the plane.

The wind swung the nose of the plane around so that it just

cleared the sampan. Lindbergh pressed the starter and began taxiing away from the starving, food-maddened Chinese who paddled after them. Soon the plane took off, leaving the desperate people far below.

For nearly two weeks Lindbergh put his plane at the service of the Chinese Relief Commission. He moved on to Hankow to continue mapping flooded areas and flying doctors to emergency stations. The river was so swift at Hankow that it was dangerous to anchor the plane. The British aircraft carrier *Hermes* was berthed there, and the captain offered to take the *Sirius* aboard each night after the day's flights. To do this, he rigged up a special sling, hoisting the seaplane out of the river to the security of the ship.

On the last day, October 2, when the *Sirius* was being lowered into the river with the Lindberghs aboard, a sudden surge in the current, a sudden shift in the wind caught the plane. The sailors couldn't release the makeshift sling. The plane's engine was turning over, and Lindbergh attempted to move the *Sirius* so there would be enough slack cable to unhook the sling. But the wind and current tilted the plane, a wing went underwater, and Lindbergh shouted to his wife to jump. They both dove clear and swam to safety.

The plane was damaged, but still flyable. Efforts were made to right it, and this was almost done. But just as the cables were being tightened, a sampan loaded with Chinese headed straight for the *Sirius*, and this time there was nothing to do but let it go under. It was later taken aboard the *Hermes* to Shanghai and shipped to the Lockheed factory in California for repairs. But the Orient flight was effectively ended there in Hankow.

The Lindberghs would probably not have flown much farther anyhow. Three days later, they got a telegram from Englewood, New Jersey. Dwight Morrow had had a stroke on the morning of October 5, 1931, and died at home that afternoon.

The Orient survey was never made the basis of a Pan American air route; the company could not get the necessary bases and concessions in Japan or the Soviet Union. Instead, with the encouragement of the Navy Department, Pan American developed a mid-Pacific route by way of Midway, Wake, and Guam islands, with a terminus at Manila, in the Philippines. As a private company, it could build elaborate installations on these outpost islands, and the Navy could defend this activity as private enterprise when the Japanese charged that it was U.S. aggression. The installations would prove extremely useful in the event of a Pacific war. The Pan American route to Manila was opened officially in 1935 and was extended to Hong Kong in 1936.

The great-circle path that Lindberg surveyed did become a commercial air route when Northwest-Orient-Airlines began flying it to Tokyo after World War II.

DEATHS IN THE FAMILY

suddenly at the height of his powers. His death was perhaps more shocking to the family because it was so unexpected.

But the family's sense of loss may have been mitigated by the fact that Morrow had been a distant man, totally absorbed in his work, his thoughts, or what he was reading. He could sit in the living room reading a book while the children played the piano and carried on loud conversations, and not hear a thing.

"Breakfast was for a long time the only meal, in fact the only time, we saw Daddy," Anne Morrow Lindbergh recalled. "I realize now, looking back on it, that it was the only time we felt ourselves as a family." And the only time he would speak at breakfast was when he was eating his poached eggs. He needed both hands to do this, so he had to put down his newspaper. At this time he usually made little jokes, or teased the children.

His most frequent gambit was to ask "Who do you like best— your mother or your father, Elisabeth?" "This," reports Anne Lindbergh, "was always agony. I could see the question coming to me next, like a bad dream, and I was never well prepared. Elisabeth was asked first and always answered honestly and courageously— perfectly frankly (which delighted him). 'I like Mother best—and *next* to Mother I like Daddy.' Then he would turn to me. I can remember the torture of trying to be honest, yet not to hurt his feelings. First I would say, evading and embarrassed, 'I like you both the same.' But Daddy would persist, 'Now, Anne, tell me the truth—Who do you love best?' Then I would protest—'But I like you—*differently!*' 'Now, Anne—' He enjoyed very much teasing me and would insist on my explaining myself, going on and on. But I never admitted liking Mother most.

" 'Well—come here and give me a kiss—anyway,' it would usually end."

After Morrow's death the Lindberghs spent a great deal of time with Mrs. Morrow. Having her daughter, grandson, and son-in-law around eased the shock of sudden loss for the widow.

Lindbergh was working a good deal in New York. His duties for the airlines had become rather routine, and if he stuck to the routine, he did not make unwelcome news. When he did anything else, he took care to keep it a secret.

On the weekends, Charles, Anne, and the baby would drive to Hopewell, New Jersey, to the new house they had built. The two-story house, an imposing structure something like C. A. Lindbergh's big house (the one that had burned down in 1906, when Charles was four), was livable but still needed work; for example, the shutter in the baby's nursery on the second floor had warped so that it could not be closed.

Normally on a Tuesday, like March 1, 1932, they would have been in Englewood. But the baby, now twenty months old, had developed a cold over the previous weekend. Anne Lindbergh, pregnant with her second child, had caught the cold. So they stayed on in Hopewell instead of returning to the Morrow house. Other than the cold, Charles, Jr., was a healthy, blond, bright baby who played happily with his nurse, his dog, and his parents. He was a perfectly normal child, except for two slightly overlapping toes.

Lindbergh went to work in New York on Monday, February 29. He called up during the day to say that he would have to stay in Englewood that night, and would drive to Hopewell the next day, Tuesday, after work. It had been widely advertised that he would attend a banquet for New York University Tuesday evening, but he got his dates mixed. He made the sixty-mile trip to Hopewell, arriving early Tuesday night. After dinner, he sat and talked for a while in the downstairs living room with his wife. Charles, Jr., had been put to bed in his upstairs nursery, carefully wrapped against the cold. It was a raw, windy night. Lindbergh heard a sudden sound around nine o'clock that seemed to come from the kitchen. He thought it was something falling off a chair.

At ten o'clock it was the custom of Betty Gow, the baby's nurse, to take the baby to the bathroom. She did not turn on the light in the nursery, but left the door open so she could see by the hall light. She entered the baby's room, closed the casement window, then plugged in an electric heater. Before touching the baby she warmed her hands.

But when "I bent over the crib I couldn't hear the baby breathe," she recalled later. "I bent down, felt all over for him and discovered he wasn't there. I thought that Mrs. Lindbergh may have him. I went out . . . met Mrs. Lindbergh . . . and asked her if she didn't have the baby. She looked surprised and said, no, she didn't.

"I said, 'Well where is the Colonel, he may have him.' I said, 'Where is he?'

"She said, 'Downstairs, in the library.' "

Betty Gow ran down the main staircase and found Lindbergh sitting at his desk, reading.

"I said, 'Colonel do you have the baby?' [Lindbergh recalled that her voice was rather excited.]

"He said, 'No. Isn't he in his crib?'

"I said, 'No.' "

Lindbergh immediately ran up the stairs to the baby's room, followed by the nurse.

Lindbergh: "From the appearance of the room I realized and from the appearance of the crib I realized something had gone wrong . . . the bed clothing in the crib was in such condition that I felt it was impossible for the baby to have gotten out for himself. . . . I knew that neither my wife nor Miss Gow had taken him because Miss Gow had asked me if I had him."

Lindbergh turned to his wife, who had come into the nursery, and said, "Anne, they have stolen our baby." He went down to a closet and got out a Springfield rifle.

The sudden assumption that the baby had been kidnaped was logical; the Lindberghs' mail had always contained a number of cranky, threatening letters among the avalanche of good wishes and requests for help or money. They had kept the baby's photograph out of the newspapers as one safeguard against his being seized and held for ransom. He had certainly disappeared from the house. He could walk, but it was unlikely that he could have climbed out of the crib without disturbing the covers.

There was an envelope propped on the radiator in the nursery, some muddy footprints—all of which reinforced the idea of an intruder. Lindbergh touched nothing. He asked the butler, Oliver Whateley, to telephone the local police while he looked for the child.

Lindbergh meanwhile called his lawyer, Colonel Breckinridge, and the New Jersey state police. Then he took his rifle and went out to search for his son. But he quickly realized he could do nothing alone, without lights, in the dark woods.

Soon came the police—local and state—and a professional search of the grounds was made. In the house, the state police opened the envelope found in the nursery. It contained a note crudely written in pencil, which read, in part:

> Dear Sir Have 50000$ ready 25000$ in 20$ bills
> 15000$ in 10$ bills and 1000$ in 5$ bills After
> 2–4 days we will inform you were to deliver the
> money We warn you for making anyding public or
> for notify the police The child is in gut care

The signature was two red circles, partly overlapped. The overlapped area was filled in with blue. In each of the three areas a square hole had been punched through the paper.

The letter had said, "Indication for all letters are singnature and three holes."

Not far from the house, the police found a wooden ladder, made in three pieces, joined by dowels. One rung was broken. There was also a carpenter's chisel, probably used to force the window in the nursery.

The police had put the crime on the teletype: "Colonel Lindbergh's baby was kidnapped from Lindbergh home in Hopewell, N.J. sometime between 7:30 and 10 P.M. this date. Baby is nineteen months old and a boy. Is dressed in sleeping suit. Request that all cars be investigated by police patrols." A New York Times reporter at the state police barracks in Somerville, New Jersey, phoned his office with the news. The night editor in New York routed the call to one reporter and, at the same time, asked an assistant to tell Deac Lyman to call Lindbergh to check the accuracy of this information. He knew that Lyman and Lindbergh were friendly.

Lyman called Colonel Breckinridge and then came over to the city desk. "It's true! It's true!" he shouted.

Lyman and another reporter were immediately dispatched to Hopewell in a rented car with a chauffeur. Another correspondent was assigned to meet them at Princeton and guide them to the Lindbergh house.

On the way, in Elizabeth, New Jersey, Lyman saw a policeman, stopped the car, and identified himself. He said they were on the way to cover the kidnaping and asked if there was any news. The policeman had not yet heard of the kidnaping; and Lyman made a mental note of how easy it would have been for the kidnaper to use a main highway for escape.

Two Associated Press men from Trenton beat the *Times* to the scene and put out a report that a kidnap note had been found. Lindbergh admitted Lyman to his house to use the telephone. The *Times* in New York wanted more about the kidnap note. Lyman went out to talk to Lindbergh and found that the state police were going to ban all reporters and photographers from the grounds, but Lindbergh intervened to allow them to stay.

It seemed that the kidnaper had threatened to harm the baby if the note were made public; so the *Times* decided to keep the contents out of the paper and merely report that a note existed. William Randolph Hearst, Jr., was in Hopewell on the story and spoke to Lyman about the note; his father, in San Simeon, California, was on the telephone. Young Hearst said to his father, "Pop, I don't think the *New York Times* will use this thing." Then he turned to Lyman: "Pop said we're not using it either. He said we aren't going to print anything that might interfere with the return of the baby." However, other New York papers reasoned that the contents of the note had been syndicated on the wire and that somebody would be bound to break it. So they printed the kidnaper's message.

Of course, the kidnaping was immediate front-page news and kept enlarging as fast as reporters could write and typesetters could set their stories. More and more reporters and photographers were sent to cover Hopewell. The other wire services and every daily paper in New York and Philadelphia dispatched men and women and automobiles; there were nearly fifty newspaper people in Hopewell within a couple of hours. One service hired two ambulances to rush photographs back and forth to New York, the backs of the vehicles equipped as darkrooms.

The kidnaping was a matter of moment not only to the newspapers—sales of newspapers went up about 20 per cent, meaning millions of extra copies and a great deal of windfall revenue—but to politicians, gangsters, ministers, movie stars, anyone who had to have the public's attention. Governor Franklin D. Roosevelt, of New York, put the New York state police at the disposal of the Lindberghs. President Herbert Hoover said that federal authorities would help as much as they could; there was then no legal sanction for their participation in a case of kidnaping unless they were invited by local police to do so. Bishop Manning, of New York, issued a special prayer for "immediate use" by the public. (Sunday was still more than four days off.) Al Capone, the gangster, in a Chicago jail, told Arthur Brisbane, Hearst newspapers' leading columnist, that he and Mrs. Capone felt sorry for the Lindberghs and offered $10,000 to try to get the baby back. Brisbane ran the offer in his column with the statement that if the government would pardon Capone's conviction on income-tax evasion, the chances were good that the baby would be returned.

Lindbergh read the piece and called Ogden Mills, the Secretary of the Treasury, to find out if anything could be done. Mills sent the head of Treasury enforcement, Elmer Irey, to see Lindbergh in Hopewell the next day. Lindbergh made it clear that in asking about Capone he was not requesting any favors, just exploring possibilities. He said he wouldn't ask for Capone's freedom as the price of saving his son's life.

The Lindberghs tried to cooperate with the newspapers. The night of the kidnaping, they admitted reporters to the living room of their house. They asked them to assist the police by leaving the grounds so that any clues would not be obliterated. The reporters obliged.

The day after the baby's disappearance, March 2, Anne Lindbergh gave the papers a list of the foods the baby was supposed to get. Just the recital of the diet was enough to wring anyone's heart:

"A half cup of orange juice on waking.

"One quart of milk during the day.

"Three tablespoons of cooked cereal morning and night," and so on, down to, "Fourteen drops of Viosterol, a vitamin preparation, during the day."

Every leading newspaper carried the list on its front page of March 3.

That day, the Lindberghs wrote an open letter and gave it to the newspapers.

Mrs. Lindbergh and I desire to make a personal contact with the kidnapers of our child.

Our only interest is in his immediate and safe return and we feel certain that the kidnapers will realize that this interest is strong enough to justify them in having complete confidence and trust in any promises that we may make in connection with his return.

We urge those who have the child to select any representatives of ours who will be suitable to them at any time and at any place that they may designate.

If this is accepted, we promise that we will keep whatever arrangements that may be made by their representative and ours strictly confidential and we further pledge ourselves that we will not try to injure in any way those connected with the return of the child.

CHARLES A. LINDBERGH
ANNE LINDBERGH

The New Jersey state police did not like the idea of seeming to promise the kidnapers immunity. They said that whether the Lindberghs prosecuted or not, they would prosecute anyone they caught.

The Lindbergh letter was widely published on March 4. That same day the Lindberghs received a second note from the presumed kidnaper, with the same signature of interlocking circles. A whole series of such communications, dealing with the ransom (the demand was increased to $70,000), methods of procedure, etc., followed—not only to Lindbergh but to his lawyer.

Reporters continued to flood into tiny Hopewell, combing the countryside for news. They had to have copy; as much as fifty thousand words were filed on days when there wasn't enough hard news to fill a half column of type.

Once again the Lindberghs were in the center of a cyclone of speculation and manufactured sensation. Once again the reportage was so out of proportion to the scope of events that it became a force of its own, stronger than the circumstances that summoned it up.

Much of the writing was improvisation; most of it had to be

fiction. On one particularly dull day, a lady writer for a well-known chain of newspapers was searching about for nonexistent news. She came across Deac Lyman, of the *Times*. Lyman had been a visitor at the Lindbergh house in Hopewell. The lady, sniffing a good feature story, asked him some questions about the interior of the house, which she had never seen. Lyman answered her without thinking too much about it. The next day, her newspaper carried a page 1 story under her by-line on "My Visit to the Lindbergh House." It was a great news beat at the time. It was also almost totally incorrect in its details, aside from the fact that the woman claimed to have seen something that she had not.

The area around Hopewell was overrun by sightseers and souvenir hunters in literally tens of thousands. Cars clogged the roads; the curious hunted for whatever they could find to prove to other neurotics that they had been in the area. In this mob scene, most clues were soon erased and the police were impeded in their work.

Colonel Breckinridge believed with Capone that the underworld was involved in the kidnaping and found a couple of hoodlums named Salvy Spitale and Irving Bitz to act as go-betweens. The chief of their gang, Morris Rosner, gave out a statement that he had definite knowledge that the baby was alive and well. Spitale and Bitz made trips to many cities with the announced intention of making contact with the kidnapers.

These gangsters were only the first of a number of people who said they knew who had kidnaped the baby and could get the child back safely.

The second offer came from a man named Gaston B. Means, a paunchy former agent of the Department of Justice, a payoff man in the high councils of the bribe-ridden administration of President Harding, and an ex-convict. Means got in touch with Evalyn Walsh McLean, owner of the Hope diamond and wife (separated) of the publisher of the Washington *Post*. Means had shrewdly estimated that Mrs. McLean would be susceptible to his pitch. (Her own son had been killed not long before, and she was close to a Lindbergh cousin.) He told her that the kidnaper was a man who had been Means' fellow-convict in the Atlanta penitentiary. For $100,000, Means said, he could arrange to have the baby delivered to a priest.

Mrs. McLean got in touch with a priest, and with Lindbergh's cousin, and they both agreed that Means seemed anxious to help. His connections with gangsters were undeniable. So Mrs. McLean withdrew $100,000 in old bills from her bank, plus $4,000 in new money for Means' expenses, and gave it all to Means.

A third major go-between in the case was a boatbuilder—John Hughes Curtis, of Norfolk, Virginia. He claimed to have made contact with the kidnapers through a former rumrunner; the kidnapers were, by his account, local Virginia rumrunners who feared intervention by the New York, Detroit, and Chicago mobs.

There was one other contact. He was a tall, erect, white-haired gentleman by the name of Dr. John F. Condon, a retired school-teacher. Condon was an eccentric, yet much admired in his community, which was the Bronx, New York. Condon's motivations were probably the purest of any of those who volunteered to help. He was an old-fashioned, flag-waving patriot who believed in God, his country, and motherhood. All of these things had been violated by the kidnaping. In Condon's mind, Lindbergh was identified with the very essence of America's virtues. The kidnaping of his child had somehow sullied the nation's honor. Condon sought to wipe out this blot by offering his services in getting the Lindbergh baby back.

Early in March, 1932, around the sixth or seventh, Condon wrote a letter to the Bronx *Home News*, which published it in its weekly edition. Condon offered his total cash savings—$1,000—in addition to the Lindbergh ransom money, for the return of the baby. He wrote that he would go anywhere at his own expense to meet the kidnapers. He promised total secrecy, and he was well known in the Bronx as a man of his word.

The *Home News* had barely come out when a reply came by mail to Condon's house. It was a penciled note, which turned out to be identical in handwriting and signature with the original Lindbergh ransom letter. But only the Lindberghs and the police—and the kidnaper—could have known that at the time; the signature had not been made public when Condon got his reply. Condon did not get this letter until after 10 P.M. on March 9. He had been out lecturing. When he read the letter, which gave instructions as to the payment of money, and which contained an enclosed letter to Lindbergh saying that the kidnaper would accept Dr. Condon as liaison, Condon "was pleased to think I had been so honored."

The letter for Lindbergh began: "Dear Sir: Mr. Condon may act as go-between. You may give him the 70,000$ make one packet. . . ." The letter to Condon contained the instruction that when he had the ransom he was to put an advertisement in the New York *American* reading "MONEY IS READY."

Condon went to the house of a man named Al Reich, who owned a car in which he had often chauffeured the old teacher. Reich was not at home, but a restaurant owner friend was there. Condon called the Lindbergh house from Reich's home. By this time, according to their joint recollection, it was after eleven.

Lindbergh did not answer the telephone. The phones in the Hopewell house had been arranged, Lindbergh said, so that a number of people could answer them. The idea was to avoid the numerous cranks who pestered the Lindberghs while leaving a line of communication open to the real kidnaper.

Lindbergh did not remember talking to Condon on the telephone at all. But Condon said that he had refused to deliver his message to anyone else and that eventually Lindbergh did get on the line.

According to Condon's recollection, he described the signature on the letter to Lindbergh:

"'Colonel, I do not know whether this is important or not, but there are what I'd call a secantal circle, that is, one circle cutting in the other, the same as a secant cuts through a circle,' and I said, 'Is it important? Shall I bring it down to you?'

"And he said to me 'I will get the automobile and come up to you. Where are you?'

"'I am in the Bronx, but you don't have to. You have enough to do and I will come down to you, to Hopewell.'"

The restaurant keeper got another man with a car and they drove Condon to Hopewell after midnight.

There was a long discussion at Hopewell, between Condon, Lindbergh, and Breckinridge. Condon sent his two friends back to the Bronx, but he was asked to stay the night. Lindbergh fixed him a makeshift bed on the floor of the nursery. The next day Lindbergh handed him a note dated March 10, 1932, authorizing Condon to act as a go-between. It was signed by both Charles and Anne Lindbergh.

On March 11, Condon ran the ad in the *American:* "MONEY IS

READY." He signed it "Jafsie," a code name he made up with the Lindberghs out of the phonetics of his initials.

A series of messages brought Condon face to face with a man who identified himself as "John," first in Woodlawn Cemetery, in the Bronx, and afterward on a park bench. John kept his face shielded and it was dark. But Condon had a good chance to learn his voice and accent; also he was able to assure himself, through the man's knowledge of details that had not been published, that his man had been in the baby's room.

After this, there was a good deal of correspondence between Condon and John, always with many precautions on John's part. The letters were all similar in their Germanic grammar, misspellings, and handwriting to the original kidnap note found at Hopewell. John's conversation with Condon also contained many German locutions, and his voice had a distinct German accent.

There were weeks of negotiations, cryptic advertisements, attempts by Condon to see John again. Finally, on Thursday, March 31, Condon got a letter that told him to have the money ready on Saturday, April 2. He would receive instructions about where and how to deliver it.

Meanwhile the newspapers were printing all sorts of rumors. One was that the Morgan bank had offered $250,000 to Lindbergh to pay the ransom. Breckinridge was livid; stories like that might make the kidnapers think they were pikers in asking for only $70,000. (Though Lindbergh was well off, he was not a rich man. He had more than $70,000, of course, and his wife's family had millions. Still, $70,000 was a huge sum to him; although, needless to say, he never had any hesitancy about paying it.)

Elmer Irey, of the Treasury, insisted that Lindbergh put gold notes in the ransom bundle; gold notes, yellow U.S. currency, were scarce and easier to trace. Lindbergh at first demurred, but he yielded when Irey threatened to step out of the case. Two ransom packages of 5,150 bills, totaling $70,000, were made up at J. P. Morgan & Company. That international banking firm had plenty of the scarce gold notes on hand. Samples of the paper and string used in making the bundles were put in a Morgan vault for later use as evidence. A list of the bills' numbers was kept.

On April 2, Condon put the message demanded by his correspondent in the *American*: "Yes. Everything O.K. Jafsie." That afternoon, he and Lindbergh stuffed the two packages of bills into a wooden box. And then they waited. And waited. At Condon's house in the Bronx.

The time crawled. An hour passed. Another. It was nearly eight o'clock when the doorbell rang. Condon's daughter opened the door to a short, thin man with dark hair, a taxi driver. After handing the girl an envelope the man drove off.

Lindbergh opened the envelope. It contained a note of instructions for Condon. He was to go to a nursery on Tremont Avenue. "Bergen Greenhauses florist." There would be another envelope there with instructions. They had three-quarters of an hour to reach the greenhouse, and they were warned not to notify the police. The signature was exactly the same as the others—the interlocked circles.

They took the same car in which Condon had been driven to his first meeting with John, a Ford coupé. Lindbergh drove. He was wearing a shoulder holster with a gun in it.

The message at the greenhouse told Condon to walk down a dirt road, which ran alongside St. Raymond's Cemetery, adjacent to the florist's. Condon started to do so, with Lindbergh sitting in the car, waiting. The money was still in the Ford, too. Condon thought the dirt road might lead him into a trap, so he turned and walked in a different direction past the cemetery, staying on the main road, Tremont Avenue. He walked back and forth past the cemetery gates, then called to Lindbergh, "I guess there's no one here. We'd better go back."

A man's voice from the cemetery shouted, "Hey, Doctor!" A figure could be seen crouching behind a tombstone within the cemetery.

"Hey, Doctor, over here!" the voice shouted, loud enough for Lindbergh to hear.

Condon went into the cemetery. It was John again. They had a brief, sharp bargaining talk. Condon suddenly got an impulse to try to save Lindbergh's money and told John he couldn't get $70,000, but had $50,000. He got him to agree to accept the smaller sum. Then, when he left to get the money, John went to get the note he was supposed to give in exchange—a memorandum of the baby's whereabouts. Lindbergh took the $20,000 package from the wooden box, leaving the promised $50,000 ransom.

John handed over an envelope as Condon gave him the box. But he told Condon not to open the letter for six hours. Condon agreed, and John looked over some of the ransom bills to see if they were marked; then he shook hands with Condon and told him he had done a good job. "Your work was perfect," he said.

When Condon handed the unopened note to Lindbergh in the car, he told him of his promise not to open it for six hours. Lindbergh held the envelope and thought. "Well," he said, "if that was the agreement [we will] live up to it."

They drove to a deserted house owned by Condon, and talked it over. Then they decided to open the note to see if it was a fake. If it was, and they waited, they would have no chance of retrieving the ransom. So they opened it and read a handwritten letter:

the boy is on Boad Nelly. it is a small Boad 28 feet long. two persons are on the Boad. the are innosent. you will find the Boad between Horseneck Beach and Gay Head near Elizabeth Island.

Lindbergh and Condon were overjoyed. They thought they had received accurate instructions for finding the baby.

However, days of search by Lindbergh in an airplane, and by Coast Guard boats, failed to turn up the "Boad Nelly" or the baby.

Meanwhile, Gaston Means claimed to have got rid of Mrs. McLean's $104,000 through some mischance, a story the authorities did not believe. He tried for another $35,000 from Mrs. McLean, but was frustrated by one of her suspicious friends.

John Hughes Curtis, the Virginia boatbuilder with the rum-running connections, claimed he had made contact with a man called Dynamite on April 18. Dynamite, a Scandinavian, had a schooner on which the Lindbergh baby was being held, Curtis said. Also, he met a man called John, who tallied with the by then published accounts of Condon's graveyard John, and saw some of the ransom bills. He even tallied them with some of the ransom-bill numbers published in the newspapers. John and Dynamite wanted more money, it seems. They had never intended to be satisfied with only one ransom payment.

For the next twenty-four days, Curtis kept Lindbergh occupied with comings and goings, alarms and excursions. The family was in a constant state of agonized hope. A boat was chartered, the *Cachalot,* to make rendezvous with the kidnapers. Lindbergh was aboard the *Cachalot* at Cape May, New Jersey, trying to get in touch with the kidnapers when he got word that his son had been found, dead.

It was early that day, on May 12, 1932, that a truck driver stumbled on the baby's body in a shallow grave in some woods about a mile from the Lindbergh house. It was taken to a Trenton funeral home which served as the county morgue. Mrs. Lindbergh and her mother were told of the discovery by the state police, who said it was not necessary for them to see the body. Betty Gow identified the baby. An autopsy revealed the cause of death as a fractured skull.

Lindbergh had been notified too late to get there that day. The next day he went to the morgue to identify the body, along with the doctor who had delivered the baby.

Lindbergh wore no hat. His face was pale, drawn. It showed no emotion, only fatigue. He walked over to a table on which something was covered by a sheet. "Take that off," he said. Somebody picked up the sheet and stepped back.

Lindbergh stared at the body. His face flushed. He bent over, looked into the mouth, and counted the teeth. He looked at the foot with the overlapping toes.

He walked into the next room. Erwin E. Marshall, Mercer County prosecutor, asked, "Colonel Lindbergh, are you satisfied that it is the body of your baby?"

"I am perfectly satisfied that it is my child," Lindbergh answered.

The body was cremated.

Then the police began to check up on the various people, like Curtis, Means, Rosner, et al., who had forced themselves into the case—not excepting Dr. Condon.

John Hughes Curtis was the first to crack. He signed a full confession that he had created his story from a "distorted mind." He regretted the "inconvenience" he had caused Colonel Lindbergh, and trusted he would be forgiven the "worry and injustice I did him in his time of grief." All the hopes he had cruelly aroused had been a fraud. Now everyone who had anything to do with the case was under suspicion. Colonel Schwarzkopf, of the New Jersey state police, said that he had been holding back in the hope of recovering the baby alive. Now that hope was gone, he intended to dig and grill and pursue every clue to find the murderer.

There were many questions raised about Condon. Why had he

been so anxious to help? Why had everything happened in the Bronx? Why had he risked his life? The insinuation was that he had been connected with the kidnaper, perhaps had even kept part of the money. He was called in for questioning by the police. His mail became filled with hate letters. He got so many telephone threats he had to change his phone number to an unlisted one. Colonel Breckinridge told the Lindberghs how the old man was suffering for his good deed, and said that something should be done. Lindbergh took time out in the midst of his grief to write Condon a letter.

MY DEAR DR. CONDON:

Mrs. Lindbergh and I want to thank you for the great assistance you have been to us. We fully realize that you have devoted the major portion of your time and energy to bring about the return of our son. We wish to express to you our sincere appreciation for your courage and cooperation.

Sincerely,

CHARLES A. LINDBERGH

The letter was released for publication.

Police work became much more intensive in other directions after the child's body was found. A famous handwriting expert was called in to examine the ransom notes; there were fourteen of the letters, all apparently written by the same hand. The wood from the three-piece extension ladder that had been used to reach the baby's bedroom was sent to an expert in the Department of Agriculture. Lindbergh went back to work, looking gaunt and older.

The news pressure continued to mount. Now it was being fed by the nation-wide hunt for the kidnaper and by the trials of Gaston Means and of Curtis. Means was tried in Washington, D.C., early in June, 1932. He was convicted on two counts of larceny (for the $104,000) and sentenced to fifteen years in federal prison. It was the third conviction in his career. Later he was convicted of attempted extortion (for the $35,000) and got another two years.

Curtis was brought to trial in Flemington, New Jersey, on June 27, on the vague charge of obstructing justice. Strange as it seems, what he had done was not illegal. He hadn't been out for money; he had, in fact, spent some of his own on the hunt for the kidnapers. There was no law to cover what he had done, which was mainly to rouse the hopes of Anne and Charles Lindbergh, to keep them on tenterhooks for more than a month, to take their time and energy

Charles A. Lindbergh, Jr., at the age of eight, photographed with his father, Congressman C. A. Lindbergh. *Brown Brothers*

A photograph taken in March, 1927, several weeks before Lindbergh's historic flight. The man to Lindbergh's right is B. F. Mahoney, president of the Ryan Aircraft Company, which was building the *Spirit of St. Louis*.   *Culver Pictures*

Impelled to uncharacteristic anxiety by newspaper stories emphasizing possible disaster, Lindbergh's mother, Evangeline Land Lindbergh, visited her son a week before he took off on his New York–Paris flight.   *UPI*

Just before takeoff, early in the morning of May 20, 1927.
Lindbergh stands bareheaded beneath the wing of his plane. *UPI*

After Lindbergh's arrival at Le Bourget field outside Paris, May 21, 1927.
Brown Brothers

Right: Lindbergh with U.S. Ambassador to France Myron T. Herrick (right, with hat and cane) acknowledging the cheers of a Paris crowd.
Brown Brothers

Below: Part of the crowd around Lindbergh's plane at Croydon Aerodrome, England, just after he landed, May 9, 1927.
Brown Brothers

A hero's return: Lindbergh, in mufti, debarking from the U.S. cruiser *Memphis*, in Washington, D.C., June 11, 1927. His mother is in the background. *Brown Brothers*

Eighteen hundred tons of paper showered on Lindbergh's triumphal march up Broadway on June 13, 1927. An estimated 4,500,000 New Yorkers watched the parade, the biggest crowd in the city's history. *UPI*

Charles Lindbergh with his fiancée, Anne Morrow, and her parents,
Ambassador Dwight Morrow and Mrs. Morrow.   *Brown Brothers*

Mr. and Mrs. Charles A. Lindbergh stand in front of their plane, *Sirius,* during their 1931 flight north to the Orient from New York to China. *Brown Brothers.*

Lindbergh prophesied disaster for Army attempts to fly air mail in 1934.
Here he is shown with War Secretary George H. Dern, who asked Lindbergh's
support of government action, without success, March 10, 1934.   *UPI*

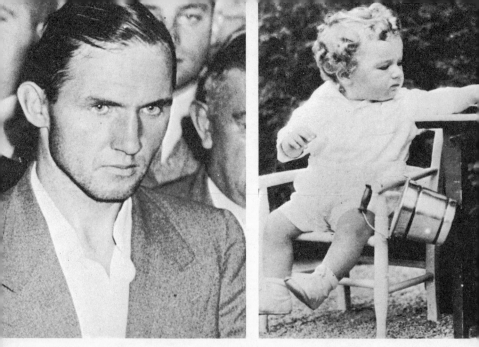

Bruno Richard Hauptmann (left), Bronx carpenter, was convicted in 1935
of first-degree murder of kidnaped Charles Augustus Lindbergh, Jr. (right).
Hauptmann was executed in the electric chair in April, 1936.   *UPI*

Part of the crowd outside Flemington, New Jersey, courthouse during the
Hauptmann trial in February, 1935. People's faces reflect the carnival
atmosphere that surrounded the proceedings.   *UPI*

Lindbergh with the other delegates to the Fourth International Congress of Experimental Cytology, August, 1936, at which the perfusion pump, developed by Lindbergh in collaboration with Dr. Alexis Carrel, was exhibited.   *UPI*

Lindbergh leaving the White House on the day of the National Advisory Committee on Aeronautics Conference, April 20, 1939. He is thought to have reported on European air strength to President Roosevelt.   *UPI*

Lindbergh was the isolationist movement's biggest draw. This is the audience at an America First rally he addressed in Chicago on April 18, 1941, where he urged that Americans "unite to stay out of war."   *UPI*

Lindbergh greets Dr. J. F. ("Jafsie") Condon, a go-between in the effort to recover the kidnaped Lindbergh baby, at an America First rally in New York City, April 23, 1941.   *UPI*

Anne Morrow Lindbergh is cheered by the audience waiting for her husband to speak at an America First rally, Philadelphia, May 29, 1941.   *UPI*

Lindbergh while he was serving as technical representative for an aircraft company in the Pacific during World War II, 1944.
United Air Craft

Lindbergh and Harry Guggenheim meet at a ceremony at the American Museum of Natural History, April 21, 1948, honoring a man they both believed in and supported: the late Robert H. Goddard, the father of modern rocketry.   *UPI*

At the invitation of the U.S. Air Forces, Lindbergh made a tour of air bases during the Berlin Airlift to suggest methods for improving the operation. Here he is shown with Lt. Gen. John K. Cannon, commanding general of the U.S. Air Forces in Europe, at the Rhine-Main Base in Frankfurt, January 21, 1949.
UPI

Lindbergh (right) next to Harry Guggenheim at an Aeronautical Sciences Institute dinner, January 25, 1954, where he received a Guggenheim medal. Mrs. Lindbergh is at table (arrow).   *UPI*

Brigadier General Lindbergh reports to the Pentagon in November, 1954, for several weeks of active duty shortly after being commissioned in the Air Force Reserve. Lindbergh held no Army rank from 1941 to 1954.   *UPI*

Jon Lindbergh, Charles Lindbergh's eldest son, aboard a Navy vessel, 1954. Jon was trained as a frogman.   *UPI*

Mr. and Mrs. Julien Feydy at their wedding in Douzillac, France, December 23, 1963. Mrs. Feydy was Anne Spencer Lindbergh; her mother, Anne Morrow Lindbergh, is at left.   *Paris Match*

and prey on their good will. He had perpetrated a cruelty on two young people that is beyond belief. Why? It would take a psychiatrist to untangle his motives. He said in a signed statement that he had been "insane . . . for the time being."

Yet, in order to convict him, the jury had to go through some mental gymnastics. They had to accept the idea that what Curtis first said about being in touch with the kidnapers was *true*. If he was to be found guilty, it had to be on the ground that after telling this lone truth he had lied and in so doing hampered the search for the kidnaper: "obstructed justice."

Lindbergh testified during Curtis's trial that he was sure Curtis had *never* been in touch with the kidnapers at any time; that he had lied from the beginning. There was other testimony to this effect. Yet the jury managed to find Curtis guilty of obstructing justice, with a recommendation for mercy.

The penalty could have been three years' imprisonment or a $1,000 fine, or both. On June 28 the judge sentenced Curtis to a year in jail and a $1,000 fine. His lawyers appealed and Curtis was set free on $10,000 bail. On November 6 he came back to Flemington. His lawyer requested that he be resentenced. The judge then suspended the jail sentence, but insisted on payment of the $1,000 fine. The grinning Curtis paid it, and gave out the statement that if he had wanted to fight the case he could have saved his money.

Meanwhile the Lindberghs, under constant surveillance by the press and the public, had to flee Hopewell. They moved to the Morrow house in Englewood, Next Day Hill, which was set in a private estate that could be guarded. Inside they were safe, but outside the roads were clogged with sightseers' cars.

When the time came for Anne Lindbergh to give birth to her second child, she was driven from Englewood in the middle of the night to her mother's town apartment in New York at 4 East Sixty-sixth Street. Jon Lindbergh was born there, August 16, 1932.

Lindbergh issued a statement to the press:

Mrs. Lindbergh and I have made our home in New Jersey. It is naturally our wish to continue to live there near our friends and interests. Obviously, however, it is impossible for us to subject the life of our second son to the publicity which we feel was in large measure responsible for the death of our first.

We feel that our children have a right to grow up normally with other children. Continued publicity will make this impossible. I am appealing to the press to permit our children to lead the lives of normal Americans.

Such appeals had no effect either on the public or on the newspapers. Lindbergh made copy just by breathing. Many lonely or desperate people focused on him in some way, good or bad. They all wanted to get in touch with him. In this large number of people, there was the usual proportion of nuts and cranks. After Jon's birth was announced, the Lindberghs began getting letters threatening to kidnap the child. Lindbergh bought a vicious watchdog to guard Jon. Some of the threats were taken seriously enough by the police to be investigated. Two men were arrested on a charge of attempted extortion, but the case was dismissed for lack of evidence. The next June the Lindberghs decided that it would never be safe to return to Hopewell; instead of selling the place (some promoters offered to buy it; they wanted to open it to the public and charge admission), they donated the estate to a nonprofit foundation set up by themselves and with some eminent people on the board. The purpose was "To provide for the welfare of children, including their education, training, hospitalization, and other purposes, without discrimination in regard to race or creed." The place, High Fields, is still run as a boys' home.

17

THE HAUPTMANN CASE

THE LINDBERGHS HAD BEEN FORCED OUT OF THEIR HOUSE into guarded seclusion. They lived under the constant threat of another kidnaping. But real life is not always intense. During the most horrendous tragedies there are uneventful moments. Life goes on.

The Lindberghs made a special effort not to be submerged by what had happened, by what was continuing to happen. They were handicapped in their effort to recapture a normal existence, but during the years that followed the taking of the baby, they managed to carry on a great many activities both separately and together. Lindbergh went about his airlines business, became involved in a large political controversy regarding air-mail contracts, and worked on two scientific projects in which he had begun to be involved before the kidnaping. (These will be discussed in following chapters.) Mrs. Lindbergh took care of her second child and began her career as a professional writer by writing *North to the Orient*.

After deeding their Hopewell house to the foundation, they left their son Jon in the well-guarded security of the North Haven summer home with Mrs. Morrow, and prepared for a second survey flight for Pan American Airways, this time over the Atlantic.

The purpose of the flight was to survey three alternative routes across the ocean—the northern Greenland route, the southern Azores route, and the great-circle route which Lindbergh had taken to Paris. Said Lindbergh in summing up the venture, "The North Atlantic is the most important, and also the most difficult to fly, of all the oceans crossed by the trade routes of men. . . . Where the distance is short, the climate is severe, as in the north; while in the south, great distances counteract the advantages of a milder season."

The flight began on July 9, 1933, in Flushing Bay, New York, went by way of Newfoundland and Labrador to Copenhagen. The plane they used was the same Lockheed they had flown to China in 1931. Only now it had been refitted with a more powerful engine of 710 horsepower, and with a variable-pitch propeller. It was rechristened *Tingmissartoq,* an Eskimo word meaning "he who flies like a big bird."

"It was necessary to be as independent as possible of outside assistance," Lindbergh wrote. "In 1933, there were no facilities for aircraft at most of the places where we landed. In fact we considered ourselves fortunate when we found a good anchorage and a well-placed buoy to moor to. . . . We often reached our destination without advance information about landing conditions. If they were bad . . . we continued on. . . . We never took off without having alternate destinations within our range. . . . On most flights our plane was heavily overloaded when measured by conventional standards. Our safety lay not in dogmatic formulas of performance and structure, but in the proper balance of constantly changing factors . . . ; sometimes . . . in a quick take-off, as among the icebergs at Angmagssalik; sometimes in a long range . . . and always in extra rations and emergency equipment." The plane carried two complete radios, one waterproof and fitted into a rubber sailboat for an emergency landng at sea. It also mounted just about every instrument available for pilots at the time: directional gyro, gyroscopic horizon, two aperiodic compasses, an ice indicator, and a great many fuel and pressure gauges, as well as the usual instruments—altimeter, rate of climb indicator, tachometer, volt-ammeter, and the like.

Lindbergh made careful studies of terrain and weather en route and sent back handwritten reports to Juan Trippe as he went. From Stockholm in September he wrote: "I believe that a transatlantic air route by way of Greenland and Iceland can be operated satisfactorily during the summer months. . . . Even with existing equipment, it should be possible to compete advantageously with the Atlantic steamship schedules." He said only by flying experimentally the year round could it be determined whether steady winter service could be maintained. "I believe that such flying should be done between bases rather than from one base, and that it is of utmost importance to use only personnel who like the north country and have confidence in its future."

"Stefansson has already stated that one side of Iceland is frequently clear even tho the other is covered with fog," Lindbergh reported. "Our experience and inquiries tended to confirm this."

On their tour, the Lindberghs visited the Faeroe and Shetland islands, Denmark, Sweden, Finland, Russia, Norway, England, Ireland, Scotland, France, the Netherlands, Switzerland, Spain, Portugal, the Azores, the Canary Islands, Río de Oro, and the Cape Verde Islands. It was late November by the time they reached this last spot. Lindbergh picked the island of Santiago as an ideal takeoff point for the long hop to South America. Santiago was two hundred miles off the coast of Africa. Leaving from there would make the difference between a secure flight of sixteen hundred miles across the South Atlantic and a hazardous flight of eighteen hundred miles (from the African mainland)—hazardous because of the plane's limited range.

But at Santiago he found that the wind blew too strongly and steadily to allow them to take off with enough fuel for the transatlantic flight. So they flew back to Bathurst, British Gambia, in Africa—only to be held up there by lack of wind. Without some wind, the heavily loaded plane could not take off. After waiting several days and stripping the plane of every useless ounce, Lindbergh did manage to nurse it into the air with enough gasoline to reach Natal, Brazil, eighteen hundred miles to the southwest.

Mrs. Lindbergh made a book, *Listen! the Wind,* out of the ten-day segment of the trip between Santiago, Bathurst, and Natal, from November 27 to December 6, 1933. From Natal they flew by easy stages to Flushing Bay, landing there on December 19. The entire trip had covered more than twenty-nine thousand miles, and had lasted five months. The plane was placed on exhibit in the Hall of Ocean Life in the Museum of Natural History, in New York City, soon after the Lindberghs' return. In 1955 it was moved to the Air Force Museum at Wright-Patterson Air Force Base, in Dayton, Ohio.

Meanwhile there were some new developments in the kidnaping case. The wood expert from the Department of Agriculture patiently, by intricate scientific devices, traced the different woods in the kidnap ladder to their source. Lindbergh ransom bills began turning up in various places during 1933 and 1934; many were gold notes, now rapidly becoming illegal. The nation was going off the gold standard and the Treasury was calling in such bills. The police asked that any filling station getting a gold note from a motorist jot down on the note the license number of the motorist's car. In September, 1934, one such note turned up at a New York City bank with the license number 4U–13–41 penciled in the margin. The license belonged to a car owned by Richard Hauptmann, a German carpenter who lived at 1279 East 22nd Street, Bronx, New York. Hauptmann, whose full name was Bruno Richard Hauptmann, was interrogated and his house and garage were searched; more than $13,000 of Lindbergh ransom money was found hidden there. The wood in the ladder left near the Hopewell house and the chisel found nearby were traced to Hauptmann. The holes punched in the overlapping circles on the ransom letters were made by one of his tools. Hauptmann was positively identified by Dr. Condon as John.

Hauptmann was arrested. The Lindberghs were in California at the time. They went into seclusion in Will Rogers' house. They came east to Next Day Hill a few days later.

Harold Nicolson arrived in America at this time to write the biography of Dwight Morrow. He had been invited to do so by Mrs. Morrow.

Nicolson came to stay at the Morrow house on September 30, 1934, soon after Hauptmann was caught. He found the Lindberghs there alone; Mrs. Morrow was out to dinner. Anne, he decided, was—"shy, Japanese, clever, gentle, obviously an adorable little person. Charles Lindbergh—slim (though a touch of chubbiness about the cheek), schoolboyish, yet with those delicate prehensile hands which disconcert one's view of him as an inspired mechanic. . . . Lindbergh's hand was resting upon the collar of a dog. I had heard about that dog. . . . He is a police dog of enormous proportions. His name is Thor. . . . Not for a moment did Lindbergh relax his hold upon the collar. It is this monster which guards Jon Lindbergh.

" 'What a nice dog!' I said.

" 'You will have to be a little careful at first, Mr. Nicolson,' he answered.

" 'Is he very fierce?'

" 'He's all that. But he will get used to you in time.' "

Nicolson tried saying the dog's name. It made a sound "not a growl . . . a deep pectoral regurgitation—predatory, savage, hungry."

Lindbergh said it would take the dog about a week to become used to Nicolson. He let Thor go. "If he wags his tail, Mr. Nicolson, you need have no fear," he said. Thor did wag his tail.

Later, after a steadying drink, Nicolson asked what happened if Thor didn't wag his tail. "Well," Lindbergh said, "you must be careful not to pass him. He might get hold of you."

"By the throat?" Nicolson asked.

"Not necessarily," said Lindbergh. "If he does that, you must stay still and holler all you can."

No doubt the dog was savage. But Nicolson did not know Lindbergh well enough to realize that he might have been kidding, just a little. The opportunity to scare an old-school-tie type was probably irresistible to Lindbergh.

On October 8, Lindbergh was called by the New York police to identify Hauptmann's voice, the voice he had heard calling "Hey, Doctor" in St. Raymond's Cemetery. Yet that morning he gave no sign of anything dramatic. At breakfast he helped Nicolson unload his camera, and then said, "Well, I have got to go up to New York—want a lift?" Nicolson, who had already started work on the Morrow biography, said no.

Lindbergh returned toward the end of lunch, and the family chatted gaily. After coffee, Nicolson left the room. But as he walked out, he saw Lindbergh, reflected in a mirror, take his wife's arm and lead her into the study. "Obviously he was telling her what happened in the court," Nicolson wrote to his wife, the novelist Victoria Sackville-West. "But they are splendid in the way that they never intrude this great tragedy on our daily lives. It is real dignity and restraint." What Lindbergh told his wife that day was that he had recognized Hauptmann's voice as the voice in the cemetery.

Lindbergh described Hauptmann as a "magnificent-looking man, very well built." But his eyes were small, said Lindbergh, "like the eyes of a wild boar—mean, shifty, small and cruel."

Once Mrs. Morrow broke down and talked about the kidnaping to Nicolson. It was the night she was flying to California to be with her eldest daughter Elisabeth, who was dying of pneumonia. Then Nicolson said something about her control and courage. "Courage?" Mrs. Morrow said. "Do you know that I cry about that baby of ours every night, even now? [This was two and a half years after the kidnaping.] That is not *courage!*" Elisabeth Morrow Morgan died not long after Mrs. Morrow arrived in California.

The arrest, identification, indictment, and extradition to New Jersey of Hauptmann were counterpointed by a mounting hysteria in the press. The impact of these events could be measured in the amount of mail received by the Lindberghs. When the case was on the front pages, the number of letters mounted to 100,000 a day.

To handle this mountain of mail from strangers, the Lindberghs had worked out a system of having it sent to an office in New York and winnowed by office boys. In this way, many important letters never reached them. Friends and relatives addressed them by special names at a secret address.

The court proceedings against Hauptmann began in Flemington, New Jersey, the Hunterdon county seat, on Wednesday, January 2, 1935. Hauptmann had been in the county jail since October 19. Small, rural Flemington did the best it could to cope with the influx of reporters and publicity hounds who had asked for reservations in the local hotel. At least three hundred reporters came to cover the trial. Among them were Walter Winchell, Edna Ferber, Arthur Brisbane, Fanny Hurst, Damon Runyon, Kathleen Norris, Alexander Woollcott, Adela Rogers St. John, Raoul de Roussy de Sales (*Paris-Soir*), Lionel Shortt (London *Daily Mail*), Dixie Tighe (London *Daily Express*). Café society also attended en masse—film stars, society people, singers, dancers, and perennial first-nighters.

Lindbergh had worn dark glasses and a cap when he observed and listened to Hauptmann at the police station in New York. But he attended the court proceedings in New Jersey without any disguise. He sat there alone watching as the jury was chosen, and his wife joined him when the trial started on January 3. The charge was murder. (Breaking and entering to commit a burglary is a felony, and a death caused during the commission of a felony is a capital crime. On that basis, the state Attorney General, David Wilentz, had been able to get Hauptmann charged with first-degree murder. As a kidnaper Hauptmann could have been charged only with extortion, not a capital offense.)

Anne Lindbergh was the second witness for the prosecution.

Among the questions she had to answer was one by Prosecutor Wilentz about the baby: "Was he healthy?"

Anne Lindbergh replied, "He was very healthy." She described the baby, the fact that he could walk and talk, that his hair was curly. She had to identify the child's wardrobe, and describe the events of the night the baby was kidnaped. It was an exquisitely painful examination, but it was necessary and she went through it in fine style. The defense did not cross-examine.

Lindbergh was the next witness, and his ordeal lasted much longer. He, too, was taken through the events of the night of the crime, particularly the sound he and his wife had heard while chatting in the living room—the sound, probably, of the kidnap ladder breaking or falling to the ground. Lindbergh said it sounded like "the top slats of an orange crate falling off a chair, which I assumed to be in the kitchen." He said he noticed it enough to ask his wife, "What is that?"

His testimony on how he had learned of the kidnaping: "I was reading in the library. Miss Gow called me in a rather excited voice and asked me if I had the baby. I immediately went upstairs into the nursery, and from the appearance of the crib I realized that something had gone wrong. The bedclothing in the crib was in such condition that I felt it was impossible for the baby to have gotten out for himself. The bedclothing was standing stiffly enough so that the opening where the baby had been was still there—the clothing had not collapsed." And he told of the envelope on the radiator containing the kidnap note.

Carefully the prosecutor led him along the trail of events, the second note, the visit to the cemetery with Dr. Condon when he heard the voice calling in a foreign accent, "Hey, Doctor."

"Since that time have you heard the same voice?" Wilentz asked.

"Yes, I have."

"Whose voice was it, Colonel, that you heard calling, 'Hey, Doctor'?"

"It was Hauptmann's voice," Lindbergh replied.

The prosecutor went on to the finding of the child's body, and Lindbergh's identification of it in the Trenton morgue.

Anne Lindbergh's testimony had been peripheral; Charles Lindbergh's was central to the charge of murder. Hauptmann's chief defense counsel, Edward J. Reilly, could not allow it to stand unquestioned.

He immediately went to the attack and asked Lindbergh if he

was carrying a gun. (There were rumors that Lindbergh would shoot Hauptmann.) The judge interrupted, but Lindbergh said he didn't mind answering. He was not carrying a gun.

Reilly asked Lindbergh if he was aware of any local hostility among the residents of Hopewell against him and his family. Lindbergh said he was not. Reilly pressed on, saying that the large Lindbergh estate had sealed a good part of formerly open land from local people, which they might resent. But Lindbergh did not go along with this.

Reilly tried for another opening, asking Lindbergh what he had done to check on the people he had hired as servants in the house. Lindbergh said he had talked to each of them for about half an hour.

"Beyond that, did you go any further?"

"Beyond that I never go any further," Lindbergh replied.

Reilly went into Lindbergh's actions the night of the kidnaping. Did he examine the ground for footprints? Did he want to re-examine the past histories of the servants? No reason, said Lindbergh, to do either; the area in question had been covered with loose gravel that would not reveal footprints and he depended on the thoroughness of the police check of the servants. The defense counsel asked Lindbergh if the butler, Mr. Whateley, would know he wasn't coming to Hopewell on Monday.

"He probably would," Lindbergh said.

"And Mrs. Whateley would be very likely to know—she was the cook wasn't she?"

"It is quite probable."

"But the outside world would not know that you were not coming home Monday night, would it?"

"Very few people would know that."

"Very few people would know that you were going back to New York again on Tuesday, would they, Colonel?"

"Very few people know what I do."

Reilly, the defense counsel, went into other matters. There had been a fox-terrier puppy that played with the baby. Did the dog sound any kind of alarm? Lindbergh said that the dog was not a watchdog and hadn't been trained to give an alarm. Could anyone have come into the house by the front door while the Lindberghs were dining? No, said the Colonel, the front door did not open easily and there was no door closed between the dining room and the front door.

"Then would it be possible for anyone in the house, who knew the house, to take the baby out of the crib and bring it down the main stairs—and to a window?"

"It might have been possible," Lindbergh said.

"Let's take the other course, Colonel. If there was disloyalty in your home, would it be possible for a person acquainted with the home to take the baby out of the crib and descend the servants' staircase and hand it to someone in the garage yard while you were dining?"

Lindbergh said it would have been possible.

Reilly went on to the matter of a footprint on a suitcase in the baby's room, and asked if it wasn't odd that if it was made by the man who was heavy enough to break a rung of the ladder, why hadn't he broken the suitcase? This was obviously not a question within the range of Lindbergh's competence. Reilly swung again into the possibility that some person or persons known or unknown —but not Hauptmann—committed the crime. Had the child been much exposed to strangers, he asked. No, only friends, Lindbergh replied. Had the baby cried out at any time during the evening? Lindbergh said that as far as he knew it had not. The implication that Reilly left with the jury was that no stranger had been near the baby.

Reilly also established that the nurse, Betty Gow, had spent more time with the baby than anyone else had. But when she had called Lindbergh to ask if he had the baby she wasn't hysterical—as though this indicated that she, perhaps, had been the one to hand the baby over to a kidnaper. Round and round went Reilly, circling and attempting to find openings. But the only time he aroused Lindbergh to anger was when he asked if it wasn't peculiar that Dr. Condon's letter offering to help find the kidnaper, in a small, out-of-the-way newspaper, had been almost immediately answered. He asked if Lindbergh hadn't considered the possibility that both questions and answers came from the same person.

"I think that is inconceivable from any practical standpoint," Lindbergh said.

Reilly hammered away at Condon's reliability. Lindbergh hadn't actually seen him get a note from the kidnaper. Lindbergh had said, at the earlier trial of John Hughes Curtis, the fraud from Norfolk, that he had believed that Curtis was in touch with a *gang* who had kidnaped the child.

"Yes," said Lindbergh, "but I found out later that Curtis was not telling me the truth."

When his public inquisition was over, the frenzy of public curiosity continued. Outside the Morrow place, a constant autocade of sightseers moved slowly by. And the Hopewell estate was still overrun by people who searched for souvenirs, the most prized of which were yielded by the actual spot where the baby's body had been buried.

In spite of his dislike of public appearances, Lindbergh showed up every day at the Hauptmann trial. The proceedings dragged on for six weeks as the prosecution tried to weave a tight web of circumstantial evidence around Hauptmann, and the defense retaliated doggedly with question and evasion. Finally, the hearing of evidence ended and Judge Thomas W. Trenchard charged the jury in a long, complicated lecture about the law and the case on the morning of February 13, 1935.

As he went through Hauptmann's testimony, he asked, "Do you believe that?" The charge as printed in the newspapers sounded quite impartial. But, Lindbergh said, it was not. Judge Trenchard's questions did not sound the way they were printed. What he asked was "Do *you* believe THAT?"

After hearing the charge, Lindbergh left the courtroom and drove back to Englewood to be with the family. The jury would deliberate for eleven hours and vote a rumored seven times before it reached a verdict.

The jury had been consulting for only five hours when Mrs. Morrow sat down to dine with the Lindberghs and Harold Nicolson. There were two radios turned on, one in the pantry next to the dining room, one in the dressing room, with the usual music and comedy shows coming through. The family kept up a spirited conversation, but everyone was straining to hear the radio give the newsbreak on the trial.

After dinner they sat in the drawing room talking about Dwight Morrow. Suddenly Mrs. Morrow put her head around a screen and said, "Hauptmann has been condemned to death without mercy." She looked very pale.

They all went into the dressing room, where the radio had been turned up. As Nicolson describes it: "One could hear the almost diabolic yelling of the crowd [the yells of the crowd were really terrifying, Nicolson said later. And Lindbergh replied, "That was a lynching crowd"]. They were all sitting around . . . Anne looking very white and still. 'You have now heard,' broke in the voice of the announcer, 'the verdict in the most famous trial in all history. Bruno Hauptmann now stands guilty of the foulest . . .' 'Turn that off, Charles, turn that off.' Then we went into the pantry and had ginger-beer. Charles sat there on the kitchen dresser looking very pink about the nose. [He had a terrible cold.] 'I don't know,' he said to me, 'whether you have followed this case very carefully. There is no doubt at all that Hauptmann did the thing. My one dread all these years has been that they would get hold of someone as a victim about whom I wasn't sure. I am sure about this—quite sure. It is this way . . .'

"And then quite quietly, while we all sat round in the pantry, he went through the case point by point. It seemed to relieve all of them. He did it very quietly, very simply. He pretended to address his remarks to me only. But I could see that he was really trying to ease the agonised tension through which Betty [Mrs. Morrow] and Anne had passed. It was very well done. It made one feel that here was no personal desire for vengeance or justification; here was the solemn process of law inexorably and impersonally punishing a culprit."

In the Flemington courtroom Wilentz moved for an immediate sentence. Hauptmann stood while the judge complied. "The sentence of the Court is that you suffer death at the time and place and in the manner provided by law," in March, 1935.

There was some dispute about the verdict, some feeling that the jury had come in with a murder verdict unsupported by direct evidence. The *New York Times* editorialized on it: "The charge of the judge and the verdict of the jury established a crime but did not clear away a mystery. We do not yet know exactly what happened on the tragic night at Hopewell. . . . The presiding judge . . . told the jury that the State had been unable to present positive evidence identifying the prisoner at the time and place of the original crime, and that circumstantial evidence alone had to be depended upon . . . beyond a doubt. . . . Hauptmann had guilty knowledge of the outrage and was at least an accessory. The jury [found] him guilty as a principal. . . . Nothing but a confession or the turning up of new evidence can now be expected to throw further light upon a mystery . . ."

But Hauptmann never confessed, and there was no new evidence. There was, however, a lot of legal maneuvering—appeals, stays of execution, denials. Hauptmann became a martyr to some of his fellow-German-Americans; there were rallies at which the name of Hauptmann was cheered, Lindbergh's booed. These rallies were held in German-American neighborhoods, like Yorkville in New York City, and were attended mostly by Bundist groups. The New Jersey Court of Errors and Appeals heard the arguments of Hauptmann's lawyers for a reversal of the verdict. In twelve thousand words the Court refuted the arguments and let the verdict stand. Then there was a petition to the Supreme Court to review the New Jersey decision.

Meanwhile the Governor of New Jersey, Harold Hoffman, got into the case personally. He actually went to see Hauptmann secretly in his death cell. Later he let this fact be known and made headlines with it. He said he wasn't worried about Hauptmann the individual, but about truth and justice. He issued a statement saying that Hauptmann ought to be given a personal hearing by the New Jersey Court of Pardons so he could plead his own case for life imprisonment.

There was more than the smell of politics in this. Hoffman was a Republican, a glamour-boy governor; Wilentz, the young prosecutor in the Lindbergh case, had been built up as his probable Democratic opponent by the successful handling of the trial. In this situation Hauptmann's life was almost an election issue. Meanwhile the Supreme Court of the United States rejected the plea of Hauptmann's counsel for review of the case.

Politicians still got a lot of publicity mileage out of it. Hoffman granted Hauptmann a reprieve of several months so that new evidence could be hunted. H. L. Mencken got into the act with a letter to Hoffman saying he thought Hauptmann was guilty, but that the crime could not have been committed alone. A crank outfit called the Committee of Witnesses made the fantastic charge that the crime was a reprisal against Lindbergh for having made his flight to the Orient in 1931, which, they said, was for the purpose of

stealing Chinese air routes from the German Lufthansa Airline. The
Committee's conclusion and message: vote against the Republican
party, because they had deliberately failed to catch the kidnapers.

It was in the midst of this kind of social science fiction that the
Lindberghs attempted to piece together their lives and, most particularly, to give their second son, Jon, a normal existence. A flood
of letters—part of it hate or crank mail—continued to pour in on
them at the Morrow house. Jon had to be driven to nursery school
by a teacher, but even then he was not safe from the Peeping
Toms.

One day in the fall of 1935, a black sedan came alongside the
teacher's car and pushed it to the side of the road. Men jumped out
of the sedan and onto the running board of the teacher's car. The
teacher screamed in terror—but the men were not kidnapers, only
newsreel and newspaper cameramen out for a news beat. They got
closeups of Jon which appeared on the front page of the next day's
paper, although Lindbergh had a working agreement with the press
that no photographs of his second son should be published.

After this, Jon was taken out of the school and kept at home
under armed guard. Now three years old, he had lived since birth in
an atmosphere of fear and secrecy.

Lindbergh told a friend that "we Americans are a primitive
people. We do not have discipline. Our moral standards are low.
. . . It shows in the newspapers, the morbid curiosity over crimes
and murder trials. Americans seem to have little respect for law, or
the rights of others."

The kidnaping threats against Jon, against Mrs. Lindbergh and
Mrs. Morrow fluctuated with the amount of news in the papers. But
the number and quality of threats became especially intense after
Hauptmann's conviction. Lindbergh could guard himself—he refused
a bodyguard, but did frequently carry a revolver—but he could not
guarantee the security of his family. Nobody could, although the
police made at least a dozen arrests of would-be extortionists.

Lindbergh had visited England twice, in 1927 and in 1933. He
thought that the English "had a greater regard for law and order
than the people of any other nation."

On Thursday, December 19, 1935, Deac Lyman was in the city
room of the New York Times when Lindbergh called him and invited him to come out to Englewood, where he was staying with

the Morrows. He said, "I've got something to talk about, but not on the telephone."

Lyman had to go to New Jersey anyway; he took his wife, Mab, with him. Mrs. Lyman talked to Anne and played with Jon in one room while in another Lindbergh said to Lyman, "Deac, I'm taking my family to England. I've got to get Anne and the baby away. Crank letters have started again. There have been threats against the family. I'm going to make England my home."

Lyman couldn't talk for a moment. Then he asked Lindbergh why he wasn't giving the story to C. B. Allen of the *Herald Tribune* and other reporters he trusted.

Lindbergh said, "If I give the information to a half-dozen people there will be a half-dozen versions. I know if I give it to you it will be right. If it's in the *Times* first the others will pick it up.

Lyman said, "Judas, Slim, don't you know this is one hell of a news story?"

Lindbergh said, "I don't know about that; it's up to you."

The details were worked out. Lindbergh told Lyman that he planned to sail secretly with his family on Sunday, December 22. He had booked passage on the freighter *American Importer* leaving from West Twentieth Street in New York. Nobody would know they were on board until he revealed their identity.

He asked Lyman to hold the story until the ship had been at sea for twenty-four hours. He promised to keep Lyman informed of any change in plans.

On Saturday, Lindbergh called Lyman at home to say goodbye and to assure him that they were definitely leaving.

Lyman was not working on Friday or Saturday. He came in to New York late Saturday evening, after Sunday's *Times* was on the presses, and revealed his story to the city editor, Bruce Rae.

Lyman had to do a bit of arguing with Rae to prevent him from running the story immediately, but he assured Rae that Lindbergh was totally reliable and would not give the story to anyone else. Lyman stayed in the city room until he read on the ticker that the *American Importer* was outward bound.

He came in on Sunday to write the story, which was handled with the greatest secrecy. No copy boy touched it; it was given for setting to a couple of typesetters carefully chosen for their closed mouths. It was put into the Monday *Times*, December 23. Lyman

vast vulgarity of its sensationalists, publicity-seekers, petty politicians and yellow newspapers?"

However, the New York *Daily News* disagreed: "He would have
been pestered less if he had acted more as a popular hero is
supposed to act, and been less embarrassed in the public gaze."

A few years later Lindbergh told Larry Kelly, of the Hearst
papers, that the reason for going to England was that "it was
impossible for me or for my family to lead a normal life because of
the tremendous public hysteria. . . . We couldn't go to a theater, a
store, or even for a stroll without being surrounded, stared at and
harassed.

"We came to the conclusion that it would be best to take a trip
abroad for a time until these events had been forgotten and we
could return to ordinary life." There had been no question that they
would ultimately return, Lindbergh said. "America always was and
always will be my country."

The Lindberghs were received with some excitement in England,
but after the original flurry they were allowed to settle quietly in the
country. They rented Long Barn, Harold Nicolson's house near
Sevenoaks-Weald, in Kent. They lived there quietly for two years,
until 1938, when they moved to France.

At 8:47 on the evening of April 3, 1936, Hauptmann was electro-
cuted in the State Prison at Trenton, New Jersey. The appeals and
stays of executions had given him more than a year of life beyond
the date set by Judge Trenchard for his execution. He died maintaining his innocence.

Comparing Lindbergh's actions and statements before 1932 with
those after 1935 makes it clear that it was the events of this period
that turned his aversion to publicity into a towering insistence on
privacy. An acquaintance calls his fear of the public a kind of
paranoia; if it is, it is a paranoia based on a number of persistent
reality factors, not the least of which was the threat to the life of his
child.

The kidnaping and death of his first-born, exacerbated by four
years of vulgar exploitation by the news media, some officials, and
many of his fellow-citizens, left Lindbergh with a psychic wound
that has never healed. Unlike his wife, he has never been able to
discuss the case with his children. There is one exception. This took

waited for the first papers off the press, took one and went h[...]

By a fantastic coincidence, a New York *American* reporter [...] sitting behind Lyman in the train he took to Long Island and sa[...] the front-page headline in the *Times* over his shoulder, and so th[...] *American* managed to run a paragraph on the Lindbergh departure that day.

But as Meyer Berger said, "The Times had put over one of the greatest exclusive news stories of the generation. . . . It was generally recognized that the story had come [Lyman's] way because of the character he had established as a trustworthy newspaperman." It later won Lyman the Pulitzer Prize.

The story started on page one of the *Times* under a four-column headline:

LINDBERGH FAMILY SAILS FOR ENGLAND
TO SEEK A SAFE, SECLUDED RESIDENCE;
THREATS ON SON'S LIFE FORCE DECISION

"Colonel Charles A. Lindbergh has given up residence in the United States and is on his way to establish a home in England," Lyman wrote. "Although [the family] do not plan to give up their American citizenship they are prepared to live abroad permanently, if that should be necessary." The story spoke of the ebb and flow of threats and of the final, crowning incident of the cameramen and the car. It concluded: "And so the man who eight years ago was hailed as an international hero and a good will ambassador between the peoples of the world is taking his wife and son to establish, if he can, a secure haven for them in a foreign land."

There was much editorial comment on an American hero being forced to flee his own country, but most of it blamed the press and the public. A few called Lindbergh a "quitter." There was no doubt, according to the Morrows' neighbors, that the Lindberghs had been in fear for Jon's life for months. Considering Lindbergh's strong sense of patriotism, the move had to be a desperation measure.

The consensus was probably summed up in the *Herald Tribune*'s editorial hope that the Lindberghs would find in England a "tolerable home . . . in a safer and more civilized land than ours has shown itself to be. . . . When has a nation made life unbearable to one of its most distinguished men," the *Tribune* asked, "through a sheer inability to protect him from its criminals and lunatics and the place one day about 1950 when a nameless stranger, a young man, rang the bell of the Lindbergh house in Darien. Reeve, Lindbergh's youngest daughter, then about five years old, answered the door. The man told the little girl that he was her long-lost brother, Charles A. Lindbergh, Jr. He insisted on seeing "their" parents.

Lindbergh was working in his study, and Mrs. Lindbergh was in New York. Reeve knew that her father did not like being disturbed, so she called her sister Anne instead. Anne, about ten at the time, tried to get the stranger to leave but he refused. So the two girls decided to tell their father.

Lindbergh came out immediately. He talked quietly to the man and finally got him to go. He did not become obviously upset. After the man left, Lindbergh spoke to the girls unemotionally for a while about the kidnaping—the only time he has talked of it to any of his children. When he was certain that the girls were no longer upset at the intrusion, he went back to his work.

Lindbergh is still bitter at the press for the barbarous things they did between 1932 and 1935. A few years ago he was in Washington to attend a professional conference. He was in one room; the conference was ready to begin in another. But between the two was a roomful of reporters. In order to get to the conference, Lindbergh would have had to walk through that room. He refused to budge unless the reporters left.

"But you'll only have to wave at them and say hello," a friend said.

"Get those people out of there," Lindbergh replied.

Somebody remarked that they were only doing their job.

"Yes, and they were only doing their job when they pried the lid off my son's coffin to take pictures in the morgue," Lindbergh replied.

Mention of the tragedy is enough to throw Mrs. Lindbergh into a state of complete silence, even today. And the Lindbergh children reflect this trauma. When one Lindbergh child recently found a copy of George Waller's book *Kidnap, the Story of the Lindbergh Case* in a friend's house, she methodically tore the book to pieces.

The sensational circumstances surrounding the case helped to focus attention on the legal loopholes that existed in the crime of kidnaping and furthered the passage of national legislation against the crime. Until then, only state laws had prevailed, and penalties varied. (New Jersey had no state law against kidnaping until after the crime.) But as a result of the Lindbergh case, the United States Congress passed a law in June, 1932, making kidnaping, in effect, a federal crime. Under the new statute, it was presumed that if a kidnaped person was not returned within a week, he had been taken across a state line, and federal authorities could enter the case without invitation by local police. The waiting period was later shortened by legislation to twenty-four hours. Since this law was passed, more than six hundred and seventy-five cases of kidnaping have taken place in the United States. The Federal Bureau of Investigation solved or helped to solve all but three of them. The law that gave them their authority is still known as "the Lindbergh law."

In January, 1967, the chief Federal District judge in New Haven, Connecticut, held that the Lindbergh law was unconstitutional because it stipulated that if the defendants were tried by a jury, the jury might recommend a death penalty; whereas if they elected to be tried by a judge, or pleaded guilty, they would not suffer this hazard. Thus, "the defendants must risk their lives to get a jury trial . . . [which is] a constitutional right," the Judge, William H. Timberg, said. The final disposition of the law is still in doubt.

18

DR. CARREL

ON MAY 16, 1932, SOON AFTER THE BODY OF THEIR SON was found, the Lindberghs received a letter that said, "There are no words that can properly express what I feel at the end of your great tragedy. . . . Today, the final blow has come. But life continues. I wish for you both all that the future holds in store for those who possess indomitable courage." The letter was signed "Alexis Carrel."

No stranger knew that Lindbergh knew the famous Carrel. It was a relationship he managed to keep secret from the public for five years.

It began in 1930 when Anne Lindbergh's sister, Elisabeth Reeve Morrow, was stricken with a dangerous heart condition. This was a mechanical problem, something that a surgeon might repair if he could operate on the heart. But in 1930 heart surgery was as impossible as the flight to Paris had been in 1920—the machinery simply didn't exist. An operation on a living heart means opening the chest. This collapses the lungs and requires a means of breathing for the patient in some mechanical fashion. Then, to work on the heart, that organ must be stopped. To keep the patient alive, his blood must be circulated mechanically, too. What was needed was some kind of blood and air pump.

Lindbergh asked the family doctor why, with the technology then available, a heart-lung machine had not been invented. The family doctor didn't know. Another doctor, an anesthetist who had attended Anne Lindbergh at the time of Jon's birth, seemed a more promising source of information. He offered to introduce Lindbergh to a man he knew, a medical researcher, who was working on the problem of a heart pump, or something similar. The man was at the

Rockefeller Institute, in New York City. Lindbergh eagerly assented to the meeting.

On November 28, 1930, Lindbergh was introduced to Dr. Alexis Carrel at the Rockefeller Institute. Carrel was a star performer in that famous group of scientists.* He was a Nobel Prize laureate,** the first and for a long time the only surgeon who had won that prize. He was a man of enormous erudition and self-confidence, a kind of maverick in the scientific community who was carving out new disciplines for himself. He had come to the Rockefeller Institute because he couldn't have the kind of freedom he wanted in his native France, where the scientific establishment created a rigid environment.

Carrel was a tiny man† with brilliant eyes; one was bright blue, the other dark brown. He had a way of sizing people up instantaneously; he would shake hands while peering through his pince-nez at their faces. He believed that every person has the qualities of his soul, mind, and body written on his face. This was done, he used to say, by the brain through its control of nerves and muscles which molded the features to mirror character. If his scrutiny gave him a good impression, he would begin to smile and talk. His talk consisted of questions at first. But if he had a bad opinion of a face, he would shrug and turn away.

He accepted Lindbergh immediately. And Lindbergh, not one to give his confidence quickly, had a reaction similar to Carrel's. According to Kenneth Davis, "both spoke of their [meeting],

* The Rockefeller Institute for Medical Research was established in 1901 by John D. Rockefeller to "conduct, assist and encourage investigations in the sciences and arts of hygiene, medicine and surgery . . . in the nature and causes of disease and the methods of its prevention and treatment." In 1908 the New York state legislature extended the corporate charter by special act to allow the Institute to carry on educational work as well. It has long been known for the brilliance of its research and teaching staff. Peyton Rous (another Nobel laureate) and René Dubos are two members. In 1954 the Rockefeller Institute became Rockefeller University, part of the University of the State of New York, and is empowered to grant degrees of doctor of philosophy and doctor of medical science, as well as honorary degrees. It has an endowment of more than $130,000,000.

** He won it in 1912 for his method of suturing blood vessels during surgery instead of destroying them, and for work in transplanting organs. This work was also basic to later developments in blood transfusion.

† Who stated in Man, the Unknown: "Men of genius are not tall. Mussolini is of medium size, and Napoleon was short."

shaking hands, their sharp gaze into each other's eyes, as one of the remarkable experiences of their lives: it was as if an electric current passed between them." Carrel believed in extrasensory perception, and so did Lindbergh.

Carrel worked in a black hooded monk's robe in his laboratory, as did all his assistants. The explanation was that black absorbed light instead of reflecting it, but the effect was theatrical, particularly as Carrel and his staff were the only black-robed people in the Rockefeller Institute. Carrel absent-mindedly often wore his black hood into the building's cafeteria.

Accepting Lindbergh as an equal, Carrel immediately began explaining what he was up to. His purpose, he said, was to study organs of the body *in vitro*, the scientist's description of the examination of living tissue in a glass environment. The study of organs up to that time had been in the hands of the pathologists, who had worked only on dead tissue. Living organs were something different, Carrel said, and if they could be kept alive outside the body, there was no telling what medical advances might not be possible; for example, dying organs might be removed, revived, and replaced to function once more within the body.

He told Lindbergh he had been working on this problem for more than twenty years. He had built an apparatus, a kind of pump, that would keep organs alive outside the body, but not for very long. They would soon become infected with disease and die. What he needed was a better apparatus that would keep the organs alive and free of infection, and a means of using blood in the machine without having the blood clot.

"For me," Lindbergh wrote, "that began an association with an extraordinarily great man. . . . To me, his true greatness lay in the unlimited penetration, curiosity, and scope of his mind, in his fearlessness of opinion, in his deep concern about the trends of modern civilization and their effect on his fellow men."

Lindbergh, as he does when learning something new, listened carefully and punctuated Carrel's discourse with simple but extremely pertinent questions. When he left, he immediately began to work on the problem. In a couple of weeks he had brought back a glass perfusion pump that had been blown to his specifications by a glassmaker in Princeton, New Jersey. It was designed to perfuse organs, through their blood vessels, with the fluids necessary to life. It did not work, but it was a good start.

Actually, it took about four years of trial and error before Lindbergh overcame this problem, which seemed almost insuperable to other scientists. One of his co-workers was Dr. Richard J. Bing, now chairman of the department of medicine at Wayne State University, in Detroit, Michigan. Dr. Bing recalls Lindbergh as "direct, sensitive and simple. . . . I think it is because of his simplicity that he dared to do what others had failed to attempt."

In the course of his work on the pump, Lindbergh developed a system for washing the blood used in the apparatus. He also invented a quick way of separating serum from whole blood by means of a centrifuge, replacing the laborious process of grinding plasma by hand with mortar and pestle. He was a dedicated worker who spent whole days in Carrel's laboratories, sometimes forgetting to eat.

He was well liked by the people who worked with him, but was generally removed from the life of the Rockefeller Institute by the seclusion in which Carrel carried on his researches. However, even in that monkish atmosphere Lindbergh never lost his penchant for practical jokes. One of his favorites was "a bucket of water over the door so that when you opened the door you got drenched," Dr. Bing recalls. "This I was told, since I never got a shower of that sort." But Bing, and those who did get drenched, apparently felt there was no malice in Lindbergh's horseplay. They knew he liked sour-ball candies, so they would put them in his bag.

When the perfusion pump was developed, the first announcement was made in June, 1935, in an article in *Science* magazine signed by both Carrel and Lindbergh. The names alone were enough to make news, but the description of how cats' organs—ovaries, hearts, kidneys—not only lived, but went through cycles of life in the apparatus, added a great deal of excitement.

There was a kind of chemistry in the association of the two names with a development that seemed fraught with possibilities for extending life. *Time* magazine theorized at length about the potential value of the pump. There was a spate of headlines and editorials in newspapers. Lindbergh was aloof from this; he wrote a technical article on the workings of the pump for the *Journal of Experimental Medicine,* published by the Rockefeller Institute, in

September, 1935. A year later, at the International Cytological Congress in Copenhagen (cytology is the study of cells), Lindbergh demonstrated his pump and Carrel lectured on its uses in science and medicine. Lindbergh was quite factual; Carrel theorized on how the pump might heal organs or limbs, "removed from the body and placed in the Lindbergh pump, as patients are placed in a hospital."

"You've got to understand that because Lindbergh and Carrel did this thing together, it was blown up out of all proportion," said a Rockefeller doctor. "If they had devised a new mousetrap there would have been loud screams about it." The pump was, as a colleague of Carrel's put it, "a step in the right direction, useful to study isolated organs. This study has since become an important branch of science. The pump was extremely sophisticated for its time—and quite remarkable, considering that the man who engineered it had had no training in this work. It was a very ingenious piece of apparatus that Lindbergh worked out. I got mine out the other day and looked at it—it's like looking at your grandmother's picture. We don't use that pump any more, but we do use later developments based on the same principle."

Another colleague of both men says, "The newspapers called it 'the Lindbergh heart,' but it was not a heart. It had nothing to do with the later development of the heart-lung machine. Its real worth was in a scientific area of study that was not nearly so dramatic as the newspapers made out by calling it a heart. But it was an important contribution to science, all the same."

Actually, the Lindbergh pump is much more than a museum piece even today. In the November-December, 1966, issue of *Cryobiology*, a journal devoted to reports on biological experiments at low temperatures, there is an article on Lindbergh's work in this field.* It is an extension of his work with Carrel. Researchers at the U.S. Naval Research Institute in Bethesda, Maryland, working in the field of organ transplant, had come across the Lindbergh-Carrel reports and were astonished to find that Lindbergh and Carrel had better results in keeping organs alive thirty years ago than researchers were getting currently with "new and improved" equip-

* "An Apparatus for the Pulsating Perfusion of Whole Organs," by C. A. Lindbergh, V. P. Perry, T. I. Malinin, and G. H. Mouer.

ment. They got in touch with Lindbergh, and had some of his pumps made by Corning Glass. Then they asked Lindbergh to design a new pump that would be much less expensive and withstand the cold of cryobiology. This he did successfully. Monkey hearts have been brought back to life in the equipment. The ultimate purpose of the Navy research is to bring to fruition what Carrel had dreamed of—the cultivation and reuse of organs. But cryobiology did not exist when Carrel was alive. The experimenters with the new technique hope to freeze-dry hearts of people who die in accidents, then bring the hearts back to life and implant them in person with dangerous heart conditions.

When he settled in England in 1936, Lindbergh began working on his scientific notes. He visited Carrel on the island of Saint-Gildas, in the English Channel, where Carrel had a summer house which he used for certain experiments. In December, 1937, Lindbergh returned quietly to the United States and stayed there until March, 1938. He wrote his part of a book on which he collaborated with Carrel. *The Culture of Organs* was published in 1938. Its chapters were written alternately by Lindbergh and Carrel, and signed separately. Lindbergh contributed chapters on the design, construction, and operation of the perfusion pump, as well as diagrams and other explanatory material. Carrel wrote the scientific chapters and rationale.

A good example of Lindbergh's scientific writing style is from Chapter II, "The Apparatus." "The composition of all gas in contact with the organ and the perfusion fluid is controlled. Flaming and evaporation of the fluid are prevented. The maximum and minimum pulsation pressures and the pulsation rate are adjustable. The pressure at various points in the pulse cycle can be controlled. The temperature of operation is adjustable. The rate of flow of perfusion fluid can be measured. Changes in the rate of flow through the organ are compensated for automatically with a minimum effect on pulsation pressures. The perfusion fluid is filtered during its circulation and before it enters the organ. Organs can be removed from one apparatus and installed in another aseptically. The perfusion fluid can be removed and replaced aseptically. The organ and the perfusion fluid can be observed at all times."

The perfusion pump was only one part of the collaboration between Lindbergh and Carrel, however. The relationship went deeper and lasted longer than their joint work at the Rockefeller Institute. They were friends for about fourteen years in the United States and in Europe. In 1938 the Lindberghs rented a small French island, Iliec, very near to Carrel's place on Saint-Gildas. Lindbergh set up a laboratory in the barn, and the two men did some experiments there. When the tide was low, it was possible to walk between Iliec and St. Gildas; the Lindberghs and the Carrels saw a lot of each other. The Lindberghs were very happy in the quiet seclusion of this retreat, and a friend of Lindbergh's says that the flier had planned to devote the next years to working on scientific problems. He used to spend hours talking to Carrel, the two of them all alone with the sound of the wind and the sea around them.

Dr. Simon Flexner, the late director of laboratories at the Rockefeller Institute, said, on the occasion of Carrel's retirement from the Institute in 1938, "The career which you will be leaving is one of the remarkable achievements of our period in the domain of experimental surgery and biology." The Lindbergh pump enabled Carrel to push forward his work into the study of living cells and tissues grown outside the body, and into viruses.

Dr. Raymond C. Parker, director of the Connaught Medical Research Laboratories of the University of Toronto, said recently that Carrel's tissue studies "formed the basis of all of the more recent work on cell nutrition." Carrel was also able, with the Lindbergh pump, to show how cancer cells grow, to measure their rate of growth, to show differences in their food requirements, and to illustrate how they could often look like normal cells. Dr. Parker adds, "None of the major undertakings of Dr. Carrel and his associates has been outmoded."

Carrel was without doubt a remarkably talented scientist and a most unusual man. He was a dazzling talker who could spin theories as fast as he could make sentences, and adduce all sorts of interesting data to back his ideas. He was a loner. He was arrogant, impatient. A friendly biographer, Joseph T. Durkin, S.J., says, "He was sometimes too certain regarding his own views. His convictions easily became prejudices of dogmas stubbornly held."

He therefore made a lot of enemies among pedestrian scientists. When Lindbergh met Carrel, who was about thirty years his senior, Carrel had become much more metaphysician than physician. "Carrel's earlier contributions to science were considerable," a doctor who was closely associated with Carrel said recently, "but later on he became too 'philosophical.'" This same man, a scientist, said that Carrel had long since broken the bounds of scientific discourse: "His approach to science was a real mixture of originality and almost charlatanism. He was a very imaginative man, and a lot of people don't have very much imagination—they judge such a man harshly. He was a nonconformist."

Lindbergh did not have the background to make this kind of assessment of Carrel when he met him. Carrel was taking the whole of mankind and its future as the scope of his work. He had definite ideas about genetics, diet, religion, morals, ethics, race, biology, music, motion pictures, education, and any other subject or discipline his mind chanced to light on. And, as Lindbergh has since said, his opinions were far from static; they often changed from day to day. Carrel's intuitive leaps and sweeps might carry a listener away. But in his book *Man, the Unknown* Carrel let himself get carried away by his own emotions and rhetoric into areas in which he had no competence. The book, published in 1935, was a big bestseller—and a good example of how Carrel's mind worked. It opens with some disarmingly modest statements. "The author of this book is not a philosopher. He is only a man of science. . . . He does not pretend to deal with things that lie outside the field of scientific observation.

"In this book he has endeavored to describe the known, and to separate it clearly from the plausible. . . . What he describes he has either seen with his own eyes or learned directly from those with whom he associates."

Before he got through the preface, however, Carrel had assumed "the necessity, not only of mental, political, and social changes, but of the overthrow of industrial civilization and of the advent of another conception of human progress."

One example of his combining observable phenomena with unscientific data to reach a baseless conclusion is seen on a couple of pages in the middle of the book: [The brackets are not Carrel's.]

Excessive light is dangerous. In primitive surroundings men instinctively hide from it. There is a large number of mechanisms capable of protecting the organism from sun rays [eyelids, the iris, pigmentation of skin, etc.] . . . It is possible that lessened reactivity of the nervous system

and of the intelligence may eventually result from too strong a light.
[It is possible. But it may not be true.] We must not forget that the most
highly civilized races—the Scandinavians, for example—are white, and
have lived for many generations in a country where the atmospheric
luminosity is weak during a great part of the year. [A combination of
some facts, some baseless premises, and a *non sequitur,* leading to con-
fusion. There is no proof that the Scandinavians are a "race" or are any
more "highly civilized" than dark-skinned people from countries with a
great deal of sunlight.] In France, the populations of the north are far
superior to those of the Mediterranean shores. [Who says so, besides
Carrel?] The lower races generally inhabit countries where light is violent
and temperature equal and warm. [What is a lower race? What is a
race?] It seems that the adaptation of white men to light and to heat takes
place at the expense of their nervous and mental development. [Q.E.D.]

Some of Carrel's ideas (not the ones on light) can be found in
Lindbergh's later writings, and can be discerned in his behavior as a
father. They have even cropped up in Lindbergh's professional
preoccupations. In 1954 Lindbergh served as a member of a three-
man Air Force Academy Site Election Committee. When it came
to setting up the Academy, Lindbergh tried to put forward his
ideas of cadet behavior and marriage, according to one Air Force
general. "He had some notion that the Air Force ought to screen
the girls Cadets wanted to marry," the officer said recently. "He
seemed to think that the cadets were of a different breed."*

This kind of thinking might stem from Carrel's idea of an élite.
"We ought to try to produce a certain number of individuals above
the mental stature which we observe in the best," Carrel wrote in
his *Reflections on Life,* a fragmentary work published after his
death. "No modern man has sufficient intelligence and courage to
attack the great problems of civilization.

"Instead of encouraging the survival of the unfit and the defec-
tive," Carrel also wrote, "we must help the strong: only the élite
makes the progress of the masses possible. Hitherto, no scientific
institute has devoted itself to the formation of men of superior
quality. For this reason, it is urgent to found an organization . . .
directed not by specialists in biology, psychology or any other
science, only [by] men of very comprehensive intelligence, free
from all doctrine or prejudice . . . entirely concerned with indi-

---

* The same officer said Lindbergh no longer held these ideas.

viduals belonging to the races who produced Western civilization. . . ."

If one were to take this seriously, how would one go about it?
First would come the problem of identifying the élite. By whose
standards would they be selected? Then comes the problem of
encouraging and perpetuating the desirable qualities of mind, spirit,
health, or what have you, supposing one knows what they are.
There is no known way of doing this genetically in human beings at
the present time. Certain *physical* characteristics can be bred in
plants and animals; Carrel himself tried to raise a higher breed of
dog. He came out with a bunch of oversized, stupid animals, and
gave up in disgust. If he couldn't improve a controlled population
of beasts, all of a carefully selected stock, how could he breed
moral and intellectual superiority in men and women?

There is a persistent belief that Carrel was a Nazi, or pro-Nazi.
This idea rests on some of Carrel's expressed ideas which paralleled
those of Fascist theoreticians, as for example his ideas about the
élite. He was also a strong believer in state censorship of movies and
radio; thought that the majority of dance halls, cabarets, and bars
should be closed; and had rigid ideas about how children should be
reared. Father Durkin says Carrel never perceived "how his theories
concerning the improvement of the white race could be and were
actually used by Hitler's followers for the support of their own
brutal aims."

However, one cannot select merely the similarities between Carrel's ideology and that of the Nazis without examining the many
divergences. Carrel was a devout, uncompromising Roman Catholic, which put him into opposition against the Nazis. He could also
write, "The human being has incomparably greater value than the
huge inanimate mass of the cosmic world," and, "Each human being
is a unique event in space and time," hardly Fascistic statements.
He never displayed anti-Semitism but, in fact, wrote appreciatively
of Cardozo, Einstein, and other Jews he considered worthy men.

Carrel had to leave the Rockefeller Institute in 1938 because of its
rule about retirement at the age of sixty-five. He was still energetic
and went to France in 1941, when part of the country was theoretically controlled by the Vichy Government, to make a study of the
effects of malnutrition on children in Europe. He was so appalled
by the privations of his fellow-countrymen that he decided to stay

in France and work as a physician to alleviate suffering.* His letters of 1939–40 make it clear that he hoped the United States would aid France to repel the Nazis; in this, he differed sharply with Lindbergh, who was by then making speeches against any assistance to European countries. When the Nazis occupied the rest of France in 1942, Carrel did not leave, although he could have.

The Vichy regime offered him a chance to establish his Fondation** for combining all scientific disciplines to study human problems. He accepted, and set up the foundation according to his own ideas. This inevitably put him in the position of working with Vichy. However, there is no evidence that he shared their politics; he was misled perhaps by "naïveté," as Father Durkin believes, or by arrogance, or by ambition. But Durkin insists that he "was oblivious to the real political issues involved in the Pétain government's relationship with the Nazis." The evidence is that his Fondation did not serve either the Nazis or Nazi ideas, but did some very useful work in nutrition and in trying to eradicate diseases among children transmitted by animals, such as tuberculosis in cows. He was making a genuine attempt to help humanity, albeit on his own rigidly moralistic terms.

In December, 1939, he had appealed to the French people from Paris by radio to win the war against the Nazis. In 1940 he wrote an attack on both Bolshevism and National Socialism, ending with "Still more than Marxism, National Socialism . . . is radically opposed to the fundamental principles of Western civilization." Also in 1940, he wrote that if the United States would give two or three thousand planes and aviators to France, they might beat the Germans.

There was a rumor that he was going to become Minister of Health in the Laval government, which proved baseless but tarred him as a collaborationist. And when he took over the Paris building of the Rockefeller Foundation for his Fondation, he created much bitterness against himself in America. He was apparently unaware of this.

Carrel endured a good deal of privation living in Occupied France. At his age the stringencies of daily existence—lack of heat, improper nourishment—probably shortened his life. Yet it had been

---

* He had gone back to France during World War I to serve the country. The Carrel-Dakin treatment for war wounds, developed then, is credited with saving many men from amputations.

** Fondation Française pour l'Etude des Problèmes Humains.

his choice to stay with his people although he could have had an easier life in the United States.

In February, 1944, General J. Bentley Mott, of the United States Battle Monuments Commission, managed to see Carrel in Paris. He wrote to a mutual friend: "Any foolish talk of Doctor Carrel being in sympathy with the Nazis is sheer nonsense. He is devoting his whole time and effort to developing his laboratory and to helping abate illness and disease in France."

By this time Carrel was a sick man. He died in Paris in November, 1944, in undeserved disgrace.

A disinterested observer of both men says, "Lindbergh was obviously fascinated by the complex, intuitive Carrel from the start, as many more sophisticated people were." (The fascination has lasted to this day. When Yale University had a special celebration in honor of Carrel a few years ago, Lindbergh made one of his rare public appearances; when Harper & Row were working on the galleys of a book by Father Durkin about Carrel in 1965, Lindbergh made several visits to the office to give his comments on the work. He also keeps in touch with Mme. Carrel, who lives in Buenos Aires.)

There is no doubt that Lindbergh was rather vulnerable to Carrel's charm and brilliance. Carrel with his dashing scientific exuberance was somewhat like Lindbergh's Grandfather Land, and his ideas about morality, young people, motion pictures, night clubs, and so on, were the sort of thing that Lindbergh had had drummed into him from both the Lindberghs and the Lands. Congressman C. A. Lindbergh had talked about the flabby morality of Americans; so did Carrel. Charles A. Lindbergh had been made aware of the contradictions between science and religion by Grandfather Land. In his youth, Lindbergh had chosen the scientific over the religious, but he often wondered if there wasn't something just beyond death's door. This mystical yearning in Lindbergh was evoked by Carrel's own attempt to bridge the teachings of Catholicism and the precepts of science. Carrel managed to alienate both the Catholic Church and the scientists by telling the Church that it was not nearly scientific enough in its appraisal of miracles, and at the same time stating that medical miracles had undoubtedly taken place at Lourdes. "Some cases of suppurating fistula, chronic ulcer, tuberculosis of the lungs, bones, joints and spine, and of cancer have been almost instantaneously cured at Lourdes," he wrote. He believed that the subject-patient at Lourdes "does not need to have faith," but "must be surrounded by an atmosphere of prayer." There was a bit of an echo of C. A. Lindbergh's experience in his scolding of the hierarchy in America and a somewhat similar reaction.

"Carrel," wrote Lindbergh, in the preface to Carrel's book, *The Voyage to Lourdes*, "was a man who spanned extremes in thought and action. As he could act with the precision which won him the Nobel Prize in surgery, he could act with an abandon which laid him open to the thrusts of enemies he both tactlessly and fearlessly created." This description is reminiscent of Lindbergh's father and grandfather Lindbergh. Carrel also had the same kind of digital deftness as Grandfather Land. Carrel was, in fact, so adroit that within the thickness of a piece of paper he could make tiny stitches that could not be seen from either side. Lindbergh has always admired people who were skillful with their hands.

Carrel, the surgeon skillful and brilliant enough to win the Nobel Prize, had been unanimously rejected for the job of house surgeon when he was a young man in a Lyons hospital. The reason was that he refused to abide by the rules of rote learning; just as Congressman Lindbergh had had trouble in law school because of his refusal to accept the "precedent" approach of jurisprudence.

If Lindbergh was conditioned to be receptive to a man like Carrel, he was also trained to think for himself. He tempered his admiration of Carrel with a realistic assessment of Carrel's free-wheeling blend of the real and the nominal. "Carrel spoke and wrote more freely than many scientists can think," Lindbergh stated. "At times, he used such sweeping statements to emphasize his points that only those who knew him well were able to draw the kernels of fact from the husk of fantasy and apply them to the instance he had in mind."

Lindbergh's rational mind could thus divine the instability of Carrel's thought. Yet, at the same time, he could not wholly escape its influence. Carrel was an older man, with a high position in science; he was undeniably brilliant; he was extremely persuasive. He was authoritarian, but not tyrannical. He felt that science had been put to work mainly for industry and commerce; that its potential for serving man had not been explored or exploited.

To reject Carrel as a scientist would be foolish. His work is unassailable; it has stood the test of time. As a philosopher he was often silly, but not wholly wrong. One can demolish parts of his philosophy without destroying the basic *gestalt*: he was a highly imperfect human being, but he was on the side of humanity. He was certainly not evil. No matter how many ridiculous prejudices he held about élites and races and skin color, he was a consistent opponent of tyranny in real life.

He had a tremendous influence on Lindbergh, not all for the good but not all bad either. And influence does not mean domination. Lindbergh showed in his comments that he felt he could pick what was sound from what was not in Carrel's thinking. Perhaps the largest benefit that he got from Carrel was the stimulation to think and learn. He has gone on widening his horizons of thought and scholarship constantly since Carrel's death nearly a quarter of a century ago. There are undoubtedly echoes of Carrel in Lindbergh today, but they are also echoes of attitudes that Lindbergh had inherited from his family and of ideas that he has tested for himself.

19

🌿 DR. GODDARD

IN 1929, WHEN LINDBERGH WAS WORKING FOR TWA AND Pan American, and was a trustee of the Guggenheim Aeronautics Fund, he had to do a lot of flying. "Flying cross country in good weather in those days," he recalled recently, "you had plenty of time to think." It was already obvious to him that airplanes were going to develop to the point where they would fly as high and as fast and carry as many passengers as one could wish. Then, Lindbergh speculated, men would not be satisfied just to travel in the air; they would want to try interplanetary space. "I realized the limits of the propeller," Lindbergh says, "and this led me into the field of rockets and jet propulsion."

That summer, this line of reasoning prompted him to seek out the du Pont Company in Wilmington, Delaware, which made the black powder used in certain types of rockets. Lindbergh did not approach du Pont with his fantasies. He presented a more practical problem. "Couldn't we develop a rocket that could be attached to a plane for the purpose of giving it one minute of thrust in case of engine failure on take-off, thus avoiding having to land it in a city or trees?" he asked.

Eventually he got a definitive answer from du Pont by letter: the idea seemed impracticable because "to equal the thrust for one minute of a Wasp [airplane] engine would require about 400 pounds of black powder, and the heat would be so intense that the powder would have to be burned in a fire-brick combustion chamber." This would make the rocket so heavy that its thrust would be canceled by its own weight.

Lindbergh was disappointed. He talked about this one fall afternoon in 1929 with Harry Guggenheim at Guggenheim's house on Long Island. As he recalls it, "Carol, Harry's second wife, was with us. Naturally she wasn't interested in our technical discussion, so she was sitting over to one side, reading a newspaper. I thought she was paying no attention to us at all but suddenly she said, 'Listen to this, you two,' and proceeded to read aloud an article from a back page of the newspaper."

Part of the article dealt with the events of the previous July 17, 1929, in a cow pasture in Auburn, Massachusetts. A physics professor named Dr. Robert H. Goddard had fired a liquid-powered rocket nearly 100 feet in the air. Coming down, the rocket had started a brush fire and had attracted considerable (and sensationally inaccurate) press coverage. The papers referred to it as a "Moon Rocket," which it was not—it was a twelve-foot-long affair designed to test certain new concepts in center of gravity—and jeered at it as having missed its target "by 238,799½ miles." Actually, it was probably the first rocket ever to carry aloft recording instruments; it had a camera, barometer, and thermometer.

When Carol Guggenheim finished reading aloud the somewhat humorous account of the flight, Harry Guggenheim said to Lindbergh, "May be the answer to our problem. Why don't you check up on Goddard? Go have a talk with him, if you think it's worth while."

Lindbergh visited the Massachusetts Institute of Technology in Boston later that month to find out what the scientists there thought of Goddard, who was professor of physics at Clark University in nearby Worcester. On November 22 he phoned Goddard from his rented farmhouse in Princeton, New Jersey.

Goddard, an unknown inventor (except for those pejorative press comments), had been doggedly developing rocketry with almost no money, practically no help, and against an almost universal skepticism that amounted to disbelief in his work.

He knew that Lindbergh had been asking about him. Still, when Lindbergh announced himself on the telephone, Goddard thought it was a practical joke. It took Lindbergh a little time to convince Goddard who he was. He asked if he could come up to Worcester the next day for a visit.

When Goddard told his wife that evening that Lindbergh had telephoned him, she had the same initial reaction as her husband:

"Of course, Bob," said Mrs. Goddard. "And I had tea today with Marie, the Queen of Rumania."

Lindbergh drove up the next day (Saturday, November 23, 1929) from Princeton. He met Goddard at his office in Clark University. Lindbergh told the professor about du Pont's judgment regarding the need for a firebrick burning chamber for their solid propellant. Goddard said that he wasn't using solid fuels. He was using liquids, like gasoline, which burned air or liquid oxygen carried by the rocket. In neither case was the combustion chamber of his rockets made of brick, but of an extremely lightweight metal, Duralumin, only ⅟₃₂ of an inch thick. His "birds" were thus light enough to fly many miles above the earth.

Goddard, a very thin, balding man, was extremely secretive about his work. Partly this was due to the ridicule he got in the press when his first monograph on rockets was published in 1920. In that monograph he had stated the theory that the moon might be hit with a rocket which could be seen because it would carry a small flash bomb in its nose that would explode on impact. From then on he was known as "the Moon Man."

Actually, this monograph, which he wrote in 1916, was largely a summary of his original findings on rockets, among them his discovery that a rocket could be fired in a vacuum, thus making it possible to travel through airless space. In the monograph, titled *A Method of Reaching Extreme Altitudes*, Goddard described a step or multistage rocket, on which he had taken out a patent in 1914. This was, of course, the basis of all the giant multistage rockets that the United States and the Soviet Union have fired into space.

Except for this monograph, prepared for the Smithsonian Institution to gain funds for his experiments, Goddard had published little of his work. He had the notion that his ideas would be stolen if he did. And he wouldn't work with other scientists—not only because he didn't trust them but because he was too impatient to join a team. Yet the secretive Goddard did not hold back with Lindbergh. There was something about the flier; his manner was extremely open and direct. As others had noted, he had an air that bred confidence.

Goddard talked and talked all afternooon: about the advantages of liquid fuel; about giant multistaged rockets that would boost themselves out of the earth's atmosphere, dropping off the empty fuel cells as they went. He took Lindbergh home for coffee. Mrs. Goddard saw that Lindbergh looked tired and was carrying his right arm in a sling. When she asked him about it, he told her he had thrown it out of joint crawling under a bed to retrieve a puppy. It was the same shoulder that he had dislocated in 1925 in an emergency parachute jump.

Later, Lindbergh asked Goddard what he most needed to carry forward his experiments. The inventor replied carefully, according to Lindbergh, "that, more than anything else, he wanted to be free of the classroom duties [at Clark University] which took so much of his time. Then, he would look for a place where he could set up a laboratory and launching tower and test his rockets without worrying his neighbors or being restricted by the police."

Goddard thought if he could get $25,000 a year for four years, this would cover all his expenses—his salary, those of his assistants, materials, and so on. Thus $100,000 would buy in four years what he could not otherwise hope to accomplish in a lifetime. He had a small grant from the Smithsonian Institution which was almost used up, and no hope of more money.

Lindbergh was favorably impressed, so much so that he offered help. Goddard accepted, and Lindbergh began setting up meetings with possible sources of aid before going to the Guggenheims.

He took Goddard to Wilmington to meet the du Pont people. They asked too many questions, Goddard thought, and in the end they offered no money. Next Lindbergh introduced the inventor to the Carnegie Foundation, with whom Lindbergh had already established contact for archaeological exploration. There they had a small success. The Carnegie Foundation gave Goddard a grant of $5,000, and apologized that it wasn't larger.

Goddard knew that other countries, particularly Germany, were more anxious to delve into rocketry than was the United States. He was getting inquiries constantly from German scientists. This was one area of military research that was open to them. The Versailles Treaty had not mentioned rockets, and had thereby neglected to prohibit them among the weapons forbidden to Germany. As early as 1930, the Wehrmacht appropriated $50,000 for research in rocket weapons; there was no appropriation at that time for rocket research in the U.S. Army or Navy.

Lindbergh could have asked the Guggenheim Fund (for the Promotion of Aeronautics) for money. But, as a trustee of the Fund, he hesitated to use his influence there. However, he had come to know the Guggenheim family well. In the spring of 1930, Lindbergh wrote to Harry Guggenheim, who was then the United States Ambassador to Cuba, asking if he had any objection in Lindbergh's approaching Harry's father, Daniel Guggenheim, to talk about financing Goddard's work. Harry replied promptly telling him to go ahead.

Lindbergh called on Daniel Guggenheim, the hardheaded paterfamilias, at Daniel's home, known as Hempstead House. He told Daniel about his conversations with Goddard, and his estimate of the rocket experiments.

Lindbergh recalls that the conversation went like this:

DANIEL GUGGENHEIM: "Then you believe rockets have an important future?"

LINDBERGH: "Probably. Of course one is never certain."

GUGGENHEIM: "But you think so. And this professor, he looks like a pretty capable man?"

LINDBERGH: "As far as I can find out, Mr. Guggenheim, he knows more about rockets than anybody else in the country."

GUGGENHEIM: "How much money does he need?"

LINDBERGH: "He'd like to have $25,000 a year for a four-year project."

GUGGENHEIM: "Do you think he can accomplish enough to make it worth his time?"

LINDBERGH: "Well, it's taking a chance, but if we're ever going to get beyond the limits of airplanes and propellers, we'll probably have to go to rockets. It's a chance but, yes, I think it's worth taking."

GUGGENHEIM: "All right, I'll give him the money."

He pledged $50,000 of his own money to support Goddard's work for two years. After that an advisory committee, set up by Clark University, and Lindbergh would review Goddard's work and decide if he merited the second $50,000.

Lindbergh telephoned Goddard to say that he had found a supporter willing to put up all the money Goddard had asked for. He said he would write and confirm the details in a few days.

Goddard couldn't quite believe it. He had been scrounging and scrimping and had finally run out of money altogether; the future had seemed hopeless. And here was rescue, just as he was clinging by his fingernails to the edge of the cliff.

Guggenheim followed through on his decision. Not long before his death in 1930, he put up $50,000 for Goddard to use without restriction. The money was channeled through a corporation set up and administered by Clark University. Now Goddard had enough funds to get himself a proper space to work, to locate his work in a sunny, clear climate that allowed him to shoot rockets almost at will. He moved his laboratory and staff to Roswell, New Mexico. He made progress there, but the work did not go as quickly as he had hoped. Two years later, in 1932, he went before the Guggenheim committee to ask for the second $50,000. The committee examined his work and approved his request. But Daniel Guggenheim's estate was still being settled, so the money was not immediately available. Also its assets had been depleted by the sharp drop in the stock market. Goddard was forced to close down his New Mexico operation and return to Massachusetts.

Lindbergh next tried to get the U.S. military establishment to aid Goddard; they were interested but not helpful. Lindbergh went back to the Guggenheims, this time to the Daniel and Florence Guggenheim Foundation.° The Foundation came up with $2,500 for 1933, $18,000 for 1934. Goddard moved his rocket laboratory back to Roswell, New Mexico.

Soon afterward, Lindbergh and his wife flew in to Roswell for a visit and inspection. It was a gala day for the little New Mexico town, and an encouraging one for Goddard.

A year later Goddard was able to report a vertical rocket flight of 7,500 feet. He was concentrating on accuracy, a parachute return of the rocket, and other items. He invited Lindbergh and Harry Guggenheim to come and see for themselves. This was during the time when the Lindberghs were living through the last months of the Hauptmann case. Lindbergh and Guggenheim arrived in September, 1935, to watch a test flight. On two separate days Goddard tried out two liquid-fueled rockets and both failed. Lindbergh said Goddard "was as mortified as a parent whose child misbehaves in front of company."

° There have been five different Guggenheim family foundations.

But Goddard's faith in his work was so strong that Lindbergh and Harry Guggenheim promised to return. Lindbergh assured Goddard that rocketry in 1935 was about where aviation had been in 1912. Then the two visitors flew back; Lindbergh wrote Goddard an encouraging letter. He said that he considered the visit useful, in spite of the fact that there had been no successful rocket launching. He went so far as to say that such a flight wasn't really important, although he knew how much it would have meant to Goddard.

This kind of empathy is not shown to strangers by Lindbergh, but is often given to friends and colleagues. He aided the inventor through years of tests that did not work, rockets that did not fly, developments that did not quite come off. He got Goddard to write a second paper, in 1936, on his work, for publication by the Smithsonian Institution—the only such revelation the inventor had made since 1920. This brought him some important recognition for his many pioneering contributions to rocketry.

But the work was far from perfected. Would the Guggenheim money continue when results were still more theoretical than practical? A few months later, Lindbergh, who by then was living in England, wrote Goddard asking in a casual way how long it would take to have a really successful high-altitude flight. Such an achievement, Lindbergh said, would be very good for everybody's morale.

Goddard went all out to perfect a new, large rocket that might soar many miles into the atmosphere. He wanted it, he *needed* it, to demonstrate that he was worthy of further support. But he couldn't get the new engine to work in time for the demonstration. He asked humbly for another year's support from the Guggenheim Foundation and, at the same time, wrote to Lindbergh that he felt that the Foundation had already done more than they had to.

Lindbergh, from England, wrote to Harry Guggenheim that Goddard would not feel ill used if the Foundation stopped his grant, but he reiterated his faith in the future of the work. He told Guggenheim that if he really wanted to promote aviation, no other project held greater promise. He said he was certain Goddard would be the first to send rockets to very high altitudes, and that his work would be scientifically valuable.

Guggenheim agreed to continue Foundation support for another year—a $20,000 appropriation. And he said, generously, that he did not want Goddard to waste his time on a spectacular demonstration.

In 1938 Lindbergh made an unexpected public gesture by writing a letter of appreciation about Goddard's work, and its future possibilities, to be read at the commencement exercises of Clark University. Among the things Lindbergh said in the letter were that observations taken through rocketry would become important to astronomy, meteorology, and terrestrial magnetism. He also predicted that rockets might one day carry explosives farther and faster than any other device. In a bit of lighthearted prescience he even spoke about interstellar flight. Goddard did not know of this letter until it was read aloud at the exercises. He usually masked his emotions, but on this occasion he seemed visibly moved.

By 1938, $148,000 of Guggenheim money had been invested in Goddard's work, and Harry Guggenheim was wishing plaintively that there was just a bit more to show for it. Guggenheim tried to get Goddard to work with Cal Tech scientists, but Goddard was too much the lone wolf for that. Nevertheless the Guggenheim Foundation continued to support his research.

After Lindbergh returned to the United States in 1939, he made a survey of American air power for the Army. On this trip he flew his Army P-36 into Roswell, New Mexico, to visit Goddard. He had other things on his mind, and he intended to move on quickly, but Goddard had so many interesting things to say that Lindbergh spent the night. He wrote to Guggenheim a few days later, saying that it seemed to him that Goddard had made more progress during that year than in any other. He said Goddard seemed to have better control over his rockets, and that the inventor felt that he could get them to much higher altitudes.

Lindbergh told Goddard about the secrecy he had encountered in Germany on rockets. He had been lunching with Adolf Baeumker, the Luftwaffe chief of research and development, he recalled, and the conversation had been easy until they touched on the subject of rocketry. Then Baeumker abruptly stopped talking. Both Lindbergh and Goddard guessed that the Germans had a rocket; they did not know that the Soviet Union was also far advanced in military rocketry. But they agreed that it was high time the U.S. military got involved in the subject.

On May 28, 1940, a meeting was arranged between Goddard,

Guggenheim, and various Army and Navy officers, including Brigadier General George H. Brett. Brett was sitting in for General Henry H. Arnold, Chief of the Army Air Force, who had promised to attend but had to drop out. The officers were all rather tense. This was the second day of the famous British Army evacuation of France from Dunkirk. Worried by the defeat of France and the near disaster to the British, on whom U.S. strategy depended, they were too preoccupied with their own problems to give much attention to Goddard's novel ideas about the development of rockets in military operations.

Actually, he had demonstrated as long ago as November, 1918, a small rocket in a recoilless barrel, and had so impressed the military with the potentialities of this weapon (later developed into the bazooka and other similar weapons) that he had been promised development support. But his timing had been unfortunate; the Armistice of World War I came four days after his demonstration and nothing was ever done with his invention. Now, in 1940, the officers were not much interested in the fact that Goddard had knocked out tanks with rockets in 1918. Besides, they all had other meetings to attend. They told Goddard that if he could develop a rocket to assist airplanes on quick takeoffs, they might be interested. But as for using the rocket as a missile, one officer said, "The next war will be won with the trench mortar." The meeting broke up without taking time to look at Goddard's movies of successful rocket launchings.

Later, Goddard was taken on by the government to develop liquid-fuel rocket motors to assist heavily loaded aircraft to take off in short distances and climb fast, a project known as JATO (for jet-assisted takeoff). Dr. G. Edward Pendray, co-founder of the American Rocket Society, has said it was "like trying to harness Pegasus to a plow." Goddard stayed in one or another branch of government research during the war; to keep going, he had to borrow $10,000 from Harry Guggenheim. Then Goddard got sick, a recurrence of the tuberculosis he had suffered as a young man, plus cancer of the throat. While he was in the hospital, Harry Guggenheim telephoned to Mrs. Goddard: "I want you to tell Bob that I will finance him after the war is over for whatever he wants, as much as he wants, as long as he wants." But Goddard died on August 10, 1945, before his work was ever truly recognized.

Of course, the Germans knew about it. A liquid-fueled rocket that

Goddard shot 9,000 feet into the air in New Mexico in 1941 contained almost all the features later incorporated into the German V-2 rockets, Dr. Pendray said. Wernher von Braun, one of Hitler's rocket experts at the Peenemünde laboratories during the war, said, "Every liquid-fuel rocket that flies is a Goddard rocket."

When Goddard died, he left more than two hundred patents on rockets and rocketry. Says Dr. Pendray, "Practically every one of the ideas that have since been developed successfully in large rockets and guided missiles, including gyro-controls, clustered rockets, research instrumentation, turbopumps for propellants and gimbal-mounted tail sections capable of being moved in flight for steering," had been tried out first by Goddard.

The federal government recognized this in 1960 by settling with Mrs. Goddard and the Daniel and Florence Guggenheim Foundation for infringement on the Goddard patents. The joint patent owners won an administrative award of a million dollars, the largest given up to that time.

Lindbergh's part in the Goddard story did not come to general attention until 1963 with the publication of Goddard's biography.* Lindbergh contributed information to this work, and helped the author through the more difficult moments of creation. And, as he has often done for books of other authors he has aided and with whose subjects he is sympathetic, he wrote the preface.

"This is a story of individualism," Lindbergh wrote of Goddard, "of one man's effort and almost superhuman vision in a field of science so fantastic in his day that anyone venturing much confidence in its future was considered unscientific by most scientists. . . . Robert Goddard's dual approach to astronautics is a fascinating study, now cautious and realistic, now adventurous and fictional." His assessment of Goddard is strikingly like his judgment of Carrel in his preface to The Voyage to Lourdes. Both were men of science who also ranged far afield from science: Carrel into religion, mysticism, and philosophy; Goddard into science fiction and projections of rocket travel to outer space, colonizing distant planets with men from earth, and so on. Both were men of great accomplishment; both were loners; both were mavericks.

In the Goddard preface, Lindbergh quoted an ancient Chinese

* Milton H. Lehman, This High Man—The Life of Robert H. Goddard (New York: Farrar, Straus & Co., 1963).

poem: "Am I a man who dreamed of being a butterfly,/Or am I a butterfly dreaming myself to be a man?" It is a question Lindbergh might have asked about himself. "One is constantly aware of the fact," he wrote, "that we live in a world where dreams and reality interchange."

The relationship with Goddard reveals a great deal about Lindbergh. He met Goddard as the result of a logical progression of attempts to solve a problem far in the future. His dreaming in the airplane in the summer of 1929 about the future of flight was like his musing in the mailplane in September, 1926, which led to his transatlantic flight; both times he brought together all the current factors in a situation and estimated future possibilities, then sought a solution. Once committed to Goddard, he stayed committed as long as Goddard lived; he helped the man through sixteen years of constant frustration and disappointment. He had nothing to gain from this except the intellectual satisfaction of following through on a judgment he thought correct. His support of Goddard also involved strong personal sympathy. Goddard was a highly emotional man and a highly secret one. He was an originator, a pioneer, and a recluse. He had self-doubts but never showed them. He was the sort of man who appealed to Lindbergh, because he was very much like Lindbergh.

THE AIR MAIL CONTROVERSY

CHARLES LINDBERGH'S FATHER HAD TAKEN ON THE ECO-
nomic establishment, the press, and other powerful opponents and
had often lost; Lindbergh fought the popular President of the
United States, Franklin Delano Roosevelt, and won a telling victory
over him.

It started in 1933 with an investigation of subsidies awarded by
the Post Office Department to airlines for carrying air mail. Former
President Herbert Hoover's Postmaster General, Walter F. Brown,
considered to be one of the ablest members of the Hoover Cabinet,
had had the power to award such contracts. As already mentioned,
his theory of making the awards was the same as that of his
predecessor, Harry S. New: that they should be used to consolidate
American commercial aviation, which was then in a state of chaos.
As a consequence, he did not hand out the contracts on the basis of
competitive bidding but gave them to large air carriers he held to
be worthy of support. This shut out the smaller lines that were, to
Brown, annoyances.

A Hearst reporter named Fulton Lewis, Jr., got wind of the fact
that in 1930, while Hoover was still in office, Brown had awarded an
air-mail contract between New York and Washington at three times
the rate proposed by a company which did not get the contract.

Lewis's employers, the Hearst newspapers, refused to print his
information. He continued, however, to dig for more facts. In 1933
the Senate voted a special committee, headed by Senator Hugo
Black of Alabama, to investigate the subsidy mail contracts given to
shipping companies and airlines. By this time, Lewis had compiled
extensive files and many leads to information, and was able to

supply Black with some of the background he needed for his hearings. Painstakingly, the Black committee elicited testimony of "immense salaries, bonuses and speculative profits [in the airlines]; dubious relations between the industry and the government officials who dealt with it; the avoidance of competitive bidding; the covert destruction of official records," according to historian Arthur M. Schlesinger, Jr.

The Black committee made telling use of a closed meeting of certain airline officials at the Post Office Department in 1930. At this discussion with the Superintendent of the Air Mail, one of the airline executives present wondered if they weren't violating the Sherman Anti-Trust Act. "If we were holding this meeting across the street in the Raleigh Hotel," the executive said, "it would be an improper meeting; but because we are holding it at the invitation of a member of the cabinet, and in the office of the Post Office Department, it is perfectly all right."

The Senate hearings revealed that Brown's policy had resulted in concentrating twenty-four out of twenty-seven air-mail contracts in three large holding companies: United Aircraft, Aviation Corporation of Delaware, and North American–General Motors.

"The control of American aviation," Black said, "has been ruthlessly taken away from the men who could fly and bestowed upon bankers, brokers, promoters and politicians, sitting in their inner offices, allotting among themselves the taxpayers' money."

Lunching with President Roosevelt in January, 1934, Black told him that it was within the Postmaster General's authority to cancel contracts obtained by fraud or conspiracy. Roosevelt asked his Attorney General, Homer Cummings, for a legal opinion; Cummings reported that the evidence turned up by the Black committee could justify cancellation of the air-mail contracts.

Roosevelt decided that if the contracts were crooked they ought to be canceled immediately. The Post Office Department wanted to delay until June, when they could advertise for new bids and thus avoid interruption of air-mail service. But Roosevelt insisted on immediate action.

An Assistant Postmaster General asked General Benjamin D. Foulois, head of the Army Air Corps, whether Army pilots could take over delivery of air mail immediately. Foulois said they could —a serious mistake of judgment.

Then the cancellation of private air-mail contracts was announced by Presidential order on February 9, 1934, to take effect on February 19.

Roosevelt's new Postmaster General, James A. Farley, said in explanation that the airlines who had held contracts from Postmaster General Brown had overcharged the government by nearly $47 million between July, 1930, and January, 1934. He also said that a sizable part of this money had gone to Transcontinental & Western Airways (TWA), known as "The Lindbergh Line."

TWA had hired Lindbergh in their takeover of TAT. The terms of Lindbergh's TAT contract had called for a $250,000 payment to him as head of the technical committee of the company. The contract also committed him to endorse this check to buy 25,000 shares of TAT stock at $10 a share. When TWA took over TAT, they exchanged Lindbergh's TAT shares for TWA shares.

(Lindbergh, as a consultant to Pan American Airways, had accepted stock warrants in that company which had profited him by $150,000 and which he had reinvested in the company.)

All of this was a matter of public record. Some of it had come out in the Black committee hearings. The committee had asked Lindbergh for details and he had supplied them with a full report of the transactions.

Consequently, when the President canceled the air-mail contracts on February 9, 1934, charging fraud, Lindbergh's reputation was involved. He did not take long to react to the cancellation. The next day, Saturday, February 10, he began to make notes for a reply. He went to his office in New York City on Sunday, February 11, and worked out a telegram to Roosevelt with Colonel Henry Breckinridge. He sent the telegram to the White House on Sunday night, simultaneously releasing it to the Monday morning newspapers on February 12. It made headlines.

The telegram read, in part:

YOUR ACTION OF YESTERDAY AFFECTS FUNDAMENTALLY THE INDUSTRY TO WHICH I HAVE DEVOTED THE LAST TWELVE YEARS OF MY LIFE. . . . THE PERSONAL AND BUSINESS LIVES OF AMERICAN CITIZENS HAVE BEEN BUILT AROUND THE RIGHT TO JUST TRIAL BEFORE CONDEMNATION. YOUR ORDER OF CANCELLATION OF ALL AIRMAIL CONTRACTS CONDEMNS THE LARGEST PORTION OF OUR COMMERCIAL AVIATION WITHOUT JUST TRIAL. . . . AMERICANS HAVE SPENT THEIR BUSINESS LIVES IN BUILDING IN THIS COUNTRY THE

FINEST COMMERCIAL AIRLINES IN THE WORLD. . . . THE GREATER PART OF
THIS PROGRESS HAS BEEN BROUGHT ABOUT THROUGH THE AIRMAIL. . . .
CANCELLATION OF ALL MAIL CONTRACTS AND THE USE OF THE ARMY ON
COMMERCIAL AIRLINES WILL UNNECESSARILY AND GREATLY DAMAGE ALL
AMERICAN AVIATION.

Lindbergh's reputation for integrity and knowledgeability in aviation was great. His swift public opposition to the air-mail contract
cancellation shook Roosevelt. Roosevelt's press secretary, Steve
Early, hit back by pointing out that telegrams to the President
released simultaneously to the newspapers were sent for publicity
purposes. Senator George W. Norris, who had stood with Lindbergh's father against America's entry into World War I, said, "Now
Colonel Lindbergh has earned his $250,000."

Farley went along with the administration, although he had
privately told his predecessor, Brown, that he felt the Black committee was hunting headlines, and he wrote later that he was "hurt"
that Roosevelt let the weight of the cancellation fall on his
(Farley's) shoulders. Publicly he said to Lindbergh, however, "I am
certain that if you were in possession of all the facts that you would
not feel that any injustice had been done or will be done."

A committee of a tri-state Federal Bar Association resolved that
Lindbergh had allowed himself to be exploited for publicity purposes by the airlines "in an undignified, disrespectful, absurd and
presumptuous attempt to discredit the President of the United
States."

Lindbergh had tremendous editorial support, however. The *New
York Times* denied that he could be a tool of corrupt interests. The
paper also published Lindbergh's judgment that the real issue was
the lives of Army pilots who were being called on to do a job they
hadn't been trained for, in planes and on airfields that were not
equipped for flying the mail.

But these were only words. The real test was what was happening
in the air. The Air Corps had begun flying the mail under the worst
possible circumstances. February was a savage month in 1934,
particularly so to Army fliers who were supposed to meet mail
schedules in spite of storms and who had to fly at night without
proper training, equipment, or night landing lights.

The first Army air-mail pilot was killed within a few days of the
start of operations; he crashed in flames in Idaho. At the end of the

first week of Army air-mail operation, five pilots had been killed, six pilots injured, eight planes wrecked. Eddie Rickenbacker, of Eastern Airlines, called it "legalized murder."

Arthur Krock wrote in the *New York Times* that the Roosevelt administration which had been riding a high tide of popularity was, for the first time, on the defensive. Roosevelt told Secretary of War George H. Dern that "the continuation of deaths in the Army Air Corps must stop."

Night flying of the mail was ended, but the Army air-mail planes continued to crash. Service was curtailed, even interrupted for a week to allow time for installation of new safety equipment. But nothing, it seems, could stop the series of tragedies. In less than two months there were twelve Army dead and forty-six forced landings.

Crashes were not uncommon in commercial aviation in those days, either. United Air Lines had four crashes within four months, killing eleven crew members and eleven passengers, for example. Yet the dramatic circumstances that had forced the Army into taking over from the commercial lines front-paged their fatalities and made the government seem reckless.

Colonel Billy Mitchell castigated the commercial airlines in a private speech. He said the law should have permitted the government to take over private planes and radio services. He also said that the Army should continue flying the mails; it would be excellent training for pilots and would "result in a much more efficient Air Corps. . . . The Army has lost the art of flying," he said. "It can't fly. If any Army aviator can't fly a mail route in any sort of weather, what would we do in a war?" And Mitchell attacked Lindbergh, saying that he had "disclosed himself as the 'front man' of the Air Trust," called him "a commercial flier," and said his "motive is principally profit."

But Lindbergh's reputation was unshakable. And nothing could make the government seem right against his unquestionably accurate prediction of Army disaster.

Secretary Dern asked Lindbergh to serve on a committee to study the Air Corps performance in carrying air mail. Lindbergh refused, and reiterated his stand in another publicized telegram:

I BELIEVE THAT THE USE OF THE ARMY AIR CORPS TO CARRY THE AIR MAIL WAS UNWARRANTED AND CONTRARY TO AMERICAN PRINCIPLES. THE

ACTION WAS UNJUST TO THE AIRLINES WHOSE CONTRACTS WERE CANCELED WITHOUT TRIAL. IT WAS UNFAIR TO THE PERSONNEL OF THE ARMY AIR CORPS, WHO HAD NEITHER EQUIPMENT DESIGNED FOR THE PURPOSE NOR ADEQUATE TIME FOR TRAINING. . . . IT HAS UNNECESSARILY GREATLY DAMAGED ALL AMERICAN AVIATION. I DO NOT FEEL THAT I CAN SERVE ON A COMMITTEE WHOSE FUNCTION IS TO ASSIST IN FOLLOWING OUT AN EXECUTIVE ORDER TO THE ARMY TO TAKE OVER THE COMMERCIAL AIR MAIL SYSTEM OF THE UNITED STATES.

Dern tried to persuade Lindbergh to change his mind, and got another refusal.

Hearings were held in March, 1934, on a Senate bill designed to return the air mail to the airlines. Lindbergh testified for two hours, was treated respectfully, and made no concessions. The *New York Times* reported that "whenever his face flashed in the familiar, winsome smile, a murmur of approval ran through the hall." He restated his charge about the unjustness of the government's contract cancellation. He attacked a provision in the pending bill that would refuse contracts to any company suing the government for revenue losses on the canceled contracts. He also opposed a provision that would require an Army, Navy, or Marine co-pilot in all private planes flying the mail.

Senator Kenneth D. McKellar asked him if he knew anything about the making of the contracts, and he said, "Very little."

"If they're honest, you're for them, and if not you wouldn't condone them?"

"My answer to that, Senator," said Lindbergh, "is that these contractors should have been given the right to trial before being convicted. . . ."

Senator Jeremiah T. O'Mahoney attacked from another angle, with the same objective, and got the same response. Then he tried a new assault. "If an officer of your company testified under oath that his concern paid $1,400,000 to persuade another company not to bid [as O'Mahoney was charging that TWA had done], and if it were established in the terms of the contract, would you consider that proof of the charge?"

"That's a hypothetical question and out of my field," Lindbergh said. "I don't want to answer that."

It was not long before the commercial airlines were flying air mail again. Some of them had had to reorganize, and the amounts of government mail subsidies dropped to some extent. But over all the effect was one of defeat for Roosevelt and his new administration. It was, in fact, the first large-scale public setback Roosevelt had received since his election, either politically or personally. And, as he did with all things political, he took it personally.

Aside from the merits of the controversy and the cancellation, it had been a test of Lindbergh's integrity, prestige, and judgment against Roosevelt's. Lindbergh had been proved right by the grisly results of the Army's attempt to fly the mail. Roosevelt did not like to be wrong or to seem wrong. He hated people who made him look wrong in public. Therefore he hated Lindbergh—and he never forgot his hatred or forgave Lindbergh, as later events proved.

ENGLAND, FRANCE, GERMANY

IN 1936, AFTER LINDBERGH MOVED TO ENGLAND, THE AIR
Ministry of the French government invited him to visit aircraft-
manufacturing plants in France. He was delighted to accept, but he
was appalled by what he saw. Airplane production in that country
was stagnant, a result of official disinterest and the frequent strikes
that plagued all French industry. This was at the time when Germany had violated the Locarno Pact and remilitarized the Rhine-
land; and already Europe was again vibrating to the hobnail
tread. The threat of war was definitely in the air, but France was
not in the least prepared—or preparing—to fight, at least not in the
air. The French Air Ministry had deliberately invited Lindbergh to
see just how badly off they were with the hope that he would say so
publicly and perhaps galvanize other branches of government to act
before it was too late. But with French politics in a state of chaos
and with the military thinking as well as the mood of the country
dominated by the Maginot line, nothing that Lindbergh said could
penetrate either public indifference or the hardened military mind.

One day, about the middle of May, 1936, Major Truman Smith,
the United States military attaché in Berlin, Germany,* was having

---

* Smith had been a Captain and Assistant Military Attaché in Berlin in 1922
when the United States Embassy had sent him to Munich to check up on an
obscure political agitator named Adolf Hitler. Smith noted in his diary at the
time that Hitler was "a marvelous demagogue." He reported to his superiors
that Hitler's National Socialist Labor Party "must be considered the Bavarian
counterpart to the Italian fascisti . . . a political influence quite disproportion-
ate to its actual strength." Of Hitler he said, "His ability to influence a popular
assembly is uncanny." William L. Shirer says in his *The Rise and Fall of the
Third Reich* that Smith "had a remarkable bent for political analysis."

breakfast in his Berlin apartment with his wife, Kay. Mrs. Smith noticed a small item about Colonel Charles A. Lindbergh in the Paris *Herald.* He had visited some airplane factories in France with his wife.

Mrs. Smith mentioned to her husband that the Lindberghs evidently felt secure enough to leave their son Jon at home in England with the servants in spite of the murder of their first-born in the United States.

A few days later, Smith was mulling over his air-intelligence problems. He himself was an infantry officer. He had no background in aviation, and no way of judging developments in that area. His chief air attaché was popular with the German Air Ministry but, according to Smith, "lacked intelligence training and skill in preparing aviation reports." The air attaché also had other deficiencies, from Smith's (and his own) point of view: he was a pilot, but lacked deep knowledge of air science and engineering, and his connections with the German Air Ministry stopped at an echelon below the top.

Smith saw evidence of tremendous military aviation activity in Germany, although the Versailles Treaty had prohibited Germany from building warplanes. Smith wrote later, "Everywhere one turned one saw airfields under construction. . . . Ever-increasing numbers of officers in their new blue-gray uniforms could be observed in the streets of Berlin." He knew of new factories, too, but had visited only one of these places, the Henschel airplane works at Schoenefelt, near Berlin, in 1935. Here, strangely —in a group of very modern buildings, carefully dispersed against bombing, each containing its own power plant—the most obsolete airplanes were being produced. Goering's Luftwaffe was equipped only with such fighters as the HE (Heinkel)-51 or the AR (Arado)-55—wooden biplanes with top speeds of 204 m.p.h. and 180 m.p.h., respectively—both far slower than comparable American fighters. Bombers were mainly the JU(Junkers)-52, with a speed of 150 m.p.h. None of these was any threat to the United States or even to Europe, yet Smith knew that the Germans were designing much faster, more modern aircraft secretly in contravention of the Versailles Treaty—and besides there were all those pilots in uniform, and the new factories.

Air intelligence in those days was, like the Air Corps, part of the Army, and the U.S. Army was not air-minded. Smith had no man power to do a proper air-intelligence job, and no money to spend for it.

In this situation, he began thinking about Lindbergh, remembering what Mrs. Smith had said. If Lindbergh could leave his son in England while he visited French factories, why could he not come to Germany to inspect the Luftwaffe? Lindbergh was not only technically knowledgeable; he also had the prestige to tempt the Germans to invite him. Furthermore, Berlin was seething with preparations for the Olympic games, and the Germans wanted as many foreign celebrities on hand as they could snare.

Smith was aware of certain other probable predispositions among the Germans to invite Lindbergh. Hermann Goering, the head of the Luftwaffe, was extremely vain and loved celebrities. He was, of course, an airman himself, and shared in the camaraderie of pilots. General Milch, his second in command, was pro-American, as were many other Luftwaffe people. Smith began to work on getting the German government to invite Lindbergh to inspect the Luftwaffe.

His first move was to mention the idea of a Lindbergh visit to his top contact in the Luftwaffe, Colonel F. K. Hanesse. The same day, Hanesse broached the idea to his superiors, Milch and Goering, and got an immediate and enthusiastic approval. But before going further, Smith sat down with Hanesse and worked out a list of the places he wanted Lindbergh to see—a number of installations which had not been shown to any American.

When the two men had agreed on the list, they initialed it and Smith felt free to invite Lindbergh; the Germans could not use the flier only as a celebrity to dress up the Olympic games. He also felt free for another reason. The American Ambassador, Dr. William E. Dodd, a former University of Chicago historian and a strong pacifist, although friendly toward Smith was unsympathetic with the military. He had never asked for any data on German rearmament. However, Dodd was on leave in the United States and his chargé d'affaires, Ferdinand Mayer, was receptive to the idea of a Lindbergh visit.

Smith did not know Lindbergh or where he was living in England but wrote him a letter as a fellow-officer and sent it with a personal note to Colonel Scanlon, the United States Assistant Air Attaché in London, asking Scanlon to forward the letter.

AMERICAN EMBASSY
Office of the Military Attaché
Tiergartenstrasse 30.
Berlin

May 25, 1936

Colonel Charles Lindbergh
My dear Colonel Lindbergh:

Although I have not had the pleasure of your personal acquaintance, I feel free on account of my position in corresponding with you with respect to a possible desire on your part to visit Germany. . . .

[I have been] requested to extend to you in the name of General Goering and the German Air Ministry an invitation to visit Germany and inspect the new German civil and military air establishments.

I was further instructed by General Goering to inform you that the strictest censorship would be imposed . . . with respect to your visit and that they would not allow even the slightest notice to appear . . . except with your distinct approval. . . .

I need hardly tell you that the present German air development is very imposing and on a scale which I believe is unmatched in the world. Up until very recently this development was highly secretive, but in recent months they have become extraordinarily friendly to the American representatives and have shown us far more than the representatives of other powers. General Goering has particularly exerted himself for friendly relations with the United States.

From a purely American point of view, I consider that your visit here would be of high patriotic benefit. I am certain that they will go out of their way to show you even more than they will show us. . . .

Furthermore, if this program interests you, they assure me that immediately permits will be issued for you to fly your plane to Berlin and for accommodations at all the German military airfields, where you can preserve your incognito better than on civil fields. During your stay in Berlin your plane will be kept at the Staaken airdrome of the army in a Western suburb of Berlin.

Mr. Mayer and myself will arrange furthermore that no mention of your visit reaches either the American or German press. As a matter of fact, a large part of your time here will be spent in the provinces far from Berlin, as few of the new and large German air stations are located in the immediate vicinity of the capital. . . .

I personally suggest as a time for your visit the period of June 26–

July 3. This may be extended, however, to the 6th or 7th, in case such would seem desirable to you.

With very best wishes, and with those of my wife added, who is extremely hopeful that Mrs. Lindbergh will come with you, I am,

Yours very sincerely,

Truman Smith
Major, G.S.,
Military Attaché

"In the light of events which transpired," Smith wrote later, referring to himself in the third person, "the military attaché showed himself, in this letter, far too optimistic of his ability to shroud with secrecy a Lindbergh visit to Germany. When the visit actually took place it proved to be the most publicized intelligence operation the military attaché was ever connected with."

On June 5, Lindbergh replied from France, giving as his return address the Nicolson house he had rented in England: Long Barn, Weald, Sevenoaks. He responded warmly to Smith's suggestion, saying he could come to Germany between July 21 and August 5 or any time after August 25. He and his wife would fly in their new plane, a Miles "Mohawk," then under construction. He doubted that his visit could be kept secret from the press, he said, but hoped only to avoid the type of publicity and intrusions by the public he had experienced before. He asked Smith to convey his thanks to General Goering for the invitation, and added that he wanted no special entertainment—he was coming to look into aviation developments, and if he could do this it would occupy his time and satisfy his interest.

The details of the visit were arranged. Lindbergh would come from July 22 to August 1, the day the Olympic games were to start. Hanesse insisted that Lindbergh attend the opening ceremony as Goering's special guest. It was also decided that during the whole trip Lindbergh would be a civilian guest of the Lufthansa commercial airline, rather than a military guest of the Luftwaffe. He and his wife would stay at the Smiths' apartment; the Smiths had a spare bedroom belonging to their daughter who was in school in Switzerland.

In his memoir of this period, which he wrote between 1954 and 1956, Smith summarized his reasons for inviting Lindbergh to Germany. Again speaking of himself in the third person, he wrote:

(1) He desired to build up . . . [the] prestige [of his office] with the Luftwaffe and the German aeronautical world.
(2) He wished to have Lindbergh . . . see as many air factories and other establishments as possible in the limited period of the visit.
(3) He wished to bring Lindbergh together with the élite of Germany's aeronautical scientists, designers, engineers and air officers and to have [the air attaché] always at Lindbergh's side during these meetings.
(4) He desired Lindbergh's considered opinion as to the quality of the German air rearmament.

To set Lindbergh's visit in the general perspective of the time, it should be remembered that while the Nazi government was strongly anti-Semitic, and the Nazi party violently so, some Jews were still able to live and work in, and leave, Germany. The United States was uneasy about Germany, but the governments were on fairly good terms. The fact that the Olympic games were to be held in Berlin in 1936 gives some idea of the willingness of our people and of other peoples to maintain normal relations with the Germans. Political leaders in the United States, as well as in Europe, believed that however much Germany might fret under the strictures of the Versailles Treaty, Hitler did not have the military or economic power to implement his announced (in *Mein Kampf*) objectives in the world.

Under these circumstances, and with the urging of his own military attaché, Lindbergh's visit to Germany was accepted at the time without criticism.

Smith knew he was using Lindbergh's public prestige to open doors, and he had an idea that Lindbergh was well versed in aviation. What he did not know was that Lindbergh was an extremely keen observer. He saw more than either Smith or Goering had expected. And he was able to analyze what he saw, and draw useful conclusions from it.

He brought to the survey his own original way of evaluating things. For example, in one place he and an American officer were presented with eight new prototype airplanes drawn up for their inspection.

Lindbergh turned to the officer and said, "Which is the best plane?"

The officer, not an aviator, said, "How in the hell would I know? I haven't got the technical ability to figure that."

Lindbergh said, "Then which is the most beautiful plane?"

The officer looked them over and picked one out. "That one over there," he said.

"Of course," Lindbergh said, "it's the most beautiful and it's the best. Because in aerodynamics, the line of beauty and the line of greatest efficiency parallel each other. Of course, engines will make a great deal of difference . . ."

In telling this story the officer said, "Who in hell would have said anything like that but Lindbergh? No other officer ever made a remark like that to me."

Dr. Igor Sikorsky, the airplane designer, also held a high opinion of Lindbergh's analytical ability. He told a woman at a dinner party that the extraordinary thing about Lindbergh was not that he could fly any plane, but that he could come down and correct its mistakes on the drawing board.

His dinner partner asked, "You mean to say that all of your test pilots can't do that?"

Sikorsky said, "None of them. They can fly anything, and when they bring it down they can tell me how it handles, but they don't know *why* it behaves a certain way. Charles will know where the mistake is and have a suggestion about correcting it."

These talents were to prove extremely useful to Lindbergh in Germany. He and his wife arrived in Berlin in their newly built plane on July 22. On hand to greet them at the well-protected Staaken military airfield were the Smiths, Luftwaffe officers, and other Germans and Americans.

The Germans adhered to their agreed schedule. The day following his arrival, Lindbergh was taken to visit General Milch, State Secretary of the Air Ministry. Milch told him without equivocation that "Germany intended to create an Air Force second to none."

Lindbergh was invited to a large lunch at the luxurious Air Club, in Berlin, with top German Air Ministry officers. He came prepared with a speech, in which he showed a willingness to speak his mind, even at the risk of offending his hosts.

He offered a sobering statement on the responsibility of airmen to protect their countries. He pointed out that for the first time it was no longer possible to safeguard civilian centers with troops alone; that every European city was vulnerable to air attack. This meant that the families of the men present, as well as the intellectual and artistic and religious treasures of their countries, might be destroyed in a war.

The speech was printed verbatim in many German, European, and American newspapers, but there was no editorial comment within Germany for its statement might make Germany seem vulnerable to air attack.

Later that day, Lindbergh flew an experimental four-engine plane, the "Hindenburg," which he found inferior in speed and maneuverability to a similar American plane.

The next day he visited an élite German fighter wing. The pilots were good, but they flew the obsolete HE-51, powered by a German-made Pratt & Whitney Hornet engine. However, the leader of the wing informed Lindbergh that these planes would soon be replaced by the ME (Messerschmitt)-109, and gave him what later proved to be accurate information about the impressive speed, armament, and ceiling of the 109.

At the Adlershof Air Research Institute, which had been previously closed to Americans, Lindbergh noted that German scientists would speak freely on any subject but rockets. He told this to Smith, who failed to pass it along—as Smith notes, "an oversight of some importance."

That day, Lindbergh flew an HE-111 bomber, which he thought compared favorably with British and American bombers of that type and was superior to any similar bomber he had seen in France. He thought the ME-109 inferior to the British "Spitfire," but was impressed with the HE-111, the HE-112 fighter (which Ernst Udet, the German ace and head of development for the Luftwaffe flew for him), and the HE-118 dive bomber. He reported to Smith that German aviation design was coming of age: "I have never seen four planes, each distinct in type, built by one manufacturer, which were so well designed."

At the Junkers works in Dessau, Lindbergh gathered some interesting information. He saw the new JU(Junkers)-210 900-horse-power liquid-cooled engine; the JU-86, a low-wing all-metal bomber approximately equal to the HE-111; and the JU-87. This was a dive bomber, later to become well and bitterly known as the "Stuka." It was to be a major weapon in the Nazi blitzkrieg that overran

Europe, but at the time, American and other Western military leaders were committed to the strategic bombing of cities, although dive-bombing had been an American innovation. They were not impressed by the Stuka, which was a short-range plane designed to support ground troops. (They changed their minds after Poland and Dunkirk.) Nor could they appreciate why the Germans were turning out quantities of the obsolete JU-52 bomber. They did not know then that Goering intended to use these planes for military transport of parachute battalions and airborne troops—concepts foreign to the Allied military command (although the tactic had been invented by Billy Mitchell).

These inspections by Lindbergh were of great interest to the press. To keep newspapermen out of Lindbergh's way, Smith arranged to brief them each day at 5 P.M. at his apartment on Lindbergh's activities that day. Almost every morning he would listen to Lindbergh's report of the visits of the day before, his comparisons of German planes with those of the United States, France, and Britain, and discuss them in detail, with a stenographer present. It was obvious that Lindbergh was getting what Smith had wanted—a more complete picture of the Nazi buildup in the air, and the German capability for the future.

Smith says that he wanted to keep Lindbergh out of touch with any Nazi politicos, particularly Hitler, whom Lindbergh expressed a desire to meet, and to keep his visit strictly on a pilot-to-pilot basis. But the exception to this policy had to be Goering, for he was not only head of the Luftwaffe but wore so many political hats as well: Air Minister, Minister President of Prussia, President of the Reichstag, Commissioner of the Four-Year Plan, Minister of Forests, and Director of the State Theatre of Prussia.

On July 28, Goering gave a formal luncheon for Lindbergh at his official residence on the Wilhelmstrasse. It was attended by many famous airmen and leaders of the Luftwaffe and, of course, by Goering. It gave Smith and Lindbergh a chance to meet and appraise Goering, the No. 2 Nazi, the man Hitler called "my paladin."

Goering, according to Smith, was a man of wide interests. He was "magnetic, genial, vain, intelligent, frightening and grotesque." He had once been slim and handsome; now he was pig-fat, but formidable. Unlike some of his Nazi colleagues, he made an effort to behave like a gentleman and, says Smith, frequently succeeded. Often he was kindly and thoughtful with his subordinates. However, he had an ungovernable temper and could be brutal and remorseless when he got angry. His generals feared him in these moods, for he seemed murderous and probably was. Field Marshal Kesselring, in his memoirs, says that Goering probably seized the opportunity of Hitler's bloody house cleaning among his own men (when Captain Ernst Roehm was murdered) to murder his enemy General von Schleicher.

At the lunch, Goering got out a huge album of photographs and showed it to Lindbergh. The pictures were of Germany's first seventy military flying fields. Lindbergh looked at them with interest. He had the same reaction toward Goering as Smith had, but was able to bridge the gap between those two men. Lindbergh's appeal lay in his prestige (Goering's vanity was an easy target for this), his mastery of air matters, and the fact that he was of Swedish descent. Goering was quite disappointed to find that Lindbergh could not speak Swedish, a language he himself spoke fluently. For Goering was almost desperately devoted to the memory of his late Swedish wife, a devotion that took the form "of a love of Sweden and all things Swedish," Smith says. The Nazis treated the Swedish Ambassador better than any other foreign ambassador. Smith speculates that it is possible that Sweden was never invaded by Germany in World War II because of Goering's fanatic sentimentality.

If Goering loved Sweden, he worshiped Adolf Hitler. At the end of his huge formal banquet hall, lined with Italian Renaissance paintings, a small water color held the place of honor over the fireplace: it was signed *A. Hitler*. At the luncheon, Goering remarked, "Smith, there are only three truly great characters in all history: Buddha, Jesus Christ, and Adolf Hitler." Smith recalls that this statement reduced him to speechlessness.

One result of Lindbergh's first visit was that the American air attaché established much better liaison with, and easy entry into, the Luftwaffe. Too, following Lindbergh's trail came a host of American airmen to view German aviation. Igor Sikorsky, Glenn Martin, J. H. Kindelberger, of North American Aviation, and Professor Jerome C. Hunsaker, of the Massachusetts Institute of Technology, were only a few.

On September 8, 1936, the Lindberghs, Mrs. Morrow, and Constance Morrow visited the Nicolsons at Sissinghurst Castle in Kent. Lindbergh told Nicolson that Germany "possess[ed] the most powerful air-force in the world, with which they could do terrible damage to any other country, and could destroy [British] food supplies by sinking even convoyed ships." He said the Nazis were a great menace but that they were not a menace to England. According to Nicolson, Lindbergh predicted a complete separation between Fascism and Communism, and said that "if Great Britain supports the decadent French and the red Russians against Germany, there will be an end to European civilisation."

Later that year, on December 9, Lindbergh lunched at the House of Commons with Nicolson, who was then a leading member of Parliament, Ramsay MacDonald, the former Prime Minister of Great Britain and the head of the Labour party, and Thomas Inskip, Minister of Defense. At first Lindbergh was shy, but when the talk turned to aviation matters, he became quietly impressive. He told Inskip that there was no known defense against air attack. He repeated what he had said in Germany: all fortification was useless; the only protection was in deterrents. He said that the British ought to develop night bombers as a deterrent weapon, planes that would fly at 30,000 feet and be guided by the stars. "He and Inskip get off into technicalities," Harold Nicolson wrote in his diary that day, "and I observe that Inskip ceases to regard L. as an interesting person to meet at luncheon, and regards him (as he is) as a person whom he wants to talk to again."

In February, March, and April, 1937, Lindbergh and his wife flew to India and back. They stopped off in Italy and Yugoslavia. The trip made some news, but not of the intense personal nature that Lindbergh had come to abhor.

Living in England, the Lindberghs had managed to keep so far out of the public eye that there had not even been a hint in the newspapers that Anne was pregnant. (In America, Jon's birth had been predicted four months ahead of time by Walter Winchell.) On May 12, 1937, the day King George VI was crowned, Charles and Anne Lindbergh and Mrs. Morrow drove hurriedly from Kent to a nursing home in London where Anne was registered under an assumed name. The streets were so crowded with coronation throngs that they very nearly didn't make it in time; Land Morrow

Lindbergh, their third son, was born that day. Lindbergh persuaded the English authorities not to make the usual public announcement. Mrs. Morrow couldn't understand why, she told a friend. "I said to Charles if you want to avoid being bothered by the press, why don't you simply announce the birth of your child? After all, he's normal and born within wedlock." But Lindbergh held up the announcement for nearly two weeks before telephoning the news to the American Embassy.

AIR POWER

ALMOST A YEAR HAD PASSED SINCE LINDBERGH'S FIRST fruitful visit to Germany, and Smith wanted him to return. But Smith made no move in that direction until he got an invitation from Colonel Hanesse in 1937. The occasion for the second visit would be the annual dinner of the Lilienthal Aeronautical Society, and this time Lindbergh was to be a guest of the German government. More specifically, he went as a house guest of Baron and Baroness Kramer-Klett at their thirteenth-century castle in the Bavarian Alps. This had been arranged by friends of the Kramer-Kletts to boost their stock with the Brown Shirts. The Kramer-Kletts were not popular with the Nazis.

Flying his own plane to and within Germany gave Lindbergh a chance to observe more than he was shown. On a direct cross-country flight from Munich to Stuttgart, he saw that Goering had much expanded the number of his military airfields during the year since the first visit; his plane passed over a military airdrome on an average of once every ten minutes on a line parallel to and within easy striking distance of the Swiss and French borders.

One important sortie was to the Bavarian Motor Works (BMW) plant, producing Pratt & Whitney Hornet engines under license. This production could be switched quickly to the Junkers or the Daimler-Benz liquid-cooled engines of much higher horsepower. Lindbergh judged the potential output of the plant at twenty-four liquid-cooled engines per day.

Ernst Udet invited Lindbergh to the Rechlin air testing field, in Pomerania, one of the most secret air establishments in Germany. There he found seven airplanes drawn up for his inspection:

HE-111 medium bomber
DO (Dornier)-17 light bomber and reconnaissance plane
ME-109 single-engine flighter
Storch infantry artillery-liaison plane
Two-engine Focke-Wulf trainer bomber
HE-123 dive bomber
JU-87 dive bomber

This was the first time an American had had a chance to examine in detail the ME-109 or the DO-17. Lindbergh was impressed by these and the other craft, particularly the Storch, which he thought ought to be highly useful. And he speculated that the next plane the Germans would develop would probably be a twin-engine fighter, powered by two 1,200-horsepower Daimler-Benz liquid-cooled engines, and that this plane would probably be identified as the ME-110. It turned out that his deduction was accurate. The ME-110, built as Lindbergh had guessed, was the standard two-engine German fighter plane in World War II.

Lindbergh was also the first American to inspect Focke-Wulf helicopters. He estimated that these might replace standard airplanes in many functions.

Before Lindbergh left, he helped Smith prepare a report entitled "General Estimate of Germany's Air Power" as of November 1, 1937. This document, signed by Smith alone, contained a number of startling and disturbing statements about German air progress—or at least it would seem so to many people in the United States.

M.I.D. REPORT   9180
General Estimate as of
Nov. 1, 1937
───────────────

Germany is once more a world power in the air. Her air force and her air industry have emerged from the kindergarten stage. Full manhood will still not be reached for three years.

The astounding growth of German air power from a zero level to its present status in a brief four years must be accounted one of the most important world events of our time. What it portends for Europe is something no one today can foretell and must be left as a problem for future historians.

. . . It is difficult to express in a few words the literally amazing size of the German air industry. The twenty-three known plants have a potential annual plane production of probably 6,000 planes. There is every reason to believe that the plants identified only give a part of the picture and that the truth, could it be known, would show a still higher potential production. The scale of the German airplane motor industry is no less impressive. It is ever and again the size of this industry, which forces the foreigner—and even the American who is accustomed to think in big terms—to pause, ponder and wonder as to the future.

Behind this industry stands a formidable group of air scientists, with large and well equipped laboratories and test fields, constantly pushing forward the German scientific advance. This advance is remarkable. The fact that the United States still leads in its air science and manufacturing skill must not be allowed to overshadow the German achievements between 1933 and 1937 and above all, not to lead to an underestimate of what Germany will achieve in the future.

. . . The extraordinary technical excellence of American aviation has been built up as a result of 19 years' uninterrupted progress since the Armistice. To equal this accomplishment in 48 months would be miraculous. In truth, it has not been achieved. Yet, because on November 1, 1937, the American technical level . . . has not been reached is no ground for the United States to adopt the British policy of smugness. If so, we shall be doomed to the same position of air inferiority with respect to Germany, as France now finds herself in and which Great Britain just as certainly will find herself in tomorrow—unless she realizes her own shortcomings. . . .

In general, the German air power has now reached a stage where it must be given serious consideration as a powerful opponent by any single nation. Qualified officers who have had the opportunity to inspect recently the British, German and French air forces, believe that:

1. Technically Germany has outdistanced France in practically all fields.
2. Germany is on the whole superior to Great Britain in the quality of her plants, but is still slightly inferior to Great Britain in motors, but rapidly closing the gap.
3. Both Great Britain and France are still superior to Germany in the training levels of their respective Air Forces, but Germany has cut down greatly the gap separating her from these rivals, during the past 12 months.

A highly competent observer,* well acquainted with both American and German air developments, estimates that if the present progress curves of these two nations should continue as they have in the past two

* Lindbergh.

years, Germany should obtain technical parity with the USA by 1941 or 1942. If, however, America makes a single blunder, or if some important incident, whether political or a conflict of views within the armed forces, should slow down her present development, German air superiority will be realized still sooner.

In November 1937 it appears that the development of German air power is a European phenomenon of the first diplomatic importance. The upward movement is still gaining momentum.

Truman Smith,
Major, G.S.
Military Attaché.

Report 15, 540

The U.S. General Staff took the Smith report seriously, as did the Air Corps, but Smith says that politicians did not. Their impression of Germany, based on news stories from Berlin at the time, was of a weak and divided country whose army and air force were not nearly ready for war. Smith's "General Estimate" of German air power did not shake this false confidence.

Returning to England, Lindbergh asked for and got an appointment with Stanley Baldwin, Prime Minister of Great Britain. (He had met Baldwin on his first visit to England in 1927.) He tried to warn Baldwin about the tremendous power of the German Air Force. He argued that England should speedily build up her own air force for her own safety. Britain had some excellent aircraft—the Spitfire was, for example, faster than the fastest Messerschmitt—but there were not enough Spitfires or even slower craft. Furthermore, England had too many different types of aircraft, which complicated maintenance. Too, British air production was low compared with Germany's.

Baldwin listened politely, but was not convinced to act. This warning was the same sort of thing he was hearing regularly from Winston Churchill, and he had no use for Churchill or his line. He certainly wasn't going to change his policy because of the personal opinions of an American aviator.

In May, 1938, Lindbergh told Harold Nicolson, still a member of Parliament, that Britain could not fight Germany, since defeat would be inevitable. He said, according to Nicolson, that the German Luftwaffe "is ten times superior to that of Russia, France and Great Britain. [English] defences are simply futile and the barrage balloons a mere waste of money. He thinks [Britain] should just give way and then make an alliance with Germany." Discounting Lindbergh's views as colored by his emphasis on air power, Nicolson gloomily concluded that Lindbergh was probably right in saying Britain was outmastered in the air.

Later that year, after more than two peaceful years in England, the Lindberghs moved to France, first to the Channel Island of Iliec and later to an apartment in Paris.

Alarmed by the fantastic progress in German military aviation, which seemed all the more remarkable when it was measured against the lethargy of England, France, and the United States in this area, Lindbergh determined to make a thorough study of air power in other European countries. With the help of military attachés in several U.S. embassies, he gathered data on air strength in their countries. With his wife he made survey trips to Poland, Rumania, Czechoslovakia, and the Soviet Union.

This was his third visit to the Soviet Union. The first was during his China trip in 1931; the second came in 1933 as a side excursion during the Atlantic survey flight. On the second trip the Lindberghs spent a week in the two most important Soviet cities, Moscow and Leningrad. On that trip Lindbergh had had a chance to estimate the quality of Russian aviation. He found the Russians copying planes designed in other countries, and not doing it well.

During their third trip, which was made in August, 1938, the Lindberghs saw more of Soviet air power. The Russians had bought aircraft-manufacturing plants from other countries, and were turning out planes and engines. But the rate of production was far below the plants' potential. And the maintenance of existing planes seemed to Lindbergh extremely poor. He could get no figures on the number of aircraft the Russians had. But in his judgment the organization of production and of the Soviet air force was so muddled, and the quality of maintenance so low, that numbers of planes made no difference. He concluded that the Russians were not a significant power in the air.

His assessment of the overwhelming power of the Luftwaffe as opposed to the French, British, and Soviet air forces led him to continue to warn leaders in both countries, as he helped warn those of his own country, about the dangers they were facing.

He did this in off-the-record discussions. One of these led to the first American press attack on Lindbergh's politics. *This Week* magazine ran an article stating that Lindbergh had made pro-Nazi and anti-Russian remarks at a private dinner at Cliveden, the famous house belonging to the late Lady Nancy Astor. Lady Astor denied that this had happened. The truth of the matter was that Lindbergh had conferred with a group of members of Parliament, at their request, on the relative strengths of the air arms of England, Germany, and the Soviet Union.

What Lindbergh told these people was what he had concluded after investigation: that the Russian Air Force was ineffectual. This was a tremendously explosive opinion in Great Britain, because British foreign policy was based in part on a militarily strong Russia. On this basis, many British politicians had dragged their feet over rearming their own country. If they were wrong, it meant not only political defeat for themselves but could mean disaster for the British Isles.

In the Soviet Union, where the Lindberghs had been the honored guests of the Russian aviators, he was widely denounced in the newspapers for his ingratitude.

Actually, his judgment of the Russan Air Force later proved uncomfortably accurate. Without air superiority, the Germans could never have got so far so fast as they did before they were stopped on the ground in Russia.

Leakage of this story embarrassed United States missions in England and the Soviet Union. Our military attachés in both countries asked Lindbergh to deny the *This Week* report to smooth relations with the two countries. But, according to Smith, Lindbergh decided to follow his "long-established policy of never either confirming or denying press reports."

Lindbergh made one more visit to Germany at Smith's request, in 1938. It was during this visit that he was awarded a medal by the Nazi government, an incident that, more than any other, helped change the picture of Lindbergh from the all-American hero to a pro-Nazi, a Nazi, or a defeatist. The circumstances are worth examining in detail.

In 1937, Ambassador Dodd, who left no doubt of his strong anti-Nazi views, had been replaced as U.S. Ambassador to Germany by Hugh R. Wilson. Wilson was a more pragmatic type who was willing to try to deal with the Nazis. Like Smith, he saw in Lindbergh a bridge to Goering, and he accepted the Smith-Lindbergh evaluation of Goering as a man who might be dealt with. During Lindbergh's third visit to Germany (October 11–29, 1938), Wilson set up a small stag dinner at the American Embassy to which he invited Goering and several key Nazis. The purpose of the dinner was, according to Smith, to persuade Goering to allow Jews who were forced to leave Germany to take some of their assets with them. Smith says that it was reasonable to assume that Goering could be persuaded on this—that, in fact, he had helped many Jews to escape and probably without any financial gain to himself (although Smith thinks that men close to him made money on these transactions). Of course, if Goering could be won over, then he could use his influence with Hitler.

The dinner was held on October 18, 1938, at the American Embassy. About four o'clock that afternoon an officer of the attaché section of the German Air Ministry telephoned the American Embassy—a time when no American officer was in the office—and left a message with a secretary that Goering intended to confer a German decoration on Lindbergh at the dinner that night.

The message was not delivered to either Smith or his air attaché until the following morning—after the event had taken place. Even had it been delivered in advance, Smith thinks it was probably impossible that anything could have been done gracefully to prevent the presentation.

Among those present at the dinner were Hugh Wilson; the Italian and Belgian ambassadors; various American officials, Dr. Igor Sikorsky; Professor Dr. Heinkel, German aircraft manufacturer; Professor Baeumker, chief of the air research division of the Air Ministry. Goering arrived later with several aides and adjutants.

He greeted his host and shook hands with the other guests. Then Goering went over to Lindbergh and began making a speech in German, a language Lindbergh did not understand. Goering held in his hand a small red box which his aide-de-camp had given him.

Since it could be seen that Lindbergh did not know what was going on, Wilson, Smith, and the American Consul-General, stepped forward to translate. Raymond Geist told Lindbergh that Goering was about to decorate him with the *Verdienstkreuz der Deutscher Adler* (Service Cross of the German Eagle), a high civilian medal. This was being given to Lindbergh for his services to aviation and particularly for his 1927 solo flight from New York to Paris—for which he had been decorated by many governments, but never by Germany.

"Under the circumstances," Smith wrote, "there was of course no possibility for Lindbergh to reject the decoration, even if the attaché's secretary had properly transmitted the Air Ministry's message. . . . To have done so would have been a personal affront to Ambassador Wilson . . . and to Minister Goering, who in a sense was his host in Germany."

Wilson said as much in a letter to Lindbergh from Vermont on August 4, 1941:

Neither you, nor I, nor any other American present had any previous hint that the presentation would be made.

I have always felt that if you had refused the decoration, presented under these circumstances, you would have been guilty of a breach of good taste. It would have been an act offensive to the guest of the Ambassador of your country, in the house of the Ambassador.

"At the moment," Truman Smith wrote, "the award of the medal seemed quite natural. . . . October 1938 was a month of much diminished international tension. Europe, after the Munich accord, was relaxing. The prospect of war had receded into the background. The notorious anti-Semitic riots of November 9, 1938, which were to shock the world, lay still some weeks away."

However, when Lindbergh and Smith brought the medal home that night, both their wives instantly and almost instinctively reacted against it. Lindbergh silently handed the box to his wife.

She opened it and glanced at the medal and looked away. Then she said without the slightest trace of emotion, "The albatross," a prescient description. Lindbergh gave the box to Mrs. Smith, asking, "Kay, exactly what did I get this for?"

Mrs. Smith read the German words written on the paper inside the box and repeated what the consul-general had said: that it was for his services to aviation and for the Paris flight. Later that evening, she said several times to her husband, "This medal will surely do Lindbergh much harm." Lindbergh never wore the medal, but sent it to the Lindbergh collection of the Missouri Historical Society in St. Louis, along with his other decorations, awards, trophies, and presents.

Although the award was reported by newspapers the next day,

there was not much criticism of Lindbergh for accepting it until after the government-organized anti-Semitic riots, which were followed by new, fierce, repressive measures by the Nazi government against the Jews. Then many newspapers in the United States made strong attacks on Lindbergh for accepting and, even more, for retaining the medal.

Wilson and Smith were disturbed by these attacks, but after talking it over they decided not to explain the circumstances surrounding the giving of the award. To do so, they felt, would have revealed their ulterior purposes in bringing Lindbergh and Goering together, an obviously impolitic act.

Lindbergh wrote Smith about the medal in 1953. The medal had never worried him, he said, and he doubted if it had added to his later troubles—when he was involved in anti-interventionist politics during the America First period. It had been just an excuse for attacking him. As he has since told other friends, if it hadn't been the medal, his enemies would have found something else.

Lindbergh is demonstrably wrong in this opinion. The medal was a most redolent albatross to hang around his neck, and most useful to cast doubt on his motives, his honesty, his integrity, and even his loyalty to his country. Between November, 1939, and December 7, 1941, the Nazi medal was mentioned in scores of speeches and articles, and many deductions were drawn from it about Lindbergh's politics. The damage that the albatross did to Lindbergh's reputation is incalculable.

If Lindbergh had given the medal back after Germany declared war on the United States, he might have retrieved some good will from the press and public over the matter. In 1942 an occasion presented itself for doing just that. Mayor Fiorello La Guardia, of New York City, planned an anti-Fascist demonstration. La Guardia, who had been a military pilot in Italy with U.S. forces during World War I, recruited a group of veterans of that theatre of war to meet at the New York City Hall and throw their Italian medals into a pot. The medals would be melted down and delivered to Italy in the form of bullets.

La Guardia asked Harry Bruno to invite Lindbergh to throw his *Verdienstkreuz* into the pot. Bruno passed the suggestion along to Deac Lyman. Lyman relayed the reply that Lindbergh would not participate in the ceremony.

Lindbergh's reason for not doing so is his own secret. But one of his friends says, "It would be entirely contrary to his nature to take part in a stunt designed to curry public favor." That, coupled with his stated notion that he regarded the whole thing as unimportant to begin with, is as near as we can come to an explanation of his intransigence.

The medal aside, just reporting Nazi progress in air power was, in 1938, equated with being pro-Nazi or untruthful, or both. When Lindbergh dined that year in England with the British Ambassador to Germany, Sir Nevile Henderson, the Ambassador asked him to arouse England to the "quality and magnitude of the aviation program in Germany." Henderson told Lindbergh, "They do not believe me when I describe it."

In the United States, generals George C. Marshall and H. H. Arnold were also uneasy about German air power, but were unable to get Congress or the administration to set a new U.S. air program in motion until after the fall of France in 1940.

Truman Smith's recollection of Lindbergh's views of Germany resulting from his visits in 1936, 1937, and 1938 were:

1. Lindbergh distrusted the Nazi government and found its anti-Semitic policies abhorrent. He did not want to return to Germany after the November, 1938, riots but did make two subsequent visits, without his wife, not for the United States.

2. Lindbergh admired most of Germany's aviators, scientists, and industrialists whom he had met. His views on Goering were mixed, as were Smith's.*

3. He believed that a war in Europe would be a catastrophe for Western civilization, and thought that such a war would result either in a German victory or in Russia's becoming the dominant power of Europe.

4. Lindbergh hoped that if Hitler did launch a war it would be against the Soviet Union. He thought that France, Great Britain, and the United States should remain neutral and build up their military strength, so that they could dictate terms of peace to an exhausted Germany and Russia.

Lindbergh's last two visits to prewar Germany in December,

---

* So were others'. Albrecht Bernstorff, a German diplomat in the London Embassy who was later murdered by the Nazis, thought (in 1937) that Goering was "an adventurer, pure and simple," and that if he were asked to shoot at Sandringham he might become a friend to England.

1938, and January, 1939, had nothing to do with American intelligence. They were, in fact, missions whose purpose was kept secret from Smith at the time. Lindbergh assured Smith that knowledge of his goal might be embarrassing to the military attaché.

The purpose of the visits was to buy aircraft engines for the French government to install in French fighter planes. Returning from Germany, where he had seen the JU-88 bomber with a top speed of 310 m.p.h., Lindbergh learned that the fastest military pursuit airplane in France was the Morane, which could not top 297 m.p.h. And this was only an experimental ship, not yet in production. Even the German bombers which were slower than the JU-88 were fast enough so that the Morane would have been ineffective against them.

Armed with this information, Lindbergh prodded French officials at a number of secret conferences in Paris with American Ambassador William C. Bullitt. At one of these meetings in Bullitt's house —at which Premier Daladier, M. Jean Monnet, and French Air Minister Guy Le Chambre were present, along with Bullitt and Lindbergh—the question came up of how the French might obtain aviation engines in the 1,000-horsepower range. British engine production was being totally absorbed in Britain; American production was insufficient to meet both domestic and French needs.

At this conference, which took place on October 3, 1938 (the Lindberghs were living in a Paris apartment near the Bois de Boulogne at the time), Lindbergh suggested that the French might buy the high-powered Junkers or Daimler-Benz liquid-cooled engines he had seen. Daladier and Le Chambre were doubtful that the Germans would sell them such engines, but after subsequent conferences with Lindbergh, at which he was the only foreigner present, they asked him to explore the possibility of buying four hundred engines. Le Chambre felt that the French public would never accept a purchase of German airplanes, but German engines in French airframes was a different matter.

Lindbergh said he would undertake the mission, providing that "he receive no remuneration whatsoever, regardless of the outcome." On December 19, 1938, Lindbergh flew to visit General Ernst Udet at his home in Berlin and broached the proposition. Udet took no stand on the idea, but said it was obviously political and would have to be taken up with General Milch. The next day, with Udet present, Lindbergh again stated the French proposal. Milch asked only if the French were serious. Being assured that they very much wanted to buy engines, he said he would take the matter up "at least with Goering." Later the same day, Milch called Lindbergh and asked him to return to the Air Ministry; he said he thought it best to wait to approach Goering until after the Christmas holidays. When the time was right, Lindbergh would receive, in Paris, a dinner invitation from Milch.

Lindbergh left his plane at Tempelhof Airport because of bad weather conditions (and because it would be an excuse to return to Germany) and took the train to Paris.

The dinner invitation from Milch arrived in Paris around the middle of January, 1939. When Lindbergh got off the train in Berlin on January 16, he was met by Smith but decided to stay at the Hotel Esplanade.

That afternoon, Udet telephoned asking Lindbergh to meet Milch at the Air Ministry at 6:00 P.M. Milch told Lindbergh that Germany was prepared to sell the French an unspecified number of Daimler-Benz liquid-cooled engines of 1,250 horsepower. These would have to be paid for in foreign currencies. He told Lindbergh to keep the matter secret and to use the ostensible purchase of a Storch liaison plane as a cover story.

On January 18, Lindbergh flew out of prewar Berlin for the last time. The next day he called on Minister Le Chambre and told him of the German offer. Le Chambre related the information to Daladier, who let Lindbergh know that he was greatly pleased.

The deal fell through when Germany occupied the rest of Czechoslovakia. Le Chambre later told Lindbergh that negotiations had started well with the Germans but that the French Foreign Office killed the plan as a result of the worsening of relations with Germany. Colonel (later General) Hanesse recalled in 1954 that he had heard of the airplane engine negotiations, and that the purchase had been approved by Goering but without consulting Hitler. Hanesse said that if Hitler had known about it, he would not have approved the deal.

With the collapse of negotiations, Lindbergh had no reason to return to Germany. He did not go back until after the war.

23

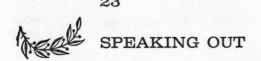

SPEAKING OUT

LINDBERGH'S JUDGMENTS OF NAZI AIR STRENGTH AND OF the air power of other countries had been given to U.S. military attachés. But his private opinions voiced to various French and British political leaders were having civilian reverberations. Joseph P. Kennedy, United States Ambassador to Great Britain, heard of Lindbergh's appraisals and wired him in France, asking him to come to London to discuss them.

Lindbergh visited Joseph Kennedy in London on September 21, 1938. He also met John F. Kennedy, who was serving as his father's aide in the Embassy.

Lindbergh followed up the visit with a letter to Ambassador Kennedy, probably at Kennedy's request. In this letter, Lindbergh sharpened and strengthened certain opinions he and Smith had worked out in Smith's estimate of German air power. The letter reveals the extent of Lindbergh's observations, and embodies the judgments which informed his actions during the next three years. In it he stated that the German air force was without question the strongest in the world—stronger than that of all other European nations combined—and that German production potential was on the order of twenty thousand aircraft a year. While the United States had once held the lead, Germany was catching up and had already outdistanced us so far as fighting planes were concerned. Germany's main point of vulnerability in wartime would be in obtaining raw materials.

Lindbergh said he thought that civilization had never been in greater danger; the great cities of Europe were threatened with extinction. France's air fleet was pitiful; England's was better, but no match for Germany's. He estimated that France was building a mere fifty aircraft a month, the English about two hundred a month.

He dismissed the Czech air force as negligible, its only up-to-date planes being Russian made, but thought that the Czechs had good antiaircraft and machine guns.

He found Russian air strength to be an unknown quantity. While Russia had enough planes to make her air force felt in any war, he felt little reliance could be placed on it. As for airplane manufacture, the Russians had American machinery and copies of American factories, but their production was inefficient.

Lindbergh concluded that it was imperative to avoid a war in Europe because such a war might wipe out civilization. He was not sure that England and France could beat Germany, but even if they could, it would be at great cost. The result would be a Europe lying prone at the feet of Russia; from his observation of life in the Soviet Union, he felt that anything was to be preferred to that. As an alternative to war with the West, he advised allowing Germany to expand to the east.

He ended by repeating that German strength must be reckoned with, that the Germans were a great and able people, and that England and France were too lacking in air power to defend themselves.

Kennedy sent a long cable to Cordell Hull, the United States Secretary of State, the same day, saying, "YOU MAY FEEL THAT THIS CONFIDENTIAL EXPRESSION OF HIS PERSONAL OPINION MAY BE OF INTEREST TO THE PRESIDENT AND TO THE WAR AND NAVY DEPARTMENTS," and quoted the paragraphs from Lindbergh's letter which pertain to his judgment of air power of the various countries. The telegram was signed "KENNEDY." It omitted Lindbergh's warnings about the consequences of a European war and his political judgments.

"Despite Ambassador Kennedy's specific request [suggestion?]," Smith writes, "there is no evidence in the State Department files that the cable was ever shown to the War Department, nor has any copy of this cable been found in War Department files. There is also no notation on the copy in the State Department files that this cable was ever shown, as Kennedy requested, to the President. Therefore, it would seem that however wide a distribution the cable may have had within the State Department, Colonel Lindbergh's views could have exerted only a small influence on the American foreign and aviation policies."

Lindbergh wrote again to Joseph Kennedy on November 9, 1938, when he returned to his Channel Island home, of his plan to take a house for his family in Berlin for the winter "to learn more about Germany."

In this letter he reiterated his concern about the air situation. He said that the Germans were making faster progress than he had reckoned and that German air supremacy had become as much a fact of politics as English sea power. And he said again that a general war would make the future of Western civilization very doubtful.

Around the same time, Lindbergh also wrote directly to General Arnold, Chief of the Air Corps of the U.S. Army, urging him to visit Germany immediately. He said Arnold ought to see for himself what was being done there not only in aviation but in other areas.

Arnold answered him a week later that he was "100% in favor of making the trip just as you outlined. As a matter of fact it is to be noted that a mission headed by the undersigned was scheduled to go to Germany about 3 months ago, but for diplomatic reasons it was called off. Upon receipt of your letter, the matter was reopened and taken up with the Chief of Staff and the Secretary of War, who stated that due to the political situation at this moment it was not deemed advisable that the Chief of the Air Corps go to Germany at this time." But he asked Lindbergh to keep sending whatever information he could about Germany.

Lindbergh agreed with this judgment, but he said that it was advisable to keep abreast of German aviation, which was undoubtedly the leader in Europe and was even ahead of the United States in certain areas.

Lindbergh wrote to Arnold again emphasizing the need for developing extremely high-speed aircraft, planes that could fly at five hundred miles per hour at altitude. He said that European bombers were now flying at speeds above three hundred miles per hour and that speeds of more than four hundred miles per hour were attributed to new pursuit craft. The whole thrust of military aircraft abroad was toward extremely high speeds, he said, even at the sacrifice of range and bombload.

Arnold never did make his visit to Nazi Germany. The same considerations that made it inadvisable for him to go there also caused Lindbergh to cancel his plans to live in Germany that winter.

From the surveys Lindbergh made, U.S. intelligence had knowledge of the existence and approximately correct characteristics of all German aircraft plants (Lindbergh and Smith missed a couple of engine factories in Austria); they knew where most German airfields were located, the approximate type and number of aircraft in the Luftwaffe; they were aware of the personnel difficulties encountered by a rapidly expanding German air force. They had learned the useful fact that the Luftwaffe was designed "for close support of the German armies in Europe, rather than as a long-range air force constructed primarily to bomb objectives far behind the front lines."

24

AMERICA FIRST

LINDBERGH'S ASSESSMENTS OF AIR POWER IN EUROPE HAD developed the data that Smith wanted. But Lindbergh was not just a passive observer. What he saw and learned led him to conclude that war was inevitable in Europe. He knew that the Luftwaffe was designed to help conquer Europe swiftly, and he estimated that the Germans could do what they planned.

He did not think that the United States could thwart a German victory. Our production of military planes was small. We had no excess fighter craft to bolster French and English defenses, or extra bombers that could help them counterattack. The only way we could help the Allies in the air would be to strip ourselves of strength. This, Lindbergh thought, would weaken this country to no avail.

His observation that the Luftwaffe was meant mainly for close support of ground troops convinced him that once the Germans had secured victory they would be no threat to the United States. Their bombers were not designed to cross the Atlantic. If the Nazis tried to establish bases in this hemisphere, we could fight them off. Their navy and air force were a threat to a sea power like England, but not to a self-contained continental power like the United States. And besides, Lindbergh thought, they really had no designs on this hemisphere.

He was in a unique position. On the one hand, he could talk the language of pilots, mechanics, and designers, and at the same time speak to the military as an officer. On the other hand, he could tell what he learned and say what he thought to leading politicians, generals, and heads of state.

His thinking was conditioned by his father's experience in World War I. His father had been right about that war: it did lead to a suppression of civil liberties in the United States and had settled nothing in Europe. Professional historians in the United States after the war tended to the view that the Germans had not been so wrong in the first place and that behind the front of a war for democracy the Allies were also preserving the French and British empires. The United States had helped them win their war (it was "their" war) but the peace had turned into something other than Wilsonian ideals had adumbrated. Both liberals and conservatives could agree on that. But they split on whose fault it was. The liberals believed that it was partly the fault of the United States that Versailles and postwar European policies were not better managed. The conservative view was that Europeans were decadent and untrustworthy and that we should have nothing to do with them. Oceans were very wide in those days.

Lindbergh sailed for the United States in April, 1939. His wife and two sons were to follow. The family was moving back to the United States permanently.

While he was aboard ship, Lindbergh got a radiogram from Major General Arnold asking for a meeting. Lindbergh called Arnold within an hour of his arrival, from the Morrow house in Englewood. They arranged to meet the next day at a hotel in West Point. There they talked for three hours, then adjourned to the Academy baseball field where a game was in progress. They kept on talking. Arnold told of the incident in his book *Global Mission,* describing how Lindbergh filled him in on the Luftwaffe while they sat unnoticed in the grandstand.

Lindbergh was then a colonel on the inactive Reserve list. Arnold asked him to take a two-week refresher course in the Air Corps, and then to go on "extended active duty," which meant remaining in uniform for a year. Lindbergh refused but agreed to continue at his own expense to work for the Air Corps and for the National Advisory Committee for Aeronautics, a civilian agency assisting U.S. Military Air Development, of which he had been a member since 1928.

Lindbergh's first major assignment was to confer with various procurement officers and others in the government connected with aviation. He attended the vital conference of the National Advisory Committee for Aeronautics on April 20. The upshot of this conference was a recommendation to Congress for a program to accelerate and expand aircraft design and production. This was almost immediately translated by Congress into an appropriation of $46 million. The money was quickly spent by the War Department for more airplanes.

In May, 1939, Lindbergh made two transcontinental inspection tours in an Army P-36 pursuit plane. (It was on one of these trips that he dropped in at Roswell, New Mexico, for a day with Dr. Goddard.) He visited almost every aircraft-manufacturing plant in the United States. He made his findings known to a military aviation board—that U.S. military planes did not equal the performances of European combat planes, but that U.S. industry had the capability to design and build the best aircraft in the world. He had joined this board, consisting of Colonel (later General) Carl ("Tooey") Spaatz, General W. G. Kilner, and two other officers, at Arnold's request. Their findings were of "inestimable value," Arnold said later, in getting new planes designed and built for the U.S. Air Corps. These were the planes that helped win the war.

Lindbergh also began telling his observations of European air power to American industrialists and politicians in private. His factual, eyewitness reports had a devastating effect on most of his listeners, and generally they agreed with his conclusion that our best course was to stay out of Europe's affairs. However, Vannevar Bush, a leading scientist, was moved to action by one of Lindbergh's reports. After listening to Lindbergh, he got together with James B. Conant, of Harvard University, Karl T. Compton, of M.I.T., and Frank B. Jewett, of the Bell Telephone Laboratories. They worked out a plan to mobilize American scientists to overtake the head start of Nazi technology in weaponry. The result was the National Defense Research Committee, which was ultimately responsible for the invention of the atomic bomb.

In July, 1939, Lindbergh was introduced to Fulton Lewis, Jr., by a mutual friend at a small private dinner. (Lewis was the former reporter who had provided the ammunition for the Black committee hearings on air-mail contracts.) Lindbergh told him how he felt about the various air forces, and about politics in general. Lewis, a radio commentator and a strong right-wing opponent of the Roosevelt administration, was delighted with what he heard.

He said, "Colonel, I am going on vacation soon and a number of prominent people are going to fill in for me as guest commentators on the air. Why don't you take over for an evening and tell the American people how you feel about things."

Lewis is reported to have expected Lindbergh to decline quickly. But Lindbergh did not reply for a minute or so, and when he did, it was to ask for a rain check on the invitation.

Early in September, 1939, after the German invasion of Poland and the quick declaration of war on Germany by England and France, Lindbergh called Lewis at his Maryland farm to say he wanted to talk about the radio broadcast Lewis had suggested.

Until that time, Lindbergh had drawn a sharp line between his public aspect, as a colonel in the Air Corps Reserve, and his private aspect, as an independent observer of European politics and air power. But with the war declared between most of the major powers of Europe, he put (as he said) his rights as a private citizen above his duty as a military man; he chose to speak out in public on a matter that crossed the frontiers between his military and private obligations.

As long as he held an Army commission, he was subject to the wishes of his Commander in Chief, and President Roosevelt let him know this quickly, albeit behind the scenes. Roosevelt's wishes were conveyed to Lindbergh by various emissaries in quiet ways as soon as Roosevelt learned that Lindbergh was going to speak in public. Secretary of war Harry Woodring reported to Roosevelt that Lindbergh was going ahead with his plan to talk on the radio, and had refused to show a copy of his speech to the War Department in advance. Harold L. Ickes, Secretary of the Interior, wrote in his diary, "Woodring was sure that he was going to take a stand against the neutrality legislation that the President wants. [This legislation was an amendment of the Neutrality Act.*] He sent word to Lindbergh that there was likelihood of his losing his position and

---

* The Neutrality Act of 1937 attempted to legislate the United States out of a future war by restricting the sale of arms to belligerent nations and preventing the United States from trading with belligerents. The President was empowered to declare when a state of war existed between other countries and to forbid export of arms, ammunition, and implements of war to the warring nations. Other trade with belligerents was prohibited, too, unless carried in foreign ships. It was the first of these provisions that Roosevelt wished to change. The new Neutrality Act was to relax the Arms Embargo and permit any country, whether at war or not, to buy matériel and remove it from the United States in foreign ships. The effect of this would be to allow France and England to buy arms from the United States.

rank as an officer in the Reserve Corps. But Lindbergh continued to be obstinate."

And Roosevelt continued to be cautious. Lindbergh's image was a little tarnished by his acceptance of the Nazi medal from Goering, but it was still magnetic. Roosevelt knew from experience that Lindbergh was a hard man to handle, and he wasn't going to give him the easy gift of martyrdom by cashiering him.

Roosevelt was sure that Lindbergh was after power—why else would he risk his commission and his good name by fighting the administration? According to C. B. Allen, the ex-New York *World* reporter and old-time friend of Lindbergh's, Lindbergh was visited by a man who said he had a message that originated in the White House. The message was that the administration was going to create a separate Air Force, a new department as important as War and Navy, and a new Cabinet post to go with it. The first Secretary of Air could be Lindbergh if he would support Roosevelt's position of aid to France and England "short of war."

Lindbergh refused, and kept silent on the offer for more than a year.

The size of the bribe was a clear indication that Roosevelt was worried—before Lindbergh had said a word in public—about the strength of his appeal. It was also an index of the lack of domestic support for Roosevelt's posture of pro-Allied neutrality.

When Lindbergh did not prove vulnerable to the offer of power, Roosevelt decided to try to reach him in another way. He gave orders to the Internal Revenue Service to go into Lindbergh's tax returns. According to one Lindbergh friend, the order was to "get Lindbergh." A newspaperman tipped Lindbergh that the story would break in the press that the government was looking into his tax returns. Would he care to comment?

Lindbergh unexpectedly said he would be delighted to talk to the press about the subject. He said he would make a statement, and that he had copies of all his income-tax returns to back it up. The newspapermen thought that at last they had Lindbergh on the defensive.

Lindbergh told the reporters that he had always felt it was a privilege to be an American, no matter what tax you paid. If you paid what you owed, you weren't really paying for the privilege of being a citizen. And, he said, he'd realized it was often difficult to figure out what you really owed for income tax. So after he had calculated his tax each year, he had made it a practice to add 10 per cent to what he thought he owed, and pay it.

He'd been doing this for many years and he'd never heard any complaints from the Internal Revenue people. He didn't expect any rebates either, he said, deadpan.

This was the end of what had seemed a promising scandal.

This was during the eight months in 1939–40 known as "the phony war." Hitler had attacked Poland; the Soviet Union had also gone into Poland and was fighting in Finland; but France and England had only declared war on the Axis without fighting it.

Harry Hopkins, who became Roosevelt's most trusted confidential aide during the war, wrote to his mother in October, 1939, "The only interest here [in Washington], as everywhere, is the war and I believe that we really can keep out of it. Fortunately, there is no great sentiment in this country for getting into it although I think almost everyone wants to see England and France win." Robert E. Sherwood, who quoted this letter in his biography of Roosevelt and Hopkins, commented, "In those two sentences Hopkins unconsciously stated the greatest problem Roosevelt had to face in his entire Administration."

Roosevelt in 1939–40 was certain that the French and British fleets were vital to United States defenses; he felt bound to help those two countries for that reason alone. His knowledge of geography told him that United States outposts on the Atlantic side were the British Isles, France, the Iberian Peninsula, and the north and west coasts of Africa, and, in the Pacific, the Netherlands East Indies, the Philippines, and the Marianas. If these fell, United States shipping was threatened, and that meant economic strangulation. So, he "risked political suicide," says Sherwood, in 1939 to get Congress to repeal the Arms Embargo provision in the United States Neutrality Act. At the time he had to say, "I hope the United States will keep out of this war. I believe that it will. And I give you my assurance and reassurance that every effort of your Government will be directed toward that end." Repeal of the Arms Embargo enabled the United States to sell "cash and carry" arms to the Allies in November, 1939.

After France fell in 1940, Roosevelt broadened his concerns to meet what he could see as the long-range threat: a Nazi attack against the Western Hemisphere. The one thing he feared was a negotiated peace in Europe. This would give Hitler time to prepare for an assault on Latin America. The Axis would have all the shipbuilding facilities in Europe and Japan to draw on. Roosevelt was also sure that, given time to consolidate his gains in Europe, Hitler would go after Africa and the Middle East.

It was obvious to Roosevelt that this was no mere European war, but total world-wide war. Oceans were no barriers except in some people's minds. Everybody was in it, like it or not.

There is no question that Roosevelt was years ahead of the great majority of Americans in his realization of the meaning of total war and of what had to be done to protect the United States. But one of the things he had to do first was to get re-elected in 1940. And in September, 1939, the majority of American voters were still about two decades off the pace of events.

Roosevelt read cables every day that told of an increasingly desperate European situation, but he could also read the Gallup Poll of September, 1939, which showed that a full 30 per cent of Americans wanted nothing to do with *any* warring country—not even trade on a cash-and-carry basis. Another 37.5 per cent wanted to take no sides, to stay out of war, but would sell to any nation cash-and-carry. Only 8.9 per cent were willing to supply England, France, and Poland while excluding Germany, and a slender 14.7 per cent would help England and France and would go to war if those countries were in danger of losing. Thus, in 1939, close to 70 per cent of our population were strongly pacifist, of which nearly half were completely isolationist.

The combination of Lindbergh's prestige and the firm popular base of his isolationist position could have been insurmountable. Roosevelt had to fight, but he could not afford to respond openly to the direct challenge of Lindbergh. In fact, he could not afford to tell the whole truth to the American public—not if he wanted to be re-elected. The Republican candidate, Wendell Willkie, was in the same fix.

Lindbergh had no such inhibition. His first speech on the war was made over the radio from a Mutual Broadcasting station in Washington, D.C., on September 15, 1939. It was carried by all three networks: Mutual, National Broadcasting, and Columbia Broadcasting, and was beamed by short wave from WIXL in Boston. It had probably the biggest single audience of any private radio broadcast of the time—even larger, probably, than some of Roosevelt's Fireside Chats.

He said on the radio, in his high, rather tense public voice, "I speak tonight to those people in the United States of America who feel that the destiny of this country does not call for our involvement in European wars." He went on to say that we should never enter a war unless it was "absolutely essential to the future welfare of the nation. . . . These wars in Europe are not wars in which our civilization is defending itself against some Asiatic intruder. There is no Genghis Khan or Xerxes." His main argument was that our entrance into a European war was against our interests and he made the cost plain. America would have to do more than merely ship armaments abroad—she would have to send her men. He predicted that "We are likely to lose a million men, possibly several million," and that we would be "staggering under the burden of recovery during the rest of our lives."

If Lindbergh overstated his case, he was at least stating it. Roosevelt, who saw the cost of entering the war clearly, had to pussyfoot all through the 1940 Presidential campaign against Willkie. Willkie predicted that if Roosevelt were re-elected, we might be in the war by April, 1941. And Roosevelt could not truthfully contradict him; he could only fudge and hedge. Roosevelt's biographer, Robert E. Sherwood, says that "This was a fight (against Willkie) that he despised. It left a smear on his record which only the accomplishments of the next five years could remove."

In his first speech Lindbergh made points that he was to reiterate in his subsequent addresses: that America did not have to enter the war to protect herself—the great oceans that surrounded her did that; that once we became involved in the war, America would have to remain forever involved in European affairs. "If we enter the quarrels of Europe during war, we must stay in them in time of peace as well. It is madness to send our soldiers to be killed as we did in the last war if we turn the course of peace over to the greed, the fear, and the intrigue of European nations."

He warned his listeners against the insidious effects of propaganda: "Much of our news is already colored. . . . We must learn to look behind every article we read and every speech we hear. We must not only inquire about the writer and the speaker—about his

personal interests and nationality, but we must ask who owns and
who influences the newspaper, the news picture, and the radio station."

He ended by saying that the future of Western civilization might
lie in America; that the war might destroy it in Europe. "Let us
look to our own defenses and to our own character. If we attend to
them, we have no need to fear what happens elsewhere. If we do
not attend to them, nothing can save us."

His first speech was received with great acclaim, and a barrage of
letters from a wide variety of people—ranging from liberal but
normally isolationist Midwesterners to rabid Roosevelt haters to the
German-American Bund, Father Coughlin, and the Fascist Silver
Shirts. He was also strongly attacked by the national administration,
although still not directly by Roosevelt. And he was immediately
forbidden active duty in the Army, but allowed to retain his rank.

He quickly established himself, Sherwood said, as "undoubtedly
Roosevelt's most formidable competitor on the radio." Fulton Lewis,
Jr., and his friends wanted Lindbergh to continue broadcasting, and
he did. He made five radio addresses over the different networks,
mobilizing such support—although he had no organization behind
him—that Roosevelt finally had to take overt notice.

In his second speech Lindbergh made it clear that he was not a
pacifist, but that "we must draw a sharp dividing line between
neutrality and war. . . . The policy we decide upon should be
as clear cut as our shorelines, and as easily defended as our continent."

He came out unequivocally for hemisphere defense, although
questioning the right of Canada "to draw this hemisphere into a
European war simply because they prefer the Crown of England to
American independence."

He also stated his belief that "our bond with Europe is a bond of
race and not of political ideology. We had to fight a European army
to establish democracy in this country. It is the European race we
must preserve; political progress will follow. Racial strength is
vital—politics, a luxury."

He translated his isolationism into four points of policy:

1. An [export] embargo on offensive weapons and munitions.
2. The unrestricted sale of purely defensive armaments.

3. The prohibition of American shipping from the belligerent countries of Europe and their danger zones.
4. The refusal of credit to belligerent nations or their agents.

In his next speech over the C.B.S. network, he said that neither the United States nor South America was threatened by air attack. Bombing planes *could* be built to cross the Atlantic and return, and either side could build them. "But the cost is high, the target [the U.S.] large, and the military effectiveness small. Such planes do not exist today in any air force. . . ."

On the political front he said, "Regardless of which side wins this war, there is no reason . . . to prevent a continuation of peaceful relationships between America and the countries of Europe."

It was known that Lindbergh was a good friend of Colonel Truman Smith, who was now in the United States. Because of the close collaboration between the two, and also because Lindbergh stayed with the Smiths whenever he was in Washington, the War Department got the idea that Smith must be writing Lindbergh's speeches, or at least helping write them. So after Lindbergh's third radio address Smith was banished to Fort Benning, Georgia, for a tour of duty. However, when Lindbergh went on making new speeches without Smith being anywhere near, it became obvious that Smith was not writing the speeches. He was brought back to Washington where his expertise in European military matters overrode the suspicions of his politics.

The French Army was defeated in 1940. The British were able to salvage an army-in-being through the magnificent rear-guard action at Dunkirk, but it cost them dear in matériel. And British gold reserves were falling fast. Under an obscure statute of 1892, it was found that the Secretary of War has the power to lease Army property "when in his discretion it will be for the public good." By this authority, the U.S. transferred munitions worth more than $43,000,000 to the British in June, 1940, to replace the mountain of supplies the B.E.F. had had to abandon in Dunkirk. The War Department did this because it was U.S. strategy to keep Britain fighting as long as possible now that France had fallen.

Roosevelt stretched the 1892 law to enable him to transfer fifty overage U.S. destroyers to the British Navy in September, 1940. These ships had cost $75,000,000 when new, and were valued at $20,000,-000 for loan. Actually, Roosevelt drove a pretty hard bargain for them. He secured U.S. rights to air and naval bases in Newfoundland, Bermuda, the Bahamas, Jamaica, St. Lucia, Trinidad, Antigua, and British Guiana.

During this time, the Battle of Britain was being fought in the air, and on and under the sea. Roosevelt was re-elected in November, 1940, for a third term, unprecedented in American history. In December he went off on a seemingly carefree fishing and inspection cruise among the new U.S. bases in the Caribbean.

During the trip he received a very long letter from Winston Churchill which turned the lighthearted cruise into a time for serious thought. Churchill outlined the position of England as desperate, and asked for more destroyers, more aid. A few days later, on December 19, Roosevelt held a press conference at which he outlined a new idea. He told the reporters that the best safeguard for the United States was to support Britain's war, and that the cash-and-carry approach was not enough. He made it very simple: "Suppose my neighbor's home catches fire, and I have a length of garden hose . . ." In other words, money was no longer to be the criterion for aid to Britain.

Out of this came the Lend-Lease bill. Some unknown genius titled it H.R. 1776. What this bill proposed to do was to give the President tremendous powers to make available to governments whose defense he deemed vital to U.S. security just about anything they needed, from war matériel to civilian supplies. And he could do this on any basis he thought fit—"payment or repayment in kind or property, or any other direct or indirect benefit."

This was a revolutionary conception, and a complete commitment to the British cause, for Roosevelt had made no bones that they were the neighbors we must help. He made a famous speech supporting the bill, calling the U.S. "the arsenal of democracy." For the first time he named the Nazis as the real enemy of this country. "A nation can have peace with the Nazis only at the price of total surrender," he said. "Such a dictated peace would be no peace at all. . . . All of us, in all the Americas, would be living at the point of a Nazi gun."

The lines were sharply drawn. Roosevelt was now supported by a united Cabinet (even former isolationists like Henry A. Wallace had been won over) strengthened by two prominent Republicans, Henry L. Stimson as Secretary of State and Frank Knox as Secretary of the Navy. He was also fresh from a smashing popular electoral victory over Willkie in which he had received 27 million votes.

Still, getting H.R. 1776 through Congress was no easy matter. The most powerful isolationists in the country had just organized themselves into the America First Committee, forming a strong pressure group. Such leading Senators as Burton K. Wheeler opposed Roosevelt. He said that the Lend-Lease bill "would plough under every fourth American boy," a reference to a New Deal farm policy. The fight went on through January and February in 1941. Public hearings were held on the bill and Lindbergh was among those who testified. He was asked which side he would like to see win the war, and replied, "I want neither side to win," an almost exact repetition of what his father had said a quarter of a century earlier.

His assessment of Great Britain was not much different from that of William Allen White, the newspaper editor, who later took a position almost diametrically opposed to Lindbergh's. White wrote in 1940, "What an avalanche of blunders Great Britain has let loose upon the democracies of the world! . . . Unless a new government takes the helm in Britain, the British empire is done."

But not long after this diatribe, White came out for U.S. aid to keep the British fleet intact, to buy time for our defense.

Lindbergh, in testifying against the Lend-Lease bill, in 1941, said, "Personally, I do not believe that England is in a position to win the war. If she does not win, or unless our aid is used in negotiating a better peace than could otherwise be obtained, we will be responsible for futilely prolonging the war and adding to the bloodshed and devastation of Europe, particularly among the democracies."

In spite of the strong opposition of Lindbergh and other isolationists, the Lend-Lease bill was passed by Congress on March 11, 1941. Aid under the bill was not limited to belligerents, but eventually went to thirty-eight countries in all, including many in Latin America. Through this new channel, fifty billion dollars' worth of equipment and supplies was eventually loaned to friendly powers, of which more than thirty-one billion went to Great Britain and eleven billion to the Soviet Union. Without this aid it is generally agreed that neither country could have resisted Germany.

Lindbergh's opposition to the bill, particularly on the grounds he gave, was galling to the British, as he had sought asylum in their country only five years before. His statement aroused a good deal of resentment there. Harold Nicolson is quoted as writing of Lindbergh: "It was almost with ferocity that he struggled to remain himself, and in the process of that arduous struggle his simplicity became muscle-bound, his virility-ideal became not merely inflexible, but actually rigid; his self-control thickened into arrogance, and his convictions hardened into granite."

H. R. Knickerbocker, the war correspondent, said that Lindbergh saw nothing to be ashamed of in allowing Britain to fall, which made him sincere. But that this was nevertheless a policy "as cynical as any Nazi could invent."

These were some of the milder attacks on Lindbergh. He was a prime target of men in the administration and of their supporters in the press. He was called everything from "ignorant," "blind," and a "coward" to our "number one fifth columnist," and worse. Robert E. Sherwood castigated him as "a Nazi with a Nazi's Olympian contempt for all democratic processes." Harold L. Ickes, who stated in his diary that he never liked Lindbergh, berated him in public as "a peripatetic appeaser who would abjectly surrender his sword even before it is demanded."

There were other, more sober criticisms of Lindbergh's politics. Walter Lippmann wrote in April, 1941, "A day or two after Colonel Lindbergh had announced that Britain was defeated and the war practically over, Hitler in his birthday proclamation to the German people announced that 'a year of heavy conflict stands before us' in which 'historic decisions of a unique scale will be made entailing immeasurable demands once again on our men folk, our people of the German homeland.' In the difference between these two estimates of what lies ahead there is all the difference between those who, like Col. Lindbergh, have never understood this war and those who, like Hitler himself or his great antagonists—Churchill and Roosevelt—actually do understand this war." Lippmann pointed out what has since been widely documented by historians from German documents as the true war aim of Hitler; namely, world conquest.* Lindbergh continued to regard the conflict as only another European struggle.

The names Lindbergh was called got stronger. Harold Ickes

* Lippmann himself had been a strong advocate of isolationism. As late as 1940, according to the biography of General George C. Marshall, the Supreme U.S. Commander, Marshall was alarmed at a Lippmann column that said: "All popular doubts, political confusions, all ambiguity, would be removed by a clear decision to shrink the Army and concentrate our major effort upon the Navy, the air force, and lend-lease."

began referring to him as a "Knight of the German Eagle," an allusion to the medal given by Goering. He used this phrase in three successive speeches around July, 1941, and provoked a reaction from Lindbergh. "Up to that time," Ickes wrote, "I had always admired Lindbergh in one respect. No matter how vigorously he had been attacked personally he had never attempted an answer. . . . I had begun to think that no one could get under his skin enough to make him squeal. But at last I had succeeded."

What gave Ickes this satisfaction was an open letter Lindbergh wrote to President Roosevelt.

It was mailed from Lindbergh's rented house at Lloyd's Neck, Long Island; copies were also given to the newspapers by Lindbergh's secretary. "For many months, and on numerous occasions," Lindbergh wrote, "your Secretary of the Interior has implied in public meetings that I am connected with the interests of a foreign government, and he has specifically criticized me for accepting a decoration from the German government in 1938.

"Mr. President, is it too much to ask that you inform your Secretary of the Interior that I was decorated by the German government while I was carrying out the request of your Ambassador to that Government? Is it unfair of me to ask that you inform your secretary that I received this decoration in the American Embassy, in the presence of your Ambassador . . . ?

"If I have any connection with a foreign Government, the American people have a right to be fully acquainted with the facts. . . .

"Mr. President, I give you my word that I have no connection with any foreign Government. I will willingly open my files to your investigation . . . if there is a question in your mind. I ask that you give me the opportunity of answering any charges."

The letter was, Ickes wrote, "a whining one. Instead of striking at me boldly and sharply, he complainingly asked the President to [set things right]."

Ickes' analysis of the letter was on the mark. Lindbergh's declaration, though true, made him suddenly appear vulnerable, where he had always seemed unassailable.

The Lindbergh letter made the front pages. Ickes was questioned about it at his regular press conference. He piously denied calling Lindbergh a Nazi agent. His denial was technically true. Then he opened the wound a little wider. Ickes reiterated his belief that "in preaching defeatism and helping to bring about disunity he [Lindbergh] was doing what a certain foreign government, namely, Germany wanted." He also said that "it did not matter how or when . . . he had received the Nazi decoration. The point was that he should have returned it long ago."

Ickes recorded in his diary that his exchange with Lindbergh had been widely publicized and that as a result Lindbergh had "slipped badly. He has now made it clear to the whole country that he still clings to this German decoration. He is now in a position where he is damned if he gives it back and damned if he doesn't. . . . [Instead of writing to Roosevelt] he should have slammed right back at me. For the first time he has allowed himself to be put on the defensive and that is always a weak position for anyone."

However, Lindbergh continued to be an effective opponent of Roosevelt's. Roosevelt was finding it increasingly difficult to get his aid-short-of-war bills passed by Congress, particularly with Lindbergh talking to huge radio audiences over the N.B.C. network against them. "There is a saying that grew in the old west to the effect that a man who enjoys life should never touch his gun unless he means business," Lindbergh said, "that he should never draw unless he is ready to shoot, and that he should never shoot unless he is ready to kill. . . . Our present danger results from making gestures with an empty gun after we have already lost the draw." He spoke about "mortgaging the lives of our children and our grandchildren"; he saw the need for hundreds of thousands of airplanes, if we entered the war, of millions of men in the Army, of a huge Navy, and of other expensive armaments.

Lindbergh also referred to "an organized minority in this country" which "is flooding our congress and our press with propaganda for war." He would spell this out in embarrassing detail a few months later.

Nevertheless, as the interchange with Ickes demonstrated, Lindbergh was not only creating pressure; he was feeling it. His speeches and his articles became progressively less temperate during his isolationist campaign. For example, in his early speeches he called England and France democracies. Later, he used "democratic" in quotes and referred to the "so-called democratic nations." He said he had seen "the military strength of Germany growing like a giant at the side of an aged and complacent England. France was awake to her danger, but far too occupied with personal ambitions, industrial troubles, and internal politics. . . . In England there was organization without spirit. In France there was spirit without organization. In Germany there were both."

In 1940, Lindbergh's wife published a small book called *The Wave of the Future—A Confession of Faith*. It is worth mentioning here because the book's thesis has become identified in the public mind with Lindbergh's thinking. He has never affirmed or denied this. *The Wave of the Future* is an odd little book, different from anything else Mrs. Lindbergh has published. It is a kind of manifesto, but rather tentative and cloudy. The most memorable thing about it is its title, which comes from a sentence near the end: "The wave of the future is coming and there is no fighting it." What she meant by this would be hard to define, except that some kind of revolution was taking place. She stated that she did not embrace Nazism, Fascism, or Communism but regarded them as inevitable manifestations of the "wave of the future." She spoke of the "spirit" of Germany as being as important as its mechanized might. She hoped that America could stand aside from the war and build a new kind of society, peaceably, that could be able to deal with the "new order."

"We have waked from one [dream]," she wrote, "and not yet started the other. We still have our eyes, our minds, our hearts, on the dream that is dying—How beautiful it was, tinting the whole sky crimson as it fades into the west. But there is another on its way in the gray dawn. Is it not, perhaps, America's mission to find 'the dream that is coming to birth'?"

The criticism one might make of the book is that it is muddled. It takes so astral a view of the world that it makes the crimes of the Nazis seem to bulk no larger than the inadequacies of the "democracies." (Mrs. Lindbergh never used the word without the quotation marks.) She makes it clear that she does not excuse the Germans, but she never specifically denounces anything they did.

There was a distinct parallel between the book and her husband's views when he said, "There is a proverb in China which says that 'when the rich become too rich, and the poor too poor, something happens.' This applies to nations as well as to men. When I saw the wealth of the British Empire, I felt that the rich had become too rich. When I saw the poverty of Central Europe, I felt that the poor had become too poor."

Much was made of the fact that Lindbergh's statements were sometimes like those of Axis leaders. For example, Goering announced, after Lindbergh had said the same thing, that "America simply cannot be invaded by air or sea. That is particularly true if her armaments and national defense are appropriate to or commensurate with the country's size. . . . If America's air force is properly developed, built up, organized and strategically based, America can defy any group of powers."

A Lindbergh supporter said, at the time, "I presume that [Lindbergh's critics] would have to call Christ a Nazi if Hitler happened to quote the Bible."

Nevertheless, one cannot beg the question of the quality of Lindbergh's influence. As observers had noted ever since his first public appearance at the American Embassy in France, in 1927, his presence had a kind of hypnotic effect on people. His utterances, therefore, had more force than those of others. It was not enough for him to say, as he did to friends, that he was "Just a private citizen" expressing his opinion. He had charisma, like it or not, and he must have known it.

Certainly the Germans and Japanese knew it. Translations of his speeches were sometimes circulated in Latin America by the Nazis. The Japanese rained copies of a Lindbergh speech on Chungking, China, along with incendiary bombs. The German military attaché in Washington, General Friedrich von Boetticher, mentioned Lindbergh often in his dispatches to Germany. "*July 20, 1940:* . . . As the exponent of the Jews, who especially through Freemasonry control the broad masses of the American people, Roosevelt wants England to continue fighting and the war to be prolonged. . . . The circle about Lindbergh has become aware of this development and now tries at least to impede the fatal control of American policy by the Jews. . . . I have repeatedly reported on the mean and vicious campaign against Lindbergh, whom the Jews fear as their most potent adversary." On September 18, 1940, Hans Thomsen, the German chargé d'affaires in Washington, reported on what (he said) Lindbergh told several American General Staff officers. According to Thomsen, Lindbergh thought that England would soon collapse under German air attacks. However, the officers to whom he spoke did not agree that German air power would be the decisive factor, Thomsen said.

For eighteen months Lindbergh continued to make his speeches unaffiliated. This period started with the Nazi invasion of Poland on September 1, 1939.

Meanwhile, as noted, an organization of prominent Americans was formed to promulgate ideas similar to those Lindbergh was advocating. It was called, in the beginning, the Emergency Committee to Defend America First, and later the America First Committee.

America First is generally remembered in the distorting mirrors of polemic or advocacy. There was much criticism of America First while it existed. (Its short life ran only from September, 1940, until December 7, 1941.) But much of the contemporary criticism was leveled at personalities rather than policies, and the organization was tarred by associations with groups it repeatedly tried to avoid and disown.*

History provides a clearer picture. To see this, it is necessary to know who belonged to America First, what their policies were, what they said, and what they did.

The Committee was organized after the fall of France by R. Douglas Stuart, Jr., who had studied at Princeton and Yale and was the son of a vice-president of Quaker Oats. The money to start the organization was put up by General Robert E. Wood, chairman of the board of Sears, Roebuck & Company; by William H. Regnery, president of the Western Shade Cloth Company, and others. Senator Burton K. Wheeler consulted with Stuart on organizing the Committee.

When the organization was announced on September 4, 1940, its national committee consisted of Wood; Regnery; General Thomas S. Hammond, president of the Whiting Corporation; Jay C. Hormel,

---

* Laura Ingalls, convicted in 1942 for failure to register as a German agent was an America First speaker. Frank B. Burch, similarly convicted, was a sponsor of the Akron, Ohio, chapter of the organization. Ralph Townsend, later convicted for failure to register as a Japanese agent, spoke at two meetings of America First on the West Coast. So far as is known, these were the only Axis agents who penetrated America First. Says Professor Cole, in his authoritative study "America First," of Miss Ingalls, "For every meeting addressed by this German agent during the Committee's history, patriotic America First speakers addressed dozens."

president of Hormel Meat Packing Company; Hanford MacNider, former national commander of the American Legion (the Legion later denounced the Committee); Mrs. Janet Ayer Fairbank, author and former National Democratic committeewoman; Edward L. Ryerson, Jr., of the board of Inland Steel Corporation; Sterling Morton, of the Morton Salt Company; Mrs. Alice Roosevelt Longworth, daughter of Theodore Roosevelt; John T. Flynn, author and adviser to the Senate Investigating Committee on munitions; Edward Rickenbacker, the aviation expert; Louis Tabor, Master of the National Grange; Bishop Wilbur E. Hammaker, head of the Methodist Church in the Denver area; Thomas N. McCarter, president of the Public Service Corporation of New Jersey; Avery Brundage, president of the Olympic Association; Dr. Albert W. Palmer, president of the Chicago Theological Seminary; Mrs. Burton K. Wheeler; Dr. George H. Whipple, a Nobel Prize winner in medicine; Oswald Garrison Villard, former editor of the *Nation;* Ray McKaig, head of the Grange in Boise, Idaho.

Others associated with local chapters of the organization, or advisers or members of the national committee, were Samuel Hopkins Adams, Irvin S. Cobb, Henry Ford, William Benton, then vice-president of the University of Chicago, and Benton's former advertising partner Chester Bowles. Philip La Follette was an influential adviser, as were Senator Wheeler, Senator Bennett Champ Clark, Senator Gerald P. Nye, Congressman Karl Mundt, and Robert M. Hutchins. Others who joined the national group later, or belonged to local chapters, were George N. Peek, former head of the A.A.A.; Kathleen Norris; Lillian Gish; General Hugh S. Johnson (first head of NRA); Amos R. E. Pinchot.

Some, but certainly not all, of these people were reactionary in their politics. But there seems to be no evidence that the Committee stood for anything more or less than its stated principles:

1. The United States must build an impregnable defense for America.
2. No foreign power, nor group of powers, can successfully attack a *prepared* America.
3. American democracy can be preserved only by keeping out of the European war.
4. "Aid short of war" weakens national defense at home and threatens to involve America in war abroad.

The Committee's statement of objectives:

1. To bring together all Americans, regardless of possible differences on other matters, who see eye-to-eye on these principles. [It specifically excluded Nazis, Fascists, and Communists, or other groups "that place the interest of any other nation above those of our own country."]
2. To urge Americans to keep their heads amid rising hysteria in times of crisis.
3. To provide sane national leadership for the majority of the American people who want to keep out of the European war.
4. To register this opinion with the President and with Congress.

The Committee kept to its principles. It rejected membership of and money from known Fascists or Fascist groups, but the national organization was not always efficient in policing contributions to local chapters. Some America First leaders, such as John T. Flynn, denounced in public, to their faces, the Silver Shirts, the German-American Bund, and followers of Father Coughlin, the jingo priest, who attended America First public meetings in large numbers. However, denunciation did not dissuade these Fascist types from attending the meetings, and their presence gave the gatherings an atmosphere that clouded the reputation of America First. Lindbergh once offered to go into the audience and personally throw Joe Williams, head of the Silver Shirts, out of Madison Square Garden, but was persuaded not to do so. There is no evidence that the Committee did anything, openly or covertly, to encourage Fascist support. In fact, it had a well-enforced policy of keeping itself nonpartisan, even as between Democrats and Republicans. America First did, in fact, include many prominent—even liberal— Democrats. Once, John T. Flynn wanted the Committee to sponsor an anti-Roosevelt (but not pro-Willkie) broadcast, and he was turned down by the board of directors. The Committee's effect was not felt as a political machine taking active part in local, state, or national politics, but more as an organizing voice of public opinion, the major portion of which was certainly noninterventionist at the time. (It should be remembered that both Roosevelt and Willkie were avowedly noninterventionist, too. Their differences with America First were on Lend-Lease, guarded convoys, and similar policies.)

The Committee scotched attempts by members to try to impeach

Roosevelt. There was talk of mass marches on Washington (America First had perhaps 850,000 members, most of them within a 300-mile radius of Chicago), but no actual demonstrations of this type took place. One influential member summed up the prevailing attitude of the group when he said that America First should not take sides in the Presidential election, since "the Committee is concerned with the establishment of a principle and not with the election of candidates." Besides, most America Firsters felt there was little choice between Willkie and Roosevelt.

The Committee later entered politics in a tentative way by deciding to use its influence in the 1942 Congressional elections. The Selective Service Act had been renewed by a margin of a single vote in Congress. Other measures were passed by narrow margins. There was thus a possibility that, given enough time, America First might have decisively affected this country's foreign policies by its political activity.

However, the Committee never became that effective. It never succeeded in stopping any of Roosevelt's important prewar measures. But it did help to fight him to a standstill. In 1941, Roosevelt had become listless and dispirited at the opposition he could not fully answer or squelch. Robert Sherwood writes that "as the world situation became more desperately critical, and as the limitless peril came closer and closer to the United States, isolationist sentiment became ever more strident in expression and aggressive in action. And Roosevelt was relatively powerless to combat it. He had said everything 'short of war' that could be said. He had no more tricks left. The hat from which he had pulled so many rabbits was empty." In short, Roosevelt could get no nearer to war than war itself.

Lindbergh was invited to head the America First national committee in April, 1941, a year and a half after he had started his one-man isolationist movement. He turned down the chairmanship, but joined the board and began speaking under Committee auspices. His first major address for the group took place on April 17, 1941. In this speech he predicted that Britain would lose the war, and reiterated his opposition to aiding her.

He made another speech a week later expanding on these themes. He pointed out that France had been defeated and said again that Britain was losing (in spite of British victories over the Italians in the Mediterranean and North Africa). He said that the British had only one last desperate ploy: "to persuade us to send another American Expeditionary Force." He went into the military difficulties of landing on a hostile coast and maintaining an army there. Our air force "might be based on the British Isles; but it is physically impossible to base enough aircraft in the British Isles alone to equal in strength the aircraft that can be based on the continent of Europe." This was one of his military analyses that turned out to be wrong. It may be said in justice that he was not always so far off the mark, but he was certainly fallible—even in his own specialty—as on the day he derided Franklin Roosevelt's call for 50,000 warplanes as "hysterical chatter."

However, Lindbergh made it plain that he would consider Britain's defeat a tragedy, and said he was not for a German victory. But he wanted us to stay out of war, a wish shared by other Americans of as varied opinions as Norman Thomas, the German-American Bund, Harry Elmer Barnes, Charles A. Beard, Stuart Chase, John L. Lewis, and—until June 22, 1941, when the Soviet Union was invaded—the Communist party of the United States. Norman Thomas appeared on several platforms with Lindbergh at America First rallies, although he was not a member of the Committee; his affiliation was with a pacifist group called Keep America Out of War.

With Lindbergh focusing isolationist sentiment like a burning glass, the America First Committee kept growing stronger, and the administration seemed feeble by comparison. Roosevelt was frustrated, maneuvering by ear in a fog of discontent.

He vented his anger against Lindbergh at a press conference on Friday, April 25, 1941. It was recognized, a reporter said, that Lindbergh was the spiritual leader of isolationist sentiment. Then, asked the reporter, since Lindbergh was an Army officer, why wasn't he called into uniform by his Commander in Chief?

Roosevelt was reported as obviously ready for this question about Lindbergh; like many press conference questions, it may well have been planted. At the time, Presidential remarks at press conferences were paraphrased, not quoted, in newspapers. During the American Civil War, Roosevelt said, liberty-loving people had fought on both sides; but there were some people who were deliberately ignored. They were not asked to serve in the war for the very good reason that they were defeatist. He mentioned the name of Vallandigham, referring to an Ohio congressman of the era named Clement L. Vallandigham, who had made violent speeches against Lincoln and had said the North could never win. He was the chief spokesman of the group known as Copperheads, people who thought as he did and opposed the war. The name of the group was that of a poisonous snake: "A rattlesnake rattles, a viper hisses, an adder spits, a black snake whistles, a water-snake blows but a copperhead just sneaks!" Thus the anti-war Democrats of the time were also called "sneak Democrats."

The Copperhead movement in its worst phases was ritualistic, secret, and paramilitary; it employed terrorism. Vallandigham was arrested and deported to the Confederacy. He finally returned to the North by way of Canada and continued his anti-war speechmaking. There were demands that he be jailed for treason, but Lincoln did not do this.

Roosevelt did not give all this background about Vallandigham but let the reporters dig it out themselves. He did say that there were people at Valley Forge who wanted Washington to give up, and he referred to the famous Tom Paine pamphlet about "summer soldiers and sunshine patriots."

He was asked if he was still talking about Lindbergh. And Roosevelt said that he certainly was.

The story made the front pages; with very little distortion headline writers could say that the President had called Lindbergh a Copperhead, in effect a traitor.

The Copperhead attack was perhaps triggered by an article Lindbergh had written in *Collier's* the month before, as well as by his joining the America First Committee's board.

In *Collier's*, Lindbergh had published "A Letter to Americans" which said, in part, "While our leaders have shouted for peace, they have consistently directed us toward war. . . . The men who entice us on to war have no more idea of how that war can be won than the governments of France and England had when they declared war on Germany."

The America First Committee came to Lindbergh's support: "President Roosevelt's remarks about Colonel Lindbergh today do not exhibit the spirit of tolerance, or of respect for freedom of conscience and freedom of belief that the American people have admired in him. . . . Colonel Lindbergh is an American first, last, and always." Roosevelt's statement was also criticized by the *New York Times* and by many other newspapers.

Three days later, Lindbergh sent a letter to the White House, simultaneously releasing it to the newspapers:

Your remarks at the White House press conference on April 25 involving my reserve commission in the United States Army Air Corps have of course disturbed me greatly. I had hoped that I might exercise my right as an American citizen to place my viewpoint before the people of my country in time of peace without giving up the privilege of serving my country as an Air Corps officer in the event of war.

But since you, in your capacity of President of the United States and Commander in Chief of the Army, have clearly implied that I am no longer of use to this country as a reserve officer, and in view of other implications that you, my President and superior officer, have made concerning my loyalty to my country, my character, and my motives, I can see no honorable alternative to tendering my resignation as Colonel in the United States Air Corps Reserve. . . .

I take this action with the utmost regret, for my relationship with the Air Corps is one of the things which has meant most to me in my life. I place it second only to my right as a citizen to speak freely to my fellow countrymen. . . . I will continue to serve my country to the best of my ability as a private citizen.

Lindbergh continued to speak. He did not submit his speeches to America First leaders for approval before he made them. Thus when he spoke in Des Moines, on September 11, 1941, at an America First rally, no one but Lindbergh knew what he was going to say. It, more than any other of his speeches (and his speeches were the most important ones made by any America Firster, invariably drawing overflow crowds), smeared his reputation and that of America First.

In this speech Lindbergh, who had been referring darkly for many months to "powerful elements" which were trying to lead the United States into war, identified specifically the interventionist groups. These groups, "responsible for changing our national policy from one of neutrality and independence to one of entanglement in European affairs . . . are the British, the Jewish and the Roosevelt administration," he said to the enthusiastic Iowans. "Behind these groups, but of lesser importance, are a number of capitalists, Anglophiles, and intellectuals who believe that their future, and the future of mankind, depends upon the domination of the British Empire. . . . [This] . . . minority . . . control . . . a tremendous influence."

Then he went on to speak his mind, with the same kind of pointless "courage" his father had used to "help" the Catholics—the kind of bluntness that gave their enemies a bludgeon with which to beat them into impotence: "It is not difficult to understand why Jewish people desire the overthrow of Nazi Germany. The persecution they suffered in Germany would be sufficient to make bitter enemies of any race. No person with a sense of the dignity of mankind can condone the persecution the Jewish race suffered in Germany. But no person of honesty and vision can look on their pro-war policy here today without seeing the dangers involved in such a policy, both for us and for them.

"Instead of agitating for war the Jewish groups in this country should be opposing it in every possible way, for they will be among the first to feel its consequences. Tolerance is a virtue that depends upon peace and strength. A few farsighted Jewish people realize this and stand opposed to intervention. But the majority still do not. Their greatest danger to this country lies in their large ownership and influence in our motion pictures, our press, our radio, and our government."

Professor Wayne S. Cole, in his detailed book *America First, the Battle Against Intervention, 1940–1941*, says, "It would be difficult to exaggerate the magnitude of the explosion which was set off by this speech. . . . Undoubtedly much of this uproar was due to genuine disapproval of Lindbergh's key statement regarding the Jews. Many may have denounced the speech publicly to protect themselves from any possible charge of anti-Semitism. But there can be no doubt that interventionists exploited this incident."

In an editorial, the Des Moines *Register* said, "It may have been courageous for Colonel Lindbergh to say what was in his mind, but it was so lacking in appreciation of consequences—putting the best interpretation on it—that it disqualifies him for any pretensions of leadership in policy-making." There were pamphlets, statements by such men as Willkie and Thomas E. Dewey, speeches by opposition groups—all aimed at Lindbergh. He was called everything from a Hitlerite to a fool; even many of America First's leading members disapproved publicly.

However, Norman Thomas said in his defense that Lindbergh was "not as anti-Semitic as some who seize the opportunity to criticize him." This was a tack taken by several people who disliked Lindbergh's statement but felt the attacks on him were extreme. Professor Gregory Mason, of a Connecticut America First chapter, pointed out that "Many . . . supporters . . . of the Committee to Defend America by Aiding the Allies and of the Fight for Freedom Committee . . . belong to . . . social clubs from which Jews are strictly barred," and that money for six English ambulances was raised in a part of Greenwich (Connecticut) "which opposes renting or selling houses to Jews."

The national committee of America First did not repudiate the speech, in spite of some agitation by Committee members to do so. But they felt compelled to say that "Colonel Lindbergh and his fellow-members of the America First Committee are not anti-Semitic. We deplore the injection of the race issue into the discussion of war or peace."* Lindbergh was even defended publicly by a prominent Jewish physician, former B'nai B'rith president Dr. Hyman Lischner of San Diego, California. Dr. Lischner said that the Jewish group was pressing toward war.

Lindbergh himself did not attempt to explain or amplify his statement, and he never made another like it. However, a few days later in Fort Wayne, Indiana, he said that he had always spoken what he believed to be the truth, and that his statements had been distorted and his motives and meanings "falsely ascribed." He also said he did not "speak out of hate for any individuals or any people."

This did not wash away the stain, a stain that is still implicit in the wrongheadedness of some of his Des Moines statements.

That speech destroyed Lindbergh's effectiveness for America First and greatly damaged the organization and its cause. Between September and December 7, 1941, America First was shrill but less and less effective.

Roosevelt had announced his "shoot-on-sight" order (that American ships should immediately fire on any hostile vessel) on September 11, 1941, the same night as Lindbergh's disastrous speech. Such

---

* Anti-Semitism was constantly associated with America First. Many local chapter leaders were guilty of openly anti-Semitic remarks, and were often reprimanded but never expelled by the national committee.

men as Philip C. Jessup, Edwin S. Corwin, Ray Lyman Wilbur, Charles A. Beard, and Igor Sikorsky signed a statement that called Roosevelt's new policy "a grave threat to the constitutional powers of Congress and to the democratic principle of majority rule." However, the order stood.

In October, with the war at sea getting hotter, Roosevelt asked Congress to repeal more of the Neutrality Act. He wanted the right to arm U.S. merchant vessels, and to send our ships into war zones— two things expressly prohibited by the act. America First put all the weight it could muster against these revisions. But it lost when Congress gave Roosevelt what he wanted in November. However, the anti-administration vote was larger against this measure than it had been against Lend-Lease; a shift of ten votes in the House of Representatives would have meant defeat for Roosevelt.

The closeness of the vote on this measure encouraged the America First Committee to take up an earlier Lindbergh suggestion: to participate actively in elections. They came to this decision on December 1, 1941, having made some movements in that direction while the Neutrality Act was still being debated in Congress. However, the decision, like America First, had only a few more days to live. When Japan attacked Pearl Harbor on December 7, 1941, she also effectively torpedoed the Committee. There was some intramural debate about whether the Committee should stay alive, but most of its leaders believed it should not. The board issued a statement on December 11, 1941, that said: "Our principles were right. Had they been followed, war could have been avoided. No good purpose can now be served by considering what might have been. . . . We are at war . . . the primary objective is . . . victory.

"Therefore," the statement concluded, "the America First Committee has determined immediately to cease all functions and to dissolve as soon as that can legally be done. And finally, it urges all those who have followed its lead to give their full support to the war effort of the nation, until peace is attained."

The Committee organization was dismantled, was almost non-existent by February, 1942, and the Committee was at last legally dissolved on April 22, 1942. (The members had had legal advice that to end their corporate life precipitately would allow the Committee name to be used by other groups.) A number of prominent members of America First joined the Roosevelt administration during the war. Lindbergh was not among them, but not out of choice.

It is interesting to speculate on what might have happened if the Japanese had not attacked the United States, and/or if Hitler had not declared war on the United States. Certainly, the mood of the electorate being what it was, no leader could have taken us into a declared war against Japan without a Pearl Harbor. And any problem we might have had in deciding what to do about Germany and Italy was decided for us. There was actually no compelling reason for Hitler to declare war on the United States. His commitment to Japan was against aggression, not to support Japan in an attack, as British historian A. J. P. Taylor has pointed out. Moreover, he was not known to be punctilious about treaty obligations when they did not suit his immediate purposes. If Hitler had not declared war on the United States, it is questionable whether Roosevelt could have procured a declaration of war from the Congress against Germany, even after Pearl Harbor. And what would Roosevelt have done if Hitler had used the occasion of Pearl Harbor to disown Japan and throw in with the United States against the yellow peril? This would have been a logical stroke on Hitler's part, and one that would have furthered his interests. We are fortunate that Hitler wasn't always logical.

Lindbergh's fight against intervention in what he considered "Europe's war" and for isolationism almost certainly had its roots in his father's isolationism during World War I. C. A. Lindbergh had been certain that we could stay out of war were it not for certain sinister interests. He was sure that war would bring out the worst side of America, that it would result in the suppression of free speech and other civil liberties. He did not suffer less for being right about this.

Lindbergh had seen the same strain of barbarism in his own time. He had felt its force in his private life. He had seen what anti-Semitism could do in Germany. There was certainly reason to fear it in the United States. His warning to the Jews could be read, in this context, as the advice of a friend, not the threat of an enemy.

In a critical article published in *Life* magazine some months before the Des Moines speech, Roger Butterfield reported that Lindbergh "believes Jews will be blamed for American entry into the war and will suffer for it. If that happens, he has said, the anti-Jewish outbreaks that will occur here will surpass those in Nazi Germany, for Americans are 'more violent' than the Germans.

"Yet [the Butterfield article continued] Lindbergh is not anti-Semitic. In personal conversation he has expressed indignation over the German treatment of Jews in Europe." But Butterfield pointed out that Lindbergh had never condemned these persecutions publicly. When friends and associates pleaded with him to do so, Lindbergh invariably refused, saying, "I must be neutral."

Much later, after the war, one of Lindbergh's daughters was dating a Jewish boy. The boy's parents made him stop seeing the Lindbergh girl because they said her father was an anti-Semite. The girl, naturally troubled by this, asked Lindbergh about it.

Lindbergh told her it was not true. He had never been anti-Semitic. It was just a convenient peg for his enemies to hang their attacks on, he said.

Lindbergh, in his Des Moines speech, had identified the Jews as a "race," though there is no scientific definition of race that would encompass all Jews. Further, he had assumed that Jews needed "tolerance" to exist. This could seem like a threat: behave or you won't be tolerated. Yet it could also be traced to Lindbergh's firsthand experience with the lack of tolerance in this country and the Nazi demonstration of what this could mean to the Jews. His assumption that Jews controlled the press, movies, and radio, and were using this control to push the country toward war to get even with the Nazis, was certainly erroneous. Jews did not exert nearly as much control of the press and radio as he said, and they were certainly not united on interventionism. The Keep America Out of War Congress had at least four Jews on its governing committee.

Lindbergh had used some of the language of anti-Semites, but this does not make him an anti-Semite. His own private statements exculpate him of the charge; it would be out of character for him to lie on a subject as vital as this. His actions before and since do not add up to bigotry.

Nevertheless he suffered because he got the reputation of an anti-Semite, and also because of his isolationism. Some of his closest friends, both Jewish (Harry Guggenheim) and Christian (Colonel

Henry Breckinridge), stopped seeing him for a time. Mrs. Dwight Morrow took a strong public stand against her son-in-law and her daughter by supporting the Committee to Defend America by Aiding the Allies, and Anne Lindbergh's sister Constance Morgan* opposed Anne and supported her own husband, who was head of British Information Services in New York.

At this time, the Lindberghs lived in Long Island with their three children; a daughter, Anne Spencer ("Angie"), had been born in 1940. The neighbors were not sympathetic; when they drove by the Lindbergh gateway, they tooted their horns in the "V" signal—the opening four notes of Beethoven's Fifth Symphony made popular by the British.

But personal affront was something Lindbergh had expected. One of his friends asked him why he persisted in speaking in public when each appearance caused him almost physical agony. He replied, "There are some things you have to do no matter what the consequences." The same idea could be extended; he knew from his father's experience that speaking forthrightly in politics was not likely to elicit gentle treatment. He knew that he had entered a dangerous area, and he was aware he would be exposed again to the public and to the press.

Actually, he minimized his physical exposure. He traveled privately and stayed in private houses or clubs. He appeared in public only long enough to make his speeches, and then vanished. He wrote his speeches himself, in a lonely battle with rhetoric, using a pencil and scratch paper. There were rumors, still current today, that his wife wrote the speeches for him. But Lindbergh has never employed a ghost, not even one as close to his thinking as his wife.

Others questioned Lindbergh's motives. To explain himself, in 1941 Lindbergh gave to Larry Kelly, of Hearst newspapers, his first personal interview in ten years.

"I stopped talking for publication ten years ago because the attendant publicity made it impossible for my family and myself to lead normal lives," Lindbergh said. "I had about made up my mind then to make no more radio addresses or public appearances.

"But no one can predict the progress of the world. . . . The

* Married to Aubrey Morgan, the widowed husband of her sister Elisabeth.

thought that I might be of some aid in doing what I believe is right for our country led me to agree to this talk.

"These are not normal times," Lindbergh continued. "We are in the midst of the greatest crisis this country has faced since the Civil War. In such a case we give up our normal desires, do what we conceive as our duty to our country, no matter what the personal cost may be. I knew what I was getting into. I knew that I would be accused of many things, and that my personal life would be dragged into the open again."

"Then why are you doing it?" Kelly asked.

"The answer to that question depends upon your values in life," Lindbergh said. "To me, the most important element in this situation is the future welfare of my country, my family, my friends, and my fellow-citizens. In relation to these things, the names one is called make very little difference, after all."

No doubt Lindbergh's calculation about war and peace in Europe was limited by his information and by the range of his interest, both of which were largely in military aviation. He was no global strategist. His political judgments were narrowed by his airman's frame of reference.

On the other hand, he was never a pacifist. He came home to help his county prepare for war, and took an active and useful part in that effort. He had often stated that we should be prepared, and said we should fight if any part of the Western Hemisphere was attacked, including Greenland.

One cannot avoid the conclusion, on balancing the evidence, that Roosevelt built Lindbergh up as a pro-Nazi so he could break him. Lindbergh was a strong and dangerous political antagonist, never a potential traitor. But Roosevelt had to get rid of him at any cost. Lindbergh was so influential that his opinions might have created the very conditions he sought to avoid.

The old isolationist-interventionist argument is past, "except from an academic viewpoint," Lindbergh said in 1945. At the same time, he refused to renege on his actions or convictions. "I have not changed my belief that World War II could have been avoided," he said in his last public statement on the subject. He still says this to his friends.

However, Lindbergh pointed out in 1945 that the atomic bomb

and the development of transoceanic rockets that could carry the bomb made a "world organization for the control of destructive forces . . . imperative. The only alternative is constant fear and eventual chaos." He said at that time that he would support the Truman administration as long as he believed its policies were "to the best interest of my country."

In a speech to the Aero Club of Washington the same year, he exhibited a philosophical attitude far different from his prewar polemics. "There is little satisfaction in spending one's life developing machines which are likely to bring ruin to one's own people," he said. "The ghost of Lilienthal* must glide uneasily over German cities. The devastation that the Nazis brought to Europe, carried on the wings he loved, is a warning to us all."

He spoke then of the need for a world organization, "based on power." "But," he said, "I must confess to you that I am fearful of the use of power. . . . History is full of its misuses. There is no better example than Nazi Germany. Power without a moral force to guide it invariably ends in the destruction of the people who wield it. We need," he said, "integrity, humility, and compassion. . . . Without them, we simply sow the wind with our aircraft and our bombs."

* Otto Lilienthal, the great German aviation pioneer, killed in one of his own gliders.

LINDBERGH'S
PERSONAL WAR

ON DECEMBER 9, 1941, THE DAY AFTER HIS COUNTRY
declared war on Japan, Lindbergh issued a statement: "We have
been stepping closer to war for many months. Now it has come and
we must meet it as united Americans regardless of our attitude in
the past toward the policy our government has followed. Whether
or not that policy has been wise, our country has been attacked by
force of arms and we must retaliate. Our own defenses and our own
military position have already been neglected too long. We must
now turn every effort to building up the greatest and most efficient
Army, Navy, and Air Force in the world. When American soldiers
go to war, it must be with the best equipment that modern skill can
design and that modern industry can build."

Lindbergh was then a civilian, having resigned his commission
the previous April. He volunteered to re-enlist in the Air Corps in a
letter to General Arnold dated December 30, 1941. Arnold wanted
to accept him, but Roosevelt was implacable. The War Department
said that his statement of support was "not enough." "From
this," his friend Deac Lyman wrote some years later, "he gathered
that he was expected to retract his earlier statements [for America
First]. He did not feel he could honestly do this. He decided then
that he had better turn to the aviation industry for his war service."
He went to see Secretary Stimson and the question was discussed.
Stimson gave it as his opinion that Lindbergh would do better to
contribute to the war effort as a civilian.

Lindbergh then applied to work for the United Aircraft and
Curtiss-Wright Aeronautical corporations. Both companies requested

clearance from Washington for his employment and, according to *Newsweek*, were told that "employing Lindbergh would be frowned upon."

In a sense, Lindbergh was the J. Robert Oppenheimer of pre–World War II. Both men made real contributions to their country in their professions. Both were later denied security clearance because of past opinions and associations. The parallels are not exact, but in neither case was there any real justification for doubting the man's integrity or expecting treasonable behavior. Rather, they were both pawns in the politics of opportunism, sacrifices to the temporary failure of American constitutional freedoms in the face of irresistible current political pressures. They were not security risks; they were security victims.

The Lindbergh case was one of the least attractive manifestations of Roosevelt's penchant for personal vendetta, as Norman Thomas said not long ago—an example of a great leader stooping to petty revenge and recrimination. In satisfying his desire to frustrate Lindbergh, Roosevelt nearly deprived this country of the services of one of our most useful aviation experts.

Nevertheless, Lindbergh managed to make several contributions to the war. Henry Ford had contracted to turn Willow Run into an assembly-line plant for B-24 bombers. He invited Lindbergh to go to work at Willow Run without permission from the government. Lindbergh accepted and there were no government protests. He suggested improvements in the airplane, adapted it for line production, and helped work out the complicated problems involved in the first large-scale assembly-line mass production of aircraft. He also flight-tested the B-24.

Lindbergh also became, around the age of forty, a high-altitude test pilot for Republic Aircraft Corporation. This was extremely hazardous work that would have taxed the stamina of a much younger man. Before undertaking it, Lindbergh, with characteristic prudence, calculated the risks by having himself put through a series of tests in an altitude chamber at the Aero Medical Unit of the Mayo Clinic in Rochester, Minnesota. It was popularly believed by pilots that a flier could not detect the symptoms of anoxia (lack of oxygen), a hazard of high-altitude flying, in time to take corrective action. But Lindbergh, studying his own reactions in the altitude chamber, noted his symptoms as his consciousness drained away and counted the seconds before he blacked out. He felt that within the tiny interval of time between the onset of giddiness and total loss of control, he could act to save himself.

Working with the Mayo doctors on this problem, Lindbergh contributed to high-altitude flying in general. As a result of his tests, high-altitude jumping equipment was improved, enabling many fliers to survive the descent into air rich enough in oxygen to sustain life.

When Lindbergh was testing a Republic "Thunderbolt" fighter at 41,000 feet one day, he nearly suffocated. His previous careful training saved his life. The following is an account of this experience as he published it some years later in a small book called *Of Flight and Life*. It is a good example of the vivid literary style Lindbergh has developed over the years in order to express the excitement and danger he frequently encounters in his work:

Forty thousand feet and still climbing. I am running an ignition breakdown test on the engine of a Thunderbolt [single-place monoplane] fighter. Research in the higher air is a relief from my wartime routine of conferences, production lines, and bomber shakedown flights. At 41,000 feet, I level off, set the trim tabs, and adjust the turbo. I must hold five minutes of level flight while plane and engine settle down to normal readings.

All goes well until, tests run and readings logged, I start to descend. Then, at 36,000 feet: something happens to clarity of air, to pulse of life, perception of eye. I grow aware of that vagueness of mind and emptiness of breath which warn a pilot of serious lack of oxygen. I force myself to alertness—I must think or die! The idea lashes brain and body like the blow of a whip. Mask leaking? I shove it up with my left hand—no, tight against my face. Out of oxygen? No. (A glance at the gauge shows 50 pounds.) Then something must be wrong with the oxygen system. I know from altitude-chamber experience that I have about 15 seconds of consciousness left at this altitude—neither time nor clearness of mind to check hoses and connections. Life demands oxygen and the only sure supply lies 4 miles beneath me.

I shove the stick forward. The earth slants upward and the dive begins . . . 35,000 feet . . . 34,000 my cockpit roars through the air . . . the earth fades out . . . the instrument dials darken . . . breath's thin; lungs, empty—I'm blacking out—losing sight. . . . I push the nose down farther . . . faster . . . 33,000 . . . 30,000 . . . the dials become meaningless . . . down . . . down. . . . I am dimly aware of a great shriek, as though a steam whistle were blowing near my ears. . . . Compressibility dive? . . . I'm not thinking about compressibility . . . it's oxygen I need. . . . I'm blind . . . I can't see the needles . . . there are no more seconds left—it's a razor edge—a race between decreasing consciousness and increasing density of air . . . 17,000 . . . 16,000 . . . 15,000 . . . a white needle moves over white figures . . . it's the altimeter—I can see —I'm reading its dial again—I'm aware of the cockpit, the plane, the earth and sky—I've already begun to pull out of the dive—the stick is free; the nose rising; the seat pressing against me.

The air in my lungs has substance. Perception floods through nerve and tissue. How clear the sky is above me, how wonderful the earth below.

When he landed, mechanics told him that his oxygen tank had been empty; it was a faulty gauge that had misled him almost into death.

United Aircraft Corporation, whose Chance Vought division was building F-4U "Corsair" fighter planes for the Navy and the Marine Corps, asked Lindbergh to join them as an engineering consultant. Lindbergh accepted without official clearance or protest. He acted as aeronautical engineer, test pilot, and instructor. He demonstrated the Corsair to pilots in training.

However, he was growing restive at these peaceful activities. He had been trained as a fighter pilot but had never fought. He began to test his skill in maneuvers and mock combat. He took his plane up against two of the best Marine pilots, and, Deac Lyman says, in a high-altitude gunnery contest, "outguessed, outflew, and outshot" both of them. This was in 1943, when Lindbergh was forty-one years old.

The famous Marine ace, Major Joe Foss, told Lyman, "We wanted him to join the Marines and come right out to the Pacific with us."

Lindbergh could not join the Marines. But he could test aircraft under combat conditions as a technical representative of a manufacturer. In 1944, he got United Aircraft to appoint him a "tech. rep.," and had himself sent to the Pacific under Navy supervision. He spent time with Foss on one of his numerous test programs in the South Pacific.

His mission was "to study the performance of fighter planes under combat conditions" with the purpose of improving existing designs and providing information for new designs. If he was supposed to study a single-place airplane under combat conditions, there was obviously only one way to do it: by flying in combat.

Men of Lindbergh's age did not generally have the reflexes
needed to fly fighter planes in combat during World War II. But
since he was not in uniform, he was not subject to the same limitations as men in service. He flew a number of combat missions in
Corsairs, including strafing raids and flying cover for bombers.

But it was in the use of the Corsair as a light bomber that
Lindbergh made an important contribution. The Corsair was rated
as carrying about 2,000 pounds of bombs in addition to the ammunition for its four .50-caliber machine guns.

Lindbergh decided to take the plane up with 4,000 pounds of
bombs—exactly double the rated bombload. When he got to the
airstrip on the island of Roi, he found a 14-knot crosswind blowing,
so he reduced the bomb weight to 3,000 pounds. This was still 1,000
pounds more than the plane was supposed to lift. Lindbergh had to
wait out a rain squall that reduced visibility to nearly zero. As soon
as the squall had passed, he took off.

"Made a curving takeoff," he reported, "because of the cross wind
heading toward a point halfway along and on the windward side of
the runway. No trouble getting off . . ." Lindbergh handled the
feat deadpan, but the Marines, of whom a large number had
gathered to watch the test, were in open awe of the attempt.

Lindbergh did more than lift the bombs. He climbed until he had
reached the desired altitude, waited his turn in the bombing run on
a Japanese radio station, "maneuvered into position, rolled over at
8,000 feet, and dove on the radio station at an angle of about 60
degrees."

He released his bombs at about 1,600 feet. He was in a state of
"grayout"—lack of blood in the brain caused by the gravity pressure
of pulling out of a steep dive. When his vision cleared and he could
see his target, he noted an almost direct hit.

However, Lindbergh's original plan had called for a 4,000-pound
bombload. The next day, he took off with one 2,000-pound and two
1,000-pound bombs in a nine-knot crosswind. This was, Lyman
wrote in the United Aircraft house magazine, "probably the heaviest
bombload ever carried up to that time by a single-engine fighter."
With his squadron, he climbed at full power to 11,500 feet to get
above clouds. One of the two squadrons supposed to carry out this
mission was forced to return to the base because of storms. The
group with which Lindbergh flew reached their objective.

His personal target was a concrete gun emplacement. He started his dive at 8,000 feet at an angle of sixty-five degrees—a very steep angle under any conditions, but one that produced severe stresses in the plane because it was carrying such a heavy load of bombs.

The two 1,000-pound bombs had to be released manually (the 2,000-pounder had an electrical release). The extra weight of bombs plus the tremendous force of the steep dive were too much for Lindbergh; he simply did not have the strength to hold his sight on the target. He wanted to drop the entire two tons of bombs on the objective. But he had little choice.

"With a lighter load," he said later, "I could have pulled out and made another dive but it seemed inadvisable with 4,000 pounds of bombs." So he abandoned dive-bombing the primary target.

There were many targets of opportunity in the area, however—installations and shore activity, all Japanese. Just before Lindbergh flew over the shore, he pulled the releases and went into a sharp climb. He could see that his bombs had made a direct hit on the main naval gun installation. One portion of the gun position had been wiped out and the gun had probably been dislocated.

The sky was filled with mountainous thunderstorms. Between huge masses of black clouds there were tiny patches of clear sky. Lindbergh flew in formation with a photographic plane at 11,000 feet, heading toward Roi Island. They wound their way through tunnels of light, "like threading a needle at times," Lindbergh later reported, and finally landed at Roi two hours and twenty minutes after their takeoff. This drop of 4,000 pounds of bombs completed the test program he had laid out at Roi. The Corsairs' bomb capacity had been doubled. That afternoon he flew on to Kwajalein Island.

Lindbergh was a civilian flying combat missions. Out of uniform and piloting a warplane, had he been shot down and captured by the Japanese, he could have been executed as a spy. Because of this, the Navy did not want the responsibility for his presence in any one spot for very long. They recognized that this technical work was valuable. Too, just the sight of Lindbergh had a morale-boosting effect on personnel. To the youngsters who flew and serviced Navy and Marine fighters, he was a legend come to life. But his presence made the men in charge nervous.

The Navy shuttled Lindbergh from base to base lest the Japanese get wind of where he was and try to shoot him down. Although they were grateful for his development work, they were nervous about his safety.

Lindbergh was quite happy as one of the pilots. A photograph taken of him at a South Pacific airbase during this period shows him with an unrestrained grin—something the camera hadn't recorded for fifteen years. Anne Lindbergh said, when she saw the snapshot, that she never seen her husband look happier.

Although Lindbergh was in the Pacific as a representative of United Aircraft, working for the Navy, he was very interested in the performance of the Army P-38 twin-engine fighter known as the "Lightning." Without authorization, Lindberg managed to persuade a friendly pilot to drop him off at Nadzab, a P-38 base on New Guinea, around the end of June, 1944.* The base commander, General Whitehead, put him up and Lindbergh spent eight hours having himself checked out in P-38s.

General George C. Kenney, who was in charge of air operations for the Army in the theatre, heard from I.N.S. correspondent Lee Van Atta of Lindbergh's presence without orders. Van Atta had seen Lindbergh at Nadzab. Kenney had Lindbergh picked up and flown to Army headquarters in Brisbane, Australia. There he took him to meet General MacArthur, who issued the necessary orders allowing Lindbergh to stay in New Guinea and fly P-38s. However, Kenney warned him to keep out of combat.

Lindbergh showed up in Hollandia, New Guinea, in July, 1944. Colonel Charles MacDonald, of the 475th Fighter Group, one of the leading American aces of the war, recalled later the entrance into his tent of a tall, balding, middle-aged gentleman in civilian dress while he and another pilot were playing checkers. The tall man gave his name, but MacDonald didn't catch it. The stranger went on to say that he wanted to learn about combat operations of the P-38.

The two pilots had seen other visitors who had put such questions and quickly disappeared. They kept on playing checkers. Mac-Donald asked the stranger his name again, and to state exactly what it was he wanted.

The stranger identified himself as "Lindbergh" and said he

* From the dates given by various colleagues, it seems that he may have checked in with the Army and flown P-38s *before* he did his development work on the Corsair, although he was an official representative of United Aircraft, the Corsair's manufacturer and the P-38 was a product of their competitor, Lockheed. The P-38 had twin Allison engines which were made by General Motors.

wanted to compare range, fire power, and other characteristics of the P-38 with single-engine fighters.

MacDonald was appalled by the idea of trying to show a civilian things that could be learned only by flying the plane. "Are you a pilot?" he asked.

The tall man said he was.

"Not *Charles* Lindbergh?"

"That's my name," Lindbergh said.

The day after Lindbergh arrived at Hollandia, MacDonald asked him if he would like to join a four-plane "anti-boredom" flight to some Japanese-held territory. Lindbergh said he would like to go along, and was told to pick up a jungle kit, a .45-caliber pistol, and a canteen. This would be a sortie on which no Japanese interceptors were expected, so Lindbergh would be sticking to his word to fly only "safe" missions. Nevertheless it would be a long flight over enemy territory. If Lindbergh's engine failed, he would have to take his chances of parachuting into the jungle and being picked up.

The other pilots on his first flight were dubious about old Lindbergh's ability to keep up and react properly, particularly as he had had only a few hours of flying time in P-38s. However, he acquitted himself well in formation flying and attack, and on following days, according to MacDonald, was "indefatigable. He flew more missions than was normally expected of a regular combat pilot. He dive-bombed enemy positions, sank barges. . . . He was shot at by almost every anti-aircraft gun . . . in western New Guinea."

On one such mission, one of the youngsters flying alongside Lindbergh noticed that Lindbergh had been a touch slow in retracting his landing gear after takeoff. The other pilot radioed: "Lindbergh . . . Get your wheels up! You're not flying the *Spirit of St. Louis!*"

When he returned from missions with the 475th, MacDonald noticed that Lindbergh's tanks held a great deal more gasoline than those of the other planes in the squadron. Yet he had been flying wing to wing with the others, at the same altitude and at the same speed. The ground crews wanted to know how he managed to use so little gas.

Lindbergh's answer was that once the formation had attained altitude, he would throttle back to 1,600 r.p.m., and increase

manifold pressure and propeller bite. In that way, he would conserve fuel while maintaining air speed. These tactics were not
original with Lindbergh, but were thought bad practice. The other
pilots and the mechanics in the 475th Fighter Group believed that
they would ruin the engines. The only way to prove the point was to
have Lindbergh's engines taken apart, and they showed no more
wear than others that had logged a comparable number of flying
hours. The squadron then adopted Lindbergh's techniques and
immediately added 600 miles (says MacDonald; Lindbergh claimed
only 500 miles) to the range of their aircraft.

This not only gave pilots a greater margin of safety but allowed
the planes to fly farther afield; it permitted a change in tactics. The
P-38 could now fly cover for bombing missions hundreds of miles
beyond where the Japanese expected to find them.

Says MacDonald, "Lindbergh had, in effect, redesigned an airplane."

On one of the new long-range missions, Lindbergh was leading a
squadron covering bombers in an attack on Aboina. The bombers
were forced by bad weather to turn back, so the fighters proceeded
to find targets they could attack themselves. As they began to use
up their ammunition, they ran into some Japanese fighters. One
Sonia-type plane escaped from two attacking P-38s and turned to fly
head on at Lindbergh. Lindbergh was in a slight climb. "Of all the
attacks it is possible to make on a Japanese plane, the one liked least
is the head-on pass," MacDonald said later, "for here you and the
enemy approach with tremendous speed, each with guns blazing.
There is always a good chance for collision."

The Sonia tried to shoot Lindbergh down. He fired point-blank at
the Sonia. Then the Japanese tried for a crash at the last split
second. The planes almost met nose to nose, both firing steadily,
with Lindbergh's just clearing the top of the Sonia's wing as it
smoked into the sea. He reported the kill in his unemotional log
style: "The enemy plane banked right to attack me head on. I fired
a burst of several seconds, observing numerous hits. The Sonia then
flew under me, almost colliding, rolled over, and crashed into the
water." He said later he felt a "bump" in his tail as the planes
passed one another. It was the first plane Lindbergh had ever shot
down.

The P-38s, trying out their extra range, began flying longer and longer missions. Lindbergh apparently forgot his orders to stay out of combat situations and flew with them. They hit Balikpapan and Mindanao, and later China and Indochina from the Philippines. These places had all been outside their old radius.

Over Palau, Lindbergh was returning in a group of four P-38s headed for their Biak base, seven hundred miles across ocean. They had just left a fight in which a Zero had got on his tail while he was attacking another plane. Lindbergh was relieved to see that his plane carried no bullet holes; the Zero had been scared off by MacDonald. The sea was smooth, the sky peaceful.

The raid had been successful, Lindbergh was thinking with some satisfaction. Slipping in at 15,000 feet, they had caught the Japanese by surprise, for Palau was considered out of range of land-based fighters. They crossed Babelthuap at almost tree-top level and, off the eastern coast, shattered the decks of a patrol ship with their guns. They shot down three enemy planes in flames.*

Then [Lindbergh wrote] our fuel reserves lowering after nearly an hour of flying at battle-cruise, we headed toward open ocean. At the same moment, a Zero dove from a cloud to attack my wingman. I turn back to his defense five seconds too soon. I should have climbed and made a wider circle. Seeing a better target, the Jap pilot whips around in a bank and half rolls onto my tail. There's no use dog-fighting with a Zero. I'm too near the water to dive. I jam the throttles into war emergency power and bank toward the other unit of our flight. I have speed and I have friends, but both are seconds away—hundreds of bullets away. I can see the cylinders of the Zero's engine, feel its machine guns rising into line behind me. It is too close to miss. I pull my elbows inside the armor plate and brace for the impact of the shells—the rip of wing covering—the torch of a fuel tank—the jerky clatter of a failing engine. Seconds are frozen; time, eternal.

Why don't the bullets strike? There is no thud, no shattering of glass, no pain! The twin tails of a P-38 flash by, almost vertical in bank. A Zero climbs steeply toward the nearest cloud. A second P-38 crosses over. Tracers are spurting from a third, firing full deflection. A trail of smoke streaks out behind the Zero and it disappears in the overcast.** The air behind me is empty. Only four P-38s circle in the nearer sky. The earth becomes unfrozen. Time and space assume their old dimensions.

---

* 2 planes destroyed by Colonel Charles H. MacDonald
  1 plane destroyed by Lieutenant Colonel Meryl M. Smith.
** Shot, and probably destroyed, by Captain Danforth P. Miller.

MacDonald's view of this fight was more matter-of-fact. When the Zero got on Lindbergh's tail, MacDonald warned him to turn right—to bring the enemy within MacDonald's range. "The Jap must not have been too good a shot," MacDonald reported. "I could see the fire leap from the leading edge of his wings as he shot at Lindbergh from such a short distance it seemed impossible he could miss." The enemy pilot must have lost his nerve, MacDonald thought. It was as he was pulling away that Captain Miller shot him down.

On this combat mission (his thirty-sixth), Lindbergh fully appreciated the technical superiority of his country's aircraft. "It was the last few miles of speed, translated into degrees of aim and inches of error, that threw the enemy bullets off my plane. It was the last few hundred horsepower, translated into seconds, that brought three P-38s to me in time. It was the final perfection of our guns, the final training of our pilots, that forced the Zero off my tail and sent it smoking off for shelter. . . . That was why the four of us had been able to raid Palau against a reported strength of nearly 200 enemy fighters."

In six months in the Pacific, Lindbergh flew a full complement of 50 combat missions as a civilian—the same number that was demanded of every pilot, navigator, bomber, and gunner in the U.S. armed services. He put in 178 combat hours. He had compiled a large, useful dossier on the performance and difficulties of our fighter aircraft. His personal war was over.

Having completed his self-imposed stint of combat service, Lindbergh returned himself to the States. General Kenney had asked him not to talk about his experiences as a prerequisite of permission to fly the P-38. "Lindbergh," says Kenney, "said he had no intention of telling the story, as he too was anxious not to have any publicity in regard to his activities in the Pacific, particularly while the war was on." Lindbergh has, in fact, never told the full details of his war experiences. He has made only one reference in print to his combat missions—in *Of Flight and Life*. This was not published until 1948.

In 1954, as already noted, President Eisenhower nominated Charles A. Lindbergh, A0215724 (Formerly Colonel, Air Corps Reserve), for a commission as Brigadier General in the U.S. Air Force Reserve, a nomination later approved by the U.S. Senate. General Kenney praised the appointment.

"When Lindbergh joined us," Kenney said, "the P-38s were considered to have a range of 400 miles. Under his training P-38s were able to escort bombers all the way to Balikpapan, Borneo, fight over the target, and get home with a reserve supply of fuel, for a 950-mile mission." This, said Kenney, let the United States get to the Philippines much sooner than planned. "Lindbergh's contribution shortened the war by several months," Kenney said not long ago, "and saved thousands of American lives."

FAMILY LIFE

ONCE, AT A DINNER PARTY IN THE LINDBERGH HOUSE, Mrs. Lindbergh was talking to Igor Sikorsky about family life. "You know," she said, "my husband doesn't think a family really exists unless there are twelve children." Lindbergh was at the other end of the table, engaged in a conversation of his own. But he immediately broke off what he was saying to reply to this statement. "Who can say that a family exists without twelve children?" he asked. Another member of the dinner party recalls, "You could see that this had been a subject of family debate for a long time."

It is a debate which Lindbergh has only half won. He has fathered six children, five of whom are living. Jon Morrow Lindbergh, born 1932; Land Morrow Lindbergh, born (in England, the only Lindbergh child born out of the country) 1937; Anne Spencer Lindbergh, born 1940; Scott Lindbergh, born 1942; Reeve Lindbergh, born 1945.

The first three of these are married, and parents. Jon has four children, Land two, Anne one, a total of seven grandchildren. Grandpa Lindbergh affects a tough, careless attitude toward his children's children. He refers to them not by name but by the old Armed Forces phonetic alphabet—Able, Baker, Charlie, Dog, Easy, Fox, George. (According to the new alphabet, they would be Alpha, Bravo, Charlie, Delta, Echo, Foxtrot, Golf.) But no matter what identification Lindbergh employs, he says he wants twenty-six grandchildren, one for every letter in the alphabet. This would work out an average of five and a fifth children for each of his children.

Lindbergh, in these numerical calculations, is, of course, not entirely serious. He is hardly ever entirely serious with his family.

But there is more than a grain of sincerity in his hankering for a large number of children, a comment on his own status as an only child.

He was an extremely lonely child, emotionally split in his loyalties to his parents, physically shuttled between residences and so many different schools in so many different places. In *We,* he said, "Through these years I crossed and recrossed the United States, made one trip to Panama, and had thoroughly developed a desire for travel, which has never been overcome."

Lindbergh's bland description reveals an unstable childhood environment that can only be characterized as traumatic. It is the sort of experience that either breaks the spirit or forges an iron will. Obviously, it didn't break Lindbergh, but it couldn't have been pleasant. He hasn't wanted that kind of life for his children.

For them he planned a permanent home in a small town and a continuity of normal public school and social relationships. He and his wife had considered these relationships basic, and had started off with these goals in Hopewell. But that home was shattered by tragedy, and they could not then establish another that would be safe for children—not in this country. For the next fourteen years, the Lindberghs lived in various houses and apartments in Europe and America. It was only after the birth of their sixth child, Reeve, that they felt they could settle into a permanent home of their own.

In 1946, Lindbergh bought a large Tudor-style house on several acres of land in Darien, Connecticut. The house was near that of a Pan American World Airways vice-president. It was in an area, marked "Private," known as Tokeneke. This is a secluded piece of woods and fields south of the right of way of the New Haven Railroad. It borders on Scott's Cove, an arm of Long Island Sound. The Lindbergh property had its own waterfront; its cost, according to stamps on the deed, was $85,000.

The house contained a bedroom for each of the five Lindbergh children and one each for Charles and Anne Lindbergh. There was also a room for one full-time servant, a cook. A cleaning woman came in twice a week to help out.

By staying completely out of the news after 1941, the family was able to achieve the privacy and security they had long sought. They could settle in Darien, and Lindbergh could blend into the background of suburban living and commuting to New York. His children went to the local public schools.* They played with the neighboring children, made friends with schoolmates, brought their friends home to play and eat. In short, the family did not have to live like the families of celebrities. They continued the same sort of quiet existence they had found in France and England.

When he was at home, Lindbergh worked in a small trailer, a present from Henry Ford, parked in the back yard. But he was not often at home; that is, he was not around in the sense that the average commuting father is there every day for a quick glimpse of the kids in the morning, a fast good night during the evening cocktail. When Lindbergh was at home, it might be for days or weeks at a time. But, absent or not, his presence was felt, his principles were known. The Lindbergh children never doubted that they had a strong, demanding, protective father.

His wandering, secretive ways were accepted by the children when young as normal, although as they have grown older and have seen how other families live, they have tended to question his behavior.

"Actually, he wasn't away as much as it seemed," one of the Lindbergh children said recently. "It's just that we never knew where he was or when he was coming back. He likes to be *mysterious*."

"He's the original jet-age man," one of his friends says. "He's just as at home in Nairobi as New York, and he doesn't see why he should be in either unless it suits him to be there." Lindbergh does not believe in writing letters. "If they don't hear from you, they know you're all right," he says. Not long ago, Lindbergh was in Scotland at the same time as one of his daughters. But she didn't know where to reach him, and he didn't even know she was in the country.

His sudden disappearances, unheralded reappearances, and frequent disassociation from the daily routines of family life may even have sharpened the children's awareness of his presence when he came home. "It's so nice to go away," he was once heard to say to one of his children. "You always like me better when I come back."

Lindbergh presented himself in terms of principle, rather than achievement. His example has been one of individualism, integrity, self-reliance, and excellence in physical mastery of the environment.

* Except Reeve, who went to day-school.

He never gave the children the idea that they were living in the shadow of a symbol, or a national hero. In fact, he has never been one to discuss with his children either his present work or his past achievements. When one of the children was accosted in the first grade by a schoolmate who said, "I hear your father discovered America," the Lindbergh child placidly accepted this statement as historical fact and added, "Yes, and he flew across the ocean, too."

"There was a chapter in our schoolbook on Father," said one of the Lindbergh children recently. "We felt kind of funny about it, but nobody made too much of it. We knew he flew the Atlantic, but he didn't talk about it much or about anything else seriously." To his children he seems to be either too serious, or not serious enough.

Believing that all his children should know how to handle firearms, as he has done from the age of six, Lindbergh gave them target-shooting lessons with a small-caliber rifle. The shooting took place in the garage at Darien. Once, when it came the turn of young Anne Spencer Lindbergh to shoot, she pointed the rifle, closed her eyes, and fired. She scored a bull's-eye. Lindbergh took the gun away from her. "That's all for you," he said. "You're perfect."

Lindbergh deprecates women's interest in and understanding of mechanical problems, although he took his wife along as radio operator on two long flights. "He knew Mother really hated it all. She likes nothing better than to fly in a Pan American plane with someone else doing the work," one Lindbergh child said. He might discuss mechanical problems with the boys, who, he felt, understood such things.

Back in 1930, Lindbergh told the *Pictorial Review* magazine that he didn't want his son to be anything he had no taste or aptitude for. "I believe that every boy should have complete freedom in the choice of his life's work," he said.

Certainly he has never encouraged any of his children to follow his path in aviation and astronautics. He did teach Jon to fly when the boy was sixteen. He gave him twelve hours of instruction in a two-place airplane. (Jon says, "This was the first time I had a chance to admire his ability.") Then one day Lindbergh walked away from the plane and said, "You go alone today."

Jon soloed successfully. Later he asked if he might try a parachute jump.

"Not *try*," Lindbergh said. "Make."

He took Jon up to 2,000 feet and then waited for the boy to jump. Although he was wearing two chutes, Jon couldn't bring himself to leave the plane. Lindbergh did not look back, but circled the landing spot a second time. This time Jon was able to jump. He landed not far from where he was supposed to.

Jon earned a pilot's license, but Lindbergh told him that he would prefer it if Jon stayed out of flying. "It's become too automatic, too push-button," Lindbergh told him. "Find something new, a field that needs research, and hasn't been well studied. Without a challenge a man isn't getting the most from his life."

When the children were small, he used to play games with them, usually animal games. The games would often take place in the dark, possibly so that the children would not have Lindbergh's early fear of darkness. He would be a bear, or a lion, or some other kindly animal, making appropriate animal noises. His children remember him, too, from their younger days, as a creative storyteller. His stories, like his games, were mostly about animals. But he had a disconcerting habit of occasionally falling asleep while he was telling a story.

The children played baseball without him. He has never been a man for team activity, his only team sports being the rifle and pistol squads of the University of Wisconsin, hardly in the team category. But he has often skied with the children, and the family has frequently gone on ski trips together—to Switzerland, to Austria, to Canada, to Aspen, Colorado. On such trips, the Lindberghs traveled incognito and registered at resorts under an assumed name that is part of his mother's family tree. Once, at a Canadian resort, a man penetrated the Lindbergh *nom d'emprunt* and came up to him on the slope in evident excitement saying, "Why, hello, Mr. Lindbergh!" Lindbergh immediately took off his skis, collected his brood, marched them to the hotel, packed, and left—all within a space of an hour or so. His children are sure that he is recognized oftener than this, but so long as no overt move is made to disclose his identity he does not feel threatened.

On skis, Lindbergh is adequate but not proficient. He can get down slopes, but does so in his own inelegant style. He skis from one side to the other, then sits down or does a jump turn, and skis back across the slope. In order to learn speed skiing, to schuss down steep trails, it is necessary to take risks and to fall down. His children have learned to ski this way. Lindbergh is a cautious skier, however. "In my business," he says, "you're allowed only one fall."

Local ski trips were often made in a Volkswagen, a favorite Lindbergh family vehicle. At one time there were several Volkswagens parked in the Lindbergh driveway. One of the Lindbergh children has one at school. Lindbergh himself often favors a Ford station wagon. He once told a friend that of American cars he preferred the Ford over all other makes. This brand loyalty undoubtedly goes back to his first family car, a Model T Ford, as well as to his long friendship with the late Henry Ford, Sr. Lindbergh told the same friend not only to buy Fords but also never to use anything but regular-grade gasoline in the engines, no matter what the manufacturer's instructions said. The friend says, "I ruined two Ford engines that way."

A friend recalls being driven to the Lindberghs' on a snowy day, and Lindbergh demonstrating the control he could exert over the car while skidding. "Want to bet five dollars I can't skid it through the gate?" he asked. He then proceeded to do just that. The friend thinks of this as one of Lindbergh's practical jokes, but actually his purpose was more practical than funny. He not only deliberately put the car into a skid so he could control it; he taught his children to do the same and how to react when a car they are driving begins to skid. As a result, one of his children was recently saved from an accident when her car hit a slick spot on an icy road. "I just knew what to do automatically, without thinking," she said. He has given them driving lessons starting at a very early age—around twelve years, almost as young as the age he started to drive.

On the road, Lindbergh is apt to be impatient with other drivers. Since he can maneuver the Volkswagen through snow, he becomes irritated with drivers who get themselves bogged down and halt traffic.

Not many years ago, Lindbergh rented a small plane at the Danbury, Connecticut, airport and took his youngest daughter, Reeve, for a ride. As always, he first had himself checked out in the plane and tried it in the air before boarding his passenger. Then he took off with Reeve and flew around. He was demonstrating climbing stalls when the engine died and could not be restarted. His daughter asked him if they were in danger, if they would crash. Lindbergh, who, of course, had several times been in a single-engine plane that had lost its power, said firmly, "No." The child was completely reassured.

He had sufficient altitude to locate a pasture, and was able to glide the plane into it without damaging it, his daughter, or himself. But the landing area was so small the plane couldn't be flown out. The wings had to be removed and they and the fuselage had to be trucked out.

Lindbergh's way of bringing up his children reflects his attitude toward life in general: he believes in sound minds in healthy bodies; in inculcating independence and responsibility in young people; in the benefits of a sound nutrition; in calculating risks but not worrying about dangers; in the relationship between physical skills and mental stability (i.e., people skillful with their hands do not have nervous breakdowns); in intellectual honesty; in fiscal responsibility; in public school education; in outdoor activities; and in many more.

Probably some of Lindbergh's ideas on child-rearing derive from the very strong opinions of his friend the late Dr. Alexis Carrel. (Carrel was also certain that the development of physical skills strongly influenced one's mental health.) But the ideas also go back to the Lindberghs, the Lands, and the Lodges.

A visitor at Long Barn, the house the Lindberghs occupied in England in 1936 and 1937, recalls being awakened in the morning by a loud hammering. She wondered what the noise could be. Later in the morning, after breakfast, she was talking to Lindbergh when Jon, then about five years old, came in and stood waiting. His father said, "What is it, Jon?" Jon said, "Well, sir, would you put some more nails in the boards for me?"

Lindbergh said, "But I've put some in for you."

"I've used them up, sir," said the boy.

Lindbergh seemed a bit surprised, the visitor relates, and said, "Excuse me for a moment please." He went out to where Jon was constructing a tool house. Lindbergh believes in practical ends to his lessons, not merely learning to exercise a talent futilely. This tool house was being built of two-by-fours and full-size planks—pieces of wood too large for little Jon to handle. Lindbergh would put the planks in place and fix each with one nail, marking crosses with a pencil where the other nails were to go.

The visitor saw that Jon was wielding an enormous hammer, so large that he had to use two hands to lift it. She thought he might hit himself on the head and knock himself out with it. So she said to Lindbergh later, "I think that's a fine idea, learning to use his hands in a practical way, but don't you think it would be a good idea for him to have a smaller hammer?"

Lindbergh said, "I've given him three small hammers and he's lost every one of them. Now he's just going to have to make out with that one until he finds the others."

Although there were several servants at Long Barn, Lindbergh did not like having them in the room while the family was dining. The servants would put the food on a sideboard in the long Tudor dining room and retire. Lindbergh would then carve and serve.

One night, the family and guests were eating, having been served by Lindbergh, but Jon's chair was vacant. The door opened and Jon came in. He was so small he had to reach up to grasp the doorknob. Lindbergh's back was to Jon, who went directly to the sideboard and took a large carving knife and fork. He reached up and began to carve himself some roast beef. The visitor saw this and did not know whether to interrupt Lindbergh to tell him what was going on—she didn't know him very well. So she sat silent and waited, expecting at any moment to hear a piercing scream indicating that the child had cut off his thumb. Not at all. Jon sliced off a huge hunk of roast beef without injuring himself and heaped his plate with vegetables. He carried it over and put it on the big table. Then he climbed up into the seat of his huge chair. He settled himself in the chair, picked up a full-sized knife and fork, and began cutting his meat and eating.

After a while his father looked at his watch and said, "Three minutes, Jon." These words were the first overt notice he had taken that the child was there.

"Yes, sir," said Jon, and shoveled food into his mouth as fast as he could.

In three minutes, Lindbergh rang the bell and the butler came in and cleared the plates. He brought dessert, of which Jon had a full-sized portion.

Later, the guest said to Anne Lindbergh, "You know, I was appalled when I saw that child reaching up to the high sideboard with that knife."

Mrs. Lindbergh said, "Yes, it is quite frightening, isn't it? But he manages quite well."

In this small incident can be glimpsed the application of several of Lindbergh's principles. Jon was late for dinner, but was made aware of his lapse only by being forced to serve himself and eat faster. His mother didn't show that she was concerned with his handling the big knife. Nobody helped him into his chair. Nobody cut the food on his plate. At the age of five, he accepted the responsibility for his own behavior that many children years older are not ready to do. In a way, this repeats Lindbergh's own enforced precocity. But there is an important difference: his children have been brought up with the support of a continuity which he did not have.

On another occasion, in Paris a year or two later, Jon was taken up to the top of the Eiffel Tower by his father, along with a couple who had a daughter a few years older than the boy. As they rode up the inclined elevator, Jon wanted to get up on a seat so that he could look out. The seat was quite high for him to reach, and noting his difficulty, the mother of the other child helped Jon onto it.

Lindbergh saw this out of the corner of his eye and, without saying a word, he pulled Jon off. He said, holding on to him, "You want to get up on there?"

"Yes, sir," said Jon.

"Well, then," said Lindbergh, letting go of his son, "get up." And Jon did manage to scramble onto the seat by himself, while Lindbergh said to the woman, "I've the greatest difficulty with mothers, preventing them from trying to help their children too much."

Descending from the Eiffel Tower, the three adults and the two children walked down the steep iron stairs. It had been raining, and the steps had pools of water in their worn hollows. Lindbergh and the father of the other child were striding down in advance. The mother was trailing by a flight with the two children. She was especially concerned about Jon, who might easily slip on the slick wet iron.

She said, "Jon, hold on to the railing and be careful."

Lindbergh heard her and turned around and said, "Let go of the railing, and run down, Jon."

The woman said, "For heaven's sake, why do you say that? Do you want him to break his neck?"

Lindbergh replied, as his son obeyed his command and scrambled down the stairs, "If he's going to be too careful, he is apt to have an accident. But if he'll just forget about it, he won't have any trouble at all."

With his usual single-mindedness, Lindbergh has applied his theory of calculated risks to all his children. For instance, some years after the Eiffel Tower incident, he took his two youngest children, Scott and Reeve, to visit neighbors not far from their Connecticut house. While Lindbergh sat inside talking to his friends, the children played around in the spacious yard.

There was a large ash tree near the house, the trunk two or three feet in diameter and correspondingly high. The children came in and said to Lindbergh, "Father, can we climb that tree?"

Lindbergh interrupted his conversation and excused himself. He went out with the two children and sat with them on the edge of the porch, Scott on one side and Reeve on the other, and looked up at the tree.

"Now, you want to climb this tree, don't you?" Lindbergh asked. They said they did.

He asked, "How are you going up?"

Scott looked up at the tree—he was twelve or so at the time—and said he'd first take this limb and then that one and so on.

His father said, "Then you're going to get stuck there, aren't you? You can't get any farther if you go up that way, can you?"

Scott agreed that he would be stopped part way up, and so did Reeve.

Lindbergh said, "Now, figure out how you're going to get up there for yourself."

The children calculated and theoretically tested various routes up the tree. At last they solved it. They told Lindbergh how they would climb the tree, until they had reached the top.

Then Lindbergh said, "All right, go up the tree." He arose, turned his back and walked into the house, and resumed his conversation with his friends.

His host said, "Charles, that was a great lesson in education."

Lindbergh replied, "Yes, they must learn to take calculated risks. As long as they figure out everything ahead of time and just don't go off half cocked."

The woman of the house shuddered a little as she recalled the story. "I couldn't have left them out there on that huge tree, although I must admit they did get up and down without an accident. I must say," the woman concluded, "the children don't admire him any less for their Spartan upbringing. Or love him any the less. Only I couldn't do it that way, and I don't know any other parent who could."

Lindbergh has also consistently applied the principle of self-reliance, by which he himself was raised, to his own children, starting with Jon. It was not only in the dining room, or in manual training, but in matters where the children were exposed to real danger. When he was thirteen, Jon had a dinghy and a small outboard engine. He set up a line of lobster pots in the Sound, and sold his catch in the local fishmarket. Some days he made as much as ten dollars.

Once, he was late coming back. It was getting dark, and Jon was somewhere out of sight of land, without a compass, when Lindbergh went down to the dock to look for him. The waves were rising, and the wind was strengthening. The local fishermen were worried, but Lindbergh said, "No use calling for a Coast Guard search yet. Let's wait and see if he can't make it back on his own."

Jon returned safely after dark, and Lindbergh said, "I don't see you wearing a life jacket."

"No," Jon said, "but I'm towing a rubber raft, just in case."

"Fine," said his father, "but get a jacket and compass before you go out again. Always leave yourself several ways out of possible trouble."

Afterward Lindbergh asked Jon why he always seemed to be out in storms (once the boy very nearly didn't get back). Jon replied, "It's more fun. And in bad weather more lobsters are around."

"Good reasons," Lindbergh said, "but only a fool goes against the odds consistently. They always catch up with you."

Charles and Anne Lindbergh were out of the house one evening when young Scott Lindbergh, then eleven years old, failed to return from an outboard motorboat trip with some of his friends. The cook, at home with the girls, began to get worried when Scott didn't show up for dinner. As the evening wore on, she became almost frantic wondering whether to call the Lindberghs or the police. Finally, about nine-thirty, Scott came home with his friends. They were all covered with mud. It seems the boat had got stuck in the mud and they had been trapped by low water. But somehow they had succeeded in dragging the boat home.

The next day, the cook told Lindbergh about the incident. He said, without any sign of being disturbed, "Don't worry about them. They know how to take care of themselves."

Lindbergh has stuck by his principles and seen them work—too well. Like any good father, he has found himself phased out of his parental responsibility by the growing self-reliance of his children.

For example, there is his relationship with Jon, his eldest son. Lindbergh is a strong swimmer—although his swimming, like his skiing, is more utilitarian than stylish. For years he has set a hard example for his children, particularly the boys. He could outswim them all, and dared them to swim in the coldest weather.

Jon Lindbergh took up skin diving when he was about fifteen, in the Florida keys. He became an expert underwater swimmer; he could swim three lengths of a pool without coming up for air. He got an aqualung when he was twenty and became proficient with it. After that, he served three years as a Navy officer in an underwater demolition unit.

Some years ago, when Jon was in his early twenties, he invited his father, then in his fifties, to go for a bit of skin diving on the West Coast. The two men—Jon is dark and smaller (five feet eleven, a hundred fifty pounds) than his six-foot-three-inch father: "More of a Morrow than a Lindbergh," a friend says—equipped themselves for the dive. Jon gave his father a belt of lead weights and the other equipment they would need, and both men plunged into the sea and began swimming.

A friend retells Lindbergh's description of the event in these words: "We swam and we swam about a mile out, then we got to a certain reef and Jon said, 'Now, father, now we're going to go down.'

"And I said to him, 'Jon, you're going, I'll wait for you to come up.'"

The friend continued, "Jon went down and Charles waited up on top hanging on to a buoy or something and then he swam back and was exhausted by the time he got to the beach."

Lindbergh was more than exhausted; he was also very pleased. He said it was the first time that any of the boys was able to do something that his father couldn't do better. "He had it on me," Lindbergh said with relish when he told the story.

It was a great day for Jon Lindbergh, too. "That was the day that Jon became independent of his father," the friend observes.

Jon has since gone on to make a distinguished career for himself in oceanography and deep-sea diving. In 1962 he and another diver plunged 432 feet below the surface of the Atlantic Ocean off the Bahamas and set a new world's record by staying at that depth for forty-nine hours. They were testing a new method of living underwater. By accustoming their bodies to the immense pressure of this great depth, Jon and his partner were able to dwell in a fragile fabric structure and to swim freely about without any diving gear. The apparatus and the idea were the work of Edwin C. Link, inventor of the famous Link aviation trainer. Link and Jon Lindbergh are associated in oceanographic development work, in a company called Ocean Systems, Incorporated, in Seattle, Washington.

Lindbergh often visits Jon to watch him work. He was in California the day Jon demonstrated a revolutionary new lightweight diving helmet. The helmet utilizes a mixture of oxygen and helium instead of the gases usually favored by professional divers.

Jon was taking the rig down far below the 250-foot limit considered safe for conventional equipment and breathing mixtures. Yet Lindbergh did not seem perturbed. He asked only technical questions concerning the amounts and types of gases breathed in the new helmet. That day, Jon dived to 400 feet, demonstrating that it was possible to do useful work at depths theretofore considered impossible. He has dived to 550 feet and has worked at a depth of 500 feet. He is considered a pioneer in the field, the way his father was in aviation. "Name anything that's dangerous and wet and he's been involved in it," says Admiral Edward Stephen, a business associate of Jon Lindbergh's. He is rated one of the top professional divers in the world, earning as much as $16 a minute, and is constantly on call to all parts of the world.

Jon has always demonstrated a great respect for money. He wears his father's castoff shoes (he says they're comfortable as well as free) and a $3.50 Mickey Mouse watch, owns only one suit and wears it rarely. Mostly he dresses in jeans. When he attended Stanford University (he specialized in marine biology), he lived in a tent off campus on a site for which he paid $1.00 a month rent.

Lindbergh plays jokes on his family as he does on other people. A paper cup of water balanced on the top of a door was a typical trick on the children. The drenching would be small, the danger of being hurt nil. He would also pull the girls' blond pigtails.

Many years ago he and his wife were in the kitchen of George Palmer Putnam, publisher of his first book, *We*. He was drinking a glass of water. Anne, wearing a blue silk dress, was seated drinking buttermilk and Charles was standing beside her. He let a few drops of water drip from his glass on her shoulder. Water stains silk. She said nothing. He tried it again. Still no response. After the third time, however, she suddenly swung around and let fly the buttermilk from her glass into his face and all over his tie, shirt, and jacket. A moment of shock—and then he burst out laughing.

With his friends the Truman Smiths, in Berlin, he was full of fun. Once, when he was driving them (Mrs. Smith in front with Lindbergh), Major Smith and Mrs. Lindbergh were jointly reading a copy of the Paris *Herald* in the back. Lindbergh lit a match and, reaching over the back of the seat, set fire to the paper. "This is always a surprise to people," he remarked casually to Kay Smith as her husband and Anne Lindbergh beat out the flame.

His jokes are often a comment on the people he plays them on and on customs he considers silly. Once, when his wife was giving a large sit-down dinner to a group of people, she set out the wines to breathe with the corks out of the bottles. Lindbergh observed this ritual, and indicated his reaction by secretly adding a bit of salt to each bottle. When the wine was poured, Mrs. Lindbergh, who, unlike her husband, drinks wine, tasted it and knew instantly what had happened—and, of course, who had done it. She said nothing to her husband, but ordered the bottles replaced, thereby topping the joke.

Lindbergh is a teetotaler not out of temperance convictions but mainly because he does not like the taste of whiskey, wine, or beer. He has tried the stuff—he will sip a bit for a toast if the occasion demands it—but he just doesn't care for any alcoholic beverage. He once told a friend who offered him a cup of breakfast coffee that he didn't want to become dependent on any stimulants. His favorite tipple is milk, which nourishes, does not stimulate, and is not supposed to be habit-forming. But since he has been drinking it all his life, this last attribute may be questionable.

Lindbergh never had any hobbies. "Everything always had a purpose," one of his children said recently. The same child was surprised to learn that her father had been photographing wild game in Africa. "I didn't know until a few months ago that Father had a camera," she said, "or knew how to take pictures. I'm glad he is getting an interest in that kind of thing." (Actually, Lindbergh has taken pictures since his youth.) Lindbergh has proposed to his family a trip to Kruger National Park, in Africa, "Where *you're* in the cage—inside a car—and an elephant has the right of way," another Lindbergh offspring said. "Father thinks that is very democratic."

Since his childhood in Little Falls and the hunting trips with his father, Lindbergh has always been an active outdoorsman, and he still likes to work with his hands around his house and grounds, as he did on the farm. At home, he usually wears work clothes, chinos and a shirt with an open collar. His only power tool is a mechanical saw.

Both Lindberghs have an aversion to ostentation and luxury, even to comfort. A guest recalls that they didn't even have a proper sofa in the living room, but a kind of day-bed with iron arms, slip-covered. There was a large and very good piano, however. There were also a few good paintings—the Lindberghs own works by Vlaminck, a painter of the French Fauve group—and a head of Mrs. Lindbergh by an unidentified sculptor. (A friend thinks it was not Jo Davidson or Epstein, but of the same genre.) However, the house was distinctly underfurnished for its size, location, and price. When the *Saturday Evening Post* sent a photographer to get a picture to run with the serialization of Lindbergh's autobiography in the magazine, in 1953, it was with some difficulty that a grouping of furniture could be put together to fill the photograph with a comfortable atmosphere.

The children's rooms were correspondingly ascetic. A guest recalls that each child had a kind of iron bedstead; that the row of bedrooms—all with doors open while the children slept—gave something of an impression of a barracks. Each Lindbergh child was required to make his own bed—a rule that was observed when

Lindbergh was at home but broken when he wasn't. There were no servants in the house other than the cook, a middle-aged German woman named Martha Knecht, who had a warm heart and an interest in music. The children were all fond of her, but the one who loved her most dearly was the youngest, Reeve. Almost every day Reeve left a small note for the cook—usually rhymed, often illustrated—lauding her cookies, apologizing for some misdeed, and the like. The cookies were rationed by paternal order, only three a day per child. One of the Lindbergh children wrote to the cook from Aspen, Colorado, during Christmas week of 1957, saying that their Father was pretty mad when three of them turned up with so many cookies in their bag. But the cookies were gone in three days, she said, and it was Father who ate most of them.

Lindbergh had many more specific ideas about nutrition than rationing cookies, however. He forbade the use of white sugar in the house; instead, he insisted on brown sugar. But it is impossible to cook everything with brown sugar, so some white sugar was used without his knowledge. He forbade such things as chocolate cake. But once, when he had to go away for a couple of days, the children asked the cook to bake a chocolate cake. "Make a big one," they said. When Lindbergh returned unexpectedly, the children grabbed hunks of cake and went to their rooms. The cook hid the rest of the cake in her room.

Generally, the food in the house was plain, substantial, and plentiful. A typical dinner consisted of a roast, a salad with dressing of oil, vinegar, and spices prepared by Mrs. Lindbergh. Lunch was a buffet, with many different kinds of cheese. Twenty-two quarts of milk were consumed in the Lindbergh house every two days when all the children were home.

The dog in the family—a German shepherd named Siggy (after Siegfried)—was much beloved by the children and was an integral part of their growing up for several years. Then Siggy bit a neighbor. The children said it was not his fault, but the Lindberghs were faced with a suit for damages, so he had to be given away. After that, they got a cocker spaniel.

Although the senior Lindberghs did not socialize with their neighbors, the children often invited their friends home to dinner. The children would get together on Saturday nights, roll up the rugs in the living room, and dance to records. Lindbergh would watch, but not dance. Young Anne played the piano and the flute. Scott and Land played guitars.

Reeve and Scott were also fond of rock 'n' roll and other contemporary popular music. One day, they played a favorite record of the Kingston Trio over and over. Lindbergh, who was downstairs trying to write, finally came upstairs and took the record and broke it in half without any show of anger. It was not that he was opposed to their having the music; it was just that they were playing it too loud and too often, a fact that they understood immediately and accepted without rancor.

When it came to money, Lindbergh was generous with his children, but it is the impression of others that his wife was even more so. The children's allowances were not fixed or regular, but depended on several variables. One was how much work they did around the house; they received payment for raking leaves, for example, at a dollar an hour. They could also earn money by being ready with the right answer when Lindbergh would ask, at dinner, for the author of some quotation. The usual bonus for such knowledge was five dollars. There was always a box of money in his closet, from which the children could help themselves freely. They used to leave IOUs stuck in his mirror: "I took 35¢ for ice cream." Lindbergh's only rule was that they had to account for what they took. It didn't make any difference how much money they spent, as long as they reported the amount and the purpose seemed sensible. One Lindbergh child said, "You could buy an ice cream soda for a friend, but if you bought a hundred ice cream sodas you'd have to tell him about it, so you just never did it. We all hated it, but it did teach us to handle money."

Lindbergh's purpose in making the children financially responsible was to prepare them to manage the fortunes they inherit from him and from the Morrow estate when they turn twenty-one. And his methods seem to have worked. Although all the children are well off, none is a spendthrift. The most extravagant is probably Scott, who drives an M.G. sports car and owns a great Dane. "He was able to talk Father into it that he *needed* both the dog and the car," one of Scott's siblings said. (The dog was for protection.)

Lindbergh has attempted to play the martinet but often ends by being a soft touch. A man of many principles—"I never saw so many principles," a friend said—and strong purpose, he also has a soft side. When he was being too strict, one of the children would say, "Oh, *Father,*" and he would immediately let up.

Sometimes the children would hope out loud that their stern parent would leave on one of his numerous trips. But when he was gone they missed him. A visitor accompanying Lindbergh when he came home from a trip recalls seeing young Anne barrel down the banister directly into her father's arms and hug him as hard as she could.

Lindbergh was also a man of many prohibitions. "He was always saying 'don't' to the children," a family friend recalls. " 'Don't do this and don't do that.' " He forbade the cook to buy a television set for her room, for fear the children would spend their time in her room watching it instead of doing their homework. Later, he relented and allowed the cook to have a set and told the children they must not watch it. But, as is usual in such domestic situations, his rule was only loosely obeyed, and mostly when he was around to enforce it.

Meals in the Lindbergh house were always punctual; that is, they were served punctually. But the children were not always on time, like Jon. Their punishments for infractions of the house rules were, like his, not physical. So far as is known, Lindbergh himself was never spanked by his father or mother, and his children have never been spanked. It was not necessary for him to make his point with violence, or even to shout. His voice would simply get cold and hard.

His children feared his angry voice as much as other children might fear a beating. One night young Anne went to a dance and came home after her father's curfew. She had forgotten her key, and she was afraid to wake anyone in the house to let her in. Instead, she climbed up the trellis to her room.

Neither Charles nor Anne Lindbergh is a regular churchgoer, and they have not brought up their children to attend church. Sunday was the day the children were allowed to stay in bed. They could sleep until ten o'clock. Then Lindbergh would wake them. But as they got older and began staying out later on Saturday night, this rule was stretched. They began sleeping to eleven and twelve without parental protest.

However, if there was something worth seeing, Lindbergh didn't hesitate to wake them. A few years ago Connecticut suffered violent floods. Lindbergh woke his children at two in the morning at the height of the torrent. "Come look at the flood," he said. "You may never see anything like this again."

Lindbergh doesn't swear, but he loves to shock people. Thus, when Mrs. Lindbergh entertained friends, he would walk past the room and say, *sotto voce*, "Jesus Christ on a bicycle." This is about the strongest language he has been heard to use around the house.

Lindbergh has insisted that the children be as wary of reporters as he is. He wants them to follow his lead in not giving interviews to newspapers or cooperating with magazine writers, television and radio people. Jon once got his picture on the cover of *Life* magazine in connection with his underwater work. Lindbergh was almost as upset at this publicity as another father might be if his son was arrested for juvenile delinquency.

"Jon probably didn't feel too unhappy about his picture being on the cover of *Life*," said a friend of the family, "but he probably had to defer to his father's loudly expressed opinion. To Charles it was like being seen in public with a tear in your britches. It didn't lose you total respect, but it was the sort of thing that was much better if it hadn't happened."

Jon and Land both think that their father's phobia of the press is rather far-fetched, according to one acquaintance, but they honor his desire for anonymity and generally will not discuss Lindbergh or themselves with anyone who might write about the family. One of them said not long ago, "I may disagree with him, but it's his life and that's the way he wants it. I've got to go along with him."

Scott is almost as publicity-shy as his father. Some overenthusiastic British journalists recently tracked him to his lodgings in England. Young Scott dashed from his quarters, got into his M.G., and took off at a high rate of speed. The Laurel-and-Hardy newspapermen set out in hot pursuit; they got so close, in fact, that they nearly forced the boy into a tree. Scott, dark and good-looking, is known as the least tractable of the Lindbergh children, and was always a fast driver in Connecticut. At university he is said to favor blue jeans and dark-colored shirts.

The girls are both blond and beautiful. Reeve is a student at an Eastern girl's college. Like her sister Anne before her, Reeve did not enter the college her mother would have perferred. Anne Morrow Lindbergh is a Smith alumna. But both her daughters elected to go to another school because, according to someone close to the girls, they preferred the quality of instruction there and because it is co-educational, connected with a men's university.

Reeve has lived in a dormitory and then in a house with twelve other girls. They do their own cooking or eat out in inexpensive restaurants. Reeve is an alert, bright, friendly, and very popular girl who, according to a classmate, is much more interested in literature than in science. (She thinks her father is an adequate writer on some subjects.) She shares clothes with her housemates; on one occasion recently she was wearing a green loden coat which the others describe as "a friendly coat, we all wear it." A friend said that Reeve does not think of herself as a privileged person because she is a Lindbergh. Nor does she act as though she has money, or comes from a moneyed family.

Anne Spencer Lindbergh, the elder sister, met her husband-to-be, Julien Feydy, in Switzerland in 1959 before she entered college. Then she went to college and was introduced into a world quite strange and different from the sheltered life she had been given. She met and knew many kinds of people she had never seen before. After a couple of years at college, Anne came to Paris and met Julien Feydy again, and married him. The Feydys and their one child live in Paris.

Being so far from the family home poses no problem to Anne Feydy or to the Lindberghs. One of the Lindbergh children said, "After all, Jon lives on the West Coast. Mother says that Paris is no farther than Seattle from New York. None of it takes very much time."

Land Lindbergh (tall and blond) not long ago bought a large cattle ranch in Montana. He has settled there with his wife and children. Ranching has long been his interest; he has studied it and will raise beef.

The Lindbergh children occasionally bridle at their father's high standards and rigid principles. One of them said, with just a shade of resentment, "He thinks we should all be the best at whatever we do—because we're Lindberghs." "He doesn't converse so much as he lectures," another child complained.

"We never used small names for our parents, like Mummy or Daddy," a Lindbergh child said, "always Mother and Father. It used to frustrate us, but now it seems rather distinguished."

Lindbergh used to run a pretty taut house. But as the children got older, discipline began to break down, and at last came the day when he was heard to say, just like any other parent, "I can't do anything any more with my children."

His friends agree that Lindbergh feels a twinge at seeing his children grow up. "He's got emotions even if he doesn't show them," one said. His children love him—"adore him," one friend says—but they are grown up now and they don't need him the way they once did. This fact, combined with his increasing detachment from his old friends—"it's a wonder he has so many good friends," one of his children said recently, "he sees so little of them"—makes Lindbergh seem more alone, more aloof, more lonely than ever.

Lindbergh has influenced his wife's development, as she has influenced his. When they moved to the quiet English countryside in 1935, in a house staffed with plenty of servants, Anne Lindbergh might have retreated into the life of a housewife. She told a friend, "I always had the excuse that I never had the time." But after they had settled into Long Barn, Lindbergh said to her, "Now you've got the time, and if you're ever going to be a writer, now's the time to prove it." He wanted her to write a second book.

He had her lock herself in the library with some sandwiches and milk, and told the servants to disturb her only "if the house was burning down." "If the child broke a leg, just send for the doctor," Mrs. Lindbergh says he told them.

Inside the locked library, Anne Lindbergh fiddled with the tools of writing. She sharpened pencils. Moved paper around. Organized everything. Until she had no choice but to begin. Once she began, she did not stop until, with her husband's urgings and criticism, she had finished *Listen! the Wind*. The book was published, and the Lindberghs were in Berlin when they got the critics' notices.

Anne was out walking with Mrs. Smith when the reviews came, and Lindbergh read them first. When the two women returned from their walk, they found him sitting on a bed covered with clippings. He pointed to them, his face shining with pleasure. "It's wonderful!" he said.

Lindbergh had written the foreword and drawn the maps in the book. Almost certainly, too, the appendix which detailed the plane's equipment and the log of the flight were his.

A friend remembers once saying to Anne after some demonstration of his strict discipline, "Anne, Charles makes me think of the angel with the flaming sword." She looked at the friend quickly and said, "No. Charles is *lightning.*"

Lindbergh's mother taught at Cass Technical High School, in Detroit, after 1924, with an interlude of one year (1928–29) at Constantinople Women's College in Turkey. She had the reputation of eccentricity; she wore her hat in school all the time, and sat alone at staff meetings reading a book.

In 1942 she retired from Cass without any warning and without giving a reason. She refused to submit to an annual physical checkup by a nurse, as required for all pensioners of the Detroit public school system, but received her pension in spite of this.

One of the reasons for her shyness was also the reason for her retirement. She had noticed the first paralytic symptoms of Parkinsonism, a disease for which there was no effective treatment at the time. So she retreated quietly to her house, where she lived with her brother until she died in 1954, at the age of seventy-eight.

Her will divided her $5,000 estate between her son and her brother: "My son, Charles Augustus Lindbergh, is my heir and would be the natural recipient of my estate. Such a disposition would be my preference because in an inadequate way it would recognize a devotion to me which has been full and constant and in many material and spiritual forms. My son, however, has stated that the disposition herein made would be his preference and I am happy to accede to his request."

CHANGE

LINDBERGH'S INSISTENCE ON PRIVACY HAS HAD A CURIOUS effect on his public image. Many people still think of him as a slim youth with wavy blond hair. Others recall him as an America Firster; they have a different idea about him, but the physical picture is that of a young man, less than forty years old. Most people do not think of him as gray-haired. They are always a little startled to learn that he is now sixty-six. So it is not surprising that they still attribute to him the ideas and attitudes of the young man they recall.

Perhaps this is reinforced by the fact that Lindbergh has twice written the autobiography of his early years, but both times stopped at the age of twenty-five. His other writings have not had the same impact as these revelations, because when they were published he was largely invisible to the public.

Lindbergh has always been pictured as a rather stiff, unbending young man, partly as a result of his shyness in public. Also, his refusal to explain himself has given the impression of rigidity. It is natural, therefore, for people to think that he hasn't changed.

Lindbergh is quite unlike this stereotype. He has demonstrated a marked ability to grow, to learn.

Lindbergh has educated himself. A friend of many years says, "When I first met Charles, I was struck by his originality—you might say genius. He had a fresh way of looking at everything. Yet I was better educated than he—and I do not consider myself a highly educated man. He felt this lack of knowledge keenly, and he was always trying to correct it."

Lindbergh has a tough mind, but not an impermeable or immovable one. He can be argued (by his friends) out of positions and ideas, although he is stubborn and gives up grudgingly. In fact, he likes to argue; he also likes to gossip and reminisce. He likes, in short, to talk, but only in private, only with friends or people he trusts.

Lindbergh has learned a lot from life, too, and although he has an obsession about never turning his back on any former credo or commitment in public, he has privately changed many of his ideas over the years.

Some of this can be seen in *The Spirit of St. Louis*. This book took fourteen years to write (1938–52) and went through a number of drafts before it was submitted for publication. It covered essentially the same ground as the 1927 book *We* (the first twenty-five years of his life, up to the end of the Paris flight). The motive for rewriting the earlier book was to rectify a work Lindbergh had long deplored.

Lindbergh combined his active life as aviation consultant with his literary work. He was able to do so because he can work anywhere —in a plane, a taxi, a waiting room. From his habit of marking each page with the name of the place where he wrote it, the itinerary of the literary *Spirit of St. Louis* can be traced. Some of the places he worked were aboard the S.S. *Aquitania*, in the Army and Navy Club in Washington, D.C., on an atoll in the Marshall Islands (during his combat service), in a bomber flying back from the North Magnetic Pole, in Japan, in the Florida keys, in Arabia, in the Italian Alps, in Germany.

As he finished each section of the book, Lindbergh mailed it to his wife for criticism. A typical response from her was "Keep your style, stay in character. Cut out all that is not in character even when it is good. Your style is clipped—short sentences—precise—not careless. Recognize your style, then keep to it. 'Your own style' is the style in which you speak. Imagine you are speaking to me, not writing at all."

With this kind of help, and by the most careful writing and rewriting, Lindbergh did hammer out a distinctive prose style. As to the actual construction of sentences and paragraphs, Lindbergh told a friend, "I don't know anything about those things. I play it by ear. If it sounds well and says what I am trying to say, then it is likely to be all right."

"As a matter of fact," he went on, "Anne doesn't know any more than I do about grammar and syntax."

For his authorities in such matters, Lindbergh relies on *Webster's New International Dictionary,* unabridged, and *A Dictionary of Modern English Usage,* by H. W. Fowler.

His method of writing the book was to begin by trying to recall events from memory. This was a useful first step, since it worked easily with his mobile existence; it required no research, no files. Memory was like a strong beam of light that outlined the high and low spots. There were bound to be omissions and vague areas, "But memory," says Lindbergh, "by eliminating detail, clarifies the picture as a whole." Pilots, according to Deac Lyman, who has known many, have extraordinarily keen memories for details of weather and topography. And Lindbergh has a phenomenal memory even among pilots.

After he had set down his recollections, Lindbergh began interviewing and digging up records that would give him accurate details. Often such sources were in conflict, and he had to resolve this by selecting the likeliest account of circumstances. Too, Lindbergh allowed himself several artistic licenses. For example, the latter part of *The Spirit of St. Louis* which deals with the flight from New York to Paris—is divided into hourly sections. Each of these is prefaced by a log entry giving details of speed, weather, temperature, engine r.p.m., fuel consumption, and the like. Yet the log he quoted in *The Spirit of St. Louis* is not the log of the *Spirit of St. Louis.* As noted, that precious document, stolen from his plane at Le Bourget, has never been found. The log in his autobiography is a composite of reckoning, remembrance, and recapitulation of other data.

The finished work was, as many critics noted on publication, a remarkable piece of writing. Hung on the framework of the eight months between the middle of September, 1926, and May 21, 1927, from the genesis of the idea of the flight to Paris through to the finish of the flight itself, *The Spirit of St. Louis* also tells the story of Lindbergh's life from his earliest recollections up to the age of twenty-five years, three months, and seventeen days. It achieves this by what movie theoreticians call "montage"; i.e., the careful trimming and interpolation of scenes. Lindbergh uses many flashbacks throughout the book, but not in chronological sequence.

Stylistically the work is, as many reviewers noted, a tour de force. It is told almost entirely in the historical present—both the flight and the flashbacks—giving a sense of suspense to the flight and a feeling of immediacy about his early life. The tension and excitement are sustained through approximately 250,000 words, a feat that would be envied by most professional writers.

The Spirit of St. Louis was serialized in the *Saturday Evening Post* before book publication under the title "33 Hours to Paris"; was a best-seller; was condensed in the *Reader's Digest;* won Lindbergh the Pulitzer Prize for biography in 1954; and in 1957 was made into a motion picture starring James Stewart as Lindbergh. The fact that Stewart, then around fifty, was playing Lindbergh at the age of twenty-five may have been one of the reasons that the picture lost money. Also, Lindbergh's campaign to keep himself out of the news had been so successful that in 1957 movie audiences, made up largely of young people, did not know who he was. The book and movie (and the publicity) did not go one day beyond the end of his 1927 flight to Paris, so the contemporary Lindbergh was able to preserve his privacy.

The Spirit of St. Louis reveals the doubts, fears, and difficulties Lindbergh had carefully omitted from *We*. In *Spirit*, too, he gives his philosophy of danger. He exposes some of his spiritual musings about death and life. He also tells, as he did not do at all in *We*, the full details of the many real dangers he encountered. In *Spirit* he takes more than 150,000 words to tell just the story of the flight, which he had tossed off in 4,000 or so in *We*.

But the differences between the two books are not only in size and detail, but in depth, perception, and literary skill. There is no poetry in *We*, while parts of *Spirit* rank with the most lyrical writings on flying.

The development from 40,000 words written in three weeks in 1927 to more than 250,000 words twenty-five years later is also a record of the interior growth of the author. Lindbergh has tried to preserve that unsmiling, impenetrable public face, that rigid posture of never clarifying, refuting, or denying; yet he has perhaps unwittingly given us a glimpse of a man who has matured.

A few years ago the Library of Congress, to which Lindbergh is a consultant on aeronautics, requested that he donate to the Library the manuscripts, reference material, and correspondence relating to *The Spirit of St. Louis*. Lindbergh complied, with the proviso that his papers be sealed from all people not authorized by him. He gave access to the documents to two men—John Grierson, and Marvin

McFarland of the Library staff—neither of whom has used this permission to write about Lindbergh.

Typically, Lindbergh delivered his files to the Library himself, driving them down from Connecticut in the back of his station wagon.

The Library's formal announcement accepting this material was drafted by McFarland: "Students who follow [the manuscript's evolution] through successive handwritten drafts and typescript revisions to the final edited printer's copy will find it a record of a man of action . . . discovering himself as a man of contemplation and developing talents of a high literary order."

This sums up what had been happening to Lindbergh during the war and after. He had been an empiricist, his thought deriving from and directed toward action. Starting around 1942, perhaps earlier, the quality of his thinking began to change away from the practical to the literary and philosophical. The whole basis of Lindbergh's commitment shifted, too, and with it the area and character of his concerns. As a young man he was a mechanist; at the end of the war he was a man for whom spiritual values were the highest in life.

Underneath his mechanism there had always been a certain amount of doubt and mysticism. Some of it was there from his childhood in his thoughts about God and death. Some of it was perhaps reinforced by his association with Carrel.

Once, many years ago, a friend guided the young Lindbergh through one of Europe's fine museums. His guide recalls, "I didn't think he would be interested in the Siena school of Italian painting, with all those saints and their golden halos. But this interested him immediately. 'There are those who say they can see auras around the heads of people, in different colors according to their characters,' he said quite seriously. So it seemed quite natural to him for the saints to have golden halos."

The belief in auras was originally Carrel's; he thought that someone sufficiently clairvoyant could literally see such things.

Lindbergh himself has explored the occult, though with a practical purpose in mind. He once studied Yoga to learn how bodily processes could be controlled. He had the idea that if people could learn to stop their heartbeat, it might be useful in surgery. He did learn how to stop his own pulse, or, at least, to make it imperceptible.

He demonstrated this to a friend who expressed skepticism. "Put your hand on my wrist and feel my pulse," he said.

The friend (a woman) did so and remarked on the powerful beat of Lindbergh's heart.

Then he looked off into the distance, and she could no longer feel his pulse. "I had a good grip on his wrist and could feel no pulse whatever," she relates. "It was frightening."

She said, "Charles, start it up again!"

Lindbergh kept staring off into space. "Charles, *please* start it up again," the woman pleaded.

At last, after what seemed a very long time, Lindbergh looked at her and smiled. "It's beating again," he said.

He gave up the idea of stopping the heartbeat as not practicable for surgery, because it would take a patient too long to master the technique. He never explained how he had learned to control his pulse.

Most men's opinions are eroded by time and are changed gradually by circumstances and the influence of other people. Lindbergh's shifts in ideas are often sudden, and sharp. They are usually brought on by violent, dangerous, life-threatening situations. Thus, from his nearly fatal high-altitude test of the Thunderbolt fighter, described earlier, he emerged with a new attitude toward life.

"Returning from the border of death always makes one more aware of life," he wrote a few years later. "The mechanic who told me that my [oxygen] pressure gage read 50 pounds too high carried dull news. . . . That had caused all my trouble—a quarter-inch error of a needle. I felt a sudden revulsion for such details, an impatience with needles, instruments, and readings. What fools men were to impress their minds, enslave their bodies, with figures and machines when life lay everywhere around them, free for the taking, unperceived. . . .

"This altitude flight at Willow Run taught me that in worshiping science man gains power, but loses the quality of life."

He figured out a reverse corollary to this idea the time he nearly got shot down by the Zero in the South Pacific and was saved by his friends in their fast, heavily armed P-38s. It was that "without a highly developed science modern man lacks the power to survive."

When he went to Germany after the war, to survey German aviation and rocketry for the United States government, he brought with him his firsthand prewar knowledge that the Germans had been leaders in aeronautical science and manufacturing. He had admired them then for their efficiency, their energy, their scientific exactitude. Yet, with all this, he saw the evidence of their catastrophe, tragic and inescapable. It gave him a third new thought. It wasn't enough, Lindbergh reasoned, to be the first in science, or industry, or air power. "In Germany, I learned that if his civilization is to continue, modern man must direct the material power of his science by the spiritual truths of his God."

These three conclusions are remarkable because they come from Lindbergh. They are ideas he did not have before the war; they are not the *sort* of ideas he would have had before the war. And they are not just words; they are sincere, deeply felt changes in his attitude toward life.

He recognized this himself, "To me in youth," he wrote, "science was more important than either man or God. The one I took for granted; the other was too intangible for me to understand." Today, Lindbergh has lost his scientist's arrogance. And, as for God—God may be dead for some theologians, but not for Lindbergh. He has become a God-fearing man.

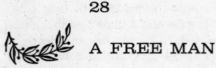 A FREE MAN

WHEN LINDBERGH MOVED TO CONNECTICUT AFTER THE war, he had three ongoing professional occupations: he was writing; he was a consultant to Pan American World Airways; and he was constantly on call for various surveys and reports to the Air Force—even though he still held no rank. Still out of uniform, he became a special consultant to the Chief of Staff of the Air Force, the newly created separate service. He visited, surveyed, and reported on American air bases in Alaska, Japan, Europe, and the Philippines. He flew the new American jet fighters and accompanied bomber missions on polar flights. He also continued to help adapt new equipment for Pan American.

In his various activities, Lindbergh's relationship with people can be gauged to some extent by how they address him and by what he calls himself. To old friends, particularly pilots and others connected with flying, he is "Slim." To newer friends, and to his wife, he is "Charles." To acquaintances, juniors, and others, he used to be "Colonel" and, after 1954, "General." He was once very proud of his rank and his uniform. Today, however, he does not like being called "General," another example of the basic change in his attitude toward life.

When he travels among strangers, he does not go as "Lindbergh." And he has two signatures. Letters are signed formally, "Charles A. Lindbergh" or, informally, "Charles." But his bank account at Morgan Guaranty Trust is credited to "C. A. Lindbergh," the way his father used to sign his name.

The bank signature is one bit of evidence supporting the charge by a psychiatrist, during the time of America First, that Lindbergh

was a "case of identification with his father." The striking parallels
between his speeches at the time and those of his father opposing
U.S. entry into World War I give further credence to the idea. His
wife noted this when she told a friend how lonely she was in her
isolationist position. "Charles at least has the memory of his father
with him," she said metaphorically during the time she was at political opposites with her mother. "I'm entirely alone." Nevertheless,
when a friend said to Lindbergh not long ago, "Slim, there's a good
deal of your father in you," Lindbergh look perplexed. He stopped
talking, concentrated on the idea, and said seriously, "You may be
right. I never thought about it before."

Another of Lindbergh's friends sees his risk-taking, his constant
drive to surpass himself, as an attempt to measure up to his father.
"If C. A. Lindbergh had lived long enough to see Slim fly the ocean,
I don't think he would be quite so driven to prove himself all the
time," this friend says.

With his father gone, Lindbergh tried to impress the other
Lindberghs—his children. He did this the way his father did it with
him, by a combination of authoritarianism and challenge.

Now that his children have all moved out on their own, Lindbergh travels more than ever, is alone more. His friendships have
usually developed out of his concerns and have been strung out
along the vectors that form his lines of interest and his routes of
travel. And, of course, these have changed. He is now less the
military man, more the philosopher; less the technical consultant,
more the conservationist. He doesn't see many of his old friends.
Knowing him, they understand the reason is simply that he is too
busy with other things and occupied with other people in other
places. Most of them accept this as inevitable, and are still as
zealously protective of him as ever. But there is some feeling in the
group of rejection, of being neglected.

Lindbergh is probably unaware of this, since it is an experience
he has not had for many years; nobody ever refuses him anything,
one man says, simply because you don't refuse a force of nature.
And that is how many of his friends regard him, as outside the
norm, above and beyond the concerns of average men. "You write
him, and he may not answer," one says. "You have to leave that up
to him."

Another tells the story of running into Lindbergh in New York one night unexpectedly some years ago. "He asked me out to the house," the man said. "It was late in the evening, about eleven-thirty. I said, 'O.K., but I don't have a damn thing with me, how about going back to the hotel for some things?'

"'What do you need?' Slim asked me. 'I can give you a tooth-brush and a razor.'

"I couldn't think of anything else I really needed, or any reason not to go. When he says go, you go. We got into his car and drove out to Darien. We got there maybe one in the morning. He bounded up the stairs the way he does. Everyone was asleep. Slim rummaged around in the bathroom and gave me a toothbrush and a razor, one that needed stropping. He stropped it right there in the middle of the night, with all those kids sleeping."

Lindbergh has long believed that the government should guarantee people the right to earn a decent living, although he has never spelled out exactly how it should happen. Sometimes he seems to think it *has* happened. For instance, he once told a friend who worked in a college and had no other source of income, "You should figure out what you and your family need to live on for the year; then you should plan to earn exactly that much money. You shouldn't draw on savings or investments." He himself needed $25,000 a year he said, and that was what he earned.

The man, recounting the incident, said, "I didn't have any savings or investments to draw on. My kids weren't coming into trust funds. I was just about making it. But that never occurred to Slim. When you needed money, all you had to do was reach out and take it."

As this suggests, his friends think that he is unsophisticated in some things. Also, he likes so much to talk with people he knows well that he often says more than he realizes. They are able to divine his activities many times when he thinks he is concealing what he is doing.

He has a quick wit, as Will Rogers once testified. Rogers was riding in a tri-engined Fokker piloted by Lindbergh many years ago, over Long Beach, California. He asked Lindbergh how he could tell the wind direction on the ground, since the wind sock at the airport was not filled. Said Lindbergh, pointing down, "Didn't you see that wash blowing on the line down there?"

Rogers, whose eyesight was not so keen, replied, "What would you do if it wasn't Monday?"

"I wouldn't fly over such a dirty place," Lindbergh retorted without hesitation.

Of course, in appraising Lindbergh's character, it is impossible to separate him from flying. He found his métier early, and has never abandoned it. It was at first his main career, and always essential to his freedom of movement; that is to say, basic to his way of life. Most men live in a two-dimensional world; Lindbergh, even more than most airmen, has the extra dimension of free flight. He is still an extremely skillful flier. His military rating is the highest, "Command Pilot." This means he can fly just about any kind of craft, including supersonic jets. He still prefers to fly small airplanes, particularly those with open cockpits—like his old Jenny.

However, he does not recommend such planes to his older friends. For example, a couple he knows well chartered a small plane and hired a pilot to fly them to some Mayan ruins in Central America. When the wife told Lindbergh about the trip, he was horrified. He said, "You oughtn't to travel in a little plane like that. The man has no instruments. If he had to land in the jungle, your husband could never walk out of there." Lindbergh knows that he is still able, at sixty-six, to walk out of almost any place. He is unbowed by his years, has great stamina and excellent vision. If he has ever been seriously ill, he has managed to keep it a secret from his closest friends.

Lindbergh voted for Coolidge and Hoover and Nixon and Goldwater, yet to stamp him automatically as a Republican would probably be wrong. He supported Coolidge and Hoover out of positive conviction that they were superior candidates. But he voted for Nixon and Goldwater because he didn't think either could win. So his current politics can be summed up as being more "against" than "for." Actually, Lindbergh liked John F. Kennedy very much as a man, and thought him a fine President. He had, as noted, known young Jack during the prewar years in London when Joseph P. Kennedy was transmitting Lindbergh's warnings to the United States. Mr. and Mrs. Lindbergh made their first public appearance in many years to attend a White House party that the John F. Kennedys gave for André Malraux, French Minister of Cultural Affairs, in 1962. On that occasion, the Lindberghs stayed overnight at the White House.

In politics, as in most other things, Lindbergh has been an

outsider. This detachment, or limited involvement, marks all of his enterprises, including his long-time association with Pan American World Airways. In that organization's management chart, Lindbergh would appear to have a direct connection with the head, Juan Trippe. Only in 1965 did he join the firm's board of directors.

This is about as much responsibility as he seems to want. Certainly he has never craved power. There were times when politicians seriously considered him as a possible Presidential candidate. Lindbergh never encouraged this. He also rejected any offers of government jobs, and has never run for public office. His most effective political activity—America First—took place outside the machinery of politics.

"A number of . . . accounts [of my life and flights] have been carefully written, but most are riddled with errors," Lindbergh wrote in the appendix of *The Spirit of St. Louis*, "some caused by carelessness, some by ignorance, some put there by intent. . . .

"Little is to be gained by recording here more of the erroneous statements that have been printed about my life and activities. . . . Few articles touching the subject have been written which do not at least in some degree conflict with fact and the story in *The Spirit of St. Louis*. No work is infallible; desire, records, and memory combined cannot produce exactness in every instance; but sufficient effort has been expended on the pages of this book to warrant that in the majority of cases where there is conflict, accuracy will rest with the account carried herein."

The detail and tone of this appendix reflect very well Lindbergh's attitude toward the writings of others about him. The calm assurance that his work must be the most accurate is also typical of his feeling about himself. It is of a piece with his refusal to recant or explain or change any of his past views. He told one of his children that his opposition to Franklin Delano Roosevelt was "a matter of principle," that Roosevelt was out to get him on any pretext, that "if it hadn't been America First, it would have been something else." Undoubtedly he believes this—and he may well be correct in one sense—but it begs the entire issue of whether he was right or not about America First.

Some reporters have doubted that Lindbergh was really sincere in trying to avoid publicity. They said that his secretive ways actually attracted more attention than an attitude of cooperation with the press. They also resented him for the reason that many felt they had "made" Lindbergh, and that he owed them his confidence in return.

Neither of these points seems valid in the light of the evidence. Lindbergh tried to give reporters and photographers cooperation within his own determination of privacy and necessity. They were never satisfied; they wanted to know all his thoughts and feelings, to invade his private life. He tried to protect the part of his life that he deemed belonged to him alone. To "cooperate" on the terms demanded would have meant abandoning this privacy.

As for being "made," there is no doubt that Lindbergh wanted publicity when he made his flight to Paris and his subsequent goodwill flights. Those were all public performances for a public purpose. He refused anything that might have been considered self-aggrandizing resulting from the publicity. And the newspapers themselves benefited a good deal from his activities. Every time he made news, they sold more papers; this was money in their pocket, and a larger base for selling advertising. It is an open question as to who used whom; or who benefited more.

Besides, he earned what he got. By any realistic test, his flight was the epic deed of a hero, one of those unique syntheses of scientific and technical progress, joined and thrust forward by the fresh perception and personal courage of one man, that help propel the entire world into a new era. It cannot be entirely accidental that before the flight U.S. civil aviation was largely a game, and that afterward it became an industry. History gave Lindbergh the opportunity to grasp the commercial possibilities of the new dimension of air and dramatize them to the world. Other men might have done the same things—other men did soon afterward—but Lindbergh was the first.

Lindbergh has always been repelled by both the positive and the negative emotional reactions he has evoked in strangers. Their gift of love—or hate—was not meant for him but was an offering to a god who had achieved the impossible through magic.

To have accepted glory on these terms would have meant trading his self-respect. Besides, it was embarrassing. A few years ago, a tough military leader was introduced to Lindbergh in the Army and Navy Club in Washington. This man said out loud that Lindbergh was to his mind the "finest human being to walk the earth since

Jesus Christ." He behaved as though he were in the presence of a deity, and succeeded in making Lindbergh thoroughly uncomfortable.

It was also obvious that bowing to hero worship meant embracing harassment. There are many celebrities who spend large sums of money to make sure they are recognized, mobbed, and badgered for autographs. With Lindbergh it was the opposite. Since he rejected this sort of exploitation, he could never understand why he had to pay the price of accepting it, in intrusiveness.

Over the years Lindbergh has cultivated detachment from society at the same time that he has felt even more deeply responsible for safeguarding civilization. His basic commitment today is to "the quality of life," a favorite and recurring phrase in his writing, as it was in the writings of Alexis Carrel. "The quality of life is more important than life itself," Carrel wrote in his posthumously published *Reflections on Life*.

He has grown a modern philosophy over the substructure of family devotion, patriotism, dedication to his profession. He is almost atavistic in his adherence to ancient virtues, values and ways of living. He has gone on making the contributions he deems necessary, in the areas he selects, at times and places of his own choosing, in spite of fog, bullets, and shifts in the consensus. It now seems to this writer that Lindbergh's many contributions, important as they are, are less significant than his attitude toward life, his insistence on doing things his own way.

His long silences, his refusal to explain or recant, have made Lindbergh an attractively impassive figure to ideologists and theoreticians. To biographer Kenneth Davis, he fulfilled the role of the classic hero, elevated by his deed, denigrated by a populace disappointed by his inability to grant the boons they craved. To Professor Daniel J. Boorstin, of the University of Chicago, Lindbergh was a convenient example of the true hero "in the best epic mold" devalued by a cheap society into a celebrity. To another professor, Paul Seabury, of the University of California (Berkeley), Lindbergh appeared as an exemplar of "the politics of nostalgia": a tremendously attractive personality without previous political commitments, a clean slate on which the public could write its own ticket.

Lindbergh can also be counted in the currency of popular

thought as an existential hero, a man with a well-developed sense of commitment but no wish for leadership or authority. He is, in another frame, as alienated as any hipster; detached, unassimilated, yet dedicated and noble.

But perhaps his true appeal to our consensus-ridden society, with its constantly eroding liberties and encroaching conformities, is his freedom. An inner-directed man in an increasingly other-directed world, Lindbergh may be more heroic for us today in his anti-heroism, doing exactly what he decides is his duty, than he was as the doer of glamorous deeds. We can find in his untrammeled way of life at least a vicarious counterpoise to our own desperate predicament. More than ever, these days, it is heroic to be oneself.

The late Henry Luce once described another thorny and controversial American, General Douglas MacArthur, in words that seem applicable to Lindbergh: "You may not like him, but he meets the test of greatness. He fills the living space around him. He cannot be trespassed upon, or toyed with, or subtracted from. Whatever ground he stands on, it is *his*."

One man, formerly a bitter enemy, calls Lindbergh a saint. Some people insist that he was, and is, a Nazi. He seems always to evoke extreme judgments, a measure perhaps of his stature. It is a mark of the man that he traded fame for privacy, to safeguard his family and explore his concerns. It is a comment on society that he had to.

Sources and Acknowledgments

The best authority on Lindbergh is Lindbergh. He researches his own works exhaustively, and is dedicated to accuracy. The bulk of material about his early years comes from his two autobiographies, *We* (G. P. Putnam's Sons, 1927) and *The Spirit of St. Louis* (Charles Scribner's Sons, 1955). Both these works are limited to the same period of his life, from birth through his Paris flight in 1927 at age twenty-five. He has also written a brief memoir of some wartime incidents, *Of Flight and Life*, published in 1948 by Scribner's. The latter two books also give a good sampling of Lindbergh's later ideas and prose. Lindbergh's public speeches and magazine articles are useful sources, too. In addition, he has worked with a number of writers who were researching subjects in which Lindbergh played some role. He has helped these people with interviews and copies of correspondence revealing facets of his interests and career. Such books as *Seed Money* by Milton Lomask, about the Guggenheim foundations (Farrar, Straus and Giroux, 1964), and *This High Man* by Milton Lehman, about Dr. Robert H. Goddard, are two good examples. Lindbergh's introductions to books (for example, *The Voyage to Lourdes* by Alexis Carrel, Harper & Brothers, 1950) are further clues to his concerns. Other good closeup material of Lindbergh can be gleaned from certain newspaper and magazine articles, in which he is not much quoted but on which he worked with the writers because he was interested in having certain material on the record. Typical stories are Lauren D. Lyman's exclusive report of the Lindbergh family's departure from the United States (*New York Times*, December 23, 1935), C. B. Allen's "The Facts About Lindbergh" (*Saturday Evening Post*, December 28, 1940), and the long memoir by Colonel Truman Smith on the Berlin years (unpublished, but available in the Sterling Library, Yale University).

There is much useful information on Lindbergh in other books and articles which are identified throughout these source notes. But such material must be sifted carefully, for a number of errors about Lindbergh have never been corrected, and continue to be repeated as later authors use the works of earlier writers for source material. The reason for the perpetuation of such errors can be laid partially to Lindbergh's refusal to cooperate with any writer not of his own choosing who may wish to write about him; and this goes back to his stated wish not to have a biography published while he is alive.

Mrs. Lindbergh's accounts of their trips together (*North to the Orient* and *Listen! the Wind*, published by Harcourt, Brace in 1938 and 1940 respectively) may be considered accurate accounts of part of her relationship with her husband. Harold Nicolson's official biography, *Dwight Morrow* (Harcourt, Brace, 1935), and his *Letters and Diaries 1930–39* (Atheneum, 1966) also provide good closeups of Lindbergh on several occasions.

Kenneth S. Davis's *The Hero: Charles A. Lindbergh and the American Dream* (Doubleday & Company, 1959) is useful to biographers because it delineates so many sources of material. Al Stump's article in *True*, "The Lone Eagle's Other Son" (December, 1966), has some good anecdotes about the character of Jon and of his relations with his father.

I would like to acknowledge personally the many debts of gratitude I owe to people who know Lindbergh more or less well and were willing to talk about him because they wish to leave a clear picture of Lindbergh on the record. This means, as noted, risking his displeasure or even the loss of his confidence and friendship; yet many, so motivated, did speak up. It is unfortunate that because of Lindbergh's well-known dislike of publicity one is least able to thank those who gave most generously of their time and recollection. I have simply indicated in the following notes that material has come "from a personal interview" when the source has requested that he not be identified.

I would like to make special mention of the generosity of my friend John Aschemeier, a collector of Lindberghiana, for the loan of his books and clippings about the flier. Jules Loh of the Associated Press was kind enough to let me use his feature story as a source, and to offer his sources to me. I wish to thank Miss Dorothy Berger, who spent long hours checking and compiling these source notes. Miss Louise Fisher typed several versions of the manuscript from rather marked-up copy; my thanks to her.

But my deepest thanks go to Miss Genevieve Young, of Harper & Row. It was Miss Young who first suggested this book, and it was she who did a most careful and complete job of editing an early version. Her searching questions resulted in a rewritten, expanded book. I am forever in her debt for her interest, her enthusiasm and her dedication to this project.

Notes

(INTRODUCTION) *The Last Hero*

PAGE

ix   time of marvelous stunts: John Lardner, "The Lindbergh Legends," in *The Aspirin Age: 1919–1941*, Isabel Leighton, ed. (N.Y.: Simon and Schuster, 1949), p. 190.

CHAPTER 1. *Lindbergh Today*

4   The description of Lindbergh's current way of life is derived from a series of interviews with various of his friends and acquaintances, as well as from a feature article written by Associated Press correspondent Jules Loh, "Lindy, Yesterday's Famous Hero, Is Today's Quiet Pioneer," which appeared in *The State Journal* of Lansing, Michigan, on May 20, 1962.

4   Report on wedding of Lindbergh's daughter: *New York Times* and New York *Herald Tribune,* December 27, 1963.

5   I got lost: from a personal interview.

5   you'd better marry him: from a personal interview.

5   Information about SST and Falcon airplane from Pan American World Airways.

5–6   Lindbergh's visit to Nairobi: reported in *East Africa Standard,* February 20, 1964.

6   For the first time: Charles A. Lindbergh, "Is Civilization Progress?," *Reader's Digest,* July 1964, p. 70.

6   Life itself is more important: *Ibid.,* p. 74.

6   Is civilization progress: *Ibid.*

6–7   Information on Lindbergh's early career may be found in his autobiographies, *We* and *The Spirit of St. Louis.*

7   Information on Lindbergh's recent Air Force career: U.S. Air Force records.

7   Selection of Yale as repository for Lindbergh's papers: from a personal interview.

7–8   Help given by Lindbergh to author of biography of Dr. C. H. Land: from a telephone interview with the author.

CHAPTER 2. *Origins*

10   When this Swedish peasant-gentleman: Lynn and Dora B. Haines, *The Lindberghs* (N.Y.: Vanguard Press, 1931), p. 4. This book is about C. A.

Lindbergh and his parents, with some references to Charles A. Lindbergh, Jr. Lynn Haines was a friend of C. A. Lindbergh's. This book is shaky on some facts, but has useful anecdotes and letters, provides insights into the character of Lindbergh's father and a good deal of background information on the family.

11   Reverend Harrison quotes: Dale Van Every and Morris De Haven Tracy, *Charles Lindbergh: His Life* (N.Y.: D. Appleton, 1927), pp. 14–15.

13   a fair-sized building: Haines, *op. cit.*, p. 32.

13   I do not think we should wait longer: *Ibid.*

13   When it came time: *Ibid.*, p. 33.

13   Conversation between teacher and C. A. Lindbergh: *Ibid.*, p. 36.

14   Ignatius Donnelly quote: *Ibid.*, p. 49.

15   He discovered *and* He could: *Ibid.*, p. 59.

15   His colleagues: *Ibid.*, p. 60.

15   could never: Walter Eli Quigley, "Like Father, Like Son," *Saturday Evening Post*, June 21, 1941. Quigley was C. A. Lindbergh's law partner, and in this personal memoir of his relationship with the two Lindberghs he draws some obvious parallels between the politics of father and son and gives an inside account of the stormier portions of Congressman Lindbergh's career.

15   Now . . . you have a head: Haines, *op. cit.*, p. 70.

16   Children manage: Walter Eli Quigley, *op. cit.*, p. 42.

16   I'm sorry you're having this trouble: Haines, *op. cit.*, pp. 78–79.

17   Haven't you: *Ibid.*, p. 76.

18   You may regret it: *Ibid.*, p. 81.

18   See if you can: *Ibid.*, p. 95.

18–19   some of [his] views: *Ibid.*, p. 101.

19   all trade: *Ibid.*, p. 102.

19   Labor gives *and* The day: *Ibid.*, p. 103.

19–20   Excerpt from C. A. Lindbergh speech against Aldrich-Vreeland Bill: *Ibid.*, p. 176.

20   whether there are not: *Ibid.*, p. 181.

20–21   Duluth editor quote: *Ibid.*, p. 141.

21   Old Guard politician quote: *Ibid.*, p. 257.

21   To a greater extent: C. A. Lindbergh, *Your Country at War and What Happens to You After a War* (Philadelphia: Dorrance & Company, 1934), p. 15. This book, published in 1917 and suppressed in 1918, was republished in 1934 with an introduction by Walter Eli Quigley. It delineates C. A. Lindbergh's central wartime ideology.

21   Trespass upon our rights: *Ibid.*, p. 16.

23   In my judgment: Quigley, *op. cit.*, p. 39.

23   the good Sisters: Haines, *op. cit.*, p. 293.

24   We must not: *Ibid.*, p. 283.

24   The 1918 campaign: Haines, *op. cit.*, p. 279.

24   punished by the press: Quigley, Preface to C. A. Lindbergh, *op. cit.*, p. 11.

25   honest, progressive: Haines, *op. cit.*, pp. 211–212.

25   Replying: Haines, *op. cit.*, p. 287.

25   I was sworn in: *Ibid.*, pp. 287–288.

25   I am not blaming: *Ibid.*, p. 286.

26   I will be here: *Ibid.*, p. 297.

CHAPTER 3. *Boyhood*

28   curve upward: Charles A. Lindbergh, *The Spirit of St. Louis* (N.Y.: Charles Scribner's Sons, 1955), p. 333.
28   As a child: *Ibid.*, p. 339.
29   You mustn't watch: *Ibid.*, p. 373.
29   Father will: *Ibid.*
29   hours on end: *Ibid.*, p. 374.
30   It's even hotter: *Ibid.*, p. 308.
30   Through the years: *Ibid.*, p. 309.
30   For me: *Ibid.*, p. 311.
32   There he is: *Ibid.*, pp. 316–317.
32   C. H. LAND, DENTIST: *Ibid.*, p. 317.
32   There's the stuffed: *Ibid.*
33   My grandfather: *Ibid.*, p. 318.
33   hum in my ears: *Ibid.*
33   These problems: *Ibid.*, p. 320.
34   Once he was riding: *Ibid.*, pp. 320–321.
34   The trouble: Haines, *op. cit.*, p. 261.
35   I'm sorry: *Ibid.*, p. 72.
35   Father thought: Lindbergh, *op. cit.*, p. 377.
36   Age seemed: *Ibid.*
36   You can't: Haines, *op. cit.*, p. 209.
36   That trip: *Ibid.*, pp. 147–148.
37   The trouble: Lindbergh, *op. cit.*, p. 392.
37   That's enough: Haines, *op. cit.*, p. 299.
37   I seem: *Ibid.*, p. 87.
38   C. A. Lindbergh: *Ibid.*, p. 86.
39   danger was a part of life: Lindbergh, *op. cit.*, p. 245.
40   How wonderful: *Ibid.*, p. 244.
40   Flying upriver: *Ibid.*, p. 245.
41–42   Anecdote about Lindbergh's motorcycle: from a personal interview.
43   I would work hard: Lindbergh, *op. cit.*, p. 403.
43   Flying is too: Kenneth S. Davis, *The Hero: Charles A. Lindbergh and the American Dream* (Garden City, N.Y.: Doubleday & Company, 1959), p. 92. This book is the only attempt at a modern, complete biography of Lindbergh. Davis did a tremendous amount of research; his bibliographical essay at the end of the book detailing his sources runs to more than 40,000 words (slightly longer than Lindbergh's early autobiography *We*). Davis's book is unfortunately marred in many places by the author's unwillingness to let his facts speak for themselves; his anti-Lindbergh bias causes him to draw palpably false conclusions. The effect is a Procrustean one, and this is unfortunate because the writer went to so much trouble to get facts.
44   All right: Lindbergh, *op. cit.*, p. 231.

CHAPTER 4. *Early Flight*

45   Information about the state of aviation in the U.S. in 1922: Lloyd W. Morris and Kendall Smith, *Ceiling Unlimited* (N.Y.: Macmillan, 1953), chaps. 2–4.

45   I can still: Lindbergh, *The Spirit of St. Louis*, p. 247.
46   Information about Hispano-Suiza, Nebraska Aircraft Corp., and Lincoln
        Standard: *Ibid.*, pp. 550, 554.
47   You had to know: *Ibid.*, p. 251.
47   A novice: *Ibid.*, p. 250.
47   I lose all: *Ibid.*, p. 249.
47   seen the earth: *Ibid.*, p. 250.
48   but watch: *Ibid.*, p. 254.
49   a feeling of anticipation: *Ibid.*, p. 255.
49   I'd like: *Ibid.*, p. 256.
50   I might want to buy: *Ibid.*
50   It isn't more dangerous: *Ibid.*
51   Slim, that was: *Ibid.*, p. 260.
51   How soundly: *Ibid.*
51   Strangely enough: *Ibid.*, p. 261.
52   Don't count: *Ibid.*, p. 263.
52   In flying: *Ibid.*, p. 262.
52   The day I stood: *Ibid.*, p. 265.
53   Information about Jenny: *Ibid.*, p. 554.
54   Let's push: *Ibid.*, p. 437.
55   But my engine: *Ibid.*, p. 441.
55   Then I rolled up: *Ibid.*
56   blood washed from his face: Davis, *op. cit.*, p. 101.
56   That was the summer; Lindbergh, *op. cit.*, p. 449.
58   AIRPLANE CRASHES NEAR SAVAGE: Lindbergh, *We*, p. 72.

CHAPTER 5. *Army*

59   Information about DH's: Lindbergh, *The Spirit of St. Louis*, p. 552.
59   They train: *Ibid.*, p. 407.
60   I heard: *Ibid.*, p. 274.
60   Where did: *Ibid.*
61   Don't fly: *Ibid.*, p. 279.
61   Information about Canuck: *Ibid.*, p. 550.
62   It was quite: *Ibid.*, p. 410.
63   After all: *Ibid.*, p. 412.
64   Photography: *Ibid.*, p. 420.
65   Their wings: *Ibid.*, p. 421.
65   He will: Quigley, "Like Father, Like Son," p. 42.
66   I saw no other ship: Charles A. Lindbergh, *We* (N.Y.: G. P. Putnam's
        Sons, 1927), pp. 144–145.
67   Then it happened: Lindbergh, *The Spirit of St. Louis*, pp. 214–215.
67   Every few seconds: *Ibid.*, p. 215.

CHAPTER 6. *Air mail*

69   an accepted: Lindbergh, *The Spirit of St. Louis*, p. 281.
69–70   Information about early air-mail business: Morris and Smith, *Ceil-
        ing Unlimited*, pp. 242–253.
70   The ground was right there: Lindbergh, *The Spirit of St. Louis*, p. 301.
71   braced for: *Ibid.*, pp. 307–308.

71   I've never chosen: *Ibid.*, pp. 268–269.
72   There was never: Kenneth S. Davis, *The Hero*, p. 128.
73   By that time: Lindbergh, *The Spirit of St. Louis*, p. 283.
73   Our contract: *Ibid.*, p. 284.
76   There's . . . nothing: *Ibid.*, p. 11.
77   Judging from the accounts: *Ibid.*, p. 14.

CHAPTER 7. *The Spirit of St. Louis*

78–80   Information about background of Atlantic flights: Morris and Smith, *Ceiling Unlimited*, pp. 230–233; also F. Alexander Magaun and Eric Hodgins, *A History of Aircraft* (N.Y.: McGraw-Hill, 1931), pp. 397–401.
78   Why shouldn't I: Lindbergh, *The Spirit of St. Louis*, p. 15.
80   Who am I: *Ibid.*, p. 17.
81   St. Louis: *Ibid.*, p. 24.
82   I can furnish: *Ibid.*, p. 25.
83   as though: Roy Alexander, speech at Lotos Club, May 16, 1967.
83   I said: *Ibid.*
84   We have: Lindbergh, *op. cit.*, p. 34.
84   We didn't: from a personal interview with Ken Boedecker.
86   Slim, you've: Lindbergh, *op. cit.*, pp. 66–67.
86   please state: *Ibid.*, p. 69.
87   WILLING TO MAKE: *Ibid.*, p. 71.
87   What would: *Ibid.*, p. 74.
87   We will sell: *Ibid.*, p. 75.
87   dumfounded: *Ibid.*
88   Good morning: *Ibid.*, p. 76.
88   Will you guarantee: *Ibid.*, p. 82.
88   The risks: *Ibid.*
88   You don't: *Ibid.*, p. 83.
89   One boy's a boy: *Ibid.*, pp. 191–192.
90   What freedom: *Ibid.*, p. 94.
91   Safety: *Ibid.*, p. 97.
91   If I get to Paris: Jules Loh, "Lindy, Yesterday's Famous Hero, Is To-day's Quiet Pioneer."
92   I don't swim: from a personal interview.
93   What started: Lindbergh, *op. cit.*, p. 113.
93   One makes errors: *Ibid.*
94   near collision *and* narrowly escaped disaster: *Ibid.*, p. 123.
94   My God! *Ibid.*, p. 119
96   Stop mail: leave address: *Ibid.*, pp. 108–110.
96   It looks: *Ibid.*, p. 135.

CHAPTER 8. *New York–Paris*

98   I've got: Harry A. Bruno, *Wings Over America: The Story of American Aviation* (Garden City, N.Y.: McBride, 1944), p. 172. Bruno's book is a history of flying that has some good personal material on Lindbergh. Most of the anecdotes originated with Bruno's partner, the late Dick Blythe, who was Lindbergh's personal press representative.
99   They're your buffers: *Ibid.*, p. 173.

99   we bedded: *Ibid.*
100   a flattened: from a personal interview.
100   Do you carry: Lindbergh, *The Spirit of St. Louis,* p. 155.
100   These fellows must think: *Ibid.,* p. 166.
100   Bruno, why: from a personal interview.
101   Good-bye, Charles: Bruno, *op. cit.,* p. 178.
101   Neither from a personal interview.
102   Accuracy: Lindbergh, *op. cit.,* p. 166.
102   taken the show: *Ibid.,* p. 159.
102   The attention: *Ibid.,* p. 165.
102   Lindbergh gave the St. Louis: Meyer Berger, *The Story of the New York Times* (N.Y.: Simon and Schuster, 1951), p. 291.
103   Up to date: Lindbergh, *op. cit.,* p. 165.
103   He *knew:* Bruno, *op. cit.,* pp. 176–177
103   The way: Lindbergh, *op. cit.,* pp. 165–166.
104   That'll teach: Bruno, *op. cit.,* 173.
104   I've always had an ambition: Harry A. Bruno, with William S. Dutton, "Lindbergh, The Famous Unknown," *Saturday Evening Post,* October 21, 1933, p. 23. Bruno also used some of the material in his book in three magazine articles in the *Saturday Evening Post* in 1933. Since Bruno wrote his book at a time when Lindbergh was being strongly criticized, and since Bruno was quite critical of Lindbergh's politics and behavior, the many good words he has to say for the young Lindbergh gain luster.
104   There's Lindbergh: Bruno, *Wings Over America,* p. 174.
105   very little room: Milton Lomask, *Seed Money* (N.Y.: Farrar, Straus and Giroux, 1964), p. 92. This is the story of the Guggenheim families' complicated philanthropies; it has important sections on Lindbergh's relationship with Dr. Goddard, background on Goddard, and some data on Lindbergh's 48-state tour.
105   when you're ready: Lindbergh, *op. cit.,* p. 169.
106   I'll take: *Ibid.,* p. 173.
106   Background on Levine-Chamberlin and Byrd: *New York Times,* June 7, 1927, and July 1, 1927.
107   Slim: Lindbergh, *op. cit.,* p. 175.
107   Are you going: Lauren D. Lyman, "Lindbergh's Flight—A Takeoff for Aviation," *Aerospace,* May 1967, p. 5.
108   We knew: C. B. Allen, speech at Lotos Club, May 16, 1967.
109   If it was fifty: from a personal interview.
109   It's less a decision: Lindbergh, *op. cit.,* p. 185.
110   Do you want: from a personal interview.
110   By God: Bruno, *Wings Over America,* p. 182.
113   To the pilot: Lindbergh, *op. cit.,* p. 289.
113   They enmesh intruders: *Ibid.,* p. 330.
114   Every cell: *Ibid.,* p. 180.
115   But the alternatives: *Ibid.,* p. 423.
116   If security: *Ibid.,* p. 433.
116   which way: *Ibid.,* p. 459.
117   Before I made: *Ibid.,* pp. 466–467.
118   like a living creature: *Ibid.,* p. 486.

CHAPTER 9. *Paris and Return*

120   Joe Humphreys: Lardner, "The Lindbergh Legends," p. 200.
121   Cars, trucks: from a personal interview.
121   When I circled: Lindbergh, *The Spirit of St. Louis*, p. 495.
121   When the *Times* bought: Berger, *op. cit.*, pp. 293–301.
122   Are there: Lindbergh, *op. cit.*, p. 495.
122   It seemed wisest: *Ibid.*, p. 496.
123   long avenue: *Ibid.*, p. 500.
124   Come on in, Mac: MacDonald, *op. cit.*, p. 108.
124   We intended to isolate: Berger, *op. cit.*, p. 304.
124   MacDonald's encounter with Lindbergh, quotes are from: MacDonald, *op. cit.*, p. 108.
124   A thousand: *New York Times*, May 12, 1927.
125   enough to have: Lindbergh, *op. cit.*, p. 548.
125   What about you: *New York Times*, May 22, 1927.
125   under Uncle Sam's roof: Davis, *The Hero*, p. 212.
125   So I did: from a personal interview.
125–126   If I had believed that: Lindbergh, *op. cit.*, p. 548.
126   *Vive* Lindbergh: Davis, *op. cit.*, p. 214.
126   I suddenly: Lindbergh, *We*, pp. 238–239.
127   aeronautical 'we': *Ibid.*, p. 302.
127   This young man: *Ibid.*, p. 241.
129   I'm going to keep on flying: from a personal interview.
130–131   Not so bad: Bruno, *Wings Over America*, pp. 182–183, and "Lindbergh, The Famous Unknown," p. 40.
132   What do you think: Bruno, "Lindbergh, The Famous Unknown," p. 40.
132   He returned: Bruno, *Wings Over America*, p. 183.
132–133   Those closest: Lindbergh, *We*, p. 272.
133   The same story: *Ibid.*, pp. 274–278.
133   Just as when: *Ibid.*, p. 285.
135   if you have: *Ibid.*, p. 301.
136   eighty of: *Ibid.*, p. 309.
137   Hello, flier: Bruno, "Lindbergh, The Famous Unknown," p. 40.
138   The visit: Davis, *The Hero*, p. 234.

CHAPTER 10. *"We"*

139   Harry, almost everyone: Lomask, *Seed Money*, p. 93.
140   I heartily approve: Berger, *op. cit.*, p. 305.
140   after the flight: Lauren D. Lyman, "How Lindbergh Wrote a Book," *The Bee-Hive*, published by United Aircraft, Summer, 1954, p. 18.
140   reinforced with secretaries: George Palmer Putnam, *Wide Margins: A Publisher's Autobiography* (N.Y.: Harcourt, Brace, 1942), p. 233.
140   a good job: *Ibid.*, p. 234.
140–141   no *and* found no fault: *Ibid.*
141   For one thing: Lomask, *op. cit.*, p. 93.
141   Irate customers: Putnam, *op. cit.*, p. 235.
141   At that juncture: *Ibid.*, p. 234.
141   at least 40,000 *Ibid.*, p. 235.

141   I didn't know: Lomask, *op. cit.*, p. 93.
141   one could almost: Putnam, *op. cit.*, p. 235.
142   Being young: Lindbergh, *The Spirit of St. Louis*, p. 547.
142   If the manuscript: Putnam, *op. cit.*, p. 236.
142   Sign it: Lomask, *op. cit.*, p. 94.
143   In one week: Bruno, *Wings Over America*, p. 185.
143   In my presence: Harry A. Bruno with William S. Dutton, "Fortunes In Flight," *Saturday Evening Post*, March 11, 1933, p. 59.
143   a home in Flushing Meadows: Lindbergh, *op. cit.*, p. 527.
144   Well, under his contract: Bruno, *Wings Over America*, pp. 185–186.
144   You're the symbol: from a personal interview.

CHAPTER 11. *Celebration*

147   For years the American people: Frederick Lewis Allen, *Only Yesterday* (N.Y.: Harper & Row, Perennial Library Edition, 1964), p. 183.
148   Ordinarily our job: Bruno, *Wings Over America*, p. 185.
148   he'd have looked: *Ibid.*, p. 187.
148   The most popular: *Ibid.*, p. 188.
149   It blinds you: Lauren D. Lyman, "The Lindbergh I Know," *Saturday Evening Post*, April 4, 1953. A good personal look at Lindbergh is taken in this article by Lyman, a longtime friend. It was the introduction to the *Saturday Evening Post*'s serialization of Lindbergh's *The Spirit of St. Louis* (serialized as "33 Hours to Paris") in 1953. Lyman's article contains many vignettes and insights into Lindbergh's character and career.

CHAPTER 12. *Forty-Eight-State Tour*

150   We'll save time: Donald E. Keyhoe, *Flying With Lindbergh* (N.Y.: G. P. Putnam's Sons, 1928), p. 6. Keyhoe's book is cloyingly adulatory. At the same time, Keyhoe's reporting is generally consistent with known facts. The book details the 48-state tour which Keyhoe and Phil Love made with Lindbergh.
151   We must remember: *Ibid.* pp, 11–12.
151   I hope you: Lomask, *Seed Money*, p. 95.
152   Don't tell: Keyhoe, *op. cit.*, p. 14.
152   Is it true: *Ibid.*, pp. 17–18.
153   You don't: *Ibid.*, p. 19.
153   lightning: *Ibid.*, p. 20.
153   We ought to: *Ibid.*, p. 22.
153   Colonel Lindbergh had the following luncheon: *Ibid.*, p. 28.
154   Do you know: *Ibid.*, pp. 32–33.
154   You're going ahead: *Ibid.*, p. 46.
155   Parachutes should not: *Ibid.*, p. 147.
155   Where's Slim: *Ibid.*, p. 54.
155   I could have landed: *Ibid.*, p. 55.
156   It's the best: *Ibid.*, p. 64.
156   Let them go ahead: *Ibid.*, p. 193.
157   Slim: *Ibid.*, pp. 103–104.
157   all these men: Professor William A. Williams, letter.
157–158   So, my mother: *Ibid.*

159   in excellent health: Lomask, *Seed Money*, p. 95.
159   Aboard 'Spirit of St. Louis': *Ibid.*, p. 239.
159   will you: *Ibid.*, p. 297.
160   Information about cost of trip, and results: Lomask, *op. cit.*, pp. 94–96.

CHAPTER 13. *Mexico*

161   I've always admired baseball players: from a personal interview.
162   I know what I can do: Harold Nicolson, *Dwight Morrow* (N.Y.: Harcourt, Brace and Company, 1935), p. 299. Nicolson's biography of Dwight Morrow is a full-length picture of an interesting man. It has some fine bits about Anne Lindbergh and her husband.
162   After returning from Europe: *Ibid.*, p. 311.
162   You get me the invitation: *Ibid.*, p. 312.
162–163   How's Dick?: Bruno, *Wings Over America*, p. 184.
163   Information about Congressional Medal of Honor: *New York Times*, December 10–13, 1927.
164   hummocky: Davis, *The Hero*, p. 257.
164   There were numerous railroads: Nicolson, *op. cit.*, p. 312.
165   Dwight and Capt. Winslow: *Ibid.*, p. 313.
166   It is just: Davis, *op. cit.*, pp. 260–261.
166   closer spiritual: *Ibid.*, p. 260.
166   I don't see why: Keyhoe, *Flying with Lindbergh*, p. 123.
167   Three short flights: Lindbergh, *The Spirit of St. Louis*, p. 512.
167   NO MORE UNLESS HE CRASHES: Lardner, "The Lindbergh Legends," p. 201.
168   The New York–Paris flight: Keyhoe, *op. cit.*, pp. 289–290.
168   The first time: Harold Nicolson, *Diaries and Letters 1930–1939* (London: Collins, 1966), Nigel Nicolson, ed., p. 182. This book, published in the United States by Atheneum in 1966, gives some closeup looks at the Lindberghs through the eyes of a trained observer. Nicolson was present during some of the most tense moments in their lives, and also was their landlord in England. He was also present at several of Lindbergh's conversations with high British officials concerning war and defense.
168   At Bolling Field: Lindbergh, *op. cit.*, p. 516.
169   Information about Ryan: Ryan Aeronautical Company.

CHAPTER 14. *A New Life*

170   Information about Kelly bill: Morris and Smith, *Ceiling Unlimited*, p. 251.
170   ill-advised: Lomask, *Seed Money*, p. 96.
171   top close to the Panama Canal: Morris and Smith, *op. cit.*, p. 268.
171–172   Information about Pan American: *Ibid.*, pp. 286 *et. seq.*
173   The moment Keys: Bruno, *Wings Over America*, p. 251.
174   Ambassador and Mrs.: Davis, *The Hero*, pp. 275–276.
174–175   Well, I see: *Ibid.*, p. 276.
175   Landing on one wheel: Lindbergh, *The Spirit of St. Louis*, p. 116.
177   Information about merger between TAT and Western Air Express and information about Walter F. Brown: Morris and Smith, *op. cit.*, p. 284.
177–178   Information about Pan Am: *Ibid.*, pp. 286 *et. seq.*

178   forty-four multi-engined: *Ibid.*, p. 287.
179   It's all right: Nicolson, *Diaries and Letters*, p. 184.
179   I have had the most horrible nightmare: Nicolson, *Dwight Morrow*, p. 124.
180   What in substance: *Ibid.*, p. 291.

CHAPTER 15. *To the Orient*

182   Information about Sirius: Lockheed Aircraft.
183   Of course: Anne Lindbergh, pp. 29–35. Anne Morrow Lindbergh, *North to the Orient* (N.Y.: Harcourt, Brace, 1938), p. 20. Three of Anne Morrow Lindbergh's books are especially revealing. This account of the 1931 flight, as well as *Listen! the Wind*, a report of ten days in the 1933 flight, gives a good picture of her relationship with her husband during the flights.
185   Think what that: *Ibid.*, p. 28.
185   Or *shoes*: *Ibid.*, pp. 28–29.
186   Don't look so: *Ibid.*, p. 45.
186–187   I like to feel that in flying: *Ibid.*, p. 62.
187   Is aviation too arrogant: Lindbergh, *The Spirit of St. Louis*, p. 288.
189   Here we are: Anne Lindbergh, *op. cit.*, p. 153.
189   Like a knife: *Ibid.*, p. 155.
189   The wind flattened: *Ibid.*, p. 156.
189   Really, it was: *Ibid.*, p. 157.
190   What's the matter: *Ibid.*, pp. 158–159.
191   Yes—a thirty-eight: *Ibid.*, pp. 216–217.
193   Northwest's use of Great Circle Route surveyed by Lindbergh: Northwest-Orient Airlines.

CHAPTER 16. *Deaths in the Family*

194   Breakfast was for a long time: Nicolson, *Dwight Morrow*, p. 160.
194   Who do you like best: *Ibid.*, pp. 162–163.
197   Dear Sir: George Waller, *Kidnap* (N.Y.: Dial Press, 1961), Giant Cardinal Edition, pp. 14–15. This book, based on newspaper stories and the transcript of the trial of Bruno Hauptmann, is a useful source for that episode in Lindbergh's life. There are several other books on the subject, but Waller's seems the most complete and dispassionate. The *New York Times* carried verbatim transcripts of most of the testimony in the Hauptmann trial starting with the Friday, March 5, 1935, issue.
197   Indication: *Ibid.*, p. 15.
197   Colonel Lindbergh's baby: Berger, *op. cit.*, pp. 384–388.
199   immediate use: Waller, *Kidnap*, p. 19.
199   A half cup: *Ibid.*, p. 27.
200   Mrs. Lindbergh and I: *Ibid.*, pp. 27–28.
203   MONEY IS READY: *Ibid.*, p. 36.
203   Dear Sir: Mr. Condon: *Ibid.*, p. 38.
203–204   Money: *Ibid.*, p. 43.
204   Yes: *Ibid.*, p. 83.
205   Bergen: *Ibid.*, p. 84.
205   I guess: *Ibid.*, p. 85.
206   your work: *Ibid.*, p. 88.

206   Well: *Ibid.*
207   Take that off: *Ibid.*, p. 123.
207   distorted mind: *Ibid.*, p. 134.
208   Mrs. Lindbergh and I: *Ibid.*, p. 186.
210   To provide for: *Ibid.*, p. 223.

CHAPTER 17. *The Hauptmann Case*

211   The North Atlantic: Charles A. Lindbergh, Introduction to *Listen! the Wind* by Anne Morrow Lindbergh (N.Y.: Harcourt, Brace & Company, 1938), Dell edition, p. 7.
212   It was necessary: *Ibid.*, p. 9.
212   I believe that: Lindbergh, report to Juan Trippe.
214   shy, Japanese, clever: Nicolson, *Diaries and Letters*, p. 180.
215   If he wags his tail: *Ibid.*, p. 181.
215   Well, I have: *Ibid.*, p. 184.
215   Obviously he was telling: *Ibid.*
215   Courage?: *Ibid.*, p. 190.
216–217   Was he healthy?: Waller, *Kidnap*, pp. 331–345.
220   Do *you* believe: Nicolson, *op. cit.*, p. 196.
220   Hauptmann: *Ibid.*
221   One could hear: *Ibid.*, p. 197.
221   The sentence: Waller, *op. cit.*, p. 570.
221   the charge: *Ibid.*, pp. 575–576.
223   we Americans: Roger Butterfield, "Lindbergh: A Stubborn Young Man of Strange Ideas Becomes a Leader of Wartime Opposition," *Life Magazine*, August 11, 1941, p. 65.
224   I've got something: Berger, *op. cit.*, pp. 414–419.
225   The *Times* had put over: *Ibid.*, p. 291.
225   tolerable home: Waller, *op. cit.*, pp. 600–601.
226   he would have: *Ibid.*, p. 601.
226   it was impossible: New York *Journal American*, August 24, 1941.
227   But you'll only have to: from a personal interview.
228   the defendants: *New York Times*, January 18, 1967, p. 1.

CHAPTER 18. *Dr. Carrel*

229   there are no words: Joseph T. Durkin, S. J., *Hope for Our Time: Alexis Carrel on Man and Society* (N.Y.: Harper & Row, 1965), p. xxiii. This study by Father Durkin of Alexis Carrel's social ideas is a scholarly book. Carrel's works, particularly *Man, the Unknown* and *The Voyage to Lourdes*, furnish source material to the student of his ideas.
230   Information about Rockefeller Institute: *Encyclopaedia Britannica*, 1958 edition, Vol. 19, p. 366.
230–231   both spoke: Davis, *The Hero*, p. 343.
231   For me that began: Charles A. Lindbergh, Preface to *The Voyage to Lourdes* by Alexis Carrel (N.Y.: Harper & Brothers, 1950), p. vi. Lindbergh has written prefaces to several works, giving indication of his interests and commitments. His preface to *The Voyage to Lourdes* is pertinent for this reason as well as for what he writes.
232   direct, sensitive: Dr. Richard J. Bing, letter.

232   a bucket of water: *Ibid.*
233   removed from: Davis, *op. cit.*, p. 347.
233   You've got to understand: from a personal interview.
233   a step in the right direction: from a personal interview.
233   The newspapers: from a personal interview.
234   The composition of all gas: Alexis Carrel and Charles A. Lindbergh, *The Culture of Organs* (N.Y.: Hoeber, 1938), p. 17.
235   The career: Durkin, *op. cit.*, p. xi.
235–236 Carrel's earlier: from a personal interview.
236   The author: Alexis Carrel, *Man, the Unknown* (N.Y.: Harper & Brothers, 1935), pp. 213–214.
237   He had some notion: from a personal interview.
237   we ought to: Alexis Carrel, *Reflections on Life* (N.Y.: Hawthorn Books, 1953), pp. 15–17.
238   how his theories: Durkin, *op. cit.*, p. xvi.
238   The human being: Carrel, *Reflections on Life*, p. 105.
238   Each human being: Durkin, *op. cit.*, p. 13.
239   oblivious to the real: Durkin, *op. cit.*, p. xvi.
239   Still more than Marxism: *Ibid.*, p. 133.
240   Any foolish talk: *Ibid.*, p. 149.
240   Lindbergh was obviously: from a personal interview.
240–241 Some cases of: Durkin, *op. cit.*, p. 115.
241   Carrel was a man: Lindbergh, Preface to *The Voyage to Lourdes*, p. vii.
241   Carrel spoke: *Ibid.*

CHAPTER 19.   *Dr. Goddard*

243   Flying cross country: Lomask, *Seed Money*, p. 141.
243   I realized the limits: Milton Lehman, *This High Man* (N.Y.: Farrar, Straus and Giroux, 1963), p. 160. This biography of Dr. Robert H. Goddard has facts about Lindbergh's relationship with the inventor. Since Lindbergh gave materials to both Lehman and Lomask (*Seed Money*), these books offer some useful information about Lindbergh.
243   Couldn't we develop: Lomask, *op. cit.*, p. 142.
243   to equal the thrust: *Ibid.*
244   Carol, Harry's second wife: *Ibid.*
244   Moon Rocket *and* by 238,799½ miles: *Ibid.*, p. 140.
244   May be the answer: *Ibid.*
245   Of course, Bob: Lehman, *op. cit.*, p. 159.
246   that more than: *Ibid.*, p. 162.
247   Mr. Dan: 'then: Lomask, *op. cit.*, p. 145.
248   was as mortified: Lehman, *op. cit.*, p. 211.
251   the next war: Lomask, *op. cit.*, p. 148.
251   like trying to: *Ibid.*
251   I want you to: *Ibid.*, p. 149.
252   Every liquid-fuel: Lehman, *op. cit.*, p. 363.
252   practically every one: Lomask, *op. cit.*, p. 146.
252   This is a story: Charles A. Lindbergh, Preface to Lehman, *op. cit.*, p. xiv.
253   Am I a man: *Ibid.*, p. xiii.

CHAPTER 20.   *The Air Mail Controversy*

255   immense salaries: Arthur M. Schlesinger, Jr., *The Coming of the New
Deal* (Boston: Houghton Mifflin Company, 1958), p. 449.
255   If we were holding this meeting: *Ibid.*, p. 450.
255   The control of American aviation: *Ibid.*, pp. 450–451.
256   YOUR ACTION: Davis, *The Hero*, pp. 333–334, and Schlesinger, op. cit.,
p. 452.
257   Now Colonel Lindbergh: Schlesinger, *op. cit.*, p. 452.
257   hurt: *Ibid.*, p. 453.
257   I am certain: Davis, *op. cit.*, p. 334.
257   in an undignified: *Ibid.*
258   legalized murder: Schlesinger, *op. cit.*, p. 452.
258   The continuation of deaths: *Ibid.*, p. 453
258   Colonel Billy Mitchell remarks: *Ibid.*, pp. 454–455.
258–259   I BELIEVE: Davis, *op. cit.*, p. 336.
259   Whenever his face: Schlesinger, *op. cit.*, p. 453.
259   Very little: Davis, *op. cit.*, p. 337.
259   If an officer: *Ibid.*, p. 338.

CHAPTER 21.   *England, France, Germany*

All quotes in this chapter, unless otherwise specified, are taken from an unpublished memoir by Colonel Truman Smith, U.S.A. (Ret.) written between 1954 and 1956. It is called "Air Intelligence Activities Office of the
Military Attaché American Embassy, Berlin, Germany, August 1935 April
1939 with special reference to the Services of Colonel Charles A. Lindbergh,
Air Corps (Res.)." There are typed copies of this manuscript in the Yale
University Sterling Library and a couple of government institutions. In the
introduction to this manuscript Smith wrote, "If I have a primary purpose
in preparing this record, it is that I wish to leave an accurate account for
history of the services of Colonel Lindbergh to American interests in connection with the birth and development of the Luftwaffe. It is my sincere hope
that Lindbergh's future biographers read this record and evaluate its facts
before they attempt to describe or comment on his activities in Germany and
America between 1936 and 1941." The document gains validity because
Lindbergh helped Smith in its preparation by lending him his diaries and
logs of the period.
265   Lindbergh's letter to Ambassador Kennedy is worth reading because it
embodies the judgments and concerns which informed Lindbergh's later
isolationist politics. It cannot be reprinted without Lindbergh's permission,
but it can be read in the unpublished Smith memoir, which is in the manuscript collection of the Sterling Library at Yale University, New Haven, Connecticut.
267   Which is the best plane: from a personal interview.
267   You mean to say: from a personal interview.
271   possess[ed] the most powerful: Nicolson, *Letters and Diaries*, p. 272.
272   I said to Charles: Davis, *The Hero*, p. 503.

CHAPTER 22. *Air Power*

Again, all quotes in this chapter are taken from Smith, "Air Intelligence," unless otherwise specified.

276–277   is ten times superior: Nicolson, *Letters and Diaries*, p. 343.
282   It would be entirely contrary: from a personal interview.
282   an adventurer, pure and simple: Nicolson, *op. cit.*, p. 302.

CHAPTER 23. *Speaking Out*

All quotes in this chapter are taken from Smith, "Air Intelligence."

CHAPTER 24. *America First*

290   extended active duty: C. B. Allen, "The Facts About Lindbergh," *Saturday Evening Post*, December 28, 1940, p. 51.
291–292   Colonel, I am going on vacation: Butterfield, "Lindbergh: A Stubborn Young Man of Strange Ideas Becomes a Leader of Wartime Opposition," p. 68.
292   Information about Neutrality Act. *Encyclopaedia Britannica*, 1958 edition, Vol. 16, p. 261.
292   Woodring was sure: Harold L. Ickes, *The Secret Diary of Harold L. Ickes*, Vol. III, 1939–1941 (N.Y.: Simon & Schuster, 1954), p. 11.
293   get Lindbergh: from a personal interview.
294   The only interest: Robert E. Sherwood, *Roosevelt and Hopkins* (N.Y.: Harper & Brothers, 1948), p. 124.
294   In those two: *Ibid.*
294   risked political suicide: *Ibid.*, p. 125.
294   I hope the United States: *Ibid.*
296   I speak tonight: *The Radio Addresses of Col. Charles A. Lindbergh* (Lake Geneva, Wisconsin: Scribner's Commentator, 1940), pp. 2, 3.
296   this was a fight: Sherwood, *op. cit.*, p. 201.
296   We must learn: Lindbergh, *op. cit.*, p. 4.
297   undoubtedly Roosevelt's: Sherwood, *op. cit.*, p. 153.
297   we must draw: Lindbergh, *op. cit.*, p. 5.
297   to draw this hemisphere: *Ibid.*, p. 6.
297   Our bond with Europe: *Ibid.*, p. 7.
297–298   Four points of policy: *Ibid.*, p. 8.
298   But the cost: *Ibid.*, p. 10.
298   regardless of which side: *Ibid.*, p. 11.
298   when in his discretion: *Ibid.*, p. 228.
299   Suppose my neighbor's home: Sherwood, *op. cit.*, p. 225.
299   payment or repayment: *Ibid.*, p. 228.
299   the arsenal *and* A nation: *Ibid.*, p. 226.
300   ploughing under: *Ibid.*, p. 229.
300   I want neither: Davis, *The Hero*, p. 398.
300   What an avalanche: Sherwood, *op. cit.*, p. 166.
300   Personally: Davis, *op. cit.*, p. 398.
301   It was almost with ferocity: Lardner in *The Aspirin Age*, p. 192.
301   as cynical: Wayne S. Cole, *America First: The Battle Against Intervention 1940–1941* (Madison, Wisconsin: University of Wisconsin Press,

1953), pp. 142–143. Strangely, there is little published material aside from newspaper stories on America First or on Lindbergh's pre-America-First isolationism. The best source for the student are the America First papers in the Hoover Library on War, Revolution and Peace at Stanford University, California. Dr. Wayne S. Cole has written a solid book based on this material.

301   ignorant: *Ibid.*, p. 476.

301   Sherwood's and Ickes' statements: *Ibid.*, pp. 142–143.

301   A day or two: Walter Lippmann, New York *Herald Tribune*, April 22, 1941.

301   All popular doubts: Thurman Arnold, "In a Democratic Society Dissent Is Not Sacred," *National Observer*, May 15, 1967, p. 12.

302   Knight of the: New York *Sun*, July 18, 1941.

302   Up to that time: Ickes, *op. cit.*, p. 58.

302   For many months: New York *Sun*, July 18, 1941.

302   Mr. President: New York *Sun*, July 18, 1941.

302   a whining one: Ickes, *op. cit.*, p. 581.

302–303   in preaching: *Ibid.*

303   slipped badly: *Ibid.*

303   There is a saying: Lindbergh, *op. cit.*, p. 12.

303   mortgaging the lives: *Ibid.*, p. 13.

303   an organized minority: *Ibid.*, p. 15.

303   so-called democratic nations: *Ibid.*, p. 17.

303–304   the . . . military strength: *Ibid.*

304   The wave of the future is coming: Anne Morrow Lindbergh, *The Wave of the Future* (N.Y.: Harcourt, Brace & Company, 1940), p. 37. This book is expository of Mrs. Lindbergh's political thinking and, perhaps, of her husband's.

304   We have waked: *Ibid.*, p. 40.

304   There is a proverb: Lindbergh, *op. cit.*, p. 17.

305   America simply cannot: Cole, *op. cit.*, pp. 120–121.

305   I presume: *Ibid.*, p. 114.

305   only one private: Butterfield, *op. cit.*, p. 67.

305   July 20, 1940: William L. Shirer, *The Rise and Fall of the Third Reich* (N.Y.: Simon & Schuster, 1960), p. 749n.

307–308   Stated principles and objectives of America First: Cole, *op. cit.*, pp. 15–16.

309   the Committee: *Ibid.*, p. 175.

309   as the world: Sherwood, *op. cit.*, pp. 382–383.

310   to persuade us to send: Davis, *op. cit.*, p. 400.

310   hysterical chatter: Sherwood, *op. cit.*, p. 153.

311   A rattlesnake rattles: *Encyclopaedia Britannica*, 1958 edition, Vol. 6, pp. 421–422.

311   summer soldiers: New York *Sun*, April 25, 1941.

311   While our leaders: *Collier's*, March 29, 1941, p. 14.

311   President Roosevelt's remarks: New York *Sun*, April 26, 1941.

312   Your remarks at the White House: New York *Sun*, April 28, 1941.

312   powerful elements: Cole, *op. cit.*, p. 143.

312–313   Excerpts from Lindbergh's Des Moines speech: *Ibid.*, p. 144.

313   It would be: *Ibid.*, p. 145.

313   It may have been: *Ibid.*, pp. 145–146.

314   not as anti-Semitic: *Ibid.*, p. 147.
314   Many . . . supporters: *Ibid.*, p. 150.
314   Colonel Lindbergh and his: *Ibid.*, p. 152.
314   falsely ascribed: *Ibid.*, p. 153.
315   a grave threat: *Ibid.*, p. 161.
315   Our principles: *Ibid.*, p. 195.
316   believes Jews will: Butterfield, *op. cit.*, p. 65.
318   There are some things: from a personal interview.
318   I stopped talking: New York *Journal-American*, August 24, 25, 1941.
319   except from an academic: *New York Times*, November 19, 1945.
319   world organization: *Ibid.*
319–320   There is little: Davis, *op. cit.*, p. 425.

CHAPTER 25. *Lindbergh's Personal War*

321   We have been stepping: Davis, *The Hero*, p. 416.
321   not enough *and* he gathered that: Lyman, "The Lindbergh I Know,
p. 86.
321   employing Lindbergh: *Newsweek*, December 5, 1949.
323–324   Forty thousand feet: Charles A. Lindbergh, *Of Flight and Life*
(N.Y.: Charles Scribner's Sons, 1948), pp. 3–7. This book presents some of
Lindbergh's wartime experiences and thoughts.
324   out-guessed: Lauren D. Lyman, "Lindbergh: 'Tech Rep,' " *The Bee-
Hive*, January 1950, p. 14.
324   We wanted: *Ibid.*
324   study the performance: *Ibid.*
325   Made a curving take-off: *Ibid.*
325   maneuvered into position: *Ibid.*
325   probably the heaviest: *Ibid.*, p. 15.
326   With a lighter load: *Ibid.*
326   like threading a needle: *Ibid.*
328   Are you a pilot: Colonel Charles MacDonald, "Lindbergh in Battle,"
Collier's, February 16, 1946, p. 11. Colonel MacDonald was Commander of
the 475th Fighter Group with whom Lindbergh flew in Dutch New Guinea.
328   indefatigable: *Ibid.*, p. 12.
328   Lindbergh . . . get your wheels up: *Ibid.*, p. 76.
329   Lindbergh had, in effect: *Ibid.*, p. 75.
329   Of all the attacks: *Ibid.*, p. 76.
329   The enemy plane: Lyman, "Lindbergh: 'Tech Rep,' " p. 15.
330   Then our fuel: Lindbergh, *op. cit.*, pp. 12–13.
331   The Jap must not have been: Colonel Charles MacDonald, "Lindbergh
in Battle," Part 2, *Collier's*, February 23, 1946, p. 30.
331   It was the last few miles: Lindbergh, *op. cit.*, p. 14.
331   Lindbergh said he had no intention: General George C. Kenney,
U.S.A.F. (Ret.), Boston *Sunday Advertiser*, September 1, 1957.
332   when Lindbergh joined us: *Ibid.*

CHAPTER 26. *Family Life*

All quotes in this chapter, except those otherwise noted, have been taken
from personal interviews with persons who requested that they not be
identified.

334   Through these years: Lindbergh, *We*, p. 22.
336   I hear your father: Lyman, "The Lindbergh I Know," p. 83.
336   This was the first time: Al Stump, "The Lone Eagle's Other Son," *True Magazine*, December 1966, p. 26.
336   You go alone today: *Ibid.*
336   Not *try*: *Ibid.*
337   It's become: *Ibid.*
343   no use calling: *Ibid.*
345   Name anything that's dangerous: *Ibid.*, p. 16.

CHAPTER 27. *Change*

355   When I first met Charles: from a personal interview.
356   Keep your style: Lyman, "How Lindbergh Wrote a Book," pp. 19–20.
356   I don't know: *Ibid.*
357   but memory: *Ibid.*
358–359   Library of Congress information: Library of Congress press release, New York *Herald Tribune*, May 21, 1954.
359   I didn't think: from a personal interview.
360   Put your hand: from a personal interview.
360   Returning from the border: Lindbergh, *Of Flight and Life*, p. 8.
360   This altitude flight: *Ibid.*, p. 10.
360   without a highly developed science: *Ibid.*, p. 14.
361   In Germany, I learned: *Ibid.*, p. 21.
361   To me in youth: *Ibid.*, p. 50.

CHAPTER 28. *A Free Man*

363   a case of identification with his father: Dr. Foster Kennedy of Bellevue Hospital, address of June 9, 1941, to American Psychopathological Association.
363   Charles . . . has . . . his father: Butterfield, "Lindbergh: A Stubborn Young Man of Strange Ideas Becomes a Leader of Wartime Opposition," p. 75.
363   Slim, there's a: from a personal interview.
363   If C. A. Lindbergh: from a personal interview.
363   You write him: from a personal interview.
364   He asked me: from a personal interview.
364   You should figure: from a personal interview.
364   Didn't you see: from a personal interview.
365   You oughtn't to: from a personal interview.
366   A number of . . . accounts: Lindbergh, *The Spirit of St. Louis*, p. 547.
366   a matter of principle: from a personal interview.
367–368   Finest human being: from a personal interview.
368   The quality of life: Alexis Carrel, *Reflections on Life* (N.Y.: Hawthorn Books, 1954), p. 11.
368   in the best epic mold: Daniel J. Boorstin, *The Image, or What Happened to the American Dream* (N.Y.: Atheneum, 1962), p. 66.
368   the politics of nostalgia: Paul Seabury, *Charles A. Lindbergh: The Politics of Nostalgia* (N.Y.: Meridian Books, 1960), p. 123.
369   You may not like him: Emmett John Hughes, *Newsweek*, March 13, 1967.

Index

Acosta, Bert, 92
Adams, Samuel Hopkins, 307
Adlershof Air Research Institute, Germany, 268
Aftonbladet, 125
Air Force, U.S., 7, 362; *see also* Army Air Corps
Air Force Academy Site Election Committee, 237
Airlines, 171–73, 177–78
Air-mail service, 69–70, 74–77, 85–86, 160, 170, 172, 177, 211, 254–60
Albert, King of Belgium, 128
Alcock, John, 79, 112
Aldrich-Vreeland Emergency Currency Act, 19–20
Alexander, Roy, 83–84
Allen, C. B., 4 n., 105, 108, 224, 293
Allen, Frederick Lewis, 146–47
Alvarez, General, 165
America (airplane), 99, 100, 106 n., 136, 146
America First, the Battle Against Intervention, 1940–41 (Cole), 313
America First Committee, 281, 300, 306–16, 321, 362, 366
American Airlines, 177
"American Clipper" (airplane), 178
American Importer, S. S., 224
American Legion, 92
American Legion (airplane), 92, 94
American Rocket Society, 251
Anti-Semitism, 313, 314, 316–18
Aquitania, S. S., 356
Army, U.S., 263
Army Air Corps, U.S., 59, 63–68, 87, 255, 257–59, 263, 276, 290, 291, 321

Arnold, General Henry H., 171, 172, 251, 282, 287, 288, 290, 321
Associated Press, 4
Astor, Lord and Lady, 129, 278
Astronauts, the, xiv
Atomic bomb, 291, 319
Auburn, Massachusetts, 244
Austria, 288
Aviation Corporation of Delaware, 255
Aviation industry, 170–71, 211–12, 321
Avions Marcel-Dassault, 5

Baeumker, Adolf, 250, 279
Bahl, Erold, 48–49
Balchen, Bernt, 99–100
Baldwin, Stanley, 129, 276
Balikpapan, 330
Banking and Currency (Charles A. Lindbergh, Sr.), 20
Barnes, Harry Elmer, 310
Baruch, Bernard, 25
Battle of Britain, 299
Bavarian Motor Works, 273
Beard, Charles A., 310, 315
Belgium, 127–28, 147
Bellanca, Giuseppe, 82, 84, 87, 92
Benton, William, 307
Berger, Meyer, 225
Biffle, Ira, 47–48
Bing, Richard J., 232
Birchall, Frederick, 103, 121, 139
Bird City, Kansas, 53
Bitz, Irving, 201
Bixby, Harold, 81, 85, 86, 87, 88, 172 n.
Black, Hugo, 254–55

Black Committee, Hugo, 254–55, 256, 257, 291
Blair and Company, 172
Blériot, Louis, 127
Blythe, Richard, 98, 99, 100, 101, 102, 104, 105, 106, 130–31, 132, 137–38, 143, 144, 148, 162–63
Boedecker, Ken, 85, 101, 107, 108, 109, 110
Boetticher, General Friedrich von, 305
Bolling Field, Washington, D.C., 136, 164, 168
Boorstein, Daniel J., 368
Boston, Massachusetts, 154
Bowles, Chester, 307
Brandewiede, Gregory, 104
Braun, Wernher von, 252
Breckinridge, Henry C., 142, 171, 197, 203, 204, 208, 256, 317–18
Brett, General George H., 251
Brisbane, Arthur, 199, 216
Brisbane, Australia, 327
British Aircraft, Ltd., 5
Bronx *Home News*, 202
Brooks Field, Texas, 62, 63
Brown, Arthur, 79, 112
Brown, Walter F., 177, 254, 255, 256, 257
Brundage, Avery, 307
Bruno, Harry, 4 n., 99, 100, 103, 105, 106, 107, 108, 110, 138, 143, 148, 162–63, 173, 281
Bruno & Blythe (press representatives), 95, 98
Brussels, Belgium, 128
Bullitt, William C., 283
Burbank, California, 182
Burch, Frank B., 306 n.
Burrage, Admiral, 132
Busch, Bishop, 23
Bush, Vannevar, 291
Butte, Montana, 157
Butterfield, Roger, 317
Byrd, Admiral Richard E., 87, 94, 99–100, 105, 106, 136

Cachalot (boat), 206
Calles, Plutarco Elías, 162, 164, 165, 166
Camp Kearney, California, 94
Camp Knox, Kentucky, 42

Camp Wood, Texas, 62–63
Cannon, Joseph, 19
Canuck airplane, 61–63, 64, 69
Cape May, New Jersey, 206
Capone, Al, 199, 201
Carnegie Foundation, 246
Carrel, Alexis, 229–42, 252, 339, 359, 368
Carrel, Mme. Alexis, 240
Cass Technical High School, Detroit, 44, 354
Caterpillar Club, 67–68
Catholic Bulletin, 23
Catholic Church, 22–23, 24
Challenge to the Poles (Grierson), 188 n.
Chamberlain, Clarence, 87, 92, 106
Chanute Field, Illinois, 61
Charles XV, King of Sweden, 10
Chase, Stuart, 310
Cherbourg, France, 121
Chicago, Illinois, 75, 86, 158
Chicago *Tribune*, 125
Chichester, Sir Francis, xiv
Chinese Relief Commission, 192
Churchill, Winston S., 276, 299, 301
Civil War, American, 14
Clark, Bennett Champ, 30, 307
Clark University, 244, 245, 246, 247, 248, 250
Cleveland Air Races (1929), 181
Coast to Coast in Forty-eight Hours (film), 173
Cobb, Orvin S., 307
Cole, Wayne S., 306 n., 313
Coli, Lieutenant, 92, 94, 95, 100, 127
Collier's magazine, 311
Colonial Air Transport, 171
Columbia (airplane), 106 n., 146
Columbia Aircraft Corporation, 85
Columbia University, 27
Commerce Department, U.S., 150
Committee of Witnesses, 222–23
Communist party, American, 310
Compton, Karl T., 291
Conant, James B., 291
Concord, New Hampshire, 155
Concorde (airplane), 5
Condon, John F., 202–06, 207–08, 214, 217, 219–20
Congress, U.S., 291, 300, 315

Coogan's Academy, 14
Coolidge, Calvin, 129, 132–33, 163, 166, 168, 179–80, 365
Corrigan, Douglas "Wrong-Way," 93
"Corsair" (F–4U) fighter planes, 324, 325
Corwin, Edwin S., 315
Coughlin, Father Charles, 308
Cryobiology magazine, 233
Culture of Organs, The (Lindbergh and Carrell), 234
Cummings, Homer, 255
Curtin, Lawrence, 80
Curtis, John Hughes, 202, 206, 207, 208–09, 220
Curtiss, Glenn H., 40
Curtiss Field, New York, 98, 108, 139
Curtiss JN–4D ("Jenny"), 53–54, 57, 60, 61, 64
Curtiss OX–5 engine, 54, 64
Curtiss OXX–6 engine, 70
Curtiss-Wright Aeronautical Company, 321
Czech air force, 286
Czechoslovakia, 277

Daimler-Benz liquid-cooled engines, 274
Daladier, Edouard, 283, 284
Danbury, Connecticut, 338
Darien, Connecticut, 1, 334–35, 336, 364
Davies, Marion, 143
Davis, Dwight F., 130
Davis, Kenneth, 230, 368
Davis, Noel, 87, 92, 94, 100
Dayton, Ohio, 138
De Havilland (DH–4B) airplanes, 59, 65, 74
Delage (French pilot), 122, 123
Denver, Colorado, 71
Denver *Post,* 125
Dern, George H., 258, 259
Des Moines, Iowa, 157, 312
Des Moines *Register,* 313
Detroit, Michigan, 31, 32, 158
Detroyat (French pilot), 122, 123
Dewey, Thomas E., 313
Dodd, William E., 263, 278
Donnelly, Ignatius, 14

Dubos, René, 230 n.
Dudley, Delos, 43
Dunkirk, France, 298
Du Pont Company, 243
Durkin, Joseph T., 235, 238, 239, 240
Dynamite, 206

Early, Steve, 257
Edward, Prince of Wales, 129
Eisenhower, Dwight D., 7, 331
Elizabeth, New Jersey, 198
England, 128–29, 147, 223, 226, 234, 251, 261, 271–72, 276–77, 278, 286, 289, 294, 295, 298, 300, 303, 304, 305
Englewood, New Jersey, 161, 176, 179, 209, 223, 290

Fairbanks, Janet Ayer, 307
Falcon airplane, 5
Farley, James A., 256, 257
Federal Bar Association, 257
Federal Bureau of Investigation, 228
Ferber, Edna, 216
Feydy, Anne Spencer Lindbergh (Lindbergh's daughter), 4–5, 227, 318, 333, 336, 349, 350, 351, 352
Feydy, Julien, 4, 352
Figaro, Le, 125
Finland, 294
Flemington, New Jersey, 208, 216, 221
Flexner, Simon, 235
Florida Airways, 172
Flynn, John T., 307, 308
Foch, Marshal Ferdinand, 127
Focke-Wulf helicopters, 274
Fokker, Anthony, 82, 87, 94, 104
Fokker airplanes, 82–83, 87, 94, 99
Fonck, René, 80, 82, 92, 100, 104
Fondation Française pour l'Etude des Problèmes Humains, 239
Force School, Washington, D.C., 38
Ford, Henry, 158, 166, 307, 322, 335, 338
Fort Benning, Georgia, 298
Fort Myer, Virginia, 40–41
Fort Snelling, 60
Fort Wayne, Indiana, 314
Foss, Joe, 324
Foulois, General Benjamin D., 255

Fowler, H. W., 357
France, 117–19, 121–27, 146, 147, 226, 238–40, 251, 261–62, 277, 283–84, 286, 294, 295, 303, 304
Frazee, Harry H., 136
French Air Ministry, 261
French Aero Club, 127, 144
Frogge, Johnny, 107

Galveston, Texas, 66
Geist, Raymond, 279
"General Estimate of Germany's Air Power" (Smith), 274–76
General Motors Corporation, 172
George V, King of England, 129
George VI, King of England, 271
German Air Ministry, 262, 279
German-American Bund, 308, 310
Germany, 246, 250, 251–52, 261, 262–71, 273–76, 278–79, 285–86, 287–88, 289, 295, 303, 304, 320, 360–61
Gish, Lillian, 307
Goddard, Robert H., 244–53
Goddard, Mrs. Robert H., 244–45, 246, 251, 252
Goering, Hermann, 262, 263, 264, 265, 266, 269–70, 281, 284, 302, 304
Goff, U.S.S., 130
Goldsborough, Brice, 99, 100
Goldwater, Barry M., 365
Gosport, England, 129
Gould, Bruce, 104
Gow, Betty, 195–96, 207, 217, 219
Grand Rapids, Michigan, 158
Granger movement, 14
Great Britain, see England
Green, Fitzhugh, 126, 133, 141, 147
Greenland, 212, 319
Grierson, John, 188 n., 358
Grimwood, I. R., 6
Guatemala City, Guatemala, 167
Guggenheim, Carol, 141, 244
Guggenheim, Daniel, 247, 248
Guggenheim, Harry, 105, 139, 141, 142, 150, 151, 170, 171, 244, 247, 248, 249–50, 251, 317
Guggenheim Foundation, Daniel and Florence, 248, 249, 250, 252
Guggenheim Fund for the Promotion of Aeronautics, Daniel, 105, 139,

Guggenheim Fund (Cont'd)
142, 150, 151, 159, 160, 171, 176, 247
Gurney, Bud, 47, 48, 51, 61, 70

Haines, Lynn, 10, 13, 24
Hall, Donald, 88–89, 92, 106
Hammaker, Bishop Wilbur E., 307
Hammond, General Thomas S., 306
Hanesse, Colonel F. K., 263, 265, 273, 284
Hankow, China, 192
Hardin, Charles, 49–50, 51, 52
Harrison, Rev. C. S., 11
Hartford, Connecticut, 151–53
Hartson, Joe, 99
Hauptmann, Bruno Richard, 214, 215, 216, 217, 218, 219, 221–22, 226
Hauptmann murder case, 213–23, 226–28
Havana, Cuba, 167
Hawks, Frank, 60
Hayden, Stone & Company, 172
Hayes, Harold T. P., xv
Hayes, Patrick Joseph Cardinal, 135
Hearst, William Randolph, 142–43, 198
Hearst, William Randolph, Jr., 198
Heinkel, Dr., 279
Henderson, Pilot, 54–55
Henderson, Sir Nevile, 282
Hermes, H.M.S., 192
Herrick, Myron, 95, 104, 123, 124, 125, 126, 127
Herrick, Parmely, 124
High Fields, Hopewell, New Jersey, 210
Hingwa, China, 190–91
Hispano-Suiza V–8 engine, 46, 64
Hitler, Adolf, 261 n., 266, 269, 270, 279, 284, 294, 295, 301, 316
Hoare, Sir Samuel, 128, 129
Hoffman, Harold, 222
Hollandia, New Guinea, 327
Homeopathic Observer, 34
Hoover, Herbert C., 177, 199, 365
Hopewell, New Jersey, 179, 195, 203, 209, 210, 218
Hopkins, Harry, 294
Hormel, Jay C., 306
Houghton, Alanson B., 128

House of Representatives, U.S., 18–21, 22, 30, 36, 163
Huff-Daland Company, 84, 87
Hughes, Charles Evans, 134, 136
Hull, Cordell, 286
Humphreys, Joe, 120
Humphrey's Field, Colorado, 71–72
Hunsaker, Jerome C., 270
Hurst, Fanny, 216

Iceland, 212, 213
Ickes, Harold L., 292–93, 301–03
Iliec Island, 235
India, 271
Ingalls, Laura, 306 n.
Inskip, Thomas, 271
Internal Revenue Service, 293, 294
International Cytological Congress (1936), 233
Ireland, 116–17, 121
Irey, Elmer, 199, 204
Italy, 271

James, Edwin L., 103, 121–22, 124, 126, 139
Janesville, Minnesota, 57
Japan, 295, 315
Jessup, Philip C., 315
Jet propulsion, 243–44, 251
Jewett, Frank B., 291
Joffre, Marshal Joseph, 127
Johnson, General Hugh S., 307
Journal of Experimental Medicine, 232

Keep America Out of War, 310, 317
Kellogg, Frank B., 21, 25, 166
Kelly, Larry, 226, 318–19
Kelly Act (1925), 170
Kelly Field, Texas, 65
Kelly Foreign Air Mail Act (1928), 172
Kennedy, John F., 285, 365
Kennedy, Joseph P., 285, 286, 287, 365
Kenney, General George C., 327, 331–32
Kesselring, Marshal Albert, 270
Ketoi Island, Japan, 190
Keyhoe, Donald E., 150, 151, 152, 153, 154, 155, 156, 157, 158, 159, 179
Keys, Clement M., 172, 173

Kidnap, the Story of the Lindbergh Case (Waller), 227
Kilmer, General W. G., 291
Kimball, Dr., 104, 106
Kindelberger, J. H., 270
Klink, Leon, 61–62, 63, 64, 69
Knecht, Martha, 348
Knickerbocker, H. R., 301
Knight, Harry, 81, 85, 88, 89, 96, 102, 105, 137, 172 n.
Knox, Frank, 299
Knutson, Harold, 26
Kramer-Klett, Baron and Baroness, 273
Krock, Arthur, 258
Kruger National Park, 347
Kusterer, Milburn, 151, 154
Kwajalein Island, 326

La Follette, Philip, 307
La Follette, Robert M., Sr., 24, 30
La Guardia, Fiorello, 281
Lambert, Major, 83
Lambert Field, Missouri, 60, 61, 70, 82, 83, 85, 97, 137, 167, 168
Land, Charles H. (Lindbergh's grandfather), 8, 32–33, 240, 241
Langley, Samuel Pierpont, 163
Lansing, E. Ray, 102
Lardner, John, 120
Latin America, 167–68, 171, 295
Lawrance, Charles, 105
Le Bourget Field, Paris, 95, 118–19, 121–23, 127, 357
Le Chambre, Guy, 283, 284
Lee, Ivy, 151
Lehman, Milton H., 252 n.
Lend-Lease bill, 299, 300
Leningrad, Soviet Union, 277
"Letter to Americans, A" (Charles A. Lindbergh, Jr.), 311
Levine, Charles A., 85, 87–88, 106 n.
Lewis, Fulton, Jr., 254–55, 291–92, 297
Lewis, John L., 310
Lewis, Sinclair, 31
Liberty engines, 74, 78–79, 158
Library of Congress, 358–59
Life magazine, 316, 351
"Lightning" (P–38) fighter planes, 327, 328, 329–30, 331, 332

Lilienthal, Otto, 320
Lilienthal Aeronautical Society, 273
Lincoln, Abraham, 311
Lincoln, Nebraska, 45, 49, 52
Lincoln Standard Turnabouts (airplanes), 43, 46, 72
Lindbergh, Anne Spencer Morrow (Lindbergh's wife), 1, 161, 166, 173–75, 351, 356, 363; articles and books by, 181, 211, 213, 304, 353; children of, 1, 4–5, 178, 209, 271–72, 318, 333–54; family life of, 333, 340–41, 346, 348, 350, 351, 353; Hauptmann case, 216–17, 221; kidnaping of Charles A. Lindbergh, III, 195–96, 199, 207, 227; marriage of, 176; radio operator on Oriental flight, 181, 183–93
Lindbergh, August (Lindbergh's grandfather), 9–12, 13, 14, 17, 32
Lindbergh, Charles Augustus, Jr., adulation of, xiii–xv, 146–49; airmail controversy, 254–60; air-mail pilot, 69–70, 74–77, 85–86; America First activities, 309–16, 321, 362, 366; American air power surveyed by, 250; ancestral and parental background, 9–26; archaeological interest, 178; Army flying school experience, 59, 61, 62, 63–68; articles and books by, 6, 126, 140–42, 143, 145, 232, 234, 256, 303, 311, 323, 331, 334, 346, 355, 356–59; 366; Atlantic Ocean survey by, 212–13; barnstorming and stunt flying, 48–49, 52–53, 59, 62–63, 70, 71–74, 78; birth of, 17, 28; boyhood of, 28–44; Brussels reception of, 128; Carrel and, 229–42; character and personality of, 69, 355–61, 362–69; children of, 1, 4–5, 178, 209, 271–72, 318, 333–54, 363; commercial exploitation rejected by, 139, 142–44, 148; commissioned Brigadier General, 331; commissioned Colonel, 130; commissioned First Lieutenant, 74; commissioned Second Lieutenant, 68; courtship of, 173–76; criticism of, 301–06, 311, 313, 316–19; education of, 38, 41–44; family life of, 333–54; flight train-

Lindbergh, Charles A., Jr. (Cont'd)
ing, 45–58, 63–68; forty-eight-state good-will flight, 142, 150–60; French air power surveyed by, 261–62, 286; German air power surveyed by, 262–71, 273–76, 278–79, 282, 285–86, 287–88; Goddard and, 244–53; Hauptmann case and, 213–23, 226–28; honors and awards, 127, 129, 133, 134, 135, 136, 137, 143, 144–45, 163, 168, 173 n., 278–82, 331, 358; invasion of privacy of, xv–xvi, 178–79, 209–10, 223; isolationism of, 295–98, 309–14, 316–17, 319; jump experiences, 49–51, 52, 53, 67–68, 70–71, 75–76; kidnapping and death of Charles A. Lindbergh, III, 195–207; Latin-American good-will flight, 167–68; Lease-Lend bill opposed by, 300–01; London reception of, 128–29; marriage of, 176, 179–80; Mexican good-will flight, 161–67; Nazi medal awarded to, 278–82; New York-Paris flight, 98–119; New York reception of, 134–37; nicknames of, 47, 53, 100, 157, 362; Oriental survey flight of, 181–93; Paris reception of, 120–27; perfusion pump developed by, 229–34; plane crashes, 56, 57–58, 62, 63, 66–67, 70, 175; plane testing, 70, 74, 93–94, 322, 323–24; present life pattern of, 1–8, 362–69; press relations of, 93, 94, 100–01, 102–03, 124–25, 152, 175–76, 199, 200–01, 225, 227, 351, 366–67; pro-Nazi criticism of, 278; public image of, 355; radio broadcasts and speeches of, on the war, 295–98, 303–06, 309–14, 316–17, 318, 319–20; residence established in England by, 223–26; rocket development and, 243–53; Roosevelt and, 292–93, 295, 298, 302–03, 310–12, 319, 321, 322, 366; St. Louis reception of, 137–38; Soviet air power surveyed by, 277, 278, 286; technical consultant for Pan American and TAT airlines, 172–73, 174, 177–78, 181–93, 195, 211–13, 243, 256, 362; transatlantic flight plans and considerations, 78–

Lindbergh, Charles A., Jr. (*Cont'd*)
97; transcontinental inspection
tours, 291; Washington reception
of, 131–34; wild-life conservation
interest, 6; World War II contributions, 321–32
Lindbergh, Charles Augustus, Sr.
(Lindbergh's father), 2, 10, 11, 12–
26, 27–28, 29, 30, 31, 32, 33, 34–
38, 43, 53, 56, 65–66, 133, 240, 241,
254, 290, 316, 363
Lindbergh, Charles Augustus, III
(Lindbergh's son), 178, 186, 195–
96, 207, 227
Lindbergh, Eva (Lindbergh's half
sister), 17, 25, 29, 31, 35
Lindbergh, Evangeline Lodge Land
(Lindbergh's mother), 27, 29, 31–
32, 34, 38, 40, 42, 44, 53, 57, 101,
125, 126, 130, 132, 133, 145, 158,
159, 166, 167, 176, 354
Lindbergh, Frank (Lindbergh's uncle), 15
Lindbergh, Jon Morrow (Lindbergh's
son), xiv, 209–10, 211, 223, 262,
333, 336–37, 339–42, 343, 344–46,
351, 352
Lindbergh, June (Lindbergh's aunt),
15
Lindbergh, Land Morrow (Lindbergh's son), 271–72, 333, 349, 351,
352
Lindbergh, Lillian (Lindbergh's half
sister), 17, 29, 31, 34, 35
Lindbergh, Linda (Lindbergh's aunt),
15
Lindbergh, Louisa (Lindbergh's
grandmother), 10, 11
Lindbergh, Mary La Fond, 15, 17, 27
Lindbergh, Reeve (Lindbergh's
daughter), 1, 227, 333, 334, 335 n.,
338, 342, 348, 349, 351, 352
Lindbergh, Scott Morrow (Lind-
bergh's son), 1, 271–72, 333, 342,
343–44, 349, 351
"Lindbergh law," 228
"Lindbergh Line," the, 256
Lindberghs, The (Haines), 10
Link, Edwin C., 345
Lippmann, Walter, 301
Lischner, Hyman, 314

Listen! the Wind (Anne Morrow
Lindbergh), 213, 353
Little Falls, Minnesota, 1, 15, 16, 26,
27, 29, 31
Locarno Pact, 261
Lodge, Albert, 34
Lodge, Edwin, 33, 34
Lodge, John C., 32
Loening, Grover, 104
London, England, 128–29, 285
London *Daily Mail*, 79
Longworth, Alice Roosevelt, 307
Los Angeles (dirigible), 132
Lost Generation, 146
Lourdes, France, 240–41
Love, Phil, 66, 74, 86, 150, 151–52,
153, 154, 155, 156, 157
Luce, Henry, 369
Lufthansa Airline, 171, 223, 265
Luftwaffe, 262, 263, 265, 268, 269,
270, 276, 277, 288, 289
Lyman, Lauren D. ("Deac"), 4 n.,
104, 108, 178, 197, 198, 201, 223–
25, 281, 321, 324, 325, 357
Lyman, Mab (Mrs. Lauren D.), 224
Lynch, H. J. ("Shorty"), 51–53, 72,
157

Maben, Mississippi, 56
MacArthur, General Douglas, 327, 369
MacCracken, William P., Jr., 150,
158–59
MacDonald, Colonel Charles H., 327–
28, 329, 330, 331
MacDonald, J. Carlisle, 122, 124, 139,
140, 142
MacDonald, Ramsay, 271
Mackay, Clarence, 136
MacNider, Hanford, 307
Madison, Wisconsin, 41–42
Macom (yacht), 134, 135
Madison, Wisconsin, 41–42
Mahoney, B. F., 88, 89, 105
Mahoney Aircraft Company, 169
Maloney, Jim, 120
Malraux, André, 365
Man, the Unknown (Carrel), 230 n.,
236–37
Manning, Bishop William T., 199
Marietta, Martin, 105
Markey, Morris, 176

Marshall, Erwin E., 207
Marshall, General George C., 282, 301 n.
Marshall, Minnesota, 56
Martin, Glenn, 270
Mary, Queen of England, 129
Mason, Gregory, 314
Massachusetts Institute of Technology, 244
Mayer, Ferdinand, 263, 264
Mayo Clinic, Rochester, Minnesota, 322–23
McAllister, Lieutenant, 66, 67, 68
McCahill, Frank, 108
McCarter, Thomas N., 307
McFarland, Marvin W., 138, 359
McGee, John F., 23
McKaig, Ray, 307
McKellar, Kenneth D., 259
McLean, Evalyn Walsh, 201–02, 206
Means, Gaston B., 201–02, 206, 207, 208
Mein Kampf (Hitler), 266
Melrose, Minnesota, 10
Memphis, U.S.S., 129, 130, 131, 132, 140
Mencken, H. L., 222
Meridian, Mississippi, 55
Method of Reaching Extreme Altitudes (Goddard), 245
Mexico, 164–67, 174, 175
Mexico City, Mexico, 164, 173
Michigan, University of, 14, 15, 27, 41
Milch, General Erhard, 263, 267, 283, 284
Miles "Mohawk" (airplane), 265
Mil-Hi Airways & Flying Circus, 71–73
Miller, Danforth P., 330 n., 331
Mills, Ogden, 199
Mindanao, 330
Minneapolis, Minnesota, 26, 29
Minnesota Public Safety Commission, 23
Missouri Historical Society, 145, 280
Missouri National Guard, 74
Mitchell, General Billy, 130, 258, 269
Mitchell Field, New York, 134, 136, 151, 159, 176
Monnet, Jean, 283
Moose Factory, Canada, 187

Morgan, Aubrey, 317 n.
Morgan, Elisabeth Reeve Morrow, 194, 215–16, 229
Morgan, J. P., 180
Morgan & Company, J. P., 204
Morgan Guaranty Trust Company, 362
Morrow, Constance, 165, 174, 271, 318
Morrow, Dwight W., 130, 139, 148, 150, 161–62, 164, 165, 179–80, 192, 194, 214
Morrow, Mrs. Dwight W., 165, 166, 176, 195, 211, 214, 215–16, 220, 221, 271, 272, 318
Moscow, Soviet Union, 277
Mott, General J. Bentley, 240
Mueller, Esther B., 143
Mulligan, Ed, 99, 101, 107, 108, 109, 110
Mundt, Karl, 307

Nanking, China, 190
Natal, 213
National Advisory Committee for Aeronautics, 290
National Aeronautic Association, 92, 106, 134
National Air Transport, 172
National Defense Research Committee, 291
National Flood Relief Commission, 190–91
National Press Club, 134
Naval Research Institute, Bethesda, Maryland, 233–34
Navy, U. S., 78, 147, 192, 193
Nebraska Aircraft Corporation, 43, 44, 45–46
Nelson, Knute, 56
Nelson, Thomas, 74
Neuman Committee, 7
Neutrality Act (1937), 292, 294, 315
New, Harry S., 134, 170, 177, 254
Newfoundland, 112
Newspaper Club of New York, 105, 106
Newsweek magazine, 322
New York, N.Y., 134–37
New York American, 203, 204, 225
New York Daily Mirror, 106, 107
New York Daily News, 226

New York *Herald-Tribune*, 224, 225–26

New York Times, The, 4, 102–03, 121, 124, 125, 139–40, 164, 167, 198, 221, 224–25, 257, 258, 259, 312

New York *World*, 67, 166

Nicolson, Harold, 168, 179, 214–15, 220, 221, 226, 271, 276–77, 300

Nixon, Richard M., 365

Nobel Prize, 230, 241

Nome, Alaska, 187, 188

Nonpartisan League, 22, 23, 24

Norris, George W., 257

Norris, Kathleen, 216, 307

North American Aviation, 172

North American–General Motors, 255

North to the Orient (Anne Morrow Lindbergh), 181, 211

Northwest-Orient Airlines, 177, 193

Nova Scotia, 111–12

Nungesser, Charles, 92, 94, 95, 100, 127

Nungesser, Mme., 127

Nye, Gerald P., 307

Ocean Systems, Inc., 345

Ochs, Adolph S., 140

Of Flight and Life (Charles A. Lindbergh, Jr.), 323, 331

O'Gorman, Juan, 166

Old Orchard Beach, Maine, 155

Olympic games (1936), 265

Omaha, Nebraska, 157

O'Mahoney, Jeremiah T., 259

Only Yesterday (Allen), 147

Oppenheimer, J. Robert, 322

Orteig, Raymond, 79, 136

Orteig Prize, 79–80, 81, 82, 83, 92, 94, 105, 137

Orteig Trustees, Raymond, 143

Ortiz, José, 166

Ottawa, Canada, 186, 187

Page, Ray, 46, 48, 49, 51, 52

Paine, Thomas, 311

Palmer, Albert W., 307

Pan American, Inc., 172

Pan American Airways, Inc., 171, 172, 174, 177–78, 181, 192–93, 211, 243, 256

Pan American World Airways, 3, 4, 362, 366

Papers of Wilbur and Orville Wright, The (McFarland), 138

Paris, France, 118–19, 121–27, 129, 277, 283, 284, 352

Paris *Herald*, 4

Parker, Raymond C., 235

Paterson, New Jersey, 84, 105, 137

Patrick, General Mason M., 130, 132

Pearl Harbor, Japanese attack on, 315, 316

Pendray, G. Edward, 251, 252

Perfusion pump, invention of, 229–34

Philadelphia, Pennsylvania, 159

Pictorial Review, 336

Pinchot, Amos R. E., 307

Pioneer Instrument Company, 99

Plummer, Richard, 43

Plymouth, England, 121

Point Barrow, Alaska, 187

Poland, 277, 294, 295, 306

Portland, Maine, 154, 155, 175

Post Office Department, U.S., 254, 255

Prensa, La, 125

Princeton, New Jersey, 179, 231, 244

Pujo Committee (1917), 20

Pulitzer Prize, 8, 225

Putnam, George Palmer, 139, 141, 142, 143, 346

Quigley, Walter Eli, 15, 21, 56, 65, 66

Rae, Bruce, 224

Reader's Digest, 358

Rechlin air testing field, Pomerania, 273–74

Reflections on Life (Carrel), 237–38, 368

Regnery, William H., 306

Reich, Al, 203

Reilly, Edward J., 217–19

Republic Aircraft Corporation, 322

Richards Field, Missouri, 71

Rickenbacker, Edward, 258, 307

Rise and Fall of the Third Reich (Shirer), 261 n.

Robertson, Bill, 70, 83

Robertson Aircraft Corporation, 70, 74–75, 86, 129, 144, 170

Rockefeller, John D., 230 n.

Rockefeller Institute for Medical Research, 230, 232, 235, 238
Rockefeller University, 230 n.
Rockets and rocketry, 243–53, 268, 319
Roehm, Ernst, 270
Rogers, Will, 165, 214, 364
Roi Island, 325
Roosevelt, Franklin D., 199, 254, 255, 256, 257, 258, 260, 286, 292–95, 296, 297, 298–300, 301, 302, 308, 309, 310–12, 314–15, 316, 319, 321, 366
Roosevelt, Theodore, 30
Roosevelt, Theodore, Jr., 104, 121
Roosevelt Field, New York, 80, 99, 108, 112, 129
Rosner, Morris, 201, 207
Roswell, New Mexico, 248, 250, 291
Rous, Peyton, 230 n.
Roussy de Sales, Raoul de, 216
Royal Air Club, 128
Royal Air Force, British, 129
Rumania, 277
Runyon, Damon, 216
Russian Air Force, 278
Ryan, T. Claude, 169
Ryan Aeronautical Company, 169
Ryan Airlines, 86, 88–89, 96, 169
Ryan M-1 monoplane, 86; see also Spirit of St. Louis
Ryerson, Edward L., Jr., 307

Sackville-West, Victoria, 215
St. Cloud, Minnesota, 12, 15
St. Cloud Democrat, 14
Saint-Gildas Island, 234, 235
St. John, Adela Rogers, 216
St. John's, Newfoundland, 112–13
St. Louis, Missouri, 60, 61, 69, 70, 74, 81, 88, 96, 97, 98, 137–38, 168
St. Louis Flying Club, 85
St. Louis Globe Democrat, 102
St. Louis Post-Dispatch, 83, 95
San Diego, California, 88, 92, 95, 96
San Pedro, California, 90
Santiago Island, 213
Saturday Evening Post, 347, 358
Sauk Center, Minnesota, 11, 14, 31
Scadta, 171
Scanlon, Colonel, 264

Schleicher, General von, 270
Schlesinger, Arthur M., Jr., 255
Schulman, Sam, 107
Schwarzkopf, Colonel, 207
Science magazine, 232
Scott, General Winfield, 27
Seabury, Paul, 368
Searle, Judge, 15
Selective Service Act, 309
Sevenoaks-Weald, Kent, England, 226, 265
Sherman Anti-Trust Act, 255
Sherwood, Robert E., 294, 296, 297, 301, 309
Shirer, William L., 261 n.
Shishmaref, Alaska, 188
Shortt, Lionel, 216
Sikorsky, Igor, 80, 92, 267, 270, 279, 315, 333
Silver Shirts, 308
Sirius (airplane), 182–92
Skidmore, Abram, 108, 110
Smith, Alfred E., 136
Smith, Kay (Mrs. Truman), 262, 263, 267, 280, 346, 353
Smith, Meryl M., 330 n.
Smith, Truman, 261–66, 267, 268, 269, 270, 273, 274–76, 278, 279, 280, 281, 282, 283, 284, 285, 286, 288, 289, 298, 346
Smith College, 174
Smithsonian Institution, xv, 30, 163, 168, 245, 246, 249
Sorenson, Ted, 155
Souther Field, Georgia, 53–55
Soviet Union, 250, 277, 278, 286, 294
Spaatz, General Carl, 291
Spirit of St. Louis (airplane), xv, 87, 92–97, 99, 102, 105, 106–07, 108, 110–19, 121, 122, 123, 124–25, 127–28, 129, 134, 136, 137, 146, 149, 150, 151, 154, 155, 156, 158, 159, 160, 161, 162, 163, 164, 167, 168–69, 357
Spirit of St. Louis, The (Lindbergh's autobiography), 8, 28, 67, 356, 357–59, 366
Spitale, Salvy, 201
Stabler, Jennie, 13
Stanford University, 346
State Department, U.S., 177, 286, 287

Stefansson, Vilhjalmur, 39, 213
Stephen, Admiral Edward, 345
Stewart, James, 358
Stimson, Henry L., 177, 299, 321
Stinson, Texas, 63, 64
Stockholm, Sweden, 212
Stout, William B., 158
Stuart, R. Douglas, Jr., 306
Stuka (airplane), 268–69
Sub-Aviation, 5
Sulzberger, Arthur Hays, 102
Svenska Dagbladet, 144

Tabor, Louis, 307
Taft, William Howard, 30, 163
Taylor, A. J. P., 316
Tempelhof Airport, Berlin, 284
Teterboro Airport, New Jersey, 151, 161
33 Hours to Paris (Charles A. Lindbergh, Jr.), 358
This High Man—The Life of Robert H. Goddard (Lehman), 252 n.
This Week magazine, 278
Thomas, Norman, 310, 314, 322
Thompson, Earl, 81–82
Thomsen, Hans, 305–06
Tighe, Dixie, 216
Timberg, William H., 228
Time magazine, 232
Timm, Otto, 47
Tingmissartoq (airplane), 212, 213
Townsend, Ralph, 306 n.
Transatlantic flight attempts, 79–81, 87, 92, 94, 100
Transcontinental Air Transport (TAT), 171, 172–73, 177
Transcontinental & Western Air Express (TWA), 177, 243, 256, 259
Travel Air Company, 86
Trenchard, Thomas W., 220, 226
Trippe, Juan Terry, 3, 4, 7, 171–72, 177, 181, 212, 366
Turner, Roscoe, 182

Udet, General Ernst, 268, 273, 283, 284
United Aircraft Corporation, 255, 321, 324, 327
United Airlines, 172, 177, 258

V–2 rockets, German, 252
Vacuum Oil Company, 99, 143
Valbuena Airport, Mexico City, 164, 167
Vallandigham, Clement L., 311
Van Atta, Lee, 327
Vaud, Switzerland, 1
Vaughan, Guy, 95
Vaughn, Wray, 71–73
Versailles Treaty (1919), 262, 266, 290
Villard, Oswald Garrison, 307
Vlaminck, Maurice, 347
Vought, Chance, 104
Voyage to Lourdes, The (Carrel), 241, 252
Vultee, Gerard F., 181

Walker, James J., 127, 135
Wallace, Henry A., 299
Waller, George, 227
Wanamaker, Rodman, 87, 136
War Department, U.S., 286, 291, 292, 298, 321
War Industries Board, 25
Washington, D.C., 30–31, 131–34, 163, 186
Wave of the Future—A Confession of Faith, The, (Anne Morrow Lindbergh), 304
We (Charles A. Lindbergh, Jr.), 126, 140–42, 143, 145, 334, 346, 356, 358
Weiss, Pierre, 123
Western Air Express, 171, 177
West Point Military Academy, 290
Whalen, Grover, 136 n.
Whateley, Oliver, 197, 218
Wheeler, Burton K., 300, 306, 307
Wheeler, Mrs. Burton K., 307
Whipple, George H., 307
White, William Allen, 300
White Bird (airplane), 95
Whitehead, General, 327
Wilbur, Ray Lyman, 315
Wilentz, David, 216, 221, 222
Williams, Al, 104
Williams, Joe, 308
Williams, William A., 157–58
Williams, William Carleton, 157
Willkie, Wendell, 295, 296, 300, 308, 313

Wilson, Hugh R., 278–79, 280, 281
Wilson, Woodrow, 30
Winchell, Walter, 216, 271
Wisconsin, University of, 41, 43, 173 n., 337
Wood, General Robert E., 306
Woodring, Harry, 292
Woollcott, Alexander, 216
Wooster, Stanton H., 87, 94, 100
Wright, Orville and Wilbur, 40, 52, 138, 169
Wright Aeronautical Corporation, 95, 99, 172 n.
Wright-Bellanca airplane, 76–77, 80, 81, 82, 84–85, 87, 92, 94, 99, 100

Wright-Patterson Air Force Base, Dayton, Ohio, 213
Wright "Whirlwind" engine (J–5), 82, 83, 89, 105, 109, 159, 169, 182

Yale University, 7, 240
York Harbor, Maine, 176
Young, Clarence M., 92–93
Young, Genevieve, xv
Your Country at War, and What Happens to You After the War, and Related Subjects (Charles A. Lindbergh, Sr.), 21–22
Yucatan, 178
Yugoslavia, 271

ABOUT THE AUTHOR

WALTER S. ROSS was born in Newark, New Jersey, in 1914. He attended Hawthorne Avenue School and West Side High School in Newark, and later attended the University of North Carolina and Rutgers University.

Mr. Ross has been in publishing since his college days, and is a free-lance writer and novelist.

His career in publishing dates back to 1947-48, when he became publisher of '47 and '48 The Magazine of the Year: he also served as Director of Public Relations of Broadcast Music, Inc.; was News and Feature Editor for Warner Bros. Pictures; was a Senior Editor for Coronet magazine, and Articles Editor for Collier's magazine.

Mr. Ross is the author of three earlier books, The Immortal, Coast to Coast and The Climate Is Hope, and his articles have appeared in national magazines, including Look, McCall's, the Ladies' Home Journal, Esquire, and the Reader's Digest. The Last Hero: Charles A. Lindbergh is his first biography.

Mr. Ross and his wife divide their time between homes in New York City, Peconic, Long Island, and Paris.

About his writing career, Mr. Ross comments, "I've always wanted to be a writer, as far back as I can remember. One would think that attaining this status would dull the edge of ambition. Not so. Banal as it sounds, there are always new challenges in the work itself, and I know that one can learn to do it better."

Section 1

"All the News That's Fit to Print."

The New

VOL. LXXVI....No. 25,320. • • •

NEW YORK, S

LINDBERGH DOES IT!
FLIES 1,000 MILES THR
CHEERING FRENCH

COULD HAVE GONE 500 MILES FARTHER

Gasoline for at Least That Much More Flew at Times From 10 Feet to 10,000 Feet Above Water.

ATE ONLY ONE AND A HALF OF HIS FIVE SANDWICHES

Fell Asleep at Times but Quickly Awoke—Glimpses of His Adventure in Brief Interview at the Embassy.

MAP OF LINDBERGH'S TRANSATLANT

LINDBERGH'S OWN STORY TOMORROW.

Captain Charles A. Lindbergh was too exhausted after his arrival in Paris late last night to do more than indicate, as told below, his experiences during his flight. After he awakes today, he will narrate the full story of his remarkable exploit for readers of Monday's New York Times.

By CARLYLE MACDONALD.
Copyright, 1927, by The New York Times Company.
Special Cable to THE NEW YORK TIMES.

PARIS, Sunday, May 22.—Captain Lindbergh was discovered at the American Embassy at 2:30 o'clock this morning. Attired in a pair of Ambassador Herrick's pajamas, he sat on the edge of a bed and talked of his flight. At the last moment Ambassador Herrick had canceled the plans of the reception committee and, by unanimous consent, took the flier to the embassy in the Place d'Iena.

A staff of American doctors who had arrived at Le Bourget Field early to minister to an "exhausted" aviator found instead a bright-eyed, smiling youth who refused to be examined.

"Oh, don't bother; I am all right," he said.

"I'd like to have a bath and a glass of milk. I would feel better," Lindbergh replied when the Ambassador asked him what he would like to have.

A bath was drawn immediately and in less than five min-

LEVINE ABANDONS BELLANCA FLIGHT

Venture Given Up as Designer Splits With Him—Plane Narrowly Escapes Burning.

BYRD'S CRAFT IS NAMED

Lindbergh Cheered at Ceremony—Commander, Now Last in Field, Waits on Weather.

Through no fault of his own, Clarence D. Chamberlin, who with Bert Acosta established a world's non-stop flying record a few weeks ago, will not fly the record-breaking monoplane in an attempt to establish a second New York-Paris non-stop flight.

G. M. Bellanca, designer of the plane, and Charles S. Levine of the Columbia Aircraft Company, owner of the ship, came to the parting of

LINDBERGH TRIU
THRILLS COOL

President Cables Pra "Heroic Flier" and Co for Nungesser and C

CAPITAL THROBS WIT

Kellogg, New, MacNider, and Many More Join in Tribute to Daring Y

Special to The New York T
WASHINGTON, May 2
triumph of Captain Charles
bergh in flying from New
Paris without a stop create
mendous sensation in the
capital and found immed
sponse in a host of official
and statements congratula
daring aviator upon his achie
President Coolidge expre
admiration in a message tra